ZOO MOMMA
by
Lori Space Day

To alice,

Enjoy!

Lori Space Day

Zoo Momma

Published by Daylite Sales
www.lorispaceday .com
New Jersey
Printed in the United States of America

Zoo Momma

Acknowledgements

Many thanks are extended to
Karen Talasco, Karen Walsh, Michele Mulder, Dr. Leonard Rue III, Jessie Goble,
Cathy Mayers Rosselli and Jackie Day for their photographic contributions to my
memoirs , and to Tom Drake for his help with the cover of my book:
"Zoo Momma" .

I would like to give credit to my mechanical genius and computer guru husband,
Doug. Without his patient tutoring and active participation this book would not be
possible. Few people know the myriad of skills Doug has performed and taught us
at the zoo.
And then there is his sense humor..

In my first book, "The Zookeeper's Daughter", I thanked the animal mentors in
my life, especially my Dad, Fred. Space. I would like to thank all of them again
now. I am still learning.

Looking towards the future "Zoo Momma" is dedicated to the next generation
who are learning or have learned animal care from me : Jackie Day, Hunter Space,
Lindsey Space, Kelsey Space, Jennie Beckman, Interns: Victoria Ciccolella,
Stephanie Guerra, Yvette Gramignano, Matthew Spinks, Allison Stapel, Sierra
Walsh and visitors to the zoo. I sincerely hope I have inspired you to learn more,
and continue to safeguard the earth and Her creatures.

Table of Contents

Zoo Momma

Chapter 1 The Russians are coming! The Russians are coming !

My family has been giving tours of the zoo as long as I can remember. As a child I was often pulled out of school to give tours to visiting school kids. I was driven back to school when the school kids got back on their busses to go home from their trip to Space Farms Zoo and Museum. We stopped giving guided tours to school groups when the zoo expanded from thirty acres to a hundred acre park. The grounds were just too large to shepherd around a thousand kids a day . For special groups other arrangements are made. These days my brother, Parker, hops in the snake den, and gives an informative snake demonstration for school kids. Dad, now 76 years old, had given up the snake den lectures when his hearing began to fade. He could no longer hear the dangerous rattle snakes' warnings. Dad or I are available to speak on other requested topics for Boy Scouts, Girl Scouts, Rotary groups or whomever.

One day I received a call from Donna Traylor, the Director of the Sussex County Agriculture Development Board and Farmland Preservation and Conservation Program. Donna often hosts visiting farmers on tours around Sussex County. She is also a good friend of mine. Donna was in charge of touring a batch of Russians around the county. The problem? A different venue had canceled on her tour for the Russians at the last minute. Did I have time to give a quick tour of the zoo? *Well, sure why not?*

Petite, but packed with agricultural knowledge and enthusiasm, Donna and the dozen or so Russians came to the zoo with an interpreter. That was good, because I don't know a word of Russian. Donna introduced me to all, names I could not pronounce, let alone spell. The visiting Russians were dressed in casual clothes, with obviously new shoes. *Why they would wear new shoes on a visit to a farm? Farmers of any ethnic group should know farms could be messy. Oh well, guess they wanted to look nice.* Donna, in her sturdy sensible shoes, turquoise calico T-shirt dress, and I in my navy blue uniform, started the tour.

The tour progressed through the main building. I explained how Space Farms Zoo and Museum got started in 1927, with my Grandfather Ralph and Elizabeth Space buying their first quarter acre in downtown Beemerville. Expanding on that, I gave a detailed history of the fox farm that evolved into the largest mink ranch east of the Mississippi and the working dairy farm that was purchased. To knowing nods, I explained how the falling milk prices determined that we sell the cows but keep the land in 1969. The Russians seemed to understand when I detailed the demise of the mink ranch in 1987. Again we kept the land for farming. I touted my Dad, Fred Space's, animal expertise, and how his father Ralph's trapped animals were the beginning of the world renowned zoo that Dad had developed. The dozen Russians were very attentive and the interpreter was constantly repeating what I had said. The nodding and gesturing Russians walked with us through the zoo, past the Syrian Grizzly bears, the foxes, porcupines, three types of fallow deer, and cougars. It was a pleasant sunny day, if

6

a little on the brisk side. Walking on the pebbled path, the ladies had a little trouble with their high heeled and pump shoes. *Why didn't the Russians wear more sensible shoes for a farm/zoo visit? Women are such slaves to fashion.*

As we walked around the Aoudad, Yak , Ostrich and Elk paddocks I gabbed up a storm on the zoo and farm business. I explained as we walked the phone call system my Dad had developed to collect the road kill deer in the area and how it was an excellent natural source of food for our animals. The interpreter repeated my words. I explained how Space Farms was actually four hundred and fifty acres, only one hundred of which is the zoo and museum, open to the public. We actively farm most of the other three hundred and fifty acres, (some land is simply open space, no pun intended!). The home grown grain and hay was utilized to feed the hoof stock. I gave out crop information that I thought the visiting farmers would appreciate. In preparation for their visit I had asked Dad to bone me up on that year's crop production statistics. I repeated the statistics verbatim. We produce 160 tons of hay, 400 round bales and 15 thousand square bales @ 300 tons, for a total of 460 tons of hay, of different types of grasses. The end of May is 1st cut, end of July is 2nd cut and on a good year, October gives us a 3rd cut. For a number of years we produced our own corn but now are buying it off our local farmers.

Questions were asked through the interpreter which I answered: How do we procure new animals? How many babies do we have per year? Do we trade or sell the animal infants? How many people do we employ? What type of machinery do we have on the farm? All questions I would expect from visiting farmers from Russia.

We were over the hill at the zoo and approaching my favorite exhibit, the tigers I had hand raised in 1998. Khyber and Tara heard me long before they saw me. They patrolled their grassy enclosure looking for me. As we finally approached their section, the Russians gathered around the guard fence. I used my keys on the padlocked guard fence to let myself inside, but stayed outside the enclosure proper. Khyber greeted me with chuffs. Tara not to be left out, rubbed her head on the fencing waiting to be petted. I commanded Khyber "Patty Cake", to show off his size with one of his favorite games. On cue he reared up, stretching tall above me, putting his dinner plate sized paws on the fence above my head. Khyber and I 'Patty Caked'. The Russians collectively "Oh-ed" and "Ah-ed" at the sight of the massive cat which towered above my head. I spoke to my babies in a tone I'm sure the Russian farmers had used on their farm stock. In front of other business men and women I would have felt embarrassed using my 'baby talk' on the animals, but I knew farmers would understand the tone no matter what their native language. Then it was time to move on.

Khyber and Tara followed us as we strolled past the long end of the enclosure. I walked backward over the uneven grass, my words interpreted as we moved. And then the expected happened: Khyber lifted his tail to mark territory. Donna and I moved quickly out of the way. *No big deal, every farmer knows basic animal behavior and these Russian farmers had worked with cows right? Every farmer on earth knows to get out of the way when a cow raises it's tail. Why aren't these people moving out of the way?* In the flash of an eyelash, it was too late. I hollered as the first drop flew, "Get out of the way, his tail is up!".

The group of Russian tourists, had stayed put by the guard fence in front of the positioned male tiger. Like deer in the head lights, the visitors did not move. Eyes wide, I watched in disbelief. Donna, the interpreter and I shoved, (not too delicately), people in all directions. Still, a few were marked, tiger style, with strong alkaline urine. Luckily everybody chuckled. I was mortified. No use yelling at the tiger. Khyber was just being a tiger.

I took Donna by the arm, still within earshot of the Russian interpreter. I sarcastically remarked, "Some batch of farmers, they didn't even move when his tail went up!" Donna and the interpreter looked at me with surprise.

"They aren't farmers, they are Russian businessmen and women!" Donna explained, "Bankers, here as guests of the Sussex County Rotary!".

"So they don't want to know about the working of the farm itself?" I asked dumbfounded.

"No, they just want to know how you make your money", explained the interpreter.

"Oh," I said, "That's easy. We make our money one admission ticket at a time. No state or federal financial subsidies. Support your local zoo!" Everyone laughed as the interpreter translated.

Yeah, the tiger spray was on the Russians, but the joke was on me.

Chapter 2 All's Well that Ends Well

Until the beginning of the 21st century, the tiger was at the absolute top of the food chain, a predator unmatched in the natural kingdom. Prior to 1900 there were eight subspecies of tigers. It is estimated that there were hundreds of thousands of wild tigers. The Caspian, Javan and Balinese tigers are now extinct. The Chinese, Corbett's, Sumatran, Siberian and Bengal tigers are now protected as endangered species.

Generic tigers are now considered any zoo tiger that does not have a paper pedigree of pure blood of one of the last five remaining species. The young tigers I raised in 1998 came to me labeled as Bengal, but they had no paper pedigree. I loved them, and their exact genealogy did not matter. Our entire human family is American Mutt, after all! We acquired Tara and Khyber for exhibit animals, not necessarily for breeding stock. The story of Khyber and Tara is in my first book, "The Zookeeper's Daughter". Since 1988, when the tiger cubs came to us, the classification for captive generic tigers changed to non-endangered due to the amounts of cross breeding that previously occurred in the United States. There are more tigers in captivity today in just the United States than there are in the wild.

The manor in which zoos garner their animals has changed drastically since the early zoos of the Egyptian times. Up until the 1970's, wild animals could legally be captured and brought to zoos in the United States, or, for that matter, anywhere (or to anyone) in the world. In 1971 President Nixon signed the Endangered Species Act to protect the endangered and threatened species in the wild. The wild kingdom was no longer available as an unending warehouse of potential zoo animals. Permits are needed for most species. Permits are impossible to obtain for the average collector, not to mention the ensuing paperwork and unending red tape.

The Endangered Species Act does protect the wild animals and inadvertently put an increasing value on captive breeding stock. The gene pool of zoo animals is now limited to those animals already in captivity that could or would breed. Many animals are capable of breeding and producing progeny in captivity but they do not. Proper diet physical condition, environment, compatible sexual partners, and psychological well being are part of the multifaceted breeding cycle. Breeding captive wild animals is not as easy as the general public thinks. It takes more than just throwing opposite sexes in a cage. My Dad, Fred Space, always said it was a combination of the five conditions I just mentioned, a lot of peace and quiet and a twinkle in their eyes! The quiet country atmosphere of our zoo is one of the reasons Space Farms has such an outstanding record of breeding difficult and endangered animals.

The only way for a zoo nowadays to obtain a new animal is to breed 'in house', trade, purchase, or a breeder loan an animal from another zoo or licensed facility. All zoos, sanctuaries and private collections in the United States must be licensed and inspected by Federal and State authorities. Each state has its" own regulations, as to where an animal can come from, even for such a common animal as a captive squirrel. All legal zookeepers complain about the paperwork, but we know it is a good thing to keep the wackoes out of the wild animal business.

The decision to neuter a zoo animal is never an easy one. To eliminate a set of genes from the captive gene pool is a major decision. However, Khyber and Tara, the tiny tigers that had arrived to us in 1998, had grown to happy, healthy, perfect specimens and produced viable cubs that we had distributed to zoos across the United States in 2003. The tiger pair had done their part for the diversity of the collective gene pool. We made sure their cubs were healthy and sent them off to responsible new homes at different zoos. Not that I didn't miss the cubs, but I knew they had to go to other zoos for the diversity of the collective gene pool. I knew that from the beginning of raising my tiger grandbabies, it just makes it easier to let them go if you know the reasons why.

Dad, Parker, Dr. Ted Spinks and I had discussed the possibility of neutering Khyber. Dr. Spinks had conferred with other zoo vets on the procedures used in other zoos. We are not talking about neutering a house cat here! Our healthy tigers were just in the beginning of their reproductive life. With the optimal food, care and condition they were in, the pair would most likely reproduce two to three litters a year for the next ten years. That is just too many tiger cubs to place. A tiger can live 18 to 22 years, in captivity. There is not that much need for new tigers in zoos. The responsibility was ours to get Khyber neutered.

We picked a day in January. Cold weather has its' advantage. There are no visitors to the zoo when we need to move dangerous animals and no pesty flies or bugs during recuperation time. Dad, Doug and Parker had moved the giant transport cage to the end of the tiger enclosure. The big pussy cats were used to that cage. Khyber and Tara had spent time using it as a den, when it was attached on the opposite end of their grassy enclosure. They had used it when they were afraid of the lions after Tara's tail accident. On the appointed day we slid the slide down. This trapped Khyber in and Tara out into the snow covered compound. Tara would have the big den to spend the next week or so alone. Khyber was going for a ride.

Parker brought over the big John Deere Tractor and deftly slid the hay forks under the transport cage floor. Now, understand this is no easy feat. The transport cage is ten feet long by six feet wide and it needed to be balanced perfectly to glide barely two feet above uneven ground. I couldn't even estimate the weight involved, although I know Khyber's estimated weight was 500 pounds. Parker maneuvered the transport cage slowly away from the door in the fence, while Dad and Doug wired the zoo enclosure door closed.

Slowly Parker drove the tractor with its' heavy, frightened, but wide awake tiger cargo up the hill past the ring tailed lemur enclosure. Dad and I walked behind the leisurely moving tractor. I knew Khyber was scared- I had raised him and watching him for four years, I could read his behavior. So could

Dad, but then Dad can read any animal.

Dad said, "Talk to him Lori, he'll be calmer". So I jibber jabbered baby talk to the huge scaredycat tiger as he 'surfed' in his transport cage to the top of the hill. Khyber faced me as I spoke, casting occasional glances over his shoulder in the direction we were traveling. He did seem to be calmer with Dad and I talking to him. Slowly our strange parade moved through the zoo. Doug was in the beat up farm pick up truck cruising ahead to open the zoo's main gate. Parker sat tall on the green tractor with the crouching tiger behind him. Dad, in his worn and patched favorite bibs, slowly walked with me, the worried mom crooning to her overgrown baby. Although the bears were sleeping in their enclosure, one picked up his head to peer out from his cave to see the unusual sight. The silver foxes sharing that enclosure, pranced curiously, then slunk away as foxes do. As we crossed the road , a car had to stop, but people around here are used to unusual things crossing the road in front of the zoo at Space Farms.

Dad, Parker, Dr. Spinks and I all knew the operation had to take place in the five bay garage. It had controllable heat. One of the problems with anesthetizing any large animal in the winter is hypothermia (the loss of body heat). We needed to make sure we could keep Khyber warm for his operation to reduce the possibility of pneumonia. Lengthwise, the transport cage was longer than the garage door was wide so the transport would have to be rolled in by hand, sideways. I mention this because the general public cannot imagine the complexity of moving a large, potentially dangerous animal. Keep in mind that Khyber was not only 500 pounds, but a good seven feet long, (9not stretched out), so a cage to keep him in for a couple of weeks of his confinement and recuperation needed to be, well, big! The transport cage was ten feet by six feet, constructed of livestock paneling with angle iron bar reinforcements. It needed to be strong to hold a tiger. The transport had a large wooden shelf and cozy cage wide enclosed wooden box six foot long by three foot square for Khyber to crawl into if he felt so inclined. But t this point Khyber was pacing around looking for reassurance from Dad and I.

Upon reaching the five bay garage, Parker gently let the transport cage down on the five telephone poles that Dad, Bruce, (another zookeeper) and Doug had previously arranged on the ground. Khyber withstood the gentle thump but was obviously nervous. I kept blabbing, giving the occasional pet as Khyber came near the side of the transport. On command we all pushed the transport cage towards the interior of the garage until one of the telephone poles, now temporary wheels, rolled out of the exterior end under the bottom of the transport cage. Then our well muscled guys moved that telephone pole to the front underside of the transport cage going into the garage. We all pushed again. This procedure was repeated over and over again until the transport was well inside the five bay garage. We gave Khyber a day or so to calm down before Parker called Dr. Spinks to schedule the castration. Not exactly like taking your housecat to the Vet in a little plastic carrier, is it now!

On the appointed day, Dr. Spinks, his Vet Techs, Sue Perras and Pam

Fagersten, Dad, hubby Doug, brother Parker, zookeeper Bruce, our photographer Karen Talasco, videographer Vic Campbell, and myself all gathered after lunch for the castration. Sue and Pam had brought the anesthesia machine from Dr. Spinks' office and all the other supplies Dr. Spinks would need. Dr. Spinks was out on other large livestock calls and met the ladies at the zoo.

Everyone had their job to do. The Vet Techs prepared the injections and anesthesia under Dr. Spinks' guidance. The punch pole or jab stick, (a hypodermic needle on the end of a long broomstick type handle) was prepared. My job was to keep Khyber distracted while Dr. Spinks injected the anesthesia into Khyber's rear flank. I had brought one of the stuffed animal toys that Khyber and Tara had played with as cubs four years earlier. I was not sure if Khyber would remember the toy but thought he might remember the smell. Or at least it was a toy he could be distracted with.

On cue, I called Khyber over to the side of the cage, wiggling the silly brown spotted puppy toy. Khyber wandered over, but we weren't fooling him any, he knew something was up. With this many people, and his strange environment, Khyber could sense the excitement in the air. He knew. 'His momma didn't raise no fool'! I got Khyber to look at the toy, talking to him all the time. Dr. Spinks saw his opportunity and poked Khyber in the butt flank with the jab stick full of anesthesia. A clean shot, we all backed off and waited for Khyber to look sleepy. After a few moments, Khyber wandered back to my position. I was strategically placed on a milk crate seat where we all figured Khyber's head should be when he finally lay down. His head was not the important part, we wanted his tail and testes to be by the transport door. This would provide a quick escape for our guys, just in case. I talked to Khyber as he grew sleepier and sleepier. Finally he laid down, his head on the other side of the bars between us. Khyber chuffed a few times and was asleep. I stroked him on the nose and announced Khyber was asleep.

Dr. Spinks chuckled at my gentle approach. Always the teacher to a willing student, Dr. Spinks told me to stroke harder and then showed me how to tickle Khyber's eyelashes to see if the blink response was 'under'. Khyber was out of it. Next Dr. Spinks pulled on Khyber's tail through the bars just to make sure Khyber was completely under. You don't get to make a mistake handling big cats. Or should I say, you don't get to make a mistake TWICE.

When Dr. Spinks pronounced the big kitty asleep, Parker took the pad locks off the transport door. More fluffy hay was taken inside to make a thicker warm bed for Khyber. Pam and Sue set up the anesthesia machine close to the cage and ran the tubing through the bars. Neomycin ophthalmic ointment was put in Khyber's eyes to prevent them from drying out and/or getting scratched from minor bits of hay as Khyber's blink response was temporarily under anesthesia also.

Dr. Spinks and the Vet Techs set Khyber up with the isoflourane gas anesthesia. The shot in the butt would not last for the duration of the operation and the metabolism of the gas was more controllable. Now I need to give credit where credit is due to Sue. She had known that we were going to castrate the tiger.

Knowing her trade, Sue knew that the gas mask for the average large dog would not fit a tiger's muzzle. Necessity being the mother of invention, Sue had brought along a gallon milk jug cut into shape for a gas mask for Khyber. Complete with a taped edge so as not to cut the tigers face with the hard plastic. Dr. Spinks also complimented Sue on her inventive thinking. Kudos to Sue.

When all was in place, Dr. Spinks started the procedure. The rhythmic pssst....pssst noise of the anesthesia vibrated though the garage. Khyber's breathing was monitored. The medical smell of the veterinary equipment, the gasoline smell of the machinery, tractors, oil etc. and the sweet smell of second cutting hay contrasted with the strong smell of tiger in the garage. Pam and Sue monitored Khyber's vitals calling out numbers and information to Dr. Spinks. Karen and Vic were busy taking pictures. Parker helped move the huge cat into position, climbing into the cage with Dr. Spinks. I watched, worrying, with the toy puppy in my hands. The toy was now consoling me. Sometimes all a mom can do is worry and pray. Doug and Dad were on hand 'just incase'. I was glad Dad was there, his expertise in animal behavior would be life saving in case of any emergency.

Khyber's scrotum was well washed with hydrogen peroxide to sterilize the area. I am always impressed with Dr. Spinks's confident, 'get it done' surgical incisions. A straight cut was made between the two testes on my giant sleeping tiger baby. Parker assisted by holding the tail out of the way, adding a hand when Dr. Spinks needed one. Parker can be a tough guy, but I saw him use his free hand to give Khyber some reassuring pats on the back, saying a macho "Sorry Buddy" only a man could understand. Up until that point we were all joking, gabbing and conferring back and forth. As Dr. Spinks made the incision, a hush fell over the room. I swear every man in the garage pressed his knees a little closer together. A trans fixation ligation was made on the spermatic cords. Dr. Spinks skillfully stitched the arteries to prevent blood loss. The testes were individually removed. There was remarkably little blood loss. My big kitty cat slept on.

The tension in the garage eased when someone made a joke about Rocky Mountain Oysters. I myself have never eaten any, nor do I plan to. The testes were about six centimeters oblong, (slightly smaller than my fist) and a healthy pink color. Dr. Spinks took a moment to demonstrate for Vic's video the different sections of the reproductive organ of a male tiger.

Returning to the procedure, Dr. Spinks and Parker cleaned up the incised scrotum and surrounding area. Parker was instructed to pack the now empty scrotum with nitofurazone, a strong antibiotic compound. Parker did not hesitate to perform the gruesome job. The scrotum would be left open, like the standard procedure on a house cat, to drain naturally. Cats lick and tigers are huge (!) cats. Khyber's licking would keep the wound clean.

Pam was still monitoring Khyber's breathing. Sue prepared antibiotic shots that were then given to Khyber. Parker and Dr. Spinks flipped Khyber to lay on his other side so the tiger's liver could more easily metabolize or defuse the anesthesia. This tiger flipping was done a couple of times while everyone else was

13

cleaning up the medical equipment in the garage. Dr. Spinks checked Khyber's teeth while Khyber was still sleeping. Khyber's teeth were clean, and his carnassials (large canine teeth) were free of tarter. The giant sandpaper tongue of the tiger was placed in such a way that the sleeping cat would not choke on it.

When all was in order, Dr. Spinks gave Khyber the reversal shot for the anesthesia. Khyber would wake up on top of a fluffy bed of hay. His body was covered by an old floral comforter to help keep him warm till he woke up. I must admit Khyber looked adorable sleeping under the multicolored floral comforter garnered from my home. Khyber was in great shape and we expected no trouble with the neutering procedure. But it was and is my duty as Khyber's mom to worry.

Everyone left after Khyber was able to raise his head on his own. The adult tiger would wake up with little distraction. We wanted him to stay as calm as possible. Dr. Spinks and the Vet Techs packed up and left. We knew we could call if there were any complications. Vic went back to his office, Karen stayed with me for the afternoon. All we needed to do was wait.

A few hours later, I bumped into Dad as I was on my way in to check on the Khyber again. Dad was on his way out from checking on the tiger.

"He's awake, and doing fine, you can stop worrying now", Dad said. I chuckled to myself, knowing Dad and Parker had checked on Khyber also, multiple times. I was the only one willing to admit to being worried. I guess that is the difference between men and women.

Khyber greeted me with chuffs and rubbing against the side of the transport. I could tell he was still groggy, but I was glad to see him standing up and moving around. Exercise and time would help him get rid of the lingering effects of the anesthesia.

Khyber stayed in the five bay garage for two weeks. Longer than that and we were afraid he would 'blow' his coat. He needed to go back outside to Tara and the large enclosure before his heavy winter coat shed due to the warmer temperature in the garage. Otherwise, he would need to be confined in the smaller transport cage until spring. We checked his incision daily, it was healing according to schedule. (When he marked territory in the transport we looked quick from the sidelines!)

After the appointed two weeks, the strange parade of trucks, tractor and Khyber in the transport cage reversed and proceeded back to the zoo. Khyber was let back into the large enclosure in the zoo proper. Tara had missed her life partner and came bounding towards him across the snowy half acre run, welcoming him with chuffs and head rubbing. Within minutes they were frolicking around the snow covered, dormant grass, a blur of playful orange, black and white stripes running and jumping in full fledged glee.

Khyber's recuperation continued without a hitch, a credit to Khyber's great physical condition, and to Dr. Spinks and his staff's veterinary skills. I am sad there will be no more tiger cubs for Tara (and I) to raise. I am grateful for the experiences I have had with all the tiger cubs, especially my first babies: Khyber and Tara. They joyfully romp through their enclosure whenever I call to them. Healthy, happy and very playful tigers. All's well that ends well.

Khyber
Photo by Karen Talasco

Chapter 3 Three Tiny Chipmunks

I had a chipmunk lost in my house in the spring of 2004. Lost you say, well, yes lost, or maybe loose would be a better word. Let me back up a bit:

A local gentleman walked into the zoo early in April with his hands clasped in front of him. I saw him coming, dressed in dirty jeans and work clothes, he did not seem the minister type, so I didn't think he was praying. The gentleman briskly strode directly to Dad sitting by the zoo doors. I was at the admission desk helping out. It was a busy day. I could not hear the conversation, with the man's back towards me, but I saw the twinkle in Dad's eye as he looked my way and pointed at me. The Praying Man came to the admission desk accompanied by my father.

"Can you raise these?" the Praying Man asked as he gently opened his palms.

"She can raise anything," Dad declared. Praise from Dad was hard to come by so I treasured the moment. *Ok that was enough moment. Curious I am.*

"Whatyagot?" My enunciation training slips when I am excited.

"I think they 're chipmunks," the praying hands presented me with three tiny, size of a peanut, chubby, pink bodies.

"They are chipmunks, Lori, see the stripes? And by their eyes?" My father must of seen the look on my face. Dad knew I was thinking : *I don't raise rats*, we *feed rat pups to snakes.*

I gently turned the little peanuts over in my palm. They were cold, but yes, the definitive white stripe bordered in black was genetically tattooed on their smooth skin. The rest of the bodies of each chipmunk infant was covered in pale pink hairless skin. *No hair, eyes still sealed closed, very small, this could be tough.*

"They are really tiny, but I'll give it a try", I assured the grateful deliverer. "Where did they come from?" I knew it would be a touch and go situation, if their birth mom was around, they would be better off with her.

"I was doing yard work with a skid loader, moving dirt, then raked out the dirt I had moved. These three were raked out, maybe there are more, but this is what I found." The stranger obviously felt bad, and had done the best he could for the three infant chipmunks. "I called some rehabbers, no one would take them, one said to try you guys."

Dad laughed and said, "Yeah, Lori has quite the reputation." With the chuckle in Dad's voice, I wasn't quite sure which of my reputations he was referring too. Oh well, looked like I had some little chipmunks to tend to.

'Thanks…I guess," I said to the grateful good Samaritan.

"Let me know how they turn out," he replied as I walked away towards the nursery office, cupping the little ones in my hand to raise their body temperatures. I nodded.

During my short walk to the nursery office, the three warmed up in my hands and started to wiggle. I enveloped the Thumbelina Chipmunks inside a scrap of fleece blanket and placed them in a six inch basket on top of a heating pad.

What to feed them was the next question. Esbilac and Kitten Milk Replacer were for omnivores and carnivores. I had some premature human formula, soy based and not loaded with animal fats so I decided to try them on that for a while. I knew the chipmunks were herbivores.

The next questions were how to feed them and would they eat? They were sooo small. I could not feed the chipmunks with the tiniest nipple I had at the zoo. I have quite the collection of nipples for all the species I might encounter, from buffalo calves to infant 'possums. A search of my nursery equipment delivered me a small plastic eye dropper. I mixed up fresh, warm formula and scooped up one squiggling little body. Face towards me, I dropped one drop of formula on his lips. He immediately sucked it in. I dropped another drip of milk. He sucked it in and collapsed in my hand. *Oh MY God, I killed him. He aspirated the milk! ...Well, wait now, don't panic, he is breathing... Oh he is just asleep.. Whew!*

After drinking three drops each, all three stopped squiggling and dozed off into chipmunk slumber land. I lay them down in their fleece blanket and went off to do other work for the next two hours. I would like to say I fed them every two hours round the clock, but I didn't. I went to bed at eleven that night, dog tired from my day at the zoo. *They are just glorified rats. God, it's your turn.* By morning they were hungry again.

It took three days of dripping drops on those tiny lips for the chipmunks to catch on that it was feeding time. At the end of the week, the youngsters were vibrantly pink and licking the milk from inside the eye dropper with their tongues, like tiny humming birds.

What a challenge for me. These common chipmunks were more challenge than the tigers and lions I had raised. Every two hours they were fed and pottied (stimulated with a cotton ball). Oh, by the way, two boys and a girl.

To my great surprise, they all survived, grew bigger and started to grow gray fuzzy hair at three weeks old. Gray fuzzy chipmunks? That is not the right color for chipmunks. I searched the internet and the library at the zoo to find information on the development of infant chipmunks and could not find any reference to the correct 'puppy' fur color. *Gray and fuzzy, like my brain in the morning.* I emailed my vet friends and they had no answers either. Dr. Spinks offered advice: Maybe chipmunks are like flamingoes and need to eat colored roots to obtain the carotenes needed to color up. Pink flamingoes need to eat shrimp to maintain their pretty pink coloration. *Ok, Dr. Spinks, I'm game.* I started the chipmunks on baby food carrots and sweet potatoes. They would lick the orange colored food off the dish, chew on some Honey Nut Cheerios and drink a few drops from the eyedropper. Their size and conformation was excellent, activity level frisky, like any other wild chipmunks I had seen. But they were still gray with the telltale white side stripes bordered by black.

By four weeks old the little pups were very active, covered in their gray fuzz running though the paper towel cardboard tubes I placed in the bottom of a twenty nine gallon fish tank. The three Musketeers would climb in the branches in the tank, scurry around and then go back to sleep in the basket with their blankie. They seemed happy, perky , roundly healthy and were certainly full of all the chipmunk noises you would expect. But they were still gray - like the dust bunnies that live (and reproduce) in my house. Gray with wimpy brushy tails. I hoped for the best, but kept them home because we could not put such rejects on display at the zoo for all the world to see. I was a failure at being a chipmunk mom.

One morning as I was having coffee in my living room, a lone chipmunk scampered to my feet, looking for his bottle. I scooped him up and put him back into the tall fish tank by the back window. I paused, *Himmmmm... better count them.* There were two, that is including the one I had just put back in. I searched the house, calling "Chippy", the terribly original name I called all three. I searched high and low, but could not find my lost chipmunk. I had been so proud they were alive, even if they were gray. I had to tell Doug and Jackie so they could be on the lookout for my lost chipmunk. Thought I felt him run across my arm one night, but I could have been dreaming. I did find a pile of seeds and chipmunk food type items in my sewing room fabric drawer. But I never found the chipmunk in my house. I am hopeful that he found his way out one of the various mouse trails that our remodeled old farmhouse has. Now come on, you've had mice in your house too. Everybody has to live somewhere, even the mice.

Then there were two. The two chipmunks grew to be a noisy nuisance in the house. Due to the great escape, I had placed a screen cover over the top of the twenty nine gallon tank. The chipmunks would travel up and down the branches, through the paper towel tubes and now, grabbing with tiny toenails, scurry across the underside of the screen cover like rodent spidermen! Their constant chirping, whistling and calling echoed in the tank, then reverberated across the living room. Chewing on branches, which is normal for a chipmunk, also added to the constant activity and noise. At five weeks they were still gray in color, despite weeks of the colorful food sources.

Eastern Chipmunks are members of the rodent family. A gnawing mammal, Tamias striatus. Tamias in Latin means 'treasurer', for the chipmunks constant hoarding. Chipmunks have large cheek pouches in which they carry food back to the tunnels to hoard for winter consumption. Striatus, meaning 'striped', also fits it's description. Adult chipmunks are about 4 ounces in weight, and maybe six inches long, nose to base of tail. They live in shallow burrows up to thirty feet long with tunnels extending to multiple entrances and exits. In winter they are not true hibernators, and wake up on warm days to eat the hoarded food stuffs in their tunnel rooms. Chipmunks seal themselves into a section of the tunnel, so predators can not get to them. Chipmunks do not come out of their tunnel system until warm weather in the spring.

Males court females early in the spring, and again later in the summer. Gestation is only thirty two days. Infants are born slightly larger than a good sized lima bean. Momma Chipmunk keeps her young underground until they are six weeks old, a at which time they are weaned, eating seeds, nuts, berries, roots, worms and insects. Perhaps the formula I gave the chipmunks did not have enough in it to color up the chipmunks, considering that the adults also eat worms and insects. Learn something new every day! I thought chipmunks were strict herbivores! Or, perhaps the shedding cycle of puppy fur applies here as they do not come above ground until six weeks. Anyway, six weeks seems to be a marker in chipmunk life.

I was very surprised to see the chipmunks finally gain their proper, or perhaps I should say, adult coloration at six weeks old! Seems I woke up one morning, fed them and as they crawled up my arms I noticed they had changed color. I'm not sure why, if it was developmental, or if the amount of carrots and sweet potatoes had finally caught up with them. I was a happy momma, my little ones now the stereotypical chipmunk orange color with racing stripes. I never read it anywhere, or talked to anyone who knew that the gray color was normal for infants. I am just putting it out there for the next generation of chipmunk raisers to know, that based on my experience, don't worry if they are gray at first.

Now that the chipmunks had their proper coloration I felt that I could take them out in public for my lecture circuit. The remaining two were very friendly to me. They greeted me with chirps, ran up and down my arms, and waiting to be petted. They were nice little pets. I was never bitten, so I felt safe taking them 'out' to the public. Though, due to my germaphobia, I never let anyone touch my babies anyway.

Their first lecture was to a group of Girl Scouts and Brownies. I presented the chipmunks. The kids "OOhed" and "Ahhed". My two Chippies were immediately afraid of the unusual noises and skittered down my arm and back into the paper towel tube in my hand. I gave the rest of my speech with the chipmunks in the paper towel tube, shaking with fear and refusing to come out. The girls did not get to see much chipmunk. Seems my Chippies liked me, but no one else. It could have been the giggly girl noise factor.

I tried to take them out for a speech one more time with the same results. It didn't seem fair to take them out if the Chippies were so scared or to keep them 'just' for pets. I thought about it for a week, then released them in the back woods of the Space Farms property. There would be plenty of food to forage, places to nest and sleep and other chipmunks to play with. It was the right thing to do. I visit the woods on a regular basis, and have not seen them since. I am all right with that. They are what they were meant to be.

But the lost chipmunk? I have no clue where he is. I never found his body in the house, so I am hopeful that he escaped to the back woods out my doors. It took me a whole year before I would set a mouse trap though. I'm sure the house mice enjoyed the reprieve.

Zoo Momma

Chapter 4 Russell Crow

It is not every day that Russell Crow walks into a gal's life. Darkly handsome, fathomless dark eyes, silent yet wary, Russell Crow came to me late one morning… in a shoe box. As happens many times every year, a neighbor brought me an orphaned infant. I quizzed him on the happenstance of his finding the little crow chick, which was a fist sized ball of slate gray fluff just starting to fledge, (grow feathers). I estimated the crow chick's age at about three weeks due to the fact that the chicks usually fledge out completely at thirty to thirty-five days. Out walking in his back woods with his dog, the gentleman's dog found the chick first. The man looked around for a nest knowing crow nests are large compilations of twigs, leaves and mud, lined with soft materials. Soft materials, not always natural materials, in today's suburban society. Dad has seen hair, strips of fabric, down feathers, string, yarn, ribbon, and anything eye catching the crow mama might find. Often colorful, crow nests are a collection of items that catch the mama crow's discriminating eye. When the neighbor didn't see a nest nearby, he brought the crow to us. At that point we had two options. One was to take the infant crow back to the wooded area and leave him for his natural mom to find. She would find the youngster and feed him on the ground.

"But there are feral cats in our area," was the gentleman's quick answer.

The other option was for me to hand rear the bird and release him later. I had fond memories of Jimmy the Crow from my youth, I must admit I was not adverse to the job. I had always wanted to raise another crow. I had visions that he would fly around the zoo, freely, and have lunch with me now and then on one of the picnic tables sprinkled throughout the zoo.

"Thank you, I have wanted to raise a crow since Jimmy the Crow. My Gramma and Dad raised Jimmy. We had kept him as a family pet when I was little," I explained to the nodding man. He was obviously happy I had accepted the charge. The man left, saying he would keep in touch. I knew crows were protected, so it would be a raise and release bird.

I busied myself with my new baby. I went outside to gather different size twigs and sticks to use as perches and grass for underbedding. The multiple diameter sticks are important to keep the chick's feet in the proper shape so the muscles in the gripping feet do not get stretched out beyond use for grasping onto branches and perches. Inside ambient temperature would be fine as the chick did not show signs of illness. A small wire cage contained my entire man made nest and the tiny fist sized chick. I named him Russell Crow, after the actor, a hot commodity in Hollywood. I have a wicked sense of humor, I mean how many women can say they have hand fed Russell Crow?

North American crows are omnivores as adults. As infants growing fast, a high protein diet is generally advised. A farm girl by birth, I knew just where to get a quick supply of a young birds favorite food - worms. I settled Russell into the office nursery and went outside in search of worms under the water dish in Pop Pop's Barnyard Nursery. I found two nice big juicy worms and brought them for my waiting charge. A quick trip to the restaurant kitchen to steal one straw of the corn straw broom and I was ready to try feeding the little crow. Skewering the squiggly worm on the broom straw I opened the top of the wire cage. Russell was waiting with tiny, so-black-they-were-blue eyes. I gently tapped the side of his beak with the worm. Russell's natural instincts kicked in. He opened his mouth wide, adding to the motion a gentle "Caaawwww". I pushed, poked and prodded the wiggling worm into his mouth, as far back as I could get it. I smiled to myself. Once again in my life I thanked Gramma's spirit for showing me all her infant feeding tricks.

Russell gurgled and swallowed the worm. Worm number two went down just as easy. Good, he would eat. As the day progressed and my ready supply of worms decreased, I went to the feed house to get a cup of the ground venison fed to some of the larger animals. I ground dry dog food into flour and mixed the powder with the venison forming small dime size meat balls. Straight meat is not good, the crow chick needed a varied diet. Mom Crow would have gathered, eaten and regurgitated directly into the mouths of her brood. But there is only so much I am willing to do for my job! By the end of the day, Russell recognized me as the food momma, opening his mouth and "Caaaawwww"-ing whenever he saw me.

Russell came home with me that night and many nights thereafter. After six worms and two dime sized meatballs, Russell fell asleep at dusk in the corner of my living room. I knew that he, like other wild crow chicks would get the moisture he needed from the damp food he was fed. Whew! First day done.

I have never needed an alarm clock in the spring, summer and fall since I was a youngster. The native birds, crows included, wake me at dawn with the accompaniment of the lions, tigers, and bugling elk (in the fall). Early the next morning Russell let me know he was awake and HUNGRY big time. I fed him, starting the next step in his training. I picked him up and put him on my finger at feeding times thereafter. I wanted him to sit on my hand to eat, the food being the positive reward for the action. After he ate, I got dressed and took Russell and myself to work. Russell would stay in his cage/nest while I performed my many duties at the zoo. Late in the afternoon, the same gentleman appeared at the admission desk again.

"Look what my dog found now!" he grimaced, opening the shoe box.

I peered into the shoe box, and smiled. *Got to feed one, two takes only a minute more.* Russell has a sibling. "That's good, now Russell will have company. I'll name this one Edgar Allen, "I stated.

The gentleman smiled catching the joke of both names. "Thank you," were the simple words he said as he turned and walked away. And now there were two.

Edgar Allen learned quickly by watching Russell eat. You could SEE Edgar watching. That amazed me. Crows are smarter than you'd think. The two chicks progressed nicely, growing their flight feathers in a few weeks. I was thrilled when both chicks hopped, then flew short distances to sit on my hands at feeding times. They would eat their fill and fly back to their nest in the cage.

The North American crow inhabits the entire continent. Crows are protected by the Migratory bird Act of 1918 so I knew that Russell and Edgar Allen would eventually be released on the farm property. There were plenty of other crows around the farm. Nationwide estimates of the crow population is thirty one million! There are many different species of crows world wide, Russell and Edgar were North American Crows or Corvus brachyrhynchos. Crows are Passeriformes or straight beaked birds. Their iridescent black feathers often look blue in the sunlight. Adult crows dot our Sussex County farmed landscape like black stitches on the patchwork quilt of fields. Wild crows have a life expectancy of eight years, while birds kept in captivity have lived as long as thirty years old. Jimmy the Crow from my childhood was around for about twenty years.

The crow is a sentinel species warning the other birds in the area when danger is near. Often the crow itself is the danger. Local crows have been seen poking their strong black beaks into turkey chick eggs, picking them up and slapping the eggs on the ground to break open and then eat them. Lately the crow has been associated with West Nile Virus, which kills birds. There has not been a recorded incident of a crow giving a human West Nile.

Crows have communal roosts and are a very social bird. A mating pair of crows are monogamous and cooperate in the feeding process for one season. Often last years offspring will assist with the feeding process. At two years the crow is sexually mature, and makes a stick and debris nest high in the top of tree branches. After an eighteen day incubation, the little quarter sized chicks are hatched. Fledging at four weeks and flying soon thereafter, the crows stay together in a flock, called a murder.

A friend of mine had wanted a pet crow to release in his back yard also. So after I felt Edgar Allen was on his feet, so to speak, with feeding and training, my friend took Edgar Allen home to his kids. It was understood that Edgar Allen would be released come fall so he could acclimate to the local crow society. Crows are notoriously messy birds. The eating process, (pecking and swallowing) and the omnivore diet causes really smelly, loose poops. The infant crow perches and poops out on a horizontal plane, which keeps the nest clean. So infant crows really stink! My friend's wife decided that Edgar Allen was not going to fit in with their family. Edgar Allen came home to me again.

In the two weeks that Edgar Allen was gone from me, Russell had truly progressed on his training to my finger at feeding times. Russell would call to me. When I approached and opened his cage, Russell would hop right up on my hand with his greedy little mouth open. I loved it. When Edgar Allen came back to me, I could tell that Edgar Allen had not been kept on the training schedule as I had hoped. Edgar Allen would eat out of the dish, but not from my hand. But crows are smart. Edgar Allen watched Russell getting fed first because Russell would fly to my hand. Edgar Allen's beady black eyes watched intently. Within a day of being back in my care, you can imagine my surprise as I opened the cage and Russell flew out to me followed by Edgar Allen, who perched on my shoulder. Wow! Edgar Allen remembered me! I was so happy I called to my hubby, Doug. "Hey honey, look at me", he was sitting in his blue chair not far from the birds and I, "Edgar Allen remembers!".

Doug, looked over from the weather channel, and did not seem to be impressed, "Humph, wow".

So Doug was not impressed. So what, I was thrilled. A human scarecrow with real crows! I guess you would have to see me in my nightie in the morning, before hairdo and make up to understand that (not so funny) comparison. I told our Vet. Dr. Ted about the happening, and he said "Lori, you have a real touch with animals". Maybe so, but I think the crow family is smarter than we humans give them credit for.

Russell and Edgar Allen grew according to crow schedule and before long I placed them in a flight cage outside in the nursery. The boys, (I did not truly know their sex as crows are not sexually dimorphic), would "Caaawww" to me every time they saw me. I constantly repeated "Hellooo, Hellooo, Hellooo" to start them on the imitation process of 'talking'. Russell caught on after a few weeks, repeating the gravelly salutation imitation three times. Edgar Allen lagged behind as usual (maybe he hatched out last). I started leaving the crow chicks at the zoo at nights when they were eight weeks old. I must admit I did not like the stink in my house either. Visitors to the nursery would talk to the boys, and Russell would "Hellooo, Hellooo, Hellooo" back. I figured once was a fluke, three repeats was indicative of learning.

Edgar Allen left the nursery one day when I opened the cage and he flew out. I called my friend to let him know just in case Edgar Allen showed up at his house. Oh well, the crows were going to be released anyway.

Russell came with me on the lecture circuit. Crows are so common I was surprised at the hit he was. Maybe it was the "Hellooo, Hellooo, Hellooo" Russell would say dipping his head and spreading his wings low. Towards the middle of the summer season, I took Russell with me to Pleasant Acres Campground just the other side of Sussex.

I love speaking at campgrounds - the friendly vacation atmosphere lightens up the crowd. Pleasant Acres is a lovely campground. Rural but with all the amenities, Pleasant Acres has a pool, store, mini restaurant, game room, fishing pond, goats, horses and a large pavilion with high beams. I spoke on snakes, raccoons and Russell. Russell behaved well for me, flying to my hand from his transport cage for his venison meatballs. He spoke to the crowd gathered in their massive pavilion, next to the pool. As Russell said his trademark "Hellooo, Hellooo, Hellooo," the two hundred people in the audience went wild with laughter. Scared by the sudden rush of human noise, Russell took off in flight from my hand to the rafter in the pavilion. *UT OH!* The crowd roared with laughter again. This time they were laughing at my red face. Russell turned his head, looked down at the people from his high perch and said his trademark phrase again. More laughter flowed from the crowd. I moved towards him and called to him with food on my finger. *Well, silly me, Russell was full, he had just eaten.* Russell stayed put.

I know the owners of the campground well. The Denman family and my family go way back for two generations. Pleasant Acres is only six miles from the zoo. My Dad, Fred, and Elmer Denman had been good friends since high school, and true characters at their ripe ages. Rich Denman, Elmer's son - who is my age, sensed my embarrassment. He stepped to the mike, putting his arm around me and said "Well, Zoomomma, it looks like your chick has flown the nest!"

Yeah, Sherlock.

"That's Ok" I said, "as long as he does not fly the coup!" I wisecracked, hoping to cover my embarrassment with humor. I finished the speech anyway, constantly watching Russell watch me. *When would I learn not to take unclipped birds out to speaking engagements?* After all the campers had left the pavilion, Rich helped me move a study picnic table under the rafter. I stood on top of the table with a long handled butterfly net I had brought with me, just in case. I knew Russell could fly and that you never can tell if an audience will scare an animal. Russell watched me climb closer to him, the five foot net in hand. Beady black eyes studied me with wary trust. I felt a little bad as I betrayed that trust, swooping the butterfly net over Russell's body in one swift move. Keeping the net in motion, so Russell could not climb out of it, I climbed down the picnic table placing the net open face down on the pavilion floor. Russell was sitting quietly in the net when I carefully disentangled the crow's jet black claws from the net. Not very upset, but just to show me he disapproved of the activity, Russell gave me a blood letting peck on my hand. *No big deal, I've been bitten by worse.*

Rich helped me pack up the animals and museum artifacts I had brought to the speaking engagement. As I pulled out of the parking lot, Russell had fully recovered from the ordeal. "Hellooo, Helloo, Hellooo" he spoke to me all the way home to the zoo. I could not cut his wings, he was a bird and meant to fly. No more speeches for him.

By the end of the summer, I opened the flight cage to let Russell free. He flew around the nursery a couple of times and ventured outside the nursery fence to the main zoo every now and then. I would leave the flight cage door open, finding Russell inside in the mornings for about a month. Occasionally in the daytimes Russell Crow would fly up to the picnic area and perch with a visiting family eating a picnic, inevitably scaring the family. I would be called on the public address system "Lori, get Russell Crow from the Picnic area". By the time I would arrive at the picnic area, the place would be packed with visitors looking for the movie star! Every one would laugh when I explained the crow's name was Russell.

Russell, like Jimmy the Crow from my youth, was becoming a pain in the butt, causing commotion in the zoo with the visitors. The public perception of crows carrying West Nile Virus, rabies or other diseases threw the visitors into fear. I brought Russell Crow home one more time, keeping him in a cage by our lilac tree. After one week, I let him go for the last time.

I see Russell every now and then, he flies with a murder of crows and visits my back yard by the lilac tree. And how do I know it is him amongst five or six of his friends? When I throw out the heals of bread I keep for him, Russell Crow spreads his wings, tips his head and says "Hellooo, Hellooo, Hellooo" then eats while the rest of the crows fly away. It is not every day Russell Crow flies in to a gal's life just to say hello, but when it does happen, it is a special day.

Chapter 5 Jenny Woodchuck

A childhood pet always conjures up warm memories. Growing up at the zoo gave me a unending list of pets, some of which were friendly and some animals were downright dangerous. When I was nine years old, we had a pet woodchuck at the zoo, her name was Jenny. I don't know how she got her name or remember where she came from, but she was friendly enough to play with. I can still see her in my mind's eye, standing erect on top of a rock in her enclosure happily eating the Lifesavers I would give her. Woodchucks in the wild only live six years, so she was a short time pet.

In early April of 2004, a gentleman casually strolled into the zoo and headed for the admission desk where I was standing. He walked right to me and called me by name, though I did not know the gentleman in blue jeans.

"Lori, I have something for you," he said.

"OK, whatyagot?" I said, eyeing the rolled blue towel in his hand, I hoped it was not a baby skunk, as he was standing inside the main building at the zoo.

"Well, I let my dog out to run in a field and he brought this little thing back to me," the gentleman sheepishly grinned. I did not know which hole to put it back into, so I thought you might help it out." His eyes implored me to say yes.

"First," I said, thinking it might be a baby skunk, cause it was their baby season, "What is it? Should we go outside?"

"I think it is a groundhog," he stated.

Whew! What a relief! I glanced at Mrs. Davis, a long time friend of mine who was working the admissions desk that day. Mrs. D. smiled and looked relieved also. You never can tell what may walk in the door at the zoo. Could have been a skunk, a porcupine, bobcat, snake, turtle, or a squirrel. We have had them all come in with people. Some things we have to turn away or refer to a wildlife rehabilitator, depending upon the laws on each specie.

I carefully took possession of the fluffy blue towel, noting the pepper like specks on the towel itself. *UT OH! Parasites, I hate parasites. One course in parasitology for veterinarians in college and I become physically sick when I am confronted with parasites, endo or ecto! I will itch and squirm for days after this....* I put the bedding down on the counter farther away from my body, *I really hate parasites.* With too fingers, I barely touched the towel in order to open it. Inside was a infant woodchuck. *How adorable*! Woodchuck, ground hog, or whistle pig, three names for the same animal. It was tiny, only the size of my fist, eyes still sealed shut from birth, soft brown hair tipped in gold, and swarming with fleas. *YUCK, YUCK, YUCK!* I knew I could keep it, legally, according to state laws, if I could mentally get past the flea problem. I checked it carefully for signs of physical damage, from the frisky dog. There were none.

"OK, I'll see what I can do," I told the gentleman, I was starting to itch already. "What kind of dog do you have?"

He looked relieved, and said "Thanks, I felt so bad when my dog brought him back to me, my dog is a Labrador retriever, " The man left rather quickly, glad, I think, to be rid of guilt from his dog's behavior. *A RETRIEVER!, gee, go figure!*

"Can you handle the desk alone, Mrs. D?" a rhetorical question, followed by "You might want to sterilize the counter." I tossed both statements over my shoulder as I headed for the office nursery (and the flea powder).

Mrs. Davis is my Dad's age, happy-go-lucky, and with a rounded grandmotherly figure. Blonde hair that seems to have an eccentric mind of it's own Mrs. D had a ready smile and always greeted the visitors to the zoo. In her day Mrs. Davis was a beauty. Her friendly personality made her perfect for the admissions desk. We weren't that busy. I had complete faith that Mrs. D would be fine for a few moments alone at the admission desk even if an onslaught of visitors suddenly appeared.

In the office nursery, I carefully examined my new charge, as I covered HER (discovered that!) with cat flea powder. I use cat flea powder on all infant animals that might lick themselves, as it is not poisonous. Dad had seen me walk into the nursery and came to check out the mystery towel I held at arms length.

"Humf! A little woodchuck, bet you're gonna call her Jenny!" Dad knew I had wanted to raise a woodchuck, I had asked him to keep an eye out for one when he was making hay in the Space Farms' fields. We reminisced over Jenny from my youth, forty some odd years ago. We were laughing, and then sneezing from the over abundant flea powder in the air.

Jenny is a natural blonde woodchuck. Woodchucks may be blonde, brown or even black in overall coloration. Each of Jenny's hairs were striped, the hair shaft closest to her body was dark brown, the next part of each hair was brown and silver, and the outer section of each hair was golden in color. This gave Jenny a bottle blonde look with dark roots. Just like her new mommy! I was instantly in love.

I cleaned the little groundhog up as best I could, examined her again for injuries from the dog's mouth, and found none. By this time the pitiful little thing looked quite silly, covered in white flea powder. A tiny girl groundhog ghost if I ever saw one. Set up in a piece of polar fleece inside a small basket on top of a heating pad, little Jenny could rest warm while I found a eye dropper and mixed up formula. Old Doc Grey, the Veterinarian we used in my youth, had told me once, "Warm will do more good than anything". I have found that to be true especially with infants.

Ground hogs are nature's most ignored rodent. Most people see them as pests in the garden, or road pizza, or buzzard brunch, rarely realizing their important place in the ecosystem. The veterinarians I've worked with hate them because of the holes they dig, endangering the legs of prize horses or dairy cows. The woodchuck is an enthusiastic digger. Woodchucks will dig a hole twelve inches in diameter, six feet deep, in less than thirty minutes. Off that vertical hole, the woodchuck creates tunnels to the left and right. Some woodchuck holes can be up to forty five feet in diameter! The groundhog creates rooms off the tunnels.

There is a high water room close to the surface in case of rain, bedrooms, and a bathroom always in the bottom of the tunnel system. When the weather is good, woodchucks will always 'do their business' outside their holes/homes.

Predators love woodchucks. Hawks, coyotes, foxes and turkey buzzards will eat woodchucks. The name whistle pig comes from the woodchuck's shrill whistle in time s of danger. If threatened by a predator, the woodchuck will zip quickly into their ornate tunnels for safety. Woodchucks always make multiple entrances and exits, just in case.

Other animals use the woodchuck holes for winter quarters. After the woodchuck goes into hibernation, in November, he seals himself into the individual room of his tunnel, using grass and dirt. That leaves the rest of the tunnel system available for skunks, snakes, foxes and other animals for dry winter quarters. If you would consider the beaver to be nature's architect, the whistle pig is nature's excavator. The created tunnels serve multiple purposes.

I mixed up premature human infant formula to feed the little powdered woodchuck. With an eye dropper, I slowly dropped one drop at time into her little black lips. Jenny quickly caught on, she was very hungry. She lapped the drops off the end of the dropper and within a day was sucking from the eye dropper. I knew then that I could switch her to a small bottle. By the end of the first week I had her, Jenny was sucking vigorously from a kitten sized tiny bottle. She was a sweetheart. Jenny would whistle and moan when she was hungry. I estimated her age to be four weeks old, since that is when the woodchucks first open their eyes. One eye opened first, giving Jenny a funny pirate look. By her fifth week, both eyes were open. I started her on solid food - Honey Nut Cheerios- my favorite food to start chewing rodents on. She quickly graduated to carrots and apples and grass. Jenny came home with me every night, my husband, Doug, baby whistle pig sitting while I prepared dinner or did housework.

Jenny grew fast, and was 5 pounds by summer's end. She was a big hit on the lecture circuit that summer. I took her with me wherever I went. Jenny would stand on my hand, and eat a carrot in front of the audience. This standing up posture was instinctual, not something I taught her. In the wild the woodchuck will stand to eat, constantly keeping an eye on it's surroundings for predators.

I had put Jenny in the large cage in the nursery which gave her access to grass and dirt to dig in. She had started a tunnel and would come up to see me whenever I called her. October of that year was exceptionally cold and Jenny went to sleep early in her tunnel. *Oh this is not good!* I could not protect her from the weather or predators if she tunneled out and was loose in the zoo. I watched for Jenny every day, worrying that she had dug out an escaped the protective cage in the nursery. Then the rains came … torrential rains, the zoo was flooded along with the rest of Sussex County. I worried more. Was Jenny already drowned in her sleep under the earth?

"Lee Lee, come quick!" I heard my nine year old nephew Hunter scream one day. The shrillness of his voice had me instantly alarmed. I hurried to the nursery where Hunter was standing, finger pointing. There was a sight for my sore eyes. Jenny was soaking wet, trying to dry off in the hay under the wild turkey chick cage suspended from the top of the little barn in the nursery! I was so happy to see her! I was smiling as I crawled on hands and knees through the turkey chick poo and chicken poo to where she was shivering in the corner. I ignored the yuck of poos, thrilled to have Jenny safely in my arms.

I had learned my lesson. I set Jenny up in a hay filled, wire bottom cage in the barn across the street. She would hibernate in safety there. Within a week Jenny had burrowed into the soft fluffy second cut hay bale I gave her. She made her own tunnel and had sealed off the entrance. I could see the woven hay across the entrance.

Hibernation is a comatose state, signified by reduced body functions. Reduced metabolism, respiration, blood pressure and body temperature help the animal reserve precious energy when not able to eat due to winter's death of plant material. Woodchucks will live off their body fat. An adult male woodchuck will weigh up to thirteen pounds at the end of the summer and fall seasons. After hibernation and the early spring wake up, that same woodchuck will weigh one third less! The extra weight/fat/energy is used to maintain the animal's body through the months of winter. Hibernation is nature's way of saying it takes less energy to sleep than to go out in cold weather conditions to gather and eat food.

Actually, that sounds darn good to me. Sleep three months of the year, no housework, work, exercise, cooking, holiday preparations AND wake up weighing one third less! Sounds like a good diet plan to me. Can I please wake up a size twelve?

But what does hibernation do? Would it wipe her memory clean? I asked Dad but he didn't know. I scoured the internet and books we had. There was no information on woodchuck memory. I called other zoos, but no one had a hand raised a pet woodchuck. Even Punxitauny Phil is handled with gloves. I had worked with Jenny all summer with bare hands. She knew and trusted me. What would her mental state be after hibernation. Would she remember me? Or would I loose my precious pet to nature's hibernation phenomenon? I wondered all winter…

Kelsey Space and Jenny Woodchuck
Photo by Karen Talasco

Chapter 6 Rhett

You never know what may happen on any given day at the zoo. Hurricane Ivan blew through the east coast two weeks before Labor Day in 2004. We all spent a couple of days cleaning up the tree branches and twig debris caused by the wind. We also were watching the flooded stream that runs through the zoo recede. It was the first time I remember the zoo being closed for a day during our open season, May through October.

Early one morning I received a phone call from Dan, the president of the Northwest New Jersey Homing Pigeon Association. He had a bird we might be interested in.

"We don't 'do' pigeons," I politely stated.

"This is not a pigeon. It is some sort of a large bird, maybe a parrot?" the voice on the other end of the phone replied. "I'm five minutes away, I'll be right there," click.

Guess there is no harm in looking.

In less than five minutes I was summoned to the main building. An older gentleman (president Dan, I assume), was flagging me from the front door. His old wood sided station wagon was parked out front. I could see the multiple animal carriers through the dusty back glass.

I introduced myself to Dan as he opened his car's back hatch. As soon as the tailgate was open I heard a welcoming "Hello" loud and clear. I peered into the crate in amazement. A large red parrot cocked his head to the side to gawk at me. It had been years since I had seen a scarlet macaw up close at one of the animal parks in Florida. Dad had taken us as children to every animal or snake roadside attraction up and down the Florida coast on our way to our annual family snake hunts. It had been years, but I knew this was definitely not a pigeon!

"You folks were the only people I could think of that would have the facilities to take care of a bird this size. Can you keep him?" the president asked.

Dan explained that he had been contacted by a elderly woman who lives on the edge of Stokes State Forest. Space Farms boarders Stokes State Forest. She thought she had a homing pigeon that had flown into her garage. That was why she called president Dan of the homing pigeon club.

Some pigeon! Must of scared the dickens out of the little old lady. Look at that beak! The bird's curved beak was massive with a wicked looking scythe like point. The beak was sandy in color, with some black highlights on it. White skin with tiny red feathers surrounded the clear pale green, almost white, eyes that were peering back at me. The rest of the bird was bright crimson, with some mottled greens and blues in its wing tips. This was a big bird, four foot total in length, including tail. Definitely a parrot. With the red coloration, it must be a scarlet macaw. She looked clean and healthy, if a little wet.

"Cracker?" the bird clearly asked. I was not sure if the bird was requesting food or making a sarcastic comment on my ethnicity. *Must be hungry.*

A quick mental inventory ricocheted through my brain. Inca the macaw,

Angie the cockatoo, Mr. & Mrs. Sweetie, two more cockatoos were already in residence at the zoo.

"All right, I have an extra cage right now, I'll keep her till we can put the word out," I told president Dan.

"You can keep the kennel till you set her up, I'll pick it up in a day or two," Dan said as he handed me the dog kennel and closed the back hatch. Dan said a quick goodbye and was gone.

"Well, guess your mine now," I reassured the frightened parrot. So there I was standing on the front porch of the zoo building with a four foot long scarlet macaw in a two foot high plastic dog kennel.

Her eyes flared, she cocked her head, studied me again and said, "CRACKER!". *Hummmm, parrots are smarter than you'd think!*

I named my new friend, "Scarlet". A play on words, for her coloration, and the strong female character in "Gone With the Wind". She did, after all, blow in on the wind after hurricane Ivan. I did not know if it was female or male. Technically it did not matter. Scarlet was still soaking wet, but it was summer so I didn't have to worry about her catching a chill. I placed the dog/parrot kennel in the office nursery for the time being. She could dry off there while I set up a larger cage. I didn't anticipate having this bird long. A nice looking bird like her, a good talker, not native to the U.S., obviously had a human caretaker. She probably just got loose from an outside aviary during Hurricane Ivan. I walked outside and hailed Doug as he was going through the gate on his John Deere green jitney. I hitched a ride to the old barn where we housed the empty cages. Scarlet would be kept in isolation until her owner picked her up. She might as well stay in the office nursery. I didn't want to put her by my other parrots just in case Scarlet was carrying a germ my birds did not need. *Yeah I am a germ-a-phobe.* I cleaned the cage and Doug circled back to help haul it into the office nursery .

Scarlet was eating well, with no obvious ill effects from her solitary sojourn into Stokes State Forest. After a day or so, Dad and I discussed Scarlet's future. I had wanted to re-design the parrot room at the zoo. We both vacillated between keeping the bird and our mouths shut, or notifying the press to put the word out that we had the found bird. She was a nice looking bird and would be a nice addition to our exhibit. Scarlet macaws range anywhere from fifteen hundred dollars to twenty five thousand dollars depending upon their age and training. She was a gorgeous bird in good shape. Somebody had loved her. Somebody was probably worried sick about her. Somebody somewhere was probably crying over her loss. Our good natures won out and I called the newspapers to let them know about our 'lost' Scarlet. I moved Scarlet to the parrot room in the zoo since she had not exhibited any signs of communicable illness. Scarlet would have company until her owner picked her up.

It was a great human interest story. The papers came to take Scarlet's picture and did a nice write up. Scarlet made all the local papers with her colorful red and white face in the picture. I told the reporters her story and that Scarlet had a leg band with numbers on it. That leg band lets reputable bird owners know that the bird was hatched in the United States. All birds that are hatched in the U.S. must legally have the leg band. If a bird does not have the leg band, it may be a contraband, smuggled bird from South or Central America. The depletion of the wild flocks due to illegal smuggling is tragic. I told the reporters that anyone that knew the numbers on the leg band could come pick the bird up. Any owner would have a record of the bird band numbers, since they would be filed with their license from the state of origin.

The amount of phone calls we received was shocking to me. Over the next week the zoo received fifty or more calls on the Scarlet. The majority of callers simply hung up when I asked for the bird band numbers. I heard many stories, "We were moving and the bird escaped," or "it's my brother's bird and he is out of town," or "the storm blew apart my aviary," each story more creative than the last. One caller told me the word was out on Parrot Find on the internet.

The most distressing calls were from people who berated me for not knowing what kind of macaw Scarlet was. I was called every kind of stupid. The newspapers called me back, asking if the macaw was a scarlet or not. Evidently, I was wrong. I admit it when I am. Didn't know it at the time, in my defense, but I was wrong. In my rush to get the word out on the missing, now found, parrot, I made a common mistake. Scarlet was not a scarlet macaw, but a green wing macaw. Same family, same red coloration, but the blue-green wings were the tip off, I discovered, after I took the time to look it up. Parrot egg on my face.

The easiest way to distinguish a scarlet macaw from a green wing macaw is by the band of yellow feathers across the wings of the adult scarlet macaw. The green wing has a band of green feathers across the wing and blue-green inner secondary and median wing coverlets. Our visiting green wing does not have a distinct band of color change, more a gradual rainbow of color on his wings. The crimson red coloration of the body is the same on both birds. Green wings also exhibit a blue edge to the red tail feathers. Scarlet macaws have green tips on feathers of their wing coverlets, but the yellow band of the wings are the striking feather factor of differentiation. Cross breeds exhibit multiple variations of color. Many birds are cross bred in the pet trade. You can see how easy it is to be confused. But still, I was wrong to label the bird before I looked it up. Oh well.

Macaws range from Central and South America, Green wings live in groups of up to twelve birds, often flocking with Scarlet, Blue and Gold, Military (kelly green with red shoulders) and other macaws. In the wild they do not interbreed. However they are often cross bred in captivity. Breeding season in the wild (south of the equator) is from November to March. In the cooler climate north of the equator, breeding often starts in April. Nests in the wild are made in hollow trees, and are often used for many years. One to three eggs are laid. Incubation is twenty three to twenty seven days. The parent birds regurgitate food into the crops of the infant chicks. Nuts, seeds, fruits and veggies comprise the adult diet in the wild. New hatched chicks are really ugly, by anyone's standards except the mom macaw's. They are all beak, pink loose skin, comic strip outsized feet with a huge grotesque neck crop that mom fills up with regurgitated gruel. Chicks grow down feathers in the first week and the fledging process takes up to twelve weeks. Macaws average two feet in length and some have a wing span of up to forty-nine inches! If you are considering them as a pet, make sure you have a cage that is large enough.

A nice lady from a parrot sanctuary volunteered to come verify the bird's ID. She confirmed my mistake. I had spent a lifetime building up my credibility and in the flash of a eyelash, it was shot to, well, you know. The lady told me that we should draw blood weekly, do stool samples weekly and feed this special diet that only she sells. Well, so much for NICE lady. The bird was not exhibiting any symptoms of illness, so why stress it out with blood tests? The giant red parrot had just survived the shock of a hurricane and being lost in the wild, after an obvious life in captivity. No need, in my opinion, to add to it's stress.

The next few weeks spun by, Labor Day weekend is a busy one for us. Many visitors came to see the bird whose story had made the papers. The phone calls to claim the perky parrot slowed down, everyone claiming her, but no one had the leg band number. Still a lot of hang ups when I asked though. How dumb do they think I am? I was assisting at the admission desk on the busy holiday weekend when Alice poked me in the elbow. Alice is a grandmotherly type, loves animals, and me. Alice has watched me grow up since I was a young chick myself. Long blonde hair tied back gives her an Old Mother Hubbard appearance, scary to some, but Alice has a heart of gold. That stiff poke got my attention.

"What's that guy doing up by the parrots?" Alice drew my attention to a scruffy man on the hill by the birds. Long frizzy hair was held back in a grungy bandana headband, hippy style. "He has binoculars! You better get up there, Miss Lori. I bet he's trying to read the leg band!"

I was up the hill in record time, I'm not that fast a runner, I took the quad that Dad and I share to cruise the zoo.

"Sir, can I help you?" I queried.

"I'm just looking at the birds," he replied as he finished tucking/hiding the binoculars in his back pack. "I think it's mine".

"Do you know the leg band numbers and have your license?" I asked. I knew he could not get the numbers with binoculars. I had trouble reading them when I was less than a foot from the bird after she first came. It took some visiting friends of mine from England a half hour studying the band to get the numbers. The band slips up and down the leg with each movement and turns like a loose ring. On top of that, this man was outside the parrot room, outside the guard fence, so he was a good ten feet away from the moving bird.

"NO, but I know he is mine," the unkempt man pouted.

" I saw your binoculars, so forget it. Unless you can produce your license from the State of New Jersey that has the leg band numbers on it, the bird stays here," I stated emphatically. I can be a bit overprotective at times, but this guy was not going to pull one over on me. The man slunk away. I never heard from him again.

We were not adverse to keeping the giant red parrot, turns out it is very friendly, hand tame, and has quite the vocabulary. But we were going to need to expand the parrot room. Five birds in separate cages were a lot for the size of the room. I knew the individual cages did not give each bird the maximum area that we could with a single large aviary.   I called Carl Morganton, owner of the Natural Bridge Zoo in Virginia. Carl is a long time friend of Dad's and an expert in parrots, parrot behavior, diet and breeding. Carl had a lot of helpful hints that Dad and I discussed. Then we designed the new parrot room.

The existing room had a window, that we would use as a portal to an outside cage. I was excited to see a design of mine come to fruition at the zoo. The inside parrot room was to be sixteen feet by five feet wide by 7 foot tall and crises-crossed with oak branches. The five parrots would have lots of room to spread their wings. Heat lamps would help when it was chilly. The back wall of the inside aviary had a mural of an ocean beach with palm trees I had painted the year before. The outside aviary was planned to be sixteen feet square with a bump out semi circle front and ten feet tall. A roof would provide shade over the grassy area. Lots of oak and locust trees branches would be used as they are hard wood. Parrots are notorious chewers, so hardwood is favored. The oak and locust trees would come from our farm's forest. The birds could be locked inside with the window portal in times of cold weather.

Construction at the zoo has to happen within a certain time frame. Fall is the best time for projects. Every spring has us inundated with winter clean up, and then, right away, school kids. Summers are always busy with visiting families and groups, so fall is our best construction time. I was, and am, very proud that I completed the inside aviary with very little help from the men folk, who were busy hunting anyway. I got the sides done and needed help getting the roof of the cage up. I waited till the men folk came in on a break from hunting. I begged for help from any of the tall guys. Scott Longhorn and his son, Dispatch came to help me lift the ceiling panel into place. Dad pouted and said they were all busy hunting. But the Longhorns were game. It's always good to have a few tall friends. My arms ached by the end of the day from using the bolt cutters to trim the thick livestock paneling to size. I will admit my hubby Doug helped me with the last few panels. My hands hurt from twisting wire to hold the panels together. At night my muscles would throb. But I was determined. I finished the inside aviary and decorated it with branches for the parrots to roost and climb on. The parrots would stay nice and warm through the winter inside the main building in separate parrot cages, as they do every year. Come spring, the birds would be placed, all at the same time, in the inside aviary. We needed to put all the birds in at the same time so one bird would not establish his territory as the whole enclosure and then bully the other parrots. All the birds would have equal time to establish a home roost. Parrots can be tricky that way.

The men built the outside aviary in the spring, the frozen ground of December not conducive to digging post holes to support the enclosure. We roped off the area to keep visiting school kids away. The kids stayed out, the birds stayed in. I was thrilled. Visitors flocked, (pun intended), to the new aviary. The birds were constant colorful choir of activity. *Oh heck, just call it noise.* God those birds can squawk!

And my new bird "Scarlet"? Yes we still have her/him. I did however change his name to Rhett, because, well, after all, he is not a "Scarlet" macaw.

Note: a few years later, Rhett laid an egg. So going back to the movie once again, I changed her name, I now call her Vivian, for Vivian Lee in "Gone with the Wind."

Vivian
Photo by Karen Talasco, background painting by Lori S. Day

Zoo Momma

Chapter 7 Big Bucks on a Bottle

In the state of New Jersey it is illegal for Joe Q. Citizen to raise white tail fawns. There is a very good reason for this. White tail fawns imprint easily on humans. With a doe (female) fawn, this is not such a big problem for humans. For the doe fawn, who is no longer afraid of cars and humans the results can be and often are - tragic. A buck fawn will often suffer the same fate. However a buck fawn raised by human hands can also be a lethal problem for we humans. Especially in the rut season, a hand reared buck will not be afraid of humans. Inflamed with hormones, human hand reared bucks have been known to attack humans. So, there are good reasons for the laws that restrict the hand rearing of white tail fawns by anyone not licensed to do so.

In late July of 2004 I received a phone call from a well intentioned lady who had raised a female fawn of that spring. The fawn was now big enough and frisky enough to be needing more room than her back yard. I explained that I could not take in little 'Snowflake' unless she got an O.K. from the state of New Jersey. I received the phone call from the state that said it was fine for Space Farms to take the fawn in. I had two other female fawns from our herd on a bottle, so once again, one more would not be that much more effort.

Snowflake arrived with her adoptive parents early one morning. I greeted the parents and immediately my heart felt for the Adoptive Mom. Her eyes were brimming with tears. I have been in that situation many times with my babies going to other zoos, so I could really empathize. Together as a group, we took Snowflake's crate up to our fawn run. Snowflake was hesitant to come out at first. After a minute or two, Snowflake was bounding around the run with the two other dappled spotted fawns.

Each fawn has it's own special markings. One may have brown rimmed eyes instead of black, or fluffier hair, slightly different crimson base color, white 'socks', or hooves, longer eyelashes etc. When you work with them every two hours, dawn to dusk, seven days a week, you learn their individual markings. The reader could equate it with a human mother of identical twins being able to tell them apart when no one else can. So I knew which one Snowflake was.

The Adoptive Mom needed time to see that her baby fawn was doing just fine, so I left them at the fawn run. I told the couple that they could take a stroll around the zoo, as I continued my other chores. Snowflake was pacing and bleating as soon as the Adoptive Mom was outside the enclosure. I reassured her that Snowflake would quite down as soon as Adoptive Mom was not there. That is why Adoptive Mom needed to stroll the zoo and observe from a distance. I knew that Snowflake would quiet down and play with her new friends. It is never easy to leave a baby behind no matter what specie. Believe me, I know.

The couple checked in with me before they left a few hours later. They asked if they could come back to visit Snowflake and bring the treats she loved.

"Sure, see yaw next weekend, she'll be fine," I tried to reassure the Adoptive mom. "It's tough, I know." I handed them more tissues as they left.

Next weekend right on opening minute, the Adoptive Mom was back at the zoo with treats in hand. She stepped outside the zoo's glass doors and called to Snowflake. Now on my life, Snowflake had not bleated a bleat during that week. Bleating is the mewing noise that fawns make, similar to a goat kid calling it's mom. Snowflake drank her bottles from me, and frolicked in the grass with the other two doe fawns, having a good time at 'zoo camp'. But now that the fawn was hearing the only mom she ever knew, Snowflake was bleating and pacing the fence! Just like a human child greeting its mom after a week at camp. I knew Snowflake had been fine, but the Adoptive Mom was having a rough time. This continued for the next few weekends. Adoptive Mom coming and baby Snowflake bleating.

Since all the fawns were female that year, I moved them into the adult white tail enclosure earlier than usual. Sometimes the adult bucks will chase unfamiliar young bucks down until the spring fawns get exhausted. The big bucks will smell, but leave the doe fawns alone as they have 'no-threat-to-my- territory' male smell, and are not sexually mature.

After a month of heart breaking reunions, I caught the Adoptive Mom before she got out the zoo doors and called to her fawn. I wanted her to see that Snowflake was not pacing the fence, crying for her mommy.

"Let's try an experiment," I implored, feeling sorry for the Adoptive Mom. She looked shook up already. "I'll get the bottles for the fawns and walk up with you. But don't say a thing once we get outside the zoo doors. Snowflake hears your voice and comes running and bleating. Just like my fawns hear the jingle of my keys and come running for their bottles." I finished saying as I tucked my key hook into my pocket. (Usually the keys just hang from my belt loop- a little redneck style, I know, but very convenient!) The jangle of my keys would not alert the fawns of our approach.

I retrieved the three fawn bottles from the kitchen and met the adoptive couple at the glass zoo doors.

"See, Snowflake is not by the fence," I pointed out. "Let's go, but remember to be quiet. We will see what they are doing when we get to the top of the hill."

Silently we walked to the top of the hill where the acre large white tail enclosure was green with waist high summer grasses. All of the white tail deer were on the other side of the hill, far away from the fence and us. I could see the Adoptive Mom was more relieved by the moment. We approached the fence. The Adoptive Mom could see the deer were all, including her 'baby', peacefully grazing in the morning sun.

"O.K. See she is fine? Now call to her." I gently whispered.

"Snowflake, come here baby," was all the Adoptive Mom had to say. Snowflake perked up her ears, bleated and then bounded towards the fence for her bottle. Big, happy leaps, straight for her mommy and the waiting bottle.

"Come on Babies," I called out as my Gramma Lizzie had taught me four decades earlier. And as I knew they would, my babies came too.

But, boy was I in for a surprise. Not only did the two doe fawns from that spring come bounding, so did every white tail I had hand reared for the last ten years. *HOLY MACKEREL! Look at 'em all come running!* I had not taken a bottle to the adult white tail pen in the years before because I had always had at least one young buck. Therefore I had not put the fawns in the large run while they were still on a bottle. Within seconds I had ten deer vying for two eight ounce baby bottles. The largest eight point buck, king of the herd, shoved the others out of the way with his antlers and started sucking from the bottle in my hand. I pulled the bottle out, giving it to the young fawn he shoved and another buck pushed that fawn away again. *WOW! This is amazing.* I had no idea that the adults would still respond to my voice, never having done this before.

I instructed the Adoptive Mom to take her bottle and Snowflake farther down the fence line. There was nothing I could do but share the two bottles, one in each hand, with the ten deer on the other side of the fence. *I'll have to come back later with bottles for the two young females, Holy Mackerel!*

The adoptive couple and I shared a good laugh coming down the hill after the feeding. Adoptive Mom had tears of joy in her eyes. She finally realized that her baby had adjusted. It was the sound of her voice that caused the young doe to react with bleating and pacing whenever the Adoptive Mom visited. Here was evidence of the love that the Adoptive Mom had poured into the fawn. Or maybe it is just positive reinforcement of the bottle. Whatever 'it' was 'it' was there.

It was a lesson for me also. My daughter Jackie was going off to college soon. On Jackie's first day of pre school I had to walk away, like Adoptive Mom walking away from her baby fawn. Like the times I had to leave lion or tiger cubs at the airport. Like the times I released squirrels, raccoons, and possums I had raised into the forests of Space Farms. Or, like Russell Crow, still circling in the sky above my back yard. I was going to have to walk away, leaving our baby girl in God's hands at college, far away from home. *Well, not that far, only two hours, but the start of a lifetime away.* I had seen so many animal babies grow and go on to their own lives. I know it is the way of life and living. I had worried and fretted to myself and hubby, but I never let Jackie know. I pushed forward positively, only expressing the great experience Jack would have at college. In my heart I prayed. I prayed and prayed that Jackie would come running, happy to see us, like the eight point buck on a bottle. Knowing that the deer and she would lead their own lives. I prayed that we would feel the joy of the reunion, the amazement of the emotion, the unabashed awe of the magic. Like watching my big bucks on a bottle. Amazing, just amazing.

Chapter 8 Holiday Hibernation Time

Holiday Hibernation Time
"Tis five days after Christmas, the leftovers have dwindled,
And oh what a mess in the wake of Kris Cringle!
So, Yes, I am very late this year,
With my annual letter to friends near and dear.
This year was a trip, crazy and fast paced,
But I'm still hanging in with a smile on my face.
Started last February with a contract - Hooray!
My dream of being published was one step away.
Signed a seven year contract in the blink of an eye,
Last time I did that, I married my guy!
Raised three little chipmunks, boy were they cute,
Big as my thumb, pink, with stripes to boot.
They grew up just fine, but stayed a funny gray,
Until they turned orange on their 56th day.
Doc Ted castrated poor Khyber the tiger,
After last year's three litters.
He's still a nice kitty, evidently not bitter.
Raised an orphaned crow, named him Russell you know,
How many women can say they hand fed Russell Crow?
Jenny the woodchuck, My sweet little pet
Is in winter sleep now, I've not seen her yet.
Fawns, Chicks, raccoons and my first fallow deer,
Named Tooter for the sound that he makes is quite queer.
On the tail wind of Ivan , a macaw blew in,
Thought it was a Scarlet, but it was a Green Wing.
So I was wrong, with egg on my face,
Can't be right all the time, with each single case.
So we built a new aviary to house all the birds
Built the inside myself, I am quite proud,
You'll not hear me brag, the birds are that loud!
Which squawk, scream and holler, though they speak lots of words.
Wrote press releases, did speeches, TV and radio,
Local FM has a shock jock, won't do that again, Oh No!
I love my work, here at the zoo
A God given talent for what I do.
Doug's still my saint, my hero, my friend.
Puts up with my family time and again.
Always fixing things the others may break,
Doug calls it job security, his own funny take.
His Grizzly Adams beard has a skunk stripe of gray,
Which he says I add to every other day.

Zoo Momma

Jack's college bound, we visited quite a few.
Now she gets to decide, what's a mother to do?
She had a fender bender that Doug helped her fix,
While I proofed my first book, how fast time does tic!
She went to the prom, a princess in her dress,
But a teenager true, her room is a mess.
An intelligent gal, with Doug's great streak of funny,
Yet a gifted writer, that other parents would envy.
I've been so blessed with my book coming out,
It's been received well, so proud I could shout.
Book signings are fun, and oh what a bother,
No one recognized me dressed up as an author.
I'd of been better off in uniform speckled in poo,
Like everyone sees me when I'm at the zoo!
OH well.
Yes Santa has come and gone, I know this is late,
You can see I've had quite a bit on my plate.
My turtle time is near, I must introspect
Of my next challenge, which I've not started yet.
Write, call or visit, you know where I am,
Uptown Beemerville, still on Space's land.
So to all my friends across the nation,
Merry Christmas, good night, time for my hibernation.
Love, Lori, Jackie and Doug.

Lori and a White Tailed Deer fawn
Photo by Jessie Goble

Zoo Momma

Chapter 9 I'm ready for my close up, Mr. DeMille

I am a worrier. Perhaps I was a Jewish mother in another lifetime. In my opinion that is a high compliment not a critical comment. My perfectionism is a problem sometimes, and worrying is my motivation. If you don't worry, you don't care…

There are few phenomenon as fascinating as hibernation. This is nature's simple way of saying that it takes less energy to sleep than it would to collect food during cold winter months. Jenny Woodchuck (she is after all a girl!) was safely ensconced in the barn all winter. Come March, she had not stirred. The other male woodchucks were kept in a separate cage next to the large glass windows, receiving the first morning sun beams. This heated the cage full of hay and the woodchucks were stirring around coming to the surface of their hay tunnels. But not my woodchuck. I was worried. I visited the barn daily to watch for signs of waking. I left a carrot to see if and when it had been eaten, to no avail. Had she frozen to death without the combined body warmth of other woodchucks? It was cold in the barn but not below freezing. I just did not know, and Jenny's fate was on my mind all winter long.

Hibernation is a prolonged, controlled state of dormancy. Animals prepare with heavy feasting during late summer and fall by storing body fat. They 'bulk up'. All the native animals, which are able to survive the cold, develop a secondary warmer fur coat. Ground squirrels, woodchucks, prairie dogs, turtles - they all hibernate. During hibernation animals have reduced body temperature, reduced respiration, circulation and metabolism. They shut down, comatose.

For instance: ground squirrels normally breathe 200 times a minute. In hibernation they have been measured at 4 or 5 breaths a minute. A hibernating animal reduces its body temperature to only a couple of degrees above ambient temperature. Keep in mind below ground temperatures are usually around 50 degrees.

Animals find an appropriate spot to hibernate. Woodchucks burrow into the ground and seal off the room of the tunnel they hibernate in. If they did not seal off the room, the other animals that use that burrow in the winter (foxes, snakes or skunks) would eat them easily. An adult male woodchuck would weigh about 10 to 13 pounds going into hibernation, and coming out, they have lost 1/3 their body weight.

My brother Eric Space, who live traps woodchucks professionally says all summer long woodchucks love apples like kids like candy. But come fall to the beginning of winter season, woodchucks will not eat them. This is Mother Nature's way of protecting them from the fermentation process when the woodchucks do not digest food in hibernation. People die of alcohol poisoning, I would assume woodchucks would also.

All this information peppered my thoughts whenever I let my mind wander to the woodchuck I have grown so fond of. Yes, I know, I have raised lions, tigers and all sorts of other animals, and it seems so silly to say that I love a woodchuck. Oh well, that is what it is.

I received a call from Dr. Leonard Rue III, a renowned photographer and close friend of the family. He wanted a picture of a woodchuck in the snow. Was Jenny awake yet? It was early March, other wild woodchucks were stirring and seen above ground. I told Lennie that Jenny was not awake yet. Ok, now I was really starting to worry since Lennie brought up the subject. We discussed which day would be good for the both of us to get together and wake Jenny up.

"Ok, but if she is dead, you have to promise not to make fun of me if I cry", I pleaded.

"Lori, you know I would not do that," Lennie replied. I did know that, and that knowledge was the only reason I agreed to wake Jenny up in front of this long time family friend who just happened to be a famous photographer. That and the fact that I really needed - wanted to know that Jenny was ok. Lennie would understand if I cried. Totally unprofessional, tears would ruin my reputation with any other photographer, but Lennie, he was family. He understood the unspoken, unusual bond our family had with many animals of different species.

On the day Lennie and his son, Len Jr., came, I was ready, steeled to the possibilities. The sun was out, the snow was fading fast, but it was still chilly. Lennie set up his camera as I went into the winter barn to bring out Jenny. I called her as I entered. No answer. I opened her cage and with a struggle, pulled out the milk crate that held the hay mound that contained Jenny. She was the only woodchuck in that cage, so I knew the lump of hay held Jenny. I carried the mounded hay filled plastic milk crate to the hill behind Dad's house. Lennie had his camera set up in the snow. Lennie and Len Jr. gathered around the silent, unmoving crate and myself. I looked at Lennie, I could feel my face flush. Worry is my middle name.

"Well, let's dig her out," Lennie suggested.

"Don't you laugh at me if I cry," I reminded him. Lennie smiled a fatherly smile and just nodded. I gently unwrapped a layer of hay. I did not know what to expect. Would Jenny be angry, snarling because I woke her up earlier than she wanted? Had she forgotten me over the winter? Did hibernation wipe her mental slate clean, deleting her memory of me? Would she dash out and run away to the nearby field? Was she even alive?

The construction of the hay mound was fascinating. The fall before I had fluffed the hay loosely into the cage with Jenny. She had rearranged it to her liking. Now I was amazed at her construction technique. Each blade of grass was placed in a circular manor, a literal woven cocoon closely surrounding her. A six inch thick cocoon. I gently plucked the individual blades of dried grass away, until I found her. I touched her ear, she was rock cold. And not moving. In a fetal position, eyes closed, previously perky nose not twitching. I was immediately heartbroken.

"OH Lennie, I think she is dead," my eyes filled to the brim, as I looked up at Lennie. Lennie's face was solemn. His eyes shown with knowledge and warmth.

"Talk to her, Lori, call her out," he simply said.

So I did. I had faith in Lennie's knowledge, and I was hoping beyond hope that he was right.

"Jenny, Jenny Woodchuck," I sang out in my standard greeting for Jenny.

"Jenny, wake up, mommy wants you to wake up now".

I looked at Lennie again. His words encouraging even if Jenny's corpse was not moving.

"Keep talking."

I did. I babbled every endearing word Jenny had ever heard from me. My baby talk. I felt a little silly standing in the snow with two photographers staring and talking to a gray plastic milk crate of hay with a cold corpse in it. But Lennie said it would work. And I was more than willing to try for my Jenny.

A whisker twitched.

"Did you see that?" I implored. *Or was it just my imagination?*

"Keep talking," was Lennie's gentle command.

Lennie, Len Jr. and I were witnesses to a sight few humans had seen. Another whisker twitch, a nose wiggle, and the beginning of a stretch. Eyes still closed, Jenny appeared to writhe in pain. She opened her mouth wide, a gasping yawn. We could see her long incisors, her tongue was barely pink. She yawned again and stretched her body in apparent pain. Her eyes opened but they were dull and dumb looking, not the normal perky hyperawareness that I was used to seeing in her eyes. I was not aware if the cameras were clicking, my total concentration was on Jenny. And I was still babbling, as my tears of fear turned into happiness.

After a couple of minutes, I entrusted Jenny's surveillance to Lennie. I ran to Dad's house, my step-mother Mira was in the kitchen pouring coffee.

"Got any carrots?" was more a command, than a question, as I pulled open the refrigerator, rudely searching the bins. I grabbed a couple of carrots and dashed out the door again. Later I found out that Mira, a registered nurse, had worked the night shift before, and was not quite awake when I made my Flash Gordon carrot grab. She told me she stood there a couple of moments wondering why Jenny our Secretary needed carrots in such a hurry! I had not mentioned that the carrots were for Jenny Woodchuck.

I returned to Jenny Woodchuck, picked her up and cuddled her to me hoping to transfer my body warmth. She was not interested in the carrots.

"It will take her a while to warm up for what we need, can you take her someplace warm?" Lennie asked. We discussed where to take her, and decided to take her to the office nursery, the warmest room on the zoo property. While I set Jenny up in a cage next to the baseboard heat for her gradual warm up, Lennie and Len Jr. packed up their cameras and met me at the office.

Dad was in his office, next door to the nursery. Lennie and Dad greeted each other as old friends do. They chatted about family matters and Dad told Lennie about a local wild bear sow that had come out of hibernation with four cubs. Lennie and Len Jr. had a couple of hours to kill until Jenny warmed up, so we all decided to go see if the guys could get some good shots of the sow and cubs. They did. A few hours later we were back to Jenny woodchuck.

Two hours after being so rudely awakened from her winter hibernation, Jenny Woodchuck was standing upright in a patch of snow chewing on a carrot.

"I'm ready for my close up, Mr. DeMille!" photogenic Jenny seemed to say.

Jenny ran once or twice, but I was able to catch her easily, her muscles still lagging from her hibernation. Afterwards, Jenny went back to the office nursery. It took Jenny a good two weeks to get her perky eyes back. I have weeks like that come spring time too.

Lori and Jenny Woodchick
Photo by Karen Talasco

Chapter 10 No Chance

Everyone always has a dream, a wish, a goal or just a plain old want. When Space Farms bought a trio of Ring tailed lemurs four years prior, I loved the look of them. Looking like a cross between a raccoon, cat, and a monkey, the Ring-tailed Lemur looks like a genetic experiment gone heavy on the cute. I wanted one. Other zookeepers I had spoken with said they made great pets, as long as you castrate if they are male. The first year, our two mothers each had twins. We were quite surprised, we knew they were old enough to reproduce, but did not know they were pregnant upon arrival to the zoo. One morning we looked and thought the one mom had developed two tumors on her breasts. Upon closer inspection, they were tiny walnut sized heads. The babies' gray coloration blended perfectly into the moms fur. Only little black heads gave away their presence. The moms were great moms, raising double sets of twins every year. I watched the process of infant raising with an envious eye. I really wanted to raise one. For four years I waited. Every year the moms raised their young expertly, not needing assistance from me. Babies clung invisibly to mom, only little black heads giving them away. Their tiny gray hands, feet with black pads and striped tails were nestled deep in the mother's gray fur. The babies piggybacked (or on the breasts in front) for two months before starting to explore the earth on their own. I did not have the heart to take a clinging, nursing baby from a mother's breast just for my own personal gratification. Out of eight young in four years, seven were male. So Space Farms Zoo had quite a population of Ring -tailed lemurs. Eleven to be exact, but I still did not have one.

Lemurs are endangered primates. The Ring tailed Lemur is one of eleven species of true lemurs and seven species of dwarf lemurs. All lemurs are found on the islands of Madagascar and the neighboring Comoro Islands off the eastern coast of Africa. They're considered primates but are on a separate branch of the evolutionary tree. Scientists speculate they evolved separately from the rest of the species on the continent after the islands shifted positions (Continental Drift Theory). Arboreal and adorable, the Ring Tailed Lemur has a gray body and a distinctive white and black striped tail. At rest the tail is often worn around the neck like a scarf. Its eyes are circled in black on a white facial mask. Crowned with cute teddy bear shaped ears, the lemur looks like a child's plush toy and is one of evolutions cutest outcomes. The ring tailed lemur has an opposable thumb on all four feet, which aids the lemur in its tree dwelling life.

Ring tailed lemur adults weigh seven to twelve pounds and are up to eighteen inches from head to base of tail. The long eighteen inch tail is not prehensile and is used for balance when jumping from branch to branch. Ring Tailed Lemurs have been known to jump ten feet vertically.

The diet of the lemur is varied with fruits, veggies, seeds, and the occasional insect. Lemurs are social and travel in troops of three to thirty. Studies have reveled over fifteen different vocal sounds, in addition to body language used for communication.

Such interesting creatures, you can understand why I dreamed of raising one. But endangered and protected animals are special. You don't take the chance of taking a healthy baby away from an attentive mom, and possibly loosing that baby, just on the whim of a wish.

Good Friday of 2005 I was sitting in my chair, drinking my morning coffee and feeling kind of blue. Another holiday and I was working, again. Why me? Never a holiday off. I asked God in a silent prayer for a sign that I should keep doing this type of work. Zoo keeping is a responsibility of care for animals, every day, 24/7,not just the normal weekday 9 to 5. But this was the life I had chosen, or perhaps the life that had chosen me. I sighed, finished my coffee, I got dressed and drove down to the zoo.

I had no sooner pulled into the parking lot when my husband Doug pulled up alongside me in his green gator jitney. He was dressed in his warm working clothes, already somewhat disheveled and dirty, after working for the previous hour.

"Hi Hon. You up for a challenge?", his eyes twinkled, "This one has <u>no chance</u> without you." Doug handed me a bunch of flannel shirt rags I had ripped for cleaning rags for the guys in our garage. I gently unrolled the rags to find a tiny Ring Tailed Lemur, his body about four inches long, with a six inch umbilical cord and placenta the size of my thumbnail still attached. His head was the size of a walnut, his tiny body half the size of a spool of thread split vertically. His fingers were curled tight on the end of two inch puny arms. Skinny grasshopper tithed legs were lank. His scrawny downy haired black and white tail made him look more like a spider than a primate. But it was too late to fall in love with this one.

"Too late Honey, It's dead," I replied, as I cradled the cold little corpse in my warm hand.

"He was breathing when I brought him from across the street," Doug sighed. We looked at the tiny creature together. Amazingly as the warmth of my hand transferred to the little lemur, it moved!

"See he is alive! I know you have wanted to raise one. His mom didn't want him. I found him on top of the wire but she was not paying this one any attention, she has the second one though." Doug and I were both smiling now. "He's got <u>no chance</u> without you", repeated the newly adopted very proud Dad.

I walked past my Dad's office with the tiny bundle. Dad was sitting in his chair.

"Whatyagot?' Dad queried.

"A little male lemur, Pop." I said, and gave him the quick run down on what Doug had told me.

"Well, you got a job ahead of you! He is tiny. Don't fret if you loose him, we have plenty of males. But you are his best bet in this life," Dad encouraged me.

I took the No Chance lemur into the nursery office and trimmed off the umbilical cord and placenta. I stuffed the lucky lemur inside my sweat shirt, (actually in my sports bra to be honest), to give him more body warmth. I knew a heating pad would cook him on one side, if he could not roll over to warm the other side, because he was that weak. *Don't get attached to this one he has no chance.* The pitiful tiny lemur was definitely alive, but I did not hold out much hope. *No Chance, don't get attached. No Chance, No Chance.* And the name stuck, half as a reminder to me, absolutely no guilt if this one doesn't make it. No Chance was my baby lemur now.

Jackie, my daughter, was playing hooky from school, a mental health day, she had called it. *Yeah, right!* I called her from the zoo office and told her where to look up the milk percentages in my files at home. I would need to figure out what to feed the No Chance lemur. He was so very tiny. Little fingers clung to my stretchy bra as he warmed up enough to hold on. Jackie read me the list I had from the Borden company of all the different animal milks they had analyzed. No Lemurs on the list. *Ok, I figured, It is a primate like a monkey.* She read me the percentages of fats to carbohydrates to proteins on primates. I took notes. Next I called Baker's Pharmacy in Sussex to see if they had premature human baby formula (humans are primates). The pharmacy did not carry any but suggested I call the A&P.

I needed some sort of milk so I decided to drive the six miles to town to read the labels myself, with the note in my pocket on the Borden analysis. I didn't have any bottle nipples small enough so I would need eyedroppers also. What to do with the little cold lemur? I could not put him on a heating pad. He could not crawl off if he got too warm. Premature human formula is expensive, what if the lemur was dead before I got to the store and back again. It is a twenty minute trip, one way. I checked my shirt in the mirror in the office hallway. The No Chance lemur bump was hardly noticeable in my sports bra. He was wiggling but not overly rambunctious. *Ok so he stays where he is nice and warm, no one will notice.* I hopped in the car and drove off to town.

First stop, the A&P baby isle. I found premature baby formula in powder, compared the ingredients and the percentages, decided it was the best I was going to find. I looked at the eye droppers they had. All the eye droppers were actually medicine droppers and were way to large for the tiny black lips I was going to feed. I purchased the formula and headed uptown Sussex to Baker's Pharmacy. I know the ladies at the pharmacy. I grew up with most of them. They knew me also. When I asked to see some eyedroppers they all gathered around. The owner, Stud, a tall, handsome man about my age, came to the counter with a selection of eyedroppers of different sizes. They all asked what I needed to feed. *I told you they knew me!*

Well, the little No Chance lemur had been tucked inside my bra, absorbing the warmth of my body for about a half hour now and was being quite wiggly. So I reached inside my sweatshirt, pulled him out of my lacy sports bra for a mouth size check with the assorted eyedroppers. The ladies behind the counter all gasped and then chuckled, knowing that the little lemur was being warmed up with boob body temperature. A natural set of all encompassing heating pads, just the right temperature! I was glad to see him moving and his little pink tongue licking his lips. He was hungry! *Great, he might drink!* I picked the size eyedropper I thought was small enough, and plastic (glass might hurt his lips or gums).

"No charge for those, Lori, take them all. Good luck with your new baby", Stud graciously said. Tucking No Chance back in his warming zone, I zoomed home and prepared formula for the little imp resting in my sports bra.

On my way home I saw my cousin Dutch Dunn in his business's driveway. I pulled over to show him my new charge.

"Keeping him warm is going to be a problem," I explained to Dutch.

"I have just what you need," Dutch winked and walked over to his black pick up truck. After returning to my car he said, "Here, this ought to do it!", as he handed me a blue camouflaged mottled motorcycle polar fleece skull cap. It was perfect, a mini sleeping bag for the No Chance lemur. I said thanks and continued home to the zoo.

After preparing the formula according to directions, I eye dropper the milk in between little black lips I could hardly see. *You know you are getting old when you need glasses to do this type of work!* The flicking pink tongue told me No Chance was taking in the milk. No Chance was not sucking, but he was taking in each individual drop, licking it off his lips. *Hallelujah!* And he was swallowing. *Even better.* After his giant meal of five drops (about one teaspoon) he settled down and cuddled in my hand. I set No Chance up in the office nursery incubator that had been donated by Newton Memorial Hospital and modified by my mechanical genius hubby, Doug. I placed him inside the blue fleece skull cap for warmth on top of a heating pad. I have to admit that No Chance looked like a demon in his Mad Hatter hat. Something about the squinty black and white rimmed honey colored eyes with ruffled sparse fur made him look like a miniature evil gremlin. But I thought he was cute anyway.

I took advantage of the sleeping baby's nap to call my friends, Butch and Lynn, the owners of the Flag Acres Zoo in New York State, to double check my procedures. Butch told me I had done everything correctly, but to call if I had any problems or questions. Butch and Lynn had raised newborn Marmosets, another small primate, but never Ring Tails. I had to ask the question, but I knew the answer. I was hoping for another answer, but the answer was "every two hours." I knew my nights of good sleep were over for quite a while.

I sent off an email that night to a lemur research group that I will not mention. I had searched their web site for information on newborns, but only finding information on eight week old lemurs, I sent off an email. Don't know what their problem was, but I never heard a word or email back. *Foley on them.*

Little No Chance drank right on schedule every two hours. Like any newborn, his main activities were drinking, sleeping and pee and poop. I used a Q-tip with warm water to stimulate his urine and bowel movements. No Chance started to fur out, but still slept inside his Harley Davidson skull cap. He was a cool dude. At two weeks old I successfully got No Chance to suck from a tiny kitten bottle. At four weeks old he had stretched out to six inches long, not including tail. He still needed to eat every two hours, but was drinking a whopping ten drops a time, maybe two teaspoons full. I loved him, and I could tell when he looked at me with those big honey colored bulging eyes that we had bonded. Oh and I changed his name, No Chance became Some Chance at week two. At four weeks old he weighed four ounces! I declared his new name: Pretty Good Chance. Chance was doing great. I started him on Cheerios at four weeks when his first teeth came through the gums. Over the next weeks I started him on human baby food fruits and vegetables. Chance was a big hit on the lecture circuit that summer, delighting audiences with his clinging abilities, never leaving my body. I trained him to wear an H shaped harness made for a ferret.

That summer I was asked to speak at the New Jersey State Fair. In order to take any animal out on the lecture circuit I need a Veterinary Certificate of Health. So I set up an appointment with our zoo Vet., Dr. Spinks. Whenever I arrive at the Animal Hospital of Sussex County, the staff gathers round. I know it's not my sparkling personality, it is the unusual animals I bring in. (This was technically Pretty Good Chance's second visit to the Vet, but that will be covered briefly in the next chapter of this book. Everybody's life is full of adventures here at the zoo.) Chance traveled with me everywhere, meetings, to Easter Breakfast at Church, home and to the zoo everyday. Only that first trip to the A&P and to Baker's Pharmacy did he ride inside my sweatshirt! I don't want to get the A&P folks in trouble, they never knew I had a hitchhiker.

The appointment at Dr. Spinks' office went well, sort of. Chance hated the leash, didn't mind the harness, but hated being restricted by the leash. At this point in his development, he did not want to be far away from mom (I.e. me) for long and always jumped back to me when I made kissy noises. So while waiting in the Vet.'s examination room, I took off his leash. Things went fine, at first. Chance was leisurely exploring the tables, the window, the window curtains and the top of the cabinets. I heard Dr. Spinks talking to one of his staff outside the door, figured I better get Chance back to me so I made kissy noises. Chance bounded quickly to my shoulder, holding his blue skull cap. Dr. Spinks entered the fifteen foot square examination room and (*thank God*) closed the door again.

"Hi Lor, so this is No Chance", Dr. Spinks calmly stated. Dr. Spinks knew of No Chance from our visit before with the kangaroo.

"Yeah, he's doing great, not sick, I just need a Veterinarian Certificate of Health, but now his name is Pretty Good Chance," I chuckled. So did the Dr.

I don't know exactly what set Chance off after that. Without warning Dr. Spinks and I were suddenly in the middle of a lemur pin ball machine. Chance was jumping from metal exam table to the curtain rods, to the cabinet, knocking over a glass container full of cotton balls in the process. Chance continued his jumping spree, lighting on my shoulder, Dr. Spinks' shoulder, the picture frame on the wall, the exam table, back to the cabinets, shoving containers full of medical equipment around and back to the curtain rods again.

"Well, his legs work fine," Dr. Spinks laughed at his own understatement. So did I.

I took the motorcycle skull cap/security blanket and held it up, knowing

Chance would return to it - eventually. On his next visit to my shoulder I put the hat over Chance's head, capturing him.

"Sorry about that, Dr. Spinks," I sheepishly grinned while holding the little lemur securely.

Dr. Spinks calmly nodded, while raising one eyebrow, then examined Chance as I held the imp. Dr. Spinks pronounced Chance healthy. *Well I knew that, but I needed the paperwork.* Chance the gremlin was not too happy when I put him back in his traveling case. He was quiet all the way home, no doubt nursing a grudge against me for all the indignities he had to physically suffer through for a piece of paper.

I had been invited to share my writing procedure with the 5th grade of the Sussex Wantage grammar school. So I took the chapter you have read so far and Pretty Good Chance to show the children. The kids were amazed when I showed them Pretty Good Chance's ability to hold on. It was a natural instinct for a little lemur. In the wild if they don't or can't hold on as momma lemur jumps from branch to branch, the infant is as good as dead. The speed and jumping ability of the lemur troop is the main defense of the lemur. The only defense little lemurs have is to hold on to mom. Don't get me wrong, they do have some nasty teeth, but if they can run away first, a lemur will. The children 'ooohed" and laughed as I took the hat Pretty Good Chance was clinging to and turned it upside down. Then I moved my arms like a roller coaster, to show how good the little lemur was at holding on. I must admit, I did hold one hand under the hat with Pretty Good Chance, well, you know, just in case.

Pretty Good Chance always traveled in the same Harley skull cap, the light blue, dark blue and black of the hat making a nice contrast with his white belly, white rimmed eyes and gray body. His little tail grew proportionately with his body. By the time he was six inches long, his fully furred out black and white striped tail was six inches also. He was beautiful. At eight weeks old I was finally able to get him to stay on the nursery baby scale. Pretty good Chance was a whopping eight ounces, so I officially changed his name once again, to Fat Chance. I was so proud of his little round belly. *Proud momma, it takes a lot of work to put that belly there.*

Fat Chance was a great crowd pleaser at my speeches that year. He clung to me or his hat. I leashed him, but he did not like it. Daytime in the zoo nursery, he stayed in his cage making pitiful "oop oop" noises whenever he saw me. I played with him when I could during the day, but night time was our playtime. Fat Chance would roam the house, looking for me in any room. After finding me, he would check out another area, then check back with me again. The only time he was in his cage was when I was sleeping, or if I was cooking. I worried about Fat Chance chewing on electrical wires or slipping off my shoulder into the stew. Strange things a lemur mom has to fret!

Fat Chance also had an affinity for Doug's increasingly bald head. Don't know why, maybe it was a warm spot to sit on, or the shiny beacon that attracted Fat Chance. Doug would get a little peeved when stretching out in his lazy boy after a hard days work and Fat Chance would jump out of nowhere onto his baldy bean. I'd hear the curse words, then see Doug reach up and pet the pesky primate.

Fat Chance was born on Good Friday, late March. By the third week of July my little family and I were going to go to the Mountain River Lodge in Canada on vacation. I was not ready to put Fat Chance in with the other lemurs and take a chance that the alpha male would kill him as a strange male coming into the troop. I needed a babysitter. Where do you find a babysitter for a spoiled lemur? My good friend, Karen Martin volunteered to stay at my house and play with Fat Chance.

Our vacation in Canada was perfect, the weather nice, the fish were biting so Doug was happy. I painted and read for a week straight. Jackie, Doug and I played card games and board games at nights after suppers out. We had a wonderful family week together. Things can get hectic at the zoo, with my infant feeding schedule, speeches, and meetings at night. So I was thrilled to have the time with Doug and Jackie to just relax. It helped me a lot to know 'my' baby animals were well taken care of, between the staff at the zoo and my good friend, Karen, at my house with Chance. I knew Karen would be an attentive mom for Chance, she had been a Vet. Tech.. She also knew Dr. Spinks just in case there was any problems.

We returned home to a major surprise. I opened the door to the house, walked through our kitchen and just stared at the amazing spider web of clothesline creatively spun around our living room. Our living room has our master bedroom directly above in the loft. A natural rock fireplace runs floor to ceiling in the two story room. The wrought iron circular staircase was interwoven with clothes line, tied conveniently in knots along the way so little lemur hands could grasp. The lines ran from the stairway to the loft, to the mantle, to the standing lamp and back again. What a spider web! I laughed out loud, knowing exactly what Karen had done. Karen had spoiled her charge with an in house playground fit for a lemur. Fat Chance was in his cage as Karen had gone to work. He "Woo"ed to me, I let him out. Fat Chance was so excited to show me his new toys. Did I mention that Karen had also strung toys on the lines ? Around and around the room Chance spun. A spider with only five legs (his four and the long tail). Quite the sight. Now that he had full run of the house, he was THE KING.

I could of lived with that. Doug could of lived with that. Jackie thought it was a trip having a lemur brother. But I could not live with the poo. Yes they were little poos. Yes they were the size of raisins. Yes they were a dryish kind of poo. But it was poo, dropping out of the sky anytime Fat Chance was above you. Not a lot, not like a rain storm, just an occasional 'plink'. Like "Here is a gift for you, Mommy." Dinner time, popcorn time, reading the newspaper, anytime. I was finding the little raisins everywhere, I especially hated finding them with my bare feet. Ffat Chance had not brought down the curtains, as our old family saying goes: "When the curtains come down the animal goes out". But once he had full run of the house, I could not get him back to the good litter box habits he had in his cage. It was late August, soon the temperature would drop, he would need to adjust to the outside temperatures gradually with the seasons. I should re-introduce him to his troop. I knew that. Dad reminded me about once a week, every week. I know that, Dad!

I was happy to leave him at the zoo overnight. No worries, he was safe, warm and dry. My house got unstrung, and cleaned. Chance was in the nursery, adjusting to the September temperatures. But he needed to go back to his troop before he became sexually mature and the other established males might fight him. So after Labor Day weekend I took the first step. I took off Fat Chance's harness, giving him a full body rub down. I put his tattered hat and a new blanket in the travel case. Fat Chance knew the routine and jumped in. I closed his door. I could of driven him to the other lemurs on my ATV Quad, but I walked, not wanting to shake Fat Chance up with the noise of the engine.

The walk up the hill was longer than usual. Seemed to take forever. It was just before closing at the zoo. The sun made orange sherbet colored streaks in the September sky. A breeze ruffled the palm sized leaves of the skyscraping oaks. The grass was still green, recently mowed, it smelled sweet. If bad things would happen, we wanted them to happen after we closed so we could take care of the problem without a dozen visitors getting in the way. *Sorry Visitors, you don't get to watch.* Fat Chance clung to the window slats of the carrying case like a child looking out the windows on a long, boring car trip. At the top of the hill, and around the Tool Museum was the 20 ft. by 12 ft. grassy enclosure with the original troop of lemurs. Fat Chance's biological mom, aunt, dad, brother and two male cousins all stared as we approached. A dozen honey colored eyes peered inquisitively, watching us, moving in unison like a school of fish.

I unlocked the guard fence, and the inside door to the lemur enclosure. The troop spun around the climbing branches, making some of the twenty one different sounds lemurs have been noted for. Their agility and acrobatics always fascinates me. Fat Chance "oip"ed, constantly, his fearful sound I had come to recognize.

"You'll be fine, you'll be fine," I constantly calmly repeated. *Let's not kid ourselves, I was reassuring myself also.*

I placed the carry case close to the enclosure door, facing away from me. I sprinkled Honey Nut Cheerios on top of the case and in front of the door of the carry case. My theory was to attract the other lemurs to come make friends. *Oh come on moms. Don't you make cookies for your kids' friends?* There was food and water inside the case for Fat Chance. I opened the carry case door from behind the case, knowing Fat Chance would stay in the back of the case, closest to me. Yeah, he did, still "oip"ing repeatedly. I backed out the enclosure door and locked the padlock.

I walked to the front of the enclosure and called Fat Chance out. He did not come out. But that was ok, he had his motley hat, and a warm blanket. Fat Chance felt safer in his familiar carrying case than he did to come out. *Ok so now what?* The other lemurs were hanging back on the branches, still staring at the case. Everyone was hesitant. I walked to the Antique School House and hid around the corner. Fat Chance stopped calling to me. *Good. Come on buddy time to make friends.*

As soon as I had hidden myself, I peeked around the red rough boards of the school house. To my horror the entire troop of lemurs was rushing towards the crate. Fat Chance was clinging to his tattered hat, like an orphan in Oliver Twist. His Security blanket/hat over his head like a protective helmet, that unbeknownst to him, would not protect him at all. I have seen monkey fights, territorial fights that are so nasty a human zookeeper can not intervene without a tranquilizer gun. They may be smaller than we humans, but a lifetime of practice with teeth, claws and climbing muscles make the primates very strong. I prayed that I had not waited too long to introduce Fat Chance to the troop. *Was my selfish love for him going to cause his death?* I could only wait and watch.

The onrushing wave of lemurs stopped about a foot from the carry case with Fat Chance still in it. There was a flurry of noises emanating from the troop, calm noises I recognized from Fat Chances vocabulary. Fat Chance was not saying a thing. Just sitting there 'listening to the music of the Titanic'. My heart was bleeding. It is hard for me to write this now, even though I know how everything turned out.

The troop sat next to the carry case eating Honey Nut Cheerios. When the supply on the ground ran out, they stretched over to the case and gently picked the Cheerios off the top. *Whew!* I walked down the hill. I knew that Fat Chance would not talk to his family if I was there. If the troop was going to attack Fat Chance they would of done it immediately. They just needed time.

If I thought the walk up the black topped path to the top of the hill was long, the next twelve hours was an eternity. First thing next morning I checked on Fat Chance. A gray head with probing eyes peeked out from under the tattered hat inside the case. The other lemurs had seen me coming and dissipated in to the branches of the exhibit. Fat Chance was fine, but had not come out of his case yet. *Some things just take time.* I left him be. Two days passed, I checked on Chance every opportunity I had. The other lemurs were not ignoring him, but they were not attacking him either. The younger cousins and brother would dash in and steal the cheerios I left in the carry case, leaving Chance with the monkey pellet food. *That's Ok, he has food. If he wants the goodies, he has to come out and play. Positive reinforcement.*

Then it started to rain. Poured actually. All night and half of the next day. The lemur troop cuddled inside their protective hut. Chance stayed in his carry case. His soft polar fleece baby blanket was a darker shade of pink and blue because it was wet. Rain had angled into the case through the window slats. The raggy hat was wet, and Chance's fur was spiked with the rain. *Ok, can't stand it, I didn't spend all this time and energy raising Fat Chance to have him die of the weather.* The lemur troop was behaving well towards Fat Chance, but the No Chance lemur was living up to his original name. He was giving the lemur troop no chance to be friends. By the time I unlocked both gates and retrieved the case with Fat Chance in it we were both cold and wet.

We walked down the hill. I felt defeated, Chance was elated. I took Fat Chance directly to the winter barn where his cousins and brother would join him in a month. I visited Chance daily, caring, petting and talking to him. I will admit, I told Fat Chance repeatedly, just like I have told our human daughter Jackie, "you are a spoiled brat". *But I said it with love in my heart, so that counts right?* I told Doug that I did not want to be there when the other young lemurs were put in the cage. Just couldn't handle it. Doug reported that the transition went smoothly, all four young lemurs jumping around, Chance amongst them. After the other sibling and cousins were in the cage, I could not safely take Fat Chance out and (more importantly) get him back in. So I didn't take him out again.

The next spring, my brother Parker told me he had found a home for our four younger lemurs, they were going to Ohio to join a troop with four female ring tailed lemurs. When the day came, I said good bye to Chance, knowing he would have a good lemur life with a lemur wife. If I ever get to Ohio… I have visitation rights. I have to stop writing now, I cannot see the page.

Chance and Lori
Photo by Karen Talasco

Chapter 11 Wrasslin' Roo

Any day at the zoo can bring mundane chores, repetitive shoveling of you know what, hauling water or hay, shepherding school kids, painting, cleaning or dusting. And then there are days you wake up and the day just starts out interesting.

On April 14, 2005, I arrived at the zoo and was in the middle of my early morning nursery chores when Dad stopped by in his car. His legs and back had been bothering him, so he uses the car a lot these days.

" Dr. Spinks, [the zoo's Veterinarian], is gonna be here in a bit to check on the male kangaroo's leg. Parker noticed this morning' that it was favorin' one leg pretty bad. Might be broke," Dad explained as he walked away towards his car with the hitch rack on the back. "I gotta get a deer". He turned in his famous faded bibs and left. Road kill pick up again. Dad was aging, but still up and out every morning to check on his beloved zoo.

"I'll be there Pop," I responded. Dad knew I was interested in the medical aspects of life at the zoo. Oh boy, a kangaroo with a broken leg. What in the world had happened? FYI - we still don't know what happened. The roos were new, one male and one female and we were hoping for joeys. A roo with a broken leg is a death sentence in the wild. In captivity... well if the roo had a chance that chance's name was Dr. Ted Spinks, V.M.D..

Later I heard the automatic gate open. I walked around the corner of the main building and followed Parker and Dr. Ted up to the Kangaroo enclosure. Both men are over six foot tall and long legged. I always seem to be a couple paces behind, not by choice, just by nature. I arrived just in time to hear Dr. Spinks pronounce.

"Yes it's broken, see how the foot is floppy? " Dr. Spinks pronounced. "Hi Lor," he greeted me. " I'll clear my schedule and we can fix it tomorrow morning. We can put a rod in it and see how it goes." Dr. Spinks went back to his Animal Hospital of Sussex County to prepare for the kangaroo procedure. We did not want to loose this roo, we had only two, one male, one female.

Darn. A roo with a broken leg. Well, we had two options. Put the roo down or try to fix it. Roos are not easy to come by in the zoological world. Ironically, they are considered pests in Australia and treated like vermin. Here in the states they are hard to get. Putting a rod in his leg and casting it was risky, but it was the five foot tall (over six foot tall if on his tippy toes) roo's only chance. All we could do was wait 'till the next morning.

The kangaroo's main defense is to hop, and they can hop fast. Average length of a kangaroo jump is eight feet. Under stress they can jump fifteen to twenty feet horizontally, eight feet high. Kangaroo hind legs are strong, solid muscle from the constant exercise of hopping. Roos can travel forty miles per hour for up to twenty miles! Constant exercise keep the legs wound tight like a spring. The massive tail is used as ballast when they hop. The tail itself is muscled. It is the size of a small musk melon at the base, tapering off at the end of the four foot fur covered tail. The thick tail is also used for balance when resting, making a tripod of the two legs and tail to support the average hundred thirty pound animal.

The hind feet of kangaroos are very interesting. They have one large center toe and a smaller toe on each side, like an ostrich or the dinosaurs. The front legs are 'wimpy', considerably smaller and have four slender finger toes on the tiny front feet. The front feet are used to steady the body when feeding off the ground on grasses and grains. The male roos box with the front feet when establishing dominance. Females clean their pouches with the little delicate fingers of their front feet.

As a side note in history: When kangaroos were first brought to the U.S. they often traveled in circus side show acts in the early 1900's. The circus 'barker' would entice macho men into a boxing ring with the come on to box with the kangaroo for a side bet gamble. The unknowing macho man would climb into the makeshift ring and attempt to box with the wimpy front legs which were conveniently encased in deceptive tiny boxing gloves. Many macho men were uncomfortably surprised. The kangaroo would balance the roo's entire body on it's tail and use the powerful back legs to 'kangaroo kick' (with both legs). The unwitting macho man would receive the full force of the kick in his stomach, knocking him off his feet and often incur severe injury to his abdomen. The kangaroo won the boxing match every time. Always bet on the kangaroo.

The next morning all of us were back at the kangaroo enclosure. My brother, Parker, in his khaki uniform and zookeeper Bruce had gently maneuvered the injured male into the den that my hubby Doug had specifically built for the roos. Filled with cushiony hay, the twenty foot square room confined the male roo. Parker and Bruce entered the inside door. Dr. Spinks joined Parker and Bruce with the jab stick full of anesthesia. (A jab stick is a hypodermic syringe on a long four foot rod.) Dad, Doug, Liz Cosh, (Spinks' Vet Tech, and also a cousin of ours), and I waited outside the den. There was only so much room inside and the roo was going to be under stress as soon as he figured out what was happening. Nobody likes a needle. Animals don't always understand or cooperate with receiving a shot.

Dad, gray with animal knowledge, Doug, grizzled gray in his beard, and I, a bottle blonde, contrasted with petite Liz's dark hair. We gabbed about family relatives that Dad had not seen for a while and that I hardly knew. Dad and Liz's father were second cousins. The conversation was stilted occasionally when we heard hard thumps against the sides of the den, and the curse words emanating from inside. The voices were muffled by the red walls of the barn and the insulating bedding hay, but we understood exactly what was going on. Moments later all three tall men emerged from the side door of the den to wait with the rest of us.

"A couple of minutes and he should be out," Dr. Spinks declared.
Parker and Bruce chuckled and relived the wrestling with the kangaroo for those of us who had waited blindly outside. Bruce was fortyish, gangly like a teenager, and could climb better than any monkey. His navy blue uniform was covered in

cottony beige touches of fur. Wisps of his reddish balding hair seemed as excited as his voice when Bruce described the 'wrasslin' injection process. Parker, staid and understated, smirked as we all intently listened to his buddy Bruce.

"Lori, go get my car so we can get him to the clinic," Dad instructed. Dad had aged and I had become his legs, and often his ears if hearing aid batteries ran out. I dutifully trotted, (Ok so I walked fast- I'm not getting any younger either!) to Gramma's Japanese crabapple tree to retrieve Dad's Ford Explorer. When I got to the SUV, there was all sorts of tools and equipment in the back, it was not terribly clean, and his famous road kill deer pick up rack was still on the rear hitch. It was gonna be hard getting a six foot roo in the back.

OK, so how mad is Doug gonna be if we put the roo in the back of our SUV ? How 'out' is the roo, will he release urine? Didn't see much blood...Oh I hope Doug understands... I headed for our SUV, a green Mountaineer. I knew there was nothing in the back seat so I could fold down the seats quickly. I flipped the back seat down but left the smaller jump seat in place. I grabbed a flannel sheet from the office nursery to act as a stretcher for the roo, our army stretcher might not fit.

I drove up to the motley group of us zookeepers, we start our work day clean, but that lasts about fifteen minutes. Dr. Spinks and Vet Tech Liz were in dressed spotless light blue scrub tops and jeans, their day had just begun. I saw my Grizzly Adams looking husband Doug's face grow darker as he realized I intended to take the roo in our relatively new SUV. I knew Doug was thinking the same thoughts I had just thought about a huge messy roo in our car. I parked next to the garage door at the old red barn. I opened the back hatch of the SUV, and grabbed the flannel sheet from the back. Doug only nodded silently. Doug being a mechanical genus, really was touchy about our vehicle. *Whew, OK got passed that!*

Moments later Dr. Spinks pronounced the roo ready to go. Parker, Bruce, Doug and Dad, rolled the roo onto the makeshift folded flannel sheet stretcher. Working quickly, worrying about the anesthesia wearing off, even though Dr. Spinks assured us the roo was 'out', the men strong armed the roo into the back of our Mountaineer. The sleeping kangaroo was relaxed, his legs stretched out making him longer. Dad gently tucked in the kangaroo's rear legs and curved the tail around so he would fit. The rear hatch door was slammed shut.

"One Kangaroo to go," Dad joked.

"OK, we'll meet you at the Animal Hospital," Dr. Spinks calmly stated.

Yeah, easy for him to be so calm, he is not riding with a roo in the car.

"Wait a minute, you all expect me to drive with a sleeping roo in the car by myself? Can you ride with me and monitor the roo?" I didn't want to seem chickenhearted in front of the men, but really now, how often do you ride with a six foot comatose roo in the car?

"All right, I'll ride with Lori and Liz will drive the Vet truck to the clinic," Dr. Spinks decided. "We'll pull around to the back door Liz." *Thank you Dr. Spinks for not making me feel foolish.* Liz nodded as she climbed into the Vet

Truck.

I nodded, Dr. Spinks hopped into the jump seat in the back, keeping an eye on the kangaroo. The parade of men and vehicles wound its way down to the zoo gate. Clearing the gate, Liz sped ahead in the Vet truck to get to the Animal Hospital before us. Ok, so I am also a pokey driver. Dr. Spinks and I chatted, the roo slept.

It is only a fifteen minute drive even for me, the pokey driver. Dr. Spinks, the roo and I arrived at the Animal Hospital of Sussex County. Liz met us at the back door. Liz and I carried the flannel printed sheet on one end and Dr. Ted grabbed the other end. That roo was heavy! We hobbled our way through the short hallway to the x-ray examination room. Quickly taking an x-ray of the broken foot/leg of the roo, we again moved the sleeping roo on the sheet to the operating room. Dr. Ted scrubbed up, prepping his hands for surgery in a nearby sink and put on latex gloves. Just as Dr. Ted had decreed, all was ready, the other Vet Techs standing by. I didn't know quite what I should do. But I really wanted to watch. So I just asked.

"Can I watch? I'll stay out of the way," I queried.

"Sure," Dr. Ted stated. "You can watch from the prep scrub room." He knew I had seen more than my share of grizzly things. Let's face it, not every day you get to watch an operation on a kangaroo.

The coordinated dance of the operation began. Pam Fagersten, Head Vet Tech, was in charge of anesthesia. She efficiently had a facemask on the kangaroo and a stethoscope on his chest. If that kangaroo woke up he would trash the hospital, glass vials and all, in panic. Other Techs and Cousin Liz were scurrying around doing what they knew to do while Dr. Ted got a good look at the broken leg. The x-ray was consulted. It amazes me to watch an operation at his hospital, the staff seemed to read Dr. Spinks' mind. They knew what equipment he would need, even before he asked for it. The roo's lower leg was cleaned of hay and debris, shaved and sterilized with iodine .

"I'm going to put a rod in it," Dr. Spinks explained loud enough for me to hear through the glass door. "Get me the drill," he stated to the Vet Tech that was already extending it for his use. To my ultimate surprise the drill was the same brand and size that I had seen my husband Doug use to build cages and fix things at the zoo. Amazing. Only difference was that Dr. Spinks' battery operated drill was sterilized. *Wait till I tell Doug that!*

Dr. Spinks began to drill in the tibia to insert the sterilized ten inch stainless steel rod and pins. This was not a gentle part of the procedure. *Just like people get. Fascinating. A bit gory perhaps for the uninitiated but fascinating none the less.*

"Somebody hold the leg up," Dr. Spinks' voice was commanding yet somehow gentle. The intense concentration showed on Dr. Spinks' face. He and I knew that this operation was the only chance for this kangaroo.

As Dr. Spinks continued on the kangaroo's leg, I observed the operation and the kangaroo.

"Take it easy Buddy," I said reassuringly to the roo.

"His name is Buddy?" Liz asked through the door.

"All the boys are 'Buddy' and all the girls are 'Sis', that is just a pet name for any creature that does not have a name, my grandfather Ralph started that. He called us kids by that also. It avoids name confusion." I answered Liz. "Affection is in the tone of voice."

Kangaroo have orange sweat. It was all over my hands and clothing. *Yuck.* I'm not sure how it got under my fingernails, but there it was. *Double Yuck.*

Pam put the stethoscope to the roo's chest and listened again and said something to Dr. Spinks I could not hear.

"He's just getting light on the anesthesia," Dr. Spinks stated, loud enough for me to hear, glancing in my direction. He calmed my fears of the roo having a heart attack on the table. He seemed to know what I was thinking. "Pam give him a little more."

Pam touched the machinery and the heart beat magically settled. Dr. Spinks continued his work stitching up the incision and the compound fracture site. Heads bent over their patient, the staff was still intent on their work. Dr. Spinks occasionally glanced up at me as he explained that he wanted to cast the leg and foot with a 45° rotation. Normally when the kangaroo hops, he turns the foot at the ankle to push off, similar to an ice skating human. Dr. Spinks did not want the leg to heal with the foot straight forward, the roo would no be able to jump as well. A complete 90° angle might throw out Buddy's hip or cause a bad limp after a time. So the decision was made to cast the leg/ankle/foot at a slight angle.

The operation complete, it was time to cast the leg. Vet Techs brought the wraps to Dr. Spinks' deft hands. Dipping the material into water, then applying the plastered wrapping to the leg, the roo was looking quite silly in one big white sock, the cast on his leg. But he was still alive.

"We need something to cover his foot or else it will wick the moisture from the ground into the cast and incision site," Dr. Ted explained to me and I guess anyone else who was listening. A plastic soda bottle with the drinking end cut off was placed in his hand. *A twelve ounce ordinary plastic soda bottle. Talk about re-cycling!! These folks are intelligent and so inventive!* The plastic soda bottle was secured to the foot of the cast with Duct Tape. *Duct Tape is absolutely amazing. Bet the manufacturer did not envision this use!* A round of antibiotic shots were given to the roo. *Poor thing, one leg in a cast and his other rump shot with multiple needles. He's gonna hurt when he wakes up. Bad night on the town Buddy!*

Everyone stepped back and drew a sigh of relief. The operation was over, the roo had lived through it. Ok, so I might have been the only one that was worried about the living part. I have complete faith in Dr. Ted Spinks abilities and those of his staff. But I worry none the less. Worrying is part of being a zoo momma. Part of Dr. Spinks and my relationship involves my occasional, pesky, worrisome questions and his reassuring answers. *Ok, so my questions are not so occasional! Sorry Dr. Spinks.*

Dr. Spinks, Liz and I trundled the still sleeping roo back into my Mountaineer. Dr. Spinks had other appointments and would not ride back to the zoo.

"Can Liz ride back with me? I'll bring her back alive," I joked.

Dr. Spinks agreed and Liz hopped in the jump seat next to the sleeping roo.

I had the Animal Hospital of Sussex County's receptionist, Joan Kiely call the zoo to tell Dad we were on the way home. The ride back was un eventful. This time. The men folk met us at the kangaroo barn and helped get the still snoozing kangaroo back into the den. The roo would stay isolated for a couple of days just to see how he would do. I drove Liz back to the Animal Hospital of Sussex County. This time I let Liz sit in the front seat. *Whew! What a day. And it wasn't even eleven a.m.*

I got back to the zoo a little late to feed No Chance the lemur his midmorning bottle. He was on an every two hours bottle schedule, so he drank readily and went back to sleep immediately in his hat. I also had raccoons on a bottle, they needed to be fed again.

Everyone kept an eye on the male roo that afternoon. In a couple of hours Dad reported that 'Buddy' was up on his feet, using his tail and good leg with the cast leg off slightly to the side. Two more days inside and Buddy was released to the outside pen to be with his sweetie. He hopped efficiently with the cast on his leg, amazing all of us.

Two weeks went by. Buddy was just as frisky as ever. He had mastered hopping with a cast on his leg. Dr. Spinks called and wanted to bring Buddy in for a check up on his leg, take another x-ray, make sure it was healing correctly, and check for infection.

Parker had been elected Mayor of Wantage Township and was at a convention in Atlantic City the week the zoo opened. We were all proud of his political accomplishment.

The rest of the zoo crew and I waited on May 2nd for Dr. Spinks and Vet Tech Cousin Liz to come. Bruce and Doug chased, yes I said chased the kangaroo with a cast on his leg into the den. Even with a cast on his leg Buddy was faster than our two strong men in their prime.

Dr. Spinks and Liz arrived. The jab stick was readied with anesthesia. Dr. Spinks, Doug and Bruce went into the den. The walls thumped again and I could hear Doug's deep voice curse. The roo was injected with the sleeping potion. Same as before, the men came out, stories were told while we waited.

"I cleaned my car, Lori, I'll drive you as far as the Animal Hospital, drop you and the roo off then go pick up a road kill deer, circle back and pick up you and the kangaroo." Dad was ready. *At least he had cleaned his car.*

The men loaded the kangaroo into Dad's Ford Explorer, I sat in the jump seat in the back to monitor Buddy. Our Vet in his truck cleared the zoo gate first and raced ahead. I had Dad stop at the kitchen door for me to pick up five week old No Chance the lemur, his hat, and bottle. No Chance was going to need a bottle before we got back. Dad drove out the zoo gates north on Route 519, right on Wykertown Road, left on Beemer Church Road, down to make a right onto 565. A straight shot through Ross's Corner and a mile to the Animal Hospital of Sussex County on the right. Five and a half miles. I could make that drive in my sleep, I've taken so many animals there.

Chance in his hat in one hand, I touched the kangaroo with my other. I deeply raked the soft cottony beige fur with my fingers, avoiding the underarms and the greasy orange sour smelling sweat. I must admit I was zoning out. Just me and the roo, stroking the soft fur. I might never get a chance to be this close to a kangaroo again. I was giving all my hope to a kangaroo that did not know me and that I had no previous connection with. The spongy cotton fur fascinated me.

Once at the hospital, everything went smoothly. I dashed up front to ask the receptionist to baby sit No Chance. I wanted to watch the next procedure through the glass doors again.

"Don't worry he won't leave his hat," I said as I dropped off the five inch baby lemur. Joan Keily looked startled at first but then saw her sweet charge and nodded. Joan had worked for Dr. Spinks for years. We knew each other. After all, Joan and I had done the snake dance together. See Chapter 91, The Zookeeper's Daughter.

The cast was removed from Buddy's leg, with a special vibrating cast saw. The saw is really neat, it stops vibrating if it touches the skin. X-rays were taken, again. All the while the large roo slept. Dr. Spinks announced that the fracture was healing well, no signs of infection and he would re cast the leg complete with new plastic soda bottle.

"That soda bottle worked out well," Dr. Spinks beamed proudly about his staff. "That was Pam's idea. She's good with inventing solutions to potential medical problems."

No Chance, Buddy and I were at the vet's for maybe an hour when Dad circled back to pick up our unusual trio. Dr. Spinks, Dad and I carried the roo back to the car. We had to haul the sleeping kangaroo over the rear hitch rack with the dead deer still on it. Buddy was not getting any lighter. *At least he ate well during his recovery.* I assumed my seat in the back of the Explorer. No Chance the lemur was in his hat on my lap. I fed him his few drops of milk from his tiny bottle.

Out of the Animal Hospital driveway we took a left towards Ross's Corner. I was happily stroking No Chance, while glancing out the window. The window was open because the sleeping roo stunk. The smell was musky, with a whiff of rabbit manure. The greasy sweat smelled like old French fry oil. The traffic light was red, a sharp contrast to the early spring greenery that polka doted the local farmland. The Chatterbox Restaurant (one of my favorites) was on our right. The chipped blue trim on the white cinderblock abandoned gas station caught my eye on our left. Tanis's white barn with green trim, accessorized with mini goats in the field, was ahead of the light on the right. One of the mini goats had a collar and a bell. I could hear it through the open window. All was good with the world.

I heard a tap. Not a loud tap, just a tap. Strange sound, I could not quite place it. The light changed and Dad slowly pulled ahead. We were maybe a mile from the Animal Hospital. *Must be a noise from the gas station.* As we passed the mini goats trailing over the rocky hill, I heard the tap again. *Odd sound. Not metal on metal. Hummmmm....* I glanced down at the roo, Buddy's eyes were still closed. Then to my horror I saw movement out of the corner of my eye. Buddy was laying on his left side, his cast right leg was jerking up and the strange sound I heard was the clash of his plastic soda bottle on glass. Glass, the back window of the   SUV!

"S#**!, Dad the Kangaroo is waking up," I said loud enough for Dad to hear over the sound of the car. I threw Chance (in his hat) in the front passenger seat.

"You worry too much, we're almost home," Dad chided me.

Almost home? We are 4 ½ miles from the turn off to the zoo. Darn! I had given those directions to visitors for years. I knew just where we were. *We are not at the zoo!*

I could see the Fetzer Farm in the distance on the left. I spun my body around kneeling with both knees on the jump seat. Buddy was looking dopey, but his eyes were blinking. We passed Dr. Castimore's horse farm. The dark brown horse fencing seemed to laugh at me, it would not contain a kangaroo. Multiple hued horses grazed contentedly, ignorant of the action in the Explorer driving past them.

Buddy's tapping was getting louder and more consistent.

" He's gonna break the window, Dad!"

"No he won't."

Don't argue with me, I'm the one kneeling here. Buddy was struggling now, his good leg and tail moving. His wimpy front legs were starting to move. Dad drove down the hill and put his left blinker on.

"What are you doing Dad? We need to get home to the zoo," I commanded.

"Thought I'd take Plains Road home in case we see another road kill deer to pick up," Dad calmly stated. "I always come home a different way than I went."

Sightseeing? I'm kneeling here with a Kangaroo and he wants to sightsee for more dead deer? The darn deer are dead, they aren't going anywhere. Double Darn.

We passed open fields, hill and dale, and made a right onto Plains Road. The Frankford Plains Methodist Church was soon on our right. The little country church had beautiful stained glass. *Glass just like the kangaroo was going to break soon.* I had visions of the kangaroo escaping and hopping across the countryside. I said a quick prayer and shifted my position and placed both hands on the shoulder of the momentarily prone animal. Buddy was really waking up now. Struggling to get out from under my hands.

The mini soap opera in the Explorer continued as we pass the Country Heritage Christmas Tree Farm. *I hope by Christmas this will be a laughable* *memory, but it ain't now. Sonofa *#(@! The roo is moving again! I must be upset to revert to my native Redneck language!* At this point I have to stop glancing out the window to see where we are. My concentration was focused on keeping Buddy laying down, exerting enough pressure to do so without breaking his ribs. I know we are passin' open fields lined with multi-floral rose next to stone fences. Dad finally passes the old white barn and makes a left onto Meyers Road. *Can this car move any slower?*

"Come on Dad, go faster, we're gonna be in big s#!t trouble here," I begged.

"Can't, there is a lady ahead of us and we are on a blind hill," Dad explained. I noticed he glanced in the rear view mirror and saw I was struggling.

"Ya better pass 'er anyhow!" I demanded. Buddy the kangaroo had gained some maneuverability and was struggling to get up on his hind feet. In the close quarters of the Explorer's back seat and cargo area, there was not going to be a lot of dancing room for me to avoid being kicked. I could envision Buddy jumping, kicking, breaking glass and/or me to get out of the car. Looking out the window I saw fields with no boundaries. No way we could catch him if he got out of the car. I had to maintain the upper hand and keep the desperately afraid and awake kangaroo on his side.

Up and down another hill. *Pokey Driver, get the heck out of the way, NOW.*

"How ya doin'? Dad asked.

"Not so good Pop, Drive faster," my curt reply.

The curve of the last corner had shifted my weight in the seat, kneeling with my butt in the air, and my shoulders pressing down. The ballast of my butt swung me sideways and relieved the pressure on Buddy's shoulders. Buddy was pushing up with his little front legs, and already standing on his one good hind leg.

"Keep him down, we're almost home," Dad said. *Yeah Right, and the check is in the mail. Keep him down? Such good fatherly advice. And I know we are not almost home. Jesus, Mary and Joseph!*

I assessed the situation. Buddy was upset, never having remembered riding in a car, in a confined space, with me - a total strange creature pushing on him, some old guy driving and a chattering lemur adding to the whir of the car engine and other unknown sounds, sights and smells. Panic was in the air, mine and his. One of us was going to get hurt. I didn't want it to be, but especially NOT to be me. I knew what I had to do. With one knee on the jump seat, my left leg braced on the flattened seat beside me, I made the sign of the cross in a flash. *Darn !I'm not even Catholic, so forgive me Dr. Spinks for screwing up all your good work.* I hastily grabbed Buddy's good leg and jerked. Whossshhh. Plop. He went down again, the cast thumping hard on the car floor. I quickly crawled over his body holding him down with mine.

"You ok?" I heard Dad ask, as I could no longer see him.

"Yeah, we are alright, but this ain't pretty," I responded.

I rode the last two miles home sumo wrestling a kangaroo in the back of

Dad's car. My head to his tail, my knees trying to hold my weight off the poor thing's head and chest. Kangaroos are not known to bite. *Don't bite me in the butt Buddy. Explain that one in the ER, Lori!* I was so happy to feel each curve and turn on the roads. I mentally checked off the turns my body felt. Oh, I should mention again how bad the butt of the kangaroo stunk. *Almost home for real now Buddy, Sorry Buddy, Sorry Dr. Spinks, Buddy I hope I didn't injure you more.* My sense of the absurdity of the situation kicked in my quirky humor as my mind raced. *Last time I wrestled in the back of a car it was with a young human man! Been a few years on that one. Wait till I tell Dr. Spinks the roo woke up! I'm gonna have a few choice words for him! This will be one to tell the grandchildren!*

Dad finally pulled up to the zoo gate. I heard the beep, beep, beep warning sound that the zoo's main gate was opening.

"I don't see the guys," Dad said. "I told them to be here. Well, we'll get the job done anyway."

You must be crazy to think I am going to wait one more minute for the guys with my nose this close to a roo's butt. God he stinks.

"Just drive up to the gate and get it open Pop," I stated. *Who me impatient?*

Dad drove to the kangaroo enclosure, as close to the enclosure gate as possible. The rear passenger door was just clear of the gate. He jumped out faster than I had seen him move in years. He was, after all, 76 years old. Pop unlocked the gate and pushed it open. Dad opened the rear passenger door.

"I'm not gonna fit through that door with the roo, Dad," I stated the obvious.

" Yes you will. Just shimmy backwards. Wait, get your knees off the sheet," Dad was in full command.

"Well, if he gets loose he'll at least be inside the zoo," I figured out loud.

Dad yanked on the sheet as I shimmied backwards on my hands and knees. Buddy was anxious and ready to go. Dad took control of the top half of Buddy, I veered to my right, putting my butt half in the jump seat, then crawled out the passenger side back door restraining Buddy's bottom half the best I could. *Good thing he is still somewhat dopey.* I am not a small woman (*understatement there!*), but we squeezed through. Dad had propped the enclosure gate open towards the car, and was standing in the small gap between the stationary post and the car. We let Buddy down to the ground and he happily hopped into the grassy enclosure, and lay down. *NOW he lays down?*

Dad closed and locked the gate. I was leaning against the passenger side of the door. I looked at Pop, Pop looked at me and we burst out laughing. Laughing so hard tears ran down my face. Oh what a father daughter bonding moment. The things we do at the zoo.

A month later it was time to take the cast off of Buddy the roo…I was not involved with the cast removal. Don't remember what I was doing at the time, I would have been there if I knew what was going to happen. Dr. Spinks relayed to me that he administered light sedation while my brother Parker and Zookeeper

Bruce held Buddy still. His prognosis was good because infection was controlled. Buddy would be absent of chronic pain because the joint had successfully fused at the 45° angle Dr. Spinks had planned and hoped for. We could expect Buddy to recover completely.

Buddy did recover completely. His fused joint caused him no trouble, and only a knowledgeable professional could detect the slight difference in his jumping gait. The operation was truly unique. So unique in fact that Dr. Voynick V.M.D. from Channel 12's "The Pet Stop" made a special two hour trip to the zoo with a TV crew to interview Dr. Spinks, and film Buddy jumping freely around his grassy enclosure. Buddy and his missus loved grapes, so I supplied the Doctors with a bag of grapes to feed the roos in order to get the roos to stand still for the cameras. Well, that was the plan. The roos were concerned with the Doctors and film crew inside their territory. The Doctors ate the grapes, while the roos hopped. The film crew got great shots of Buddy jumping and hopping.

Many of the folks on staff at Space Farms have other talents than the job they perform. 'Doc' (short for Dolson) and Barb Ayers had managed the restaurant at the zoo for almost twenty years. Doc was also the coach for the High Point High School's baseball team. Previously a minor league baseball player, he definitely had the credentials. Doc and Barb are the gentle grandparent type, advisers to all the high school kids, (and often me), that we employed on staff in the restaurant. Their white hair gives credence to life's experience. They also are gifted vocalists. Their voices frequently grace church services or other local parties.

Dr. Voynick, V.M.D., is a fabulous guitar player and plays in a band that has performed in Vegas. He is also a wonderful vocalist. I had tried to learn to read music early in life, but just could not make the connection between dots on paper and a sound in my head. So it never went anywhere for me, but I did have a guitar.

Dr. Voynick suggested that we all perform a slightly different rendition of "Tie Me Kangaroo Down, Mate" to close out the TV show segment on the kangaroo's broken leg. I drove the quick trip home and retrieved the guitar. At the end of the tape, Dad, Parker, Dr. Spinks, Dr. Voynick, Doc, Barb, zookeeper Bruce, Vet Tech Liz and myself sang "Tie me kangaroo down, Spinks, Tie me kangaroo down." Dr. Voynick accompanied the unusually diverse singing group on my old guitar. What a hoot! Just another day at the zoo, and my public singing debut. I better keep my day job.

And Buddy? He did very well. Dr. Spinks had performed an operation that saved Buddy's life. Buddy did well enough in fact, to father four offspring. After all is said and done, we have to give Dr. Spinks credit here. Dr. Spinks gave Buddy the kangaroo a leg to stand on.

Zoo Momma

Chapter 12 Khyber's Bottle

The summer of 2005 went by in a whir of activity. The zoo was busy with visitors and the constant cleaning, maintenance, painting and various small projects. I spend my early mornings feeding and cleaning in the nursery, then help the ladies at the admission desk, subbing in for them at lunch. Then more nursery feedings, and back inside answering visitor questions. Then I am back outside again for more feedings and questions. My days are hectic and fast paced. I am never bored.

In late June I was working at the admission desk on a hot day when a lady came in from the zoo huffing and puffing. She had run all the way from the tiger enclosure to tell us that one of the visiting camp group kids had thrown a plastic water bottle into the tigers. One of the tigers was now chewing on it. *Oh s#!t! OOPS, Did I say that out loud? The plastic could cut the tigers gums when he chews on it, or if a piece gets swallowed, could cut open his stomach or intestines. What were those kids thinking? Darn. Double Darn it.*

Zookeeper Andy was helping us out for the summer. Andy had previously worked in the kitchen through high school and was promoted to summer zookeeper. Tall, thin and handsome, the girls in the kitchen were sad to see him leave the kitchen for the zoo. We needed the extra manpower out in the zoo, so Parker had promoted Andy. Andy was finishing up lunch, so I haled him and explained the situation. I grabbed a pair of snake grabbers (Phlystrom tongs). We jumped in a jitney. I figured I could call the tigers to me and Andy could use the tongs to grab the bottle. It would be easier than putting the tigers in lock down inside the den. That is IF we could grab the bottle. Zookeeper Andy and I rode out to the tiger enclosure. Upon our arrival, there was no plastic water bottle to be seen in the tall grass and boulders in the tiger enclosure. There was a crowd of twenty people standing outside the guard fence. I unlocked the guard fence and walked inside by the chain link enclosure fence. Andy latched the gate and followed. I could not go inside the enclosure, my baby tigers were now full grown. Khyber and Tara trotted majestically to my side on the other side of the fence. They chuffed to me, delighted as always to see me.

"Where's the bottle?" I asked the assorted crowd of camp kids and visiting adults. No one answered. We looked and looked for a couple of minutes. We couldn't find it. *God I hope they didn't eat it!* The original reporting lady had run all the way back to the tigers again.

"It's over there between the rocks," she stated.

I did not think of the next words I said. I just spoke them automatically, out loud.

"Khyber, play fetch, bring Mommy the bottle, fetch. Bring it to Mommy good boy," I stated in my loud commanding but loving mommy voice.

Well, I'll be darned if Khyber didn't walk right over between the boulders, pick up the unseen dangerous plastic water bottle and fetch it back to me at the fence. He was holding it between his lips and canine teeth! I squatted down to receive the bottle, hooking my fingers in the chain link. *Oh, my knees- I am getting older.* Tara wanted in on the fun. She nuzzled her head against the fence and Khyber dropped the bottle before I could get it. I was disappointed. *Darn, Double Darns! Life is never easy.*

I moved around the fence corner to a section that had a larger camera hole in the chain link. Squatting, I commanded Khyber again.

"Khyber, fetch, bring Mommy the bottle. Play fetch Khyber," I said hoping against hope he would do the same again. *Son of a gun*! Khyber picked up the clear plastic bottle once again and brought it to the fence, dropped it, then stood guard. Tara circled behind Khyber.

I used the snake grabbers to grab the bottle and brought it directly to the fence. I slid my fingers in the mouth of the bottle holding it in place, all the while talking baby talk to my 600 pound tiger. I told Andy to put his finger in the lip while I wiggled my fingers against the back end of the flattened bottle. I didn't want to risk Andy's (unfamiliar human male) fingers to the tiger. The flattened bottle was wider than the chain link fence hole. I could not get it through the fence easy, I would have to push.

At this point Khyber was curious and put his big hairy face down by my fingers. I didn't know how he would respond to me taking his 'toy'. Feeling his breath on my fingers, I pulled my fingers out. Khyber then pushed the back end of the bottle through the fence with his nose. The gathered crowd applauded and cheered. I have to admit, I was still angry at the stupid kid that threw in the bottle in the first place. Too angry to realize what had just happened. Andy and I stood up, walking nonchalantly to the guard fence gate with the bottle.

"Wow Lori, that was cool!" Andy spoke in a whisper, while locking up the guard fence gate. "Did you know they would do that?"

I whispered back, not wanting the surrounding crowd to hear.

"No. I didn't even think about it. I just commanded. It worked. I haven't played fetch with them since the spring of 2000 - before they were put in the adult enclosure. I'm amazed that Khyber remembered at all. Radically Cool though, Huh?" I explained in a hushed voice. It had been five years since we'd played fetch.

Zookeepers get to witness amazing things. God and Andy as my witness.

Chapter 13 Tears of Fall

Labor Day is always a busy weekend at the zoo. The last weekend of the summer before school starts, everyone takes their family's final outing. Hopefully that includes coming to Space Farms. We are open until October, but after Labor Day the numbers of visitors slows down, drastically. My responsibilities with the previous spring's babies are also greatly reduced. Most animal babies born in the spring are weaned by fall, and are   eating solid foods. They eat and grow all summer while the food sources are plentiful in the wild. Hopefully they are strong enough to survive the winter with a sparse food supply. Of coarse zoo animals don't have to worry about the food supply since we human zookeepers bring it to them.

As my nursery feedings and time are lessoned in the fall, it gives me more opportunity to work on projects at the zoo. Fall is the best time for projects. Fall is the worst time for worrisome moms when their human child goes off to college. And Jackie was leaving home to go to Rider University near Trenton, N.J. There is even a psychological term for it, I'm sure you have heard of Empty Nest Syndrome. I never thought in a million years that I would have Empty Nest Syndrome. Let's face it, I have raised hundreds of animals, they always leave my care, whether to another zoo or to the adult section of our zoo at Space Farms, or sometimes, sadly they die.

Doug and I drove Jackie, in our Mountaineer packed to overflowing, down to Rider University on Labor Day Weekend. This was he first Labor Day Weekend we took off in the ten years since we came back to help Dad and Parker with the zoo. It was important to both of us to see her settled. All right, I admit, I needed to make sure she was settled and ok. That worrisome zoo momma applies extra to our only human child. *Poor Kid!*

On the appointed day we drove her the two hour trip to college. Longest two hours of my life. I was trying so hard to be brave, positive and just not cry. Doug was braver than I, or at least he put on a good front. Jackie was jubilant and excited having previously met her roommate. They had planned decorations for their dorm room and all that kind of stuff. Her excited chatter echoed off the car windows. We arrived and other students helped us unload the over packed car.

Doug, our computer guru hero, set up Jack's computer, but couldn't get the printer to work, so we dashed to a local computer store and bought a new one. That one worked fine. After all was said and done, Jackie and I shared a brief teary moment. It was time for us to leave our baby girl.

With hugs goodbye and Doug's urging arm pushing around my waist, we walked towards her dorm room door. *Don't look back, Don't look back, just like leaving lion or tiger cubs at the airport, don't look back. You've done this enough times, she'll be ok, don't' look back.* I looked back. I saw our Jackie standing in her doorway. The little eight pound six ounce baby girl with the wrinkly forehead had metamorphosed into a wonderfully intelligent, quirky, streaky blonde haired, tall as me, seventeen year old, green eyed beauty. Her eyes were brimmed with tears, but she courageously held them back.

I waved one more time, Doug's arm urging me forward. *Don't look back, don't look back.* I made it to the car before the first tear fell. I hopped in and faced the passenger side window. The ride was silent, Doug and I both consumed with our own emotions. Mine were more visible than his. A couple of miles up the road Doug was the first to speak.

"You ok?"

"No," my voice wavered so he knew I was tearful.

"She'll be fine, so cheer up" he commanded *(reassured ?)* me. Deep sighs emanated throughout the car. It was a long ride to Rider, a longer ride home. But Doug was not talking much either.

"Know thyself," is a well known aphorism from the ancient Greeks. I knew I would be upset, hopefully not for long. Being the workaholic I am, I had planned a major project for that fall. Work is soothing. Work keeps your mind busy and off your troubles. Work makes you tired so you can sleep. Work makes you feel good, like you accomplished something tangible. Therefore, work is good.

When my grandfather Ralph established the museums in 1976, he had the inside walls all painted white. The entire Rutgers Experimental Dairy Station was revamped to hold the museum my Gramp had envisioned. Slowly but surely over the years the walls had become dingy. I had painted many of the walls white again, but the artist in me was never content with white walls. I am not a formally trained artist. I have no training other than High School Art class with Mr. Kinney at High Point Regional, and a recent air brushing class. So wall by wall, year after year in the fall, I cleaned and painted. I love to paint, but not white walls white. When you visit Space Farms Museum you will see murals, stenciling, and signage that I have painted.

Growing up at the zoo, my grandfather's friend, Ralph Capute, and his wife Kitty, used to spend available weekends and holidays at Space Farms. "Uncle" Ralph was an aeronautical engineer, a pilot and worked for the federal government as an aeronautical parts inspector. Gramp and Elinor (my grandfather's second wife) had become good friends with Ralph and Kitty Capute. They met when Ralph and Kitty picked up their son, Milton, from Boy Scout camp at High Point State Park, which is near us. In 1939 the Capute family saw a sign for the Blue Ridge Animal Farm and stopped in, met Grampa Ralph, Elinor and Gramma Lizzie. They became friends. Milton was my dad's boyhood chum, spending the summers with Dad in exchange for room and board. Every hand was needed at the growing fox, mink and animal farm. The boys worked hard together and became chums. This is a relationship Dad and Uncle Milton still enjoy today. These two old geezers have a lot of funny stories and memories. It pleases me so to see my Dad laugh out loud. Uncle Milton is a treasure to me.

Uncle Ralph painted a lot of signs while visiting the farm. As a child I would watch Uncle Ralph delicately paint signs, using all his tools and paintbrushes. Each stroke had a purpose. It was fascinating to watch an artist at work. Uncle Ralph would sign the back of his work. and date it. I felt honored every time I repainted a sign of his, and signed my name under his on the back with the current date. His signs often lasted twenty years.

All through high school, I would help paint animal enclosures, back when the zoo was concrete block and metal bars. I've painted the snake den so many times, I can't count. I painted in the spring before the snakes were put in. The last couple of years, Doug and Parker painted the inside. I Guess they figure I'd have too much trouble getting in there and out again. *That's ok, let 'em think that.* When Doug, Jackie and I lived in Pittsburgh, I would come home on vacations and paint cages over again.

I've painted bathroom stalls, then stenciled them. I've painted signage, white buildings white, then put specially designed signs on them. Barns, dens, road signs, billboards and swing sets. You name it, I have painted it, most more than once. I painted the little red schoolhouse, you got it- red. (Even the cupola on the top.) I painted an igloo in the Eskimo exhibit. I painted rocks on the outside of the snake den. I've turned corrugated aluminum sided shacks into bamboo dens and bathrooms. I must give credit where credit is due; I learned that technique while visiting Hershey Park with daughter Jackie and my sister, Renee and chatted with an artist while he was working on a similar project. He was kind enough to show me his technique. Jack and Ney Bell got annoyed because I chatted so long, but the results are definitely cool. It is neat to see zoo visitors walk up to the bamboo bathrooms and touch the paint.

One day Dad and I had a discussion about the old red barn's windows. They were busted out or patched with naked plywood.

"NO. We are not putting new windows in an old run down barn," Dad decreed. "That barn was built in the early 1800's. It's not worth it."

" But Dad, they look so bad, it gives the whole barn a derelict look. That barn is one of the first things people see when they walk out the zoo doors," I pleaded.

"NO," Dad ended the conversation. And that was the final word. I hear that a lot.

I came up with an idea. *End Run?* I dragged a tall aluminum ladder to the barn witch is thirty feet tall, and painted the plywood white with black squares to look like windows. My feet hurt for days after standing on the rungs of the ladder for many hours. The back of my legs ached too, I must have overextended my calf muscles. Oh well. *That reminds me, need to do them again. Put it on the list.* The fake windows look good, nobody even notices them, they look so real. *Don't tell me "NO."*

So reader, you get the idea. The creative artist in me just has to come out sometimes. I enjoy creative painting. When Jackie went off to college, I knew I needed a big project with some fun built into it. I informed Dad I would work on the Plow Museum. Dad ok'd the project. The Plow Museum had, *what else?*, plows in it. Plows, and other farming equipment was hung on the walls in my grandfather's methodical, straight lined, institutional style. Everything was made of brown wood or rusty metal. There were plows, manure spreaders, goat carts, hay forks, all antiques showcasing the history of farming. During the years my little family was in Pittsburgh, my grandfather had died, and Dad had added peacocks to the open section of the barn. Encased in chicken wire, the peacocks could not escape, but little native birds could get in to feast on the peacock food. I swear each and every bird had left its mark on the walls. The plows and other farming equipment had become soiled with droppings. The white walls were no longer white, but speckled. The open shed part of the museum was eighty feet long. It would be just the kind of massive project I would need to keep my mind off of my daughter so far away. We moved the peacocks to an empty cage in the zoo and I got started.

I cleaned and sorted museum artifacts. I really don't mind cleaning the museums, I learn something new every time. *I hate cleaning my house, it is so redundant. Besides what would you rather do? Laundry, paint creatively or play with the lion cubs?* My grandfather was an eclectic collector. There is all sorts of neat stuff, *oh sorry, antiques*, in every nook and cranny of the museums. So just the cleaning of the items took time.

A month later a newly painted mural included the inside section of a barn, an old dead tree, corn, hay, tomato and zucchini fields. I added the zucchini fields as a joke for my Dad. He hates zucchini. After the antiques were put back in, I typed up labels, laminated them, and mounted the labels on the antiques. Job well done.

Sadly, I still have empty nest syndrome. It never ceases to amaze me. I am a very busy woman. I cook every night, belong to a number of organizations and write for other organizations, am an author, have zoo work that is never ending, and I do break down every now and then and clean my house. And I still have empty nest syndrome. Go figure!

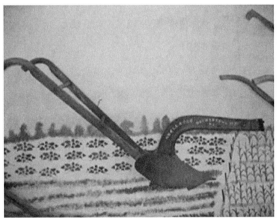

Deckertown Plow in a zucchini field!
Photo by Lori Space Day

Chapter 14 Judy's Garden

Every year since I could remember, the New Jersey Trapper's Association has held meetings at Space Farms twice a year. As kids, we helped Dad put on a chicken barbeque for the trappers. We hauled cinderblocks to make the pit, for wood or charcoal, made the rub for the chicken, grilled it, and served it with all the accompaniments. We often cooked two hundred chicken halves, which was a lot of work! I grew up knowing all the trappers, watched them age, like my dad has done, *(but not me!)* and gotten to know the next generation of trappers coming up. My Dad, brother Eric and nephew Hunter, all trap. So this is part of my family's heritage and upbringing. I trap raccoons, skunks and possums that break into my nursery at the zoo to prey upon the free ranging chickens and chickies.

Trappers are an interesting group of true woodsmen and women. A trapper is a behaviorist. A good trapper can read tracks and read trail signs (I'm not talking the printed kind), and knows the denning, mating, eating, defecating, and hunting behavior of the specie he is trapping. Identifying scent gland excretions are part of the job, smelly, though that may be.

I know my reader is asking how a zoologist is pro-trapping. Mankind has destroyed the natural balance of the species in the wild, and therefore someone correct it. The larger predators are slowly making a comeback in this area, due to the regulations of trapping of certain species set forth by the N.J. Division of Fish and Wildlife. If overabundant species are not trapped, or hunted, natural problems arise, such as starvation due to over population and depletion of the natural food source, and disease. The American beaver was responsible for the exploration of the west. Trappers were the first mountain men to go west. A wanderlust combined with extensive specie knowledge fueled by the potential profit of the trap line caused the mountain men to explore new areas, make friends and trade with the indigenous Native Americans. Leg hold traps are no longer legal in New Jersey, and regulations state that a trapper must check his traps once a day. Keep in mind folks that fur is a renewable resource. A mink or coyote will reproduce at two years old, having up to 10 babies. That nylon coat you may be wearing- is made from an oil product. Oil takes millions of years to produce and is not renewable within our lifetime. Oh and down jackets … FYI you have to kill the goose to get the down feathers. Get the point? Ok, so off my soapbox.

I have always enjoyed the days the trappers come to Space Farms. They are interesting and non pretentious folk. Trappers trade stories, and jokes, have skinning contests, educational demonstrations and there is camaraderie much like the old frontier days during a rendezvous. The men and women have become friends of mine.

Jim and Judy were a constant at the trappers' meetings. Jim was vice president of the Association for years, and Judy the secretary. Jim doted on Judy even after she had developed muscular distrophy which confined her to a wheel chair. Her smile outshone her illness. As a pair they were a study in contrast, Jim, a few years older than me, was tall, slender and silver haired. Judy in the wheelchair, had wisps of strawberry blonde hair and was slightly chunky. A sweet couple, devoted to each other and the Trapper's Association.

I heard that Judy passed away from my brother Eric. Eric and Jim were good friends scince my brother Eric is a renowned trapper and modern day mountain man. Linda, my sister-in-law and Judy were friends too. Evidently at some point when Judy and Linda were chatting shortly before she died, and Judy mentioned that she would like to have her ashes buried in the flower garden at Space Farms near where the trappers meetings were held. I'm not sure who initiated the conversation, but one day Jim stopped by to ask Dad if he could spread Judy's ashes on the flower garden.

"Sure, I don't see why not," Dad's sympathetic answer. "And Lori here, can do the funeral."

I was serving coffee to the men at the time, I almost dropped the pot.

"She's the lay minister of Beemerville, she's even preached a bunch of sermons in the church over there," Dad gushed and gestured towards the Beemerville Presbyterian Church. "She's done a funeral before," turning to me, " Huh Lori?"

"That would be great," Jim replied.

"O.K. sure, let me know when," I said. *What does one say to that conversation?*

On the appointed day, I went home from work and put on my good pants and long dark green dress coat. I added a hat because December was cold. The garden had been stripped of its flowers, first by nature's chill, then cleaned up by me. The garden looked sad and desolate, with brick bordering mustard brown dirt. A statue of a life size, beige deer stood in the middle. *Just too plain.* I thought it should be prettier for Judy. *What to do? Got it!* Returning to the zoo I brought with me my Christmas pine greenery I use on my garden. I circled the deer twice with the green artificial trimming. *Looks better than the dirt.*

Jim and his family gathered in the office with Dad, Eric and myself. I went over the short ceremony with the small group of family and friends and we proceeded to the garden across the street.

Gathered at the garden I spoke of Judy's life, her wonderful attributes as a mother, wife and friend. The breeze was chilly, folks stood on one foot then the other. We sang "Amazing Grace". The wind was kicking up, cold and chilling coming down from the hill behind the barn.

Oh my, how do I ask everyone to move up wind? I don't want Judy's ashes all over me. I'm sure they don't want Judy's ashes all over them either! Oh Please God, give me strength to say something. What to say? What to say?

I nodded to Jim. Jim had carried Judy's ashes under his coat from the car. *How sweet, he is still keeping her warm, Maybe the wind will stop just for a few minutes.* The cold had numbed Jim's normally nimble fingers. He slowly opened a cardboard box the size of a five pound sack of flour. Nestled inside was a black plastic bag full of Judy's ashes.

Zoo Momma

I should mention here that this was the first time I presided over an internment of ashes. I had never actually seen ashes before and was amazed that the human body could be reduced to so little. Judy was so much more that that, her heart full of the love for Jim, her family, friends and the trappers. Her spirit shone through her smile, and touched all that knew her. Judy was there, around us in spirit, and so much more than the little package that Jim now held so tenderly.

"Um, Folks, I think that we should all move to the other side of the garden," Dad stuttered. Everyone nodded. We all side stepped in unison to the upwind side of the garden. *Oh thanks, Dad, you saved the day.*

The plastic bag was sealed shut and hard to open. Jim was flustered, this was his wife's last request, to have her ashes spread on the garden next to the trappers' meeting place and the bag would not open. Dad once again came to the rescue, pulling his pocket knife out of his pants pocket and offering it to Jim. Jim, distinguished and regal, slowly circled the garden with the ashes. It took three times around the small garden to empty the container. The silver white of the ashes marked a distinct contrast on the mustard colored earth and fake pine greenery. The oval of the garden surrounded by red brick, the elongated circle of pine greenery, and the inner circle of silvery white ashes, all topped by the stately buck statue staring into the invisible distance, etched itself into my mind. What a fitting place for Judy, a lover of the outdoors and the wife of an outdoorsman, to be finally released from her earthly body.

I led a short prayer and concluded with the Lord's Prayer. The group dispersed, each consumed with their own thoughts.

A few weeks later, I removed the greenery. Judy's circle was still prominent. The next spring, Tommy, a high school intern, was given the job to turn the garden over in preparation for the spring flowers to be planted. He asked what the silver white circle was.

"That's Judy's special formula for fertilizing the garden," I simply stated. "We will have beautiful flowers this year."

It was the most beautiful flower garden that year, and has been ever since. Now we call it 'Judy's Garden'.

Chapter 15 Safe and Warm Out of the Storm

Staying Safe and Warm out of the Storm
Though Lions roar at the break of light,
And wolves may bay all through the night,
I'm warm and cozy, thinking of you,
As another Christmas comes to the zoo.
Spring came early way back in March,
I woke up poor Jenny, who was stiff as starch.
Friend Lennie Rue, a photog, wanted a shot
Of groundhog in the snow, could I find a spot?
I dug Jenny out of her hibernation,
Thought she was dead, much to my consternation.
Lennie said "Call to her, she'll hear your voice".
Jenny started to writhe, and we all rejoiced.
This summer Jenny tunneled out of her Nursery cage,
Adding more worry and gray hair for my age.
I searched around daily, then the rains they poured so,
And brought Jenny up from her home down below.
Had to slap myself upside the head-
"You silly old fool", she's a woodchuck I said!
Doug gave me a newborn, tiny as can be,
A 2 oz. Ring Tailed Lemur, what a challenge for me!
The "NO Chance" Lemur, with mini black lips,
Grasshopper legs, striped tail, no hips.
Head the size of a walnut, body ½ a spool of thread,
Fed every two hours, 5 drops, else he'd be dead.
Chance grew and grew, learned to jump and climb,
But Chance in the house drove me out of my mind.
Was like living inside a pinball machine,
His jumping ability was truly supreme.
He is back with his brothers down at the zoo
Couldn't housebreak him, could not stand the poo.
I sumo wrestled a Kangaroo
That had broken his leg at our family zoo.
Dad was driving on the way back from the Vet.
And the roo woke up, *"Please God, not yet!"*
In the back of Dad's car, he struggled to get free
Like I said, Dad was driving, so that left ME,
To hold the roo down in a wrestling hold,
And get him safely back to the fold.
Next time, Dr. Ted, we need more juice,
To prevent the roo from getting loose!
Roo is now jumping around like crazy,

Zoo Momma

Gonna be a daddy, he's certainly not lazy.
Ah yes Folks…
This year I turned fifty one
Give me the job, and I'll get it done.
But how many women do you know,
That can wrestle a kangaroo on the go?
Raised raccoons, fawns, and those damned Turkey Chicks
Must I forever repent killin' Dad's Tom with a stick?
Designed and installed a new parrot impound
They delight zoo visitors with their many sounds.
Zoo work I love, there is such variety,
Care, building, painting, writing & speaking, for me.
Well, my 1st book's been out for a year, what a ride,
Now the 2nd is started, though in my head I confide.
I'll type it up soon, after the New Year,
When the Holiday is over and my calendar clears.
Now Jack's off to college, having a blast
Enjoying the experience, tops in her class.
Doug's the proud papa, grinning ear to ear,
Just ask about Jack - watch that papa appear!
For me empty nest came as quite a shock,
That only happens to 'Stay at Homes' down the block.
Not to me, the Zoomama, with so much to do
A full time plus job working at the zoo.
So I painted a mural in the Museum with the plow
Frenzied, then stepped back and said "Holy Cow"!
Eighty feet by ten, Barns, fields, fences, believe it or not.
Seems a workaholic never changes her spots.
Doug's still my hero, been so sweet and kind,
A better husband for me I could never find.
He works so hard daily, strong as can be
His wit and intelligence a treasure to me.
Dad's doing fine, along with all the rest,
Though often my patience is put to the test.
Tolerance is God's greatest gift,
(Remind me that the next time I get miffed).
For this next one, hold onto your sox,
Dad volunteered me, that sly old fox
I presided a funeral, on our land,
As ashes were put to rest in the sand.
Every spring I plant flowers there,
OHHH! The concept has me in despair.
So I'm here in my nightie, cozy and warm,
Chance and Jenny asleep in the barn.

Zoo Momma

The roo and the animals down at the zoo,
Are settled in and sleeping, so how 'bout you?
(Write, call or visit, you know where I am)
To all my friends, wherever you be
Merry Christmas, Stay safe,
Love, Doug, Jack and Me.

Buddy Kangaroo in his leg cast.

Photo by Karen Talasco

Chapter 16 Space Farms began as The Blue Ridge Fox Farm

The first farm established by Ralph and Elizabeth Space in 1928 at Beemerville was a fox farm. As a trapper for the State of New Jersey, Ralph's job was to trap varmints that harassed local farm stock. Growing up in rural Sussex County at the base of the Blue Ridge of the Kittatinny Mountains, Ralph was a true naturalist, constantly studying his surroundings. His knowledge and expertise helped him trap even the wiliest predator for the local farmers. Ralph trapped bobcats, foxes and raccoons year round to help supplement his income for a growing family during the depression. Realizing that prime pelts would bring a better price in the fall, he started to keep live trapped animals until fall. Using his knowledge of natural diets and behaviors, the captive animals thrived. His children, Fred, Edna and Loretta begged him to keep certain animals alive as they had become pets. From these wild 'pets', and their mates, the Blue Ridge Fox Farm was established.

Ralph Space's first license from the Board of Fish and Game Commissioners of the State of New Jersey is dated June 6, 1928 and is on display in the Space Farms Museum. This license enabled Ralph and Elizabeth to propagate native game animals for business purposes. In a few years the Space Fox Farm was in major production of gray, red, and silver foxes. In 1930 Ralph Space was the first fox farmer in the United States to import Platinum foxes from Canada to extend the fur color range of his ranch. By cross breeding different colors of foxes, Ralph developed Cody Platinum, Pearl Platinum, La Forest Platinum, Norwegian Platinum and White Marked Silver foxes. My grandfather was recognized as a leader in the fox farm industry. In 1939 Ralph's fox farm housed thirty, individually caged, pairs of foxes.

" When I was a little girl, I could hear the foxes playing in their water dishes at night. Their cages were right behind our house. It was a pleasant sound," Ralph's daughter, Loretta Space Dunn recalls.

"As a young boy my chores included watering the foxes, cleaning up the poopie, (which I carried to our vegetable garden), and helping Dad move foxes after the breeding season," reminisces my Dad, Fred. "It was a lot of work for a little 10 year old boy."

In 1934 Ralph received his first permit for a wild Animal farm from Wantage Township for the price of $1.00 and the Space Farms Zoo was born. As neighbors found injured or orphaned native species they brought them to the zoo due to Space's knowledge of animals. These injured or orphaned animals were the next inhabitants of today's world renowned zoo. Fred's chores were to take care of the animals every day as Ralph was busy with the foxes and trapping. As the fox fur fad faded, Ralph expanded into the mink ranch business. Based on his exceptional knowledge of the natural diet and behaviors of the wild creatures he observed in Sussex County, Ralph Space received many national awards and trophies for his quality fox and mink.

Today the Space Farms Zoo is home to four breeds of foxes. The native gray fox is the most diminutive of the foxes. Red foxes are known for their vibrant orange/red coats. The sliver fox, is actually grayish black with silver flecks tipping each hair across its back. The silver fox's facial markings are distinctive extended 'eyebrows' in a silver color. The gold cross fox is a hybrid of a red fox and a silver and does not breed true, the youngsters reflecting the colors of its grandparents. The red, silver and gold cross fox have a striking white tip to their tails, while the native gray fox's tail is tipped in black.

The silver fox is a northern color phase of the red fox. In the southern states the color phase of the North American red fox is red in color with a frosted guard hair overlay down the middle of the back. Originally the native red fox's range was from Canada to northern New York State. According to Leonard Rue III's book " Fur Bearing Animals of North America", the European red fox was imported in 1650 for hunting purposes. Plantation owners in Maryland released the imported European red fox into the wilderness to continue the tradition of fox hunting in the states. In 1750 red foxes from England were again released on Long Island and in New Jersey. The red fox now ranges from Canada to Florida, and as far south as Texas and New Mexico. Here in northern N.J. the red fox is a deep russet orange. The European red fox has interbred with the native North American red fox. When the European red fox was introduced to the middle colonies, the gray fox was native to this area. The gray fox is not easily hunted since it will run into a burrow when chased by dogs. The European red fox did not behave in this manor but would run above ground until exhausted making for a 'good' hunt.

The wily red fox has a number of attributes that has enabled it to thrive in the United States. They are crepuscular, preferring to hunt for small game in the early mornings and evenings, thereby avoiding the human population. Like other members of their Canine family, they are omnivores. The fox's pupils are oval, and their sharp sight can spot prey at a distance. Intelligent, sly and skittish, the fox is acutely aware of its surroundings. Hearing is sharp, enabling a fox to hone in on a mouse at 300 feet. The sense of smell is very important to a fox. Foxes mark territory with urine and musk, giving notice to others a fox of a certain sex is in the area. This urine is very strong and will kill grasses in the marked area. The acrid smell of fox musk is easily mistaken for a skunk.

When the fire whistle blows in Beemerville or the surrounding towns, the coyotes, wolves and foxes will all howl. Foxes can be very vocal, yipping during the mating season and communicating with each other, like many of their fellow Canines.

Red foxes seldom den up preferring to sleep in the open. During snow storms, the red fox will curl up with its' tail over its nose, and is often covered in snow. Only mated pairs den up for a short time during the birthing and rearing of kits (fox puppies).

Gray foxes will inhabit burrows created by other animals such as the woodchuck. This habit exposes the gray fox to a number of diseases. Gray foxes will also climb trees and is the only fox to do so. The gray fox will also challenge a predator while the red fox relies on a speedy escape to survive.

Zoo Momma

Foxes breed in the last two weeks of January in this part of New Jersey. After a fifty-three day gestation, six to eight kits are born, weighing approximately four ounces each. Eyes open in ten to twelve days. The pair of parents work in coordination, the mother is fed by the sire for the first week, after which both parents hunt for prey for the young. The young are weaned at three months and trail after the mother while learning to hunt for themselves. By the fall, the kits are nearly full grown and strike out on their own. A large male red fox will weigh eleven pounds, the grays a mere nine pounds.

In the wild all foxes are susceptible to distemper, enteritis, rabies, mange, ticks, and fleas. Foxes are preyed upon by coyotes and kits are easy prey for hawks, owls and eagles. Readers are advised not to approach a 'friendly' fox but to call an animal control officer, since the fox may be sick.

At the Space Farms Zoo many visitors marvel at the cohabitation of a pair of silver foxes with the two male five-hundred pound Syrian Grizzly bears.

"Foxes often follow the bear trails in the wild," says my dad, Fred. "Bears are messy eaters, the foxes tag along after for the scraps".

Grampa Ralph Space and his first Platinum Fox in 1937
Photo by Space Farms

Chapter 17 Kitty Fox

In the middle of a fast food parking lot, I slowly unfolded the flaps of a plain brown cardboard box. Three balls of charcoal gray fuzz were curled up inside on top of a ratty old towel. The smallest two still had their eyes sealed shut since birth, ten days before. The largest gray fuzz ball was four weeks old. She looked over her tiny shoulder forlornly. A look that said "I'm scared". Curled tightly around her cousins, her tail tucked between her legs, she spoke to me without words. She won my heart in that moment.

"Hi, pretty Kitty," I cooed in my best loving mommy voice. I scooped her up in my hand, and she curled into a smaller ball, trying to disappear. A baby fox is called a kit.

"It's all right, baby girl," I said.

I knew the three little foxes were girls, that was what I had ordered from the fox farmer. One for our zoo and two for the Staten Island Zoo. We both wanted handle able foxes for our exhibits. *Oh, let's be honest, I ordered three in case I lost one, I had never raised foxes before.*

"These are red foxes?" I questioned the farmer. "They are so dark." I did not want my ignorance to show, but I knew I had ordered red foxes and these babies were definitely charcoal gray. Maybe he had brought me silver fox babies by mistake?

"Yep, they'll turn red at four weeks", the grizzled, bearded farmer stated. "See, this one already has red starting on her face."

I learn something new every day.

I picked up the other two babies, each not much bigger than my fist. I looked in their ears, at their sealed eyes and at their bottoms. All were clean, with no visible sign of infection or discharge. I looked for fleas and ticks, and saw none. The kits seemed to be in good shape. The parents had been wormed before giving birth, so I did not expect any problems in that area. I had known this farmer for years, and knew he took good care of his stock. After I gently placed each kit back in the box resting on the hood of the farmer's white truck, we conducted our business. I took his State of Pennsylvania Propagation License number, his truck license plate number and he took all the info he needed from me, the Space Farms U.S.D.A number, phone numbers and State of New Jersey Zoological Exhibit permit number. *Whew, the paperwork!*

We said our goodbyes, and the friendly fox farmer told me to call him if I had any problems.

"It was a six hour trip, they are probably hungry," were his parting words.

My green SUV grumbled up High Point mountain as my mind raced. If my Gramp Ralph could see me now! He would be so proud. My Gramp Ralph started Space Farms as a fox farm. I knew my Dad, Fred knew all about foxes and I could rely on him for help if I needed it. And there was always Dr. Spinks.

Upon my arrival back at the zoo, I put the kits in the nursery incubator I had prepared. I mixed up Esbilac, the formula used for the canine family, in a two to one ratio of H2O and powder. I offered the kits the bottle. They did not like the taste of the rubber nipple, but they would have to learn how to suck on a bottle instead of Momma Fox. It was a struggle, but they each drank one ounce. I put them in their incubator box bed to sleep on a heating pad covered with a clean fluffy towel. They slept soundly for the next three hours. It had been a long, exhausting day for three little girls.

The North American Red Fox is not indigenous to New Jersey. The North American Red Fox's territory was from Canada to northern New York State. When the first English settlers came to America they brought the custom of fox hunting with them. In 1650 and again in 1750, European Red Foxes were brought across the ocean in the same ships as the settlers. Some of the foxes escaped the hunt and lived in the American wilderness thereafter.

Foxes eat small rodents and vegetation, which are plentiful in this section of the country. Their sharp sense of hearing and sight can help them locate a mouse three hundred feet away. The fox has vertical pupils, like a cat, and walks like a cat, placing the hind foot in the front foot's footprint. However, foxes are a member of the canine family, along with dogs and wolves.

A full grown red fox will weigh eleven pounds, but looks much bigger due to fluffy fur and long legs. Its tail is up to one foot long and is used for balance while jumping and communication. The colorful fur of an adult red fox is made up of two sections, the under fur and the guard fur. The under fur is fuzzy and warm. The guard hairs are up to two inches long. This combination makes the fur of the fox soft as a cotton ball. The red fox has red fur on it's back, white on its' belly, and charcoal black legs. Every red fox has a white tipped tail.

But the babies I had were all charcoal gray! Boy, I hoped I had not been snookered by the fox farmer. My family trusted him, so I trusted him, sort of. I double checked with my Dad and my brother, Eric, who both had much more experience than I did with foxes. Both assured me the little girls would turn red.

By the next day, after four sloppy bottle sessions, the three foxes were drinking well from the bottle. *Whew! One worry off my mind.* On the third day the biggest, Kitty, was walking around. The two smaller foxes, Vixen and Lady, still slept most of the time. Vixen is the name for a female fox, like a female horse is called a mare, or female cattle are called cows. Lady got her name from "Lady and the Fox", Kitty's name came from the famous movie star Kitty Fox. I had the names picked out, like any expectant mom, before the kits, (babies), arrived.

A quick trip to Dr. Spinks' Veterinary Hospital confirmed that all three girls were doing well. Future visits would entail (hah, no pun intended) inoculations, but for now, the girls were just fine.

Foxes are very vocal, communicating with yips, growls and pants. Foxes are also crepuscular, active at dawn and dusk. This caused a problem in our house, since my husband, Doug, was not happy with the early morning wake up calls the kits made when they woke up hungry. Often the kits wrestled and played, screaming like a lady in distress.

They quickly grew stronger and larger. At four weeks, like magic, they started to shed their baby fur and were gradually turning the brilliant red that red foxes are known for. *Whew!* By five weeks old each kit was eating wet dog food, and running around our home after work. By day, they would travel with me to the zoo and stay in the nursery's center enclosure. The girls romped in the green grass, and rested in the shade, delighting zoo visitors.

I knew two would go to the Staten Island Zoo, but not which two. I hoped I would be able to keep Kitty, my favorite. *Yes, I know a mom is not supposed to have favorites!* I had separated her from the two smaller girls because she was two weeks older, so much stronger, and more coordinated and would beat up the other little foxes while playing. Kitty needed a playmate, so that was me, after 10 p.m. on my living room floor. I bonded with Kitty, and she with me. I gave some serious thought to keeping her as a house pet. Since I live on the zoo property, that might be o.k.. Foxes do have a scent gland, the smell slightly less offensive than a skunk. But only slightly. I considered having her scent glands removed. Somehow I could not do that, she was as God intended her to be, a fox. I hoped she would stay with me at Space Farms... But the Staten Island Zoo was to have their pick of two out of the three babies... What would I do if they wanted Kitty???

I had separated Kitty out of the grassy nursery pen, away from Vixen and Lady when I noticed that Kitty would growl and shoo the two smaller kits away from their wet dog food. Kitty was only two weeks older, but so much more aggressive. I put Kitty in another enclosure in the nursery. With plenty of stuffed toys, and a little more attention from me, she did just fine.

I had been in constant touch with the Staten Island Zoo's Acting General Curator, Bob Kurtz. I sent info and pictures back and forth like any proud momma. Bob didn't want the kits until they were off a bottle and on solid food. I do tend to overextend the bottle time on all my babies. At first the bottle is for basic nutrition. After weaning age, the bottle is a positive reward system. At twelve weeks, the kits were fine on solid food. In the wild, kits are weaned between six and eight weeks old, depending upon the small game food source availability. So my girls were more than ready to depart from the bottle. The question was- was I ready to give them up?

Bob and I set a day for him and others from the Staten Island Zoo to come see our zoo, and pick up the kits of their choice. Now I have to admit, when other zookeepers come to our zoo, it is a fun day. It is so nice to chat with other professionals, relaxed, informal, and friendly. It's a holiday for the visiting zookeepers, work away from work. We exchange husbandry tips and tidbits, grouse a little about the government intrusion into our business, chat about new regulations, complain about the paperwork, and talk about species coming up, (being born),that we may want to trade.

When Bob and the other keeper's arrived we first checked on the kits. Lady and Vixen were resting quietly in the grass until they heard my voice. Kitty, from her higher vantage point, (her enclosure was elevated), saw me and starting yipping right away. I explained why they were separated, and offered to put them all together so the visiting keepers could see the interaction. I'm sure Bob and the others noticed my affection for Kitty. But I didn't mention it. I try to be professional. At least I try.

"Don't bother," said Bob. "These look fine. Can we play with them?"

"Sure," my grateful reply as I opened the enclosure door.

After Lady and Vixen rushed to play with the visitors, the decision was made. Lady and Vixen would go to the Staten Island Zoo. *Whew, load off of my mind.* The rest of their visit was spent touring our zoo, gabbing, lunch with the visiting zookeepers, (they had buffalo burgers- what a treat!), and finally paperwork and my final goodbye to Vixen and Lady. I was not worried for them, they would have a fantastic life at the Staten Island Zoo, with all the food, medical care and spacious enclosure they could want. In the fox world, they had won the lottery! As per my Lori's Law, I have lifetime visitation rights.

During the same visit, Bob picked up a baby ground hog, (redneck terminology- a woodchuck), that I had raised on a bottle, one of Jenny Woodchuck's babies. I had named the ground hog Elvis, due to the fact that Elvis always curled his lip when I fed him a bottle. Funny how names stick. Bob loved the original human Elvis, and thought it was fate that I had named the woodchuck Elvis. Bob told me later that Elvis' name was changed to Chuck E. Groundhog, a combination of woodchuck, Elvis / Groundhog. Chuck became the hit of the curator's office. Staten Island Zoo celebrated the national holiday- Ground hogs day- with a flurry of paparazzi and Mayor Bloomberg. You know that ground hog that bit Mayor Bloomberg? That was my Elvis, now Chuck E. Groundhog. To my chagrin. Oh well.

So I still had Kitty Fox. She stayed in the Nursery exhibit until fall, when I needed the enclosure for another animal, and she needed more room. She was moved to an auxiliary enclosure until she grew big enough to go in with the other red foxes we had. I visited her daily, bringing her deer ears, tails and sticks, natural toys that foxes enjoy.

Jim Stein and Dan Bacon are partners who own Lakota Wolf Preserve in Columbia, New Jersey, about forty five minutes away from Space Farms Zoo. Jim and girlfriend Becky, are also the head curators for the Lakota Wolf Preserve. They came to visit us at the zoo. As keepers do we gabbed about our animals, the babies I had raised and I mentioned Kitty Fox. Becky wanted to meet Kitty, so we played with Kitty for a while. Their resident red fox was getting up there in years at twelve years old. Foxes in the wild live about ten years. Foxes with the added security of captivity,(medical care, constant nutrition, clean water, no predators, parasites and comfy safe enclosures) will live fifteen to eighteen years.

Jim and Becky had seen Kitty Fox when she was small and I had taken her on the lecture circuit promoting the zoo at Camp Taylor, the home of the Lakota Wolf Preserve. I knew what would happen and I let it happen, just by introducing Becky to Kitty Fox. Becky fell in love with Kitty. We had a female fox in residence at Space Farms, but did not have a friendly one, like Kitty. But I could have more foxes, anytime I wanted from the fox farmer in Pennsylvania. I knew what would happen and it was ok. Becky wanted Kitty for the Lakota Wolf

Preserve. Kitty would have a wonderful life there, living in a natural enclosure at the edge of the National Delaware Water Gap State Park with Becky to love her. Kitty would get much more attention from Becky than I could give her. So when Jim and Becky asked if Kitty was available, I said a reluctant yes. Jim and Becky would check with their partner, Dan Bacon, who is also a friend of our family, and get back to me.

The Space family, through three generations, has a great reputation for raising not just healthy stock, but excellent specimens. Only healthy, happy animals reproduce and live long lives. Space Farms Zoo holds longevity, birth, and size records on different species. With the lifelong studies of animals in their natural habitats, my Grandfather Ralph, Dad Fred, my brothers, and myself have all contributed to the family's knowledge pool. This pool of knowledge is dipped into by many writers, Veterinary specialists and other zoos.

Becky called me and we set up a day for them to pick up Kitty Fox. I said my teary farewells and promised to visit. Sometimes love is knowing it is best to let go. Jim and Becky changed Kitty's name to Sierra.

I have visited Vixen, Lady, and Kitty Fox. I didn't get to see Chuck E. Groundhog when I was at the Staten Island Zoo, he was in hibernation. I only get to visit places in the winter, during our off season. As of this writing, they are all doing well, and I am at peace with that.

Kitty Fox and Lori
Photo by Karen Talasco

Chapter 18 Baby Boas

In the spring of 2006 our new calf had just arrived from the Sytsema's Dairy Farm, which is just down the road from us. Young Will, now thirty something, hefted the fifty pound calf in his arms easily and carried the calf through the side nursery gate. I checked out the calf while Will gave me the lowdown on the week old newborn Holstein's progress on the bottle. Will was grinning, his John Deere baseball cap shading his twinkling proud eyes. Thumbs hooked into his jean pockets, Will and I chatted about possible names, looking at the coloration and spots on the black and white calf.

Suddenly, JoAnn, the restaurant cook, burst through the main building's back zoo doors.

"Did you know the boa was pregnant? And she is having babies right now?" JoAnn blurted out. JoAnn's thin body trembled with the exciting news, or maybe it was the breeze on the early spring day. She had just passed the boas while cleaning the outside bathrooms.

"No, but here anything is possible," was my reply. "Well, Willy, I gotta go!"

"Yep, you do," Willy replied knowingly, ending our conversation.

I ran to the side of the main building where the exotic snakes were kept in huge cases on wheels. Dad had built the cases and I had painted and decorated them years before. I was faster then Willy's truck, the pick-up passed the snakes a minute or two later. Headed out the main gate, I saw Will smile at me and give me the 'thumbs up' sign and drive on out of the zoo. *Yeah, I'm gonna need luck on this one! Thanks Will.*

I glanced through the plexi-glass front of the six foot high by three foot deep boa case. Yes sireee! There she was plopping out babies as she wiggled along the bottom of the mulch chip strewn floor! Wow! I had never seen a boa birth. Live birth! Double Wow! Each baby was being born individually, still encased in the chorionic membrane! The babies seemed to be having trouble wiggling out of their clear tiny sacks. In the wild a momma boa would be traveling over twigs, leaves, rocks, and vegetation on the jungle floor. The tiny boa's crystal clear chorionic membranes would be automatically ripped open as momma extruded the eggs over the rough jungle floor surfaces.

This was not the case in our exotic snake enclosures. The floor substrate we use is wood chips, landscape mulch quality- *obvious to me right then*- not a rough enough surface.

Some of the tiny babies were struggling inside their clear egg bubbles.

Both mom and her two casemates were circling the young still inside their eggs. I had no experience with boa snakes giving birth. I had no idea if mom and casemates would chow down on the trapped immobile tiny tots. My mind raced though the snake reproductive facts in my head. *Pythons protect their eggs by shimmying, but they lay eggs outside their bodies. Boas carry them inside their bodies until term. OVOVIVIPAROUS Yeah, Lor lots of good big words are gonna do ya now! I had read somewhere that boas may eat their young.. I have more than a few snake facts in my head, really I do, But not a lot on live births...So what's a gal to do? "I don't know nothing' about birthin' no boa babies!" Ricocheted inside my head.*

I ran to the kitchen, grabbed a clean bucket, turned and rushed past JoAnn again towards the kitchen door.

"'How's it going?" I think JoAnn said, but my mind was not on conversation. JoAnn knows me well enough to know I was not being rude. Back at the boas's enclosure I grabbed the snake hook. I opened the stock room door from the back porch. I knew the boas; one red tail and two regular boas. I had changed water and substrate and fed them once a week for years. Two were nicely handle-able, one, *(of coarse, there is always one!),* was nasty. I grabbed the top to a metal trash can in the stockroom that held goat feed.

Slowly unlocking the door to the snake case, I inched the door open. One ten inch wiggly baby boa fell onto the concrete porch. I grabbed the birth fluid slippery serpent with my available hand and plunked him in the tall white bucket.

Inching the door open wider, the rest of the inhabitants stayed put. Mom boa was circling the inside of the case still giving birth to more offspring. The nasty boa was nosing a couple of the still encased infants. I tapped Nasty Boa on the nose with my four foot snake hook, effectively causing him to retract his seeking head. Using the garbage can lid to shield myself and the little boas, I quickly hooked into the birth sacks, freeing the little snakes at the same time, I pulled the babies towards the enclosure door, lay the snake hook down in the case for a second, pinched the birth membranes off their noses, and plunked them into the bucket.

Pristine and beautiful, the tiny snakes heads were the size of my thumbnail. Glistening in the mid-morning air, their burnished copper, beige and black coloring was vibrant.

My moment to observe in awe was quickly over. Mom was circling by again. Nasty Boa and the other boa were all on the move. Excitement tainted the interior of the case. *Or maybe it was just me.* My snake hook hindered my agility. I put it down, using the garbage can lid to pop the two marauding snakes on the nose, backing them up. One hand with my garbage can shield, my left hand pinching birth sacks and freeing noses to breathe, I was a machine in constant motion. My total concentration was on the snakes before me. Aware of the danger of the adult boas to myself and the infants, I scooped twenty-two new baby boas into the bucket. My elbows flexed and fingers flew, grabbing the newborn boa babies. Using my jeans farmer style I quickly wiped my hand off when it became too slippery to facilitate the job at hand. *Pun intended.*

With a garbage can shield, and crazily gesticulating messy gooey hands, I'm sure I looked like Don Quixote fighting imaginary demons. The mom and other boas were not, however, imaginary. Twenty- three boa babies later, I slowed to see if there were any more in the corners or under the log inside the case. Two bright yellow- orange oval shapes caught my eye. They looked like wet Twinkies.

Didn't know what they were, so I scraped them out onto the floor.

Dad had stopped in for coffee and JoAnn told him what was happening. Not to miss the opportunity to see, teach, help and advise, Dad was suddenly at my side.

"How's it going?" Dad's standard catch phrase.

"Think I got 'em all. See any more?" I responded.

"No live ones, but there is one more dud egg, might as well clean it out while you are there," Dad instructed.

OH so that is what those Twinkies are.

"Yup, I see it now, Dad," I said quickly. "I did not know what they were before, but do now." A 'dud egg' in farmer talk, is an unfertilized egg. In zoological terminology a dud snake egg is called a 'slug'. That is why they were that bright yellow orange color. They contained the undigested yolk from a non existent embryo. *Wow learn something new every day. Learning a lot today.*

Dad and I finished up at the boas' case, closed and locked the door.

"How many ya got?" Pop asked.

"Don't know, yet, Pop, maybe two dozen?" I took a breath. "I need help getting one of the big 55 gallon aquariums out of your basement. The one I raised the little gator in. It has a top.

"OK, I'll get it here," Dad loves snakes. He always has. He is a well known authority on snakes. Hospitals call him for identification of snakes that have bitten people. Locals bring snakes to Space Farms for Dad, Parker or I to identify. I hope someday to know all that Dad knows on snakes, but I doubt I ever will.

Dad left me with the bucket of baby boas. I was checking out the babies, making sure all their noses were clear of the membranes. Within minutes the fifty-five gallon tank was at the front door. Visitors were gathering around all the activity. Sometimes the hardest thing I have to do is stay nice to visitors when I really want to say "Get out of my way, I'm working here!" DeNero style.

The fish tank in place on the table, I layered the bottom with wood chips and placed a large dog dish full of water on one end. Dad helped me hook up a heat lamp on the post behind the table. The slimy babies needed to dry off.

One by one we placed the ten inch beige, black and burnished copper baby boas in the tank. Fascinating. Some had trailing yolk sacks, Dad advised me not to cut them off. Evidently some of the babies absorb the rest of the yolk after birth.

At this point I should explain what an ovoviviparous birth is. Ovoviviparous snakes keep eggs inside their bodies. The eggs do not have a hard shell like a chicken or soft leathery shells like other reptiles, (turtles, most snakes, and lizards). The ovoviviparous snake retains the infants inside their bodies. There is no umbilical cord or nutrient exchange directly with the mother, only fluids by osmosis. The embryos are not connected to the mother by umbilical cords. They are separate little islands inside the mother. Each egg has the same basic contents and structure as a chicken egg. The embryo sits on top of the yolk sack, surrounded by albumin (the clear part of the chicken egg we are all familiar with). Extra embryonic membranes, the chorion, (the outer 'package'membrane), allantois, (similar to the mammalian placenta but retained with in the egg itself), and the yolk sack,(the embryo snake's food source), are all part of the egg retained within the mother boa. As the embryo grows it feeds upon the yolk sack which is attached to the embryo at what we would call the belly button. When the embryo has grown to size, the yolk sack is absorbed into the belly/stomach of the baby snake. The fluids surrounding the snake, the albumin is absorbed into the embryo/baby snake also. The birth and hatching occur at the same time. Our problem on this occasion was that the outer membranes of the snakes' eggs did not break upon exit of the mother snake's body.

Boa constrictors are members of the Boidae family and found in Central and South America and some Caribbean Islands. There are ten sub-species of boas all with different color patterns. A boa can grow up to fourteen feet long, or longer in captivity. In the wild the females are larger, seven to ten feet, than their male counterparts at six to eight feet long. Captive life expectancy is up to thirty years, with a record of one boa living to be forty years old.

As I put the tiny tots into the large fish tank, I noticed they all had a yellow glow in their bellies, the vibrant yellow yolk they had just absorbed. Each little boa looked like ET had just touched their tummies with his glowing finger!

I counted the youngsters as I put them into the tank. Twenty- two squiggling, slimy, shiny serpents, not knowing where they were, where to go or what they were supposed to do. One baby died inside his membranes-maybe I didn't get to him quick enough. But twenty two live births is just fine with me. A litter of boas can be up to sixty- five! And with the Twinkie slug eggs, that would have been twenty-six babies if they had all birthed. Wow! *What a mom! Better her than me.* Oh and another interesting reproductive snake fact just popped into my head: some snakes can retain sperm for up to three years, Boas only for three years. *Think about that one, Ladies.* Gestation is a hundred to a hundred-twenty days.

After all was said and done, we sat down for lunch, the infant snakes settled in their tank, coiling under the warm heat lamp. What an exciting morning.

A week later it was time for the baby boas to eat. I purchased pinky mice, which are mice the size of your pinkie finger- newborn mice. I hoped they would all eat. And they did- voraciously. Every week for the next month, I fed them on schedule just like the big boas and other snakes. Their growth rate was fabulous. At two months old they were all two foot long and eating 'hoppers'- mice that just started to hop, about the size of your thumb.

At two months old we transferred them into an empty big snake case just like their mother's. Feeding time had become a problem, all twenty snakes wanted to eat at the same time, and often the same mouse. Boas are constrictor snakes, grabbing their prey and coiling around it, squeezing tighter with each prey's exhale. When two stubborn baby boas grabbed on the same mouse, they would coil into a knot, sometimes for an hour, until one decided to give up. Since they all looked alike, it was hard to figure who had eaten and who had not gotten the mouse. I developed a system of multiple fish tanks set up behind the large snake enclosures. At feeding time, I would put a mouse and one baby boa in the tank. When that boa was coiled on the mouse, I would add another baby boa and another mouse. Three smaller fish tanks would hold twelve eating baby boas. The last six boas I could feed in their larger enclosure by separating them to different corners, and one in the front middle and one towards the door. Making sure each boa got a mouse was the challenge. After everyone got a mouse, I would put them back in their home enclosure. They all did very well and grew quickly.

Boas do make nice pets, with a big HOWEVER: Boas grow quickly. The nice little snake a parent purchases for their child grows about a foot a year, if fed properly. If handled on a regular basis the boas get used to being handled and remains 'nice'. The thrill of a new pet eventually fades, or the child goes off to college, moves to an apartment that does not allow pets, or gets married and the new bride does not want snakes in the house. Space Farms receives about fifty phone calls a season, "Will you take my pet snake?" The answer is always NO. The average boa constrictor will live twenty to thirty years, and they can get quite large. We steer callers towards other zoos that we know are looking. However the truth is there are so many older pet snakes looking for a home. We did place a number of our youngsters with homes. We sold the rest to a pet store chain.

In recent years Florida has been having an intense problem with pet snakes that have been released into the wild. The released pet snakes have eaten the small wildlife, including protected baby gators, that live naturally in the warm Florida climate. The Florida Department of Fish and Wildlife have folks whose job it is to go out and catch those now huge released pet snakes. Releasing an exotic snake in colder climates is a death sentence for the snake.

I hope our Bertha Boa does not have any more offspring. While I don't want Bertha to have more babies, I still treasure the experience of the birth that I witnessed. It was educating and fascinating. And now I can say " I do know something 'bout birthin' those baby boas!"

Bowl of Boa Babies
Photo by Lori Space Day

Chapter 19 Peafowl

The Space Farms Zoo and Museum gets an amazing number of phone calls with dumb questions:

"Do you have live animals there?"

"I just saw a bear *(substitute any native animal here).* Did you have one escape?"

"Where are you? Can I get there from here?" *I'm tempted to say "No."*

"My cat just saw a raccoon out my deck's sliding doors. What should I do?"

"I am at your bear enclosure. (*We have four?*) Where is the nearest bathroom?" O.K. so maybe that one is not so dumb, but we give every family a map of the zoo!

"There is a large bird flying overhead. What kind is it?" *Where are you?* "Home."

"Is Mr. Fox there?"

So when I was called to the phone about a peacock I was not surprised. There had been reports of feral peacocks, actually peafowl, in Vernon and Highland Lakes. Everybody thinks they escaped from us. However, Joe Q. Public can buy peafowl. Folks buy them as chicks, not realizing how large and noisy they can be. Once those two facts are discovered, they release the peafowl, or the peafowl 'escape'. We had received multiple phone calls on these escaped peafowl, sometimes the calls are quite menacing.

This gentleman on the phone, was nice, and stated that he had two peacocks in his back yard. He wanted us to come catch them. I explained that they were not ours and catching peafowl from the wild is not easy as they fly away as soon as you approach them with a net. The gentleman understood and asked if he got them into his garage would we come get them.

"Yeah, sure, get them in the garage and call us back," I told him, doubtful if he could accomplish his good deed.

Three days (!) later he called us back. The peacocks were trapped in his garage, how quickly could we come? *Holy Mackerel, did not expect to hear back from him.* Dad was having coffee, so I quickly explained the situation to him. I had not mentioned the first phone call since we get so many of those. The calls not necessarily on peacocks but on skunk, possum, raccoon, snake, you name it, in somebody's garage.

"You want peacocks? You just remodeled the barn in the museum," Dad said.

"Yeah, sure, we can put them in the auxiliary cage, for the winter, until we get another cage built," I stammered. "They're pretty and easy to care for." I felt like a little girl asking for some fancy bauble. But I left off the "please Daddy" whine.

"Where are they?" Dad's sensible question.

"Highland Lakes. I'll get some nets, and a crate," I said over my shoulder as I left him to finish his coffee, didn't want to give him too much time to think about it. Ten minutes later we were in his car, equipment in the back, flying down the road towards Highland Lakes.

Peafowl are beautiful birds. Green or Indian peafowl are what most folks call peacocks. Actually, only the males are called peacocks. The females are called peahens. The males have the distinctive five foot long train of beautiful iridescent blue-green feathers with that unique eye colored and shaped feather tip. The train of feathers is not the tail feathers. The true tail feathers are beige-brown and support the train when the male is 'showing'. Females also have the tail feathers, but not the showy beautiful train. Both sexes have a tiara of slender crest feathers with a tiny blue opalescent dot on the top, reminding one of a Dr. Seuss character. Both sexes also have a colorful neck but the males are much more distinctive and extensive in the coloration. The female's body is a motley gray brown color. Her body helps her camouflage the nest. Nests of one to eight eggs are laid on the ground and incubation is twenty eight days. Chicks have a thirty percent survival rate. Only two out of six survive despite their tawny spotted coloration. The peafowl are not powerful flyers, but they can fly short distances or to the tree branches where they prefer to roost at night. Peafowl can weigh up to thirteen pounds and live fifteen to twenty years.

Many scientists have theorized that the tail has evolved over the eons of time to court females. However some theorize that the tail is actually to intimidate other male rivals. 'My tail is bigger than your tail', kind of intimidation. *Huumm...* Be that as it may, the male peafowl's train is gorgeous. The luscious long train is held erect by the true tail feathers during courtship of a female. The six foot diameter wide saucer of color also acts as a sound reflector, like a satellite dish, funneling the courtship clucks to the peahen or peacock in front of the displaying male. A male may have a harem of five or six females. When not in courtship or show off mode, the distinctive male's train simply flows behind the male in a fluffy wave. The eyes of the train are deceptive to predators, who after grabbing on the train, find themselves with a mouth full of feathers, but no meat.

The peacock sheds its train feathers every year around the Fourth of July. When I was growing up at the zoo, *(yeah, when dinosaurs walked the earth),* our peafowl ran free on the zoo grounds. As the visitor population expanded, we cooped them up to prevent feather plucking by unwatched children. We now sell the peacock train feathers in our gift shop. The peacocks and their feathers have a special significance in my nuclear family. It was always hubby Doug and daughter Jackie's job to go collect the feathers. In honor of those special daddy daughter moments, our daughter now has a gorgeous peacock feather tattoo on her foot. *Not that I am a big fan of tattoos but this one is very nice.*

The Indian Peafowl is indigenous to South Asia. The Green Peafowl is native to Burma and Java. . *Who knows what those countries are called today, geography is not my strong suit!* They are useful birds in those areas, as peafowl eat young snakes and cobras. There is also a Congo Peafowl, a bird with a beautiful colored body but no train, and it looks like a dumpy cousin of what we commonly call a peacock. Peafowl are members of the pheasant family. *Even to me, peafowl sounds strange on my lips. I'll call them peacocks.*

While the colorful birds may have originated in Southern Asia, they have been domesticated for two thousand years. There are also white peacock variations. The peacock's all seeing eye was the basis for many different gods. In the Greco - Roman times peacocks became the prized banquet fare. There are references to peafowl in the Bible. Now there are feral populations in Japan and England. Peacocks were brought to those countries by royalty, to decorate courtyards with the peafowl's plumage. After established and gone feral, these magnificent birds were hunted and eaten. Peacock was one of Henry VIII of England's dinner dishes. (*He also ate swans, not to cast judgment here, just showing the reader the change in attitude on food sources. I'm sure the Donner Party would had been happy to have peacock or swan!*)

Mexico's feral flock dates back to the early nineteenth century. South Florida and California's wild flocks were released/escaped more recently. The flock in California has stirred up a bit of a range war. Some neighbors like them, some neighbors want them shot.

There are downsides to having these beautiful birds in your neighborhood. Peacocks roost in trees or on rooftops at night. Their rather large poo has to go somewhere. Peacocks also scratch the earth to find worms, bugs and seedlings to eat. They have three toes pointing forward, just like a garden claw trowel and one toe pointing backward. There goes your garden. The call of the male peacock sounds like a woman's elongated scream of "HELLLLLP". And that is only one of eleven different calls, clucks or sounds. Only one of said calls could be considered soft, and that is the gentle coo the hen makes to her chicks. The peafowl are an automatic alarm system, calling out loudly at the first sign of danger. They also call or crow out at dawn, dusk, or just about any time they want to.

But they are gorgeous! A group of peafowl are called a flock, pride, or, appropriately, an ostentation. The phrase 'Proud as a Peacock' comes from the strutting glory of the male bird's ostentatious show. The train when in an upright position is shimmed and quivered to enhance the light's glistening off the flashy feathers.

So did I want peacocks for the zoo? Sure I did. We had them before, but they had 'aged out'. I recall camping in the zoo as a kid. The call of the peacocks at night was petrifying even though we knew what it was. We could of bought a pair, but that would have been way too easy. And these were free for the catching. Dad and I were on our way.

We got to the gentleman's house, shook hands all round and approached the garage. Dad was in his bibs, torn, dirty, road kill deer blood stained kaki shirt, and me in my not early- morning-clean navy blue zoo uniform, I'm sure we looked like a motley crew. Dad is however graced by age, experience, and fame. We are typically accepted wherever we go in working clothes. In a time crunch, that is just the way we roll.

We entered the garage, quickly netted the excited, frightened birds and put them in the pet taxi for the ride home. No muss no fuss. At least on us. The frightened adult birds had knocked the garage supplies off shelves and the debris evident when we opened the garage door. And the poo! The neighbors and the gentleman were happy to have the birds gone.

Now all I had to do was to convince the guys that the peacocks deserved a separate enclosure. I was not going to put them back in the plow museum after I had cleaned, reorganized, and painted my mural the year before. The peafowl would poo all over it. AGAIN. I had some talking and planning to do. So I did, all that winter long…

My Dad, Fred Space and Paul Truman Peacock
Photo by Michelle Mulder

Zoo Momma

Chapter 20 Hunter on the Prairie

I cannot say where my inspiration to paint comes from. Sometimes it makes <u>me</u> wonder. I had repainted the life size fiberglass oxen, horse and man that accompanied the Prairie Schooner in our museum. They had become drab and dull since the thirty years ago when Grampa Ralph (the founder of our museum) had put them in the museum. Along the hallway going to the Prairie Schooner is a long white wall which needed painting also. So I painted it white. As I am painting the white wall white *(how boring!)*, I decided to paint a mural on it. I spent about three weeks in November and December painting the mural. On it is depicted a coiled diamondback rattlesnake, cacti, the prairie schooner, a lady and child sitting in the prairie schooner, a herd of buffalo, and a hunter taking aim at the buffalo on a background of prairie and dry mountains. As is my technique, I would sketch out the major components at home at night and transfer them onto the mural with carbon paper. *(Remember carbon paper?)* The mural went along fairly well. I had some trouble with the dimensions of the prairie schooner's bonnet. I could not get it fluffy enough for me. I remember thinking that my grandpa would be proud, but only if I got it right. *Come on Grampa help me out.* Afterwards, my fingers flew and the bonnet looked just fine.

When I was having trouble with the hunter I wanted to put on the prairie there was an easier solution.

My nephew Hunter, then age 12, came home from school one day and I asked him to hold a gun, (my family are avid hunters so we have a lot of guns), so I could look at his stance. I did not want to put the face of the hunter in the painting, it would take too much time and I am not that good with faces. Hunter stood with the gun for a couple of minutes. Good enough. I finished my day's work and went home for the night. That night I sketched out the hunter on the prairie. The next day I transferred the sketch to the wall mural. I had taken down the sketch and thrown it on the floor, with the other garbage I had accrued. It was labeled ' hunter on the prairie'.

Hunter sought me out after school that afternoon like he did every day. *He was always finding Doug or I to 'help'. Really now, what kid would want to go home, when he could come to the zoo?* He found me finishing up the mural in the hallway.

"Nice job, Lee," Hunter said and we chatted about his school day. He spied the discarded sketch on the floor. Picking it up he looked at the sketch and the wall. In his little boy voice he said "OH Lee, you put ME in the painting!"

It took me a moment to figure out what he meant. Then I saw he had the labeled sketch in his hand. 'Hunter on the prairie'. It's all in the name.

"Yep, hon, I did," was my reply. Well, it was him, he modeled for the painting.

Hunter asked if there was more painting to do and I let him paint some rocks along the trail. Hunter seemed proud of his work too. We both signed it. The prairie schooner mural is probably one of my best art works.

Zoo Momma

Chapter 21 In Mid Hibernation

In Mid Hibernation…
Just one moment before I sleep,
My note to you, my friendship keeps.
I know that this is very late,
Forgive me, quite a bit on my plate.
This year has passed in such a blur
Of feathers, scales, and often fur.
The zoo is fine, my babies grown,
Some have trotted, others flown.
This year was a first for me per say,
I was contracted by another zoo in May.
Not Dad, not Parker, but just me
To raise pet foxes, make that three.
The Staten Island Zoo wanted two,
So I bought three from a fox farmer who
Lives in PA, maybe out by you?
Three little girls, Kitty, Lady and Vixen,
(Vixen the name for a female fox kitten).
Kitty my favorite was a little older,
And compared to the others, quite a bit bolder.
They came to me gray, fuzzy and cute,
But soon the red showed up on their snoots.
North American Red Fox, really neat!
Red body, black legs on little white feet.
They are city foxes now, keepers like 'em just fine
I'd expect nothing less of babies of mine.
Kitty stayed with me for a while,
Did the lecture circuit, made 'em smile,
With her beautiful fur and foxy grin.
Then I gave her up to my chagrin,
She is now at Lakota Wolf Preserve,
Close enough to visit when time serves.
They treat her like a princess there,
She is in good hands, I know they care.
Got a phone call early one day,
A pair of peacocks showed up not far away,
Dad and I hopped in the car,
Now at the zoo is where they are.
I hope to build a whole new exhibit,
With peacocks, quail and pheasants in it.
Colorful birds will be a nice show
Now I've got to convince the guys ya know?

Zoo Momma

I birthed baby boas, a first for me
Twenty two, no make that twenty three.
One died, I did not get there fast enough
To clean their noses of gunky stuff.
Was fascinating non the less,
Although the birthing was quite the mess.
The other three big boas hung around,
Looking for lunch in the babies they found.
So I grabbed a garbage can lid to protect my hand
Like Don Quixote I took a stand.
So now I still have twenty two
Looking for new homes, how about you?
Professionally, all is the same,
My book has given me surprising fame,
A satisfying accomplishment
The story of my lifetime spent.
So on to book number two,
About all the crazy things I do.
Press releases, radio, Children's Sermons & TV
taught Grammar school classes, Yes that's ME!
Fixed skinned knees on school kids by the bunch
Painted, cleaned cages and gave breaks for lunch
Raised babies, worked the admissions desk
Painted a mural, perhaps my best.
My 'ole Gramp must of given me the call,
When I painted on the museum wall.
Rattle snake, cacti, Conestoga Wagon,
Mountains, Settlers, Buffalo with tails draggin'.
Must of been an artist in another life,
Painting sure helps me to relieve the strife.
A good friend told me to my face
"Your name is sure all over the place.
You may not have your name on the stock,
But you've made your mark on every cement block,
And cage, and sign, and painted wall,
Everyone will know you've been here after all."
Well, who knows what the future holds,
That's in God's hands so I've been told.
Jack is doing great in college,
Even if it puts Mom and Dad on edge.
She's joined every club that I did in school,
(Hummmnn could be trouble), but she is kool!
High honors Dean's List- good for her,
Enough to make her parents purrrrrr.

Zoo Momma

She's got a job at the info desk at Rider,
Call the school, you can talk to her!
Doug's doing fine, stronger by the day,
Now he has new friends with which to play,
He's helping some guys with their tractor trailers.
Comes home filthy and cursing like sailors,
But enjoys using his mechanical brain.
A genius given to him that still remains,
That he gets to use sometimes at the zoo,
Between bailing hay and scooping poo.
The rest of my family is doing fine,
Though puts me in consternation most the time.
Dad's out hunting every day still
It helps to keep the larders filled.
Doug and I went to Canada without Jack
She took summer classes 'till we came back.
Saw the most amazing thing this year,
That put our lives in mortal fear.
A storm came through our campsite
Uprooted trees, wow! Nature's might!
And horizontal lightning like a spiders web
Beneath the clouds when the storm did ebb.
Really cool, not seen that before,
Watched it all from our cabin door.
As trees were crashing, our adrenaline spent
We were so happy we weren't in a tent!
The electric was out around us for miles away
But our campground was saved by my Doug Day
Who hooked up an RV generator to the wires
So we had running water, I'm no liar.
I'm in mid-hibernation right now,
So again before to sleep I bow
To say hello, now how about you?
Drop a line and let me know how you do.
I know this is late but you know why?
Because I missed the sleigh when reindeers fly.
So once again I'm sending the invitation
To all my friends across the nation,
Come visit when you have the time,
Witness my crazy life, not just this silly rhyme.

Love, Lori Doug and Jackie

Chapter 22 Buck on the Run

Every fall here is a rush to beat the weather. We close the zoo on October 31st and the race begins. Fronts go on all the open dens, leaving a small door for the cougars, leopards, jaguars and foxes to enter. This helps keep the snow and cold weather out. The guys stuff all the dens full of hay and the animals stay nice and warm. It is a two week process during which we are trying to beat the cold weather to come.

Snakes are a different story. The large exotic snake cases are rolled inside the main building. Parker jumps in the iconic snake den outside and brings in the non-poisonous constrictor snakes, poisonous cotton mouth moccasins and rattlesnakes. They go in a spare case in the restaurant also.

Since the parrots are my bailiwick, I bring them in the restaurant, setting them up in individual cages by the large picture windows. Inside they, are a lot more work, requiring cleaning every day. And the bird feathers, such a mess, but that is not the story.

One day in early December I was cleaning the unusually noisy birds. I looked out the front windows seeing a sight I had never seen before. The danger of the situation quickly registered.

Running down the road was a jogger. No big deal. This same jogger, Rich, is a neighbor and jogs through town every day. He usually follows his wife, but today he seemed to be without her.

But he was not alone. Close on his heels was a six point buck deer. I read the deer's signals. It was mating season, which is the time of year when bucks go into a hormonal rut, fighting other males. The buck's head was down, his nostrils flaring. His hooves pointed straight forward as he ran. The buck was chasing Rich. I saw Rich glance over his shoulder at the buck and continue running. Not jogging now, Rich was full out running as fast as he could. So was the buck. I watched the uneasy pair as they came down the hill from dad's house and passed the windows in front of me. *God, this is trouble! If Rich stops the buck will gore him. That buck is looking for a fight. I've heard my Dad talk about situations like this. There is no fighting back - that just encourages the buck to fight more.*

I grabbed my car keys out of my discarded jacket pocket and ran to my car. *No time to put a jacket on.* I started the car and drove as fast as I could to catch up with the buck and Rich. About a block away, at the intersection of Route 519 and Wykertown Road, I caught up right behind the nasty hormonally high buck. I simply beeped my car horn a few blasts and the deer veered off into the Beemerville Cemetery.

Rich stopped in his tracks, bent over, hands on his knees huffing and puffing. Rich waved his hand to let me know he was ok. I turned my car around and went back to work with the squawking birds.

A couple days later, Rich stopped in while Dad and I were having coffee to say thanks. We all had a good laugh about it. Yeah, now we can laugh.

Chapter 23   The Train Tunnel Mystery

The hairs on the back of my neck rose in unison. I sat up a little straighter on the milk crate precariously perched upon the shelf. *Must be a breeze*, I thought. The day was very chilly for October, necessitating a union suit under my sweat pants and multiple layers of shirts. I had waited all summer for the opportunity to paint this mural, but did not have the opportunity. The swarms of visitors at the Zoo and Museum on cozy warm days, along with last spring's animal offspring, had taken all my time. A little chill was not going to stop me now. Weeks earlier I had cleaned and labeled the train gauges in the Museum on a rainy day. That was a half hour job which turned into weeks of contemplating the mural waiting to be born now before me. I had sketched out the keystone of the stonework edging the train tunnel. My cold fingers tingled with the anticipation of the first few creative strokes.

Perched on the green milk crate on the narrow shelf four feet high , I dipped my brush and began. I let my mind flow with every stroke. I was Edward Sissorhands crafting in colors. Although totally immersed in my painting, the chill permeated my bones. Every now and then the outside breeze would open the doors to the museum in the hallway, blowing in stray leaves and dust. I felt the door open more than heard it. *Must be one of the guys coming in to talk to me.* I looked around. No one there. Hummmn.... *Look at that Circus train set. Wow, it would be really neat if we could set it up like Roadside America, but we don't have enough track.* I happily painted more. I am a hobbyist painter with no formal training, but I sure do enjoy it. My Gramp, Ralph Space, used to draw bunnies and other animals for myself and the other grandkids. I must have inherited his artistic tendencies. I thought of Gramp and the collections that he had amassed and preserved by creating the museum. The Space Farms' Museums were the last project Gramp completed before his death in 1986. Amazing man, eccentric, but amazing none the less. *Gramp would be proud of my paintings. I was glad that I was improving HIS Museum. Wouldn't it be great to set a miniature train track with a moving train? Oh well, we have other projects that take priority in the year's budget.*

I had painted for an hour or so, focusing on the train tunnel and the surrounding scenery. I was painting the disappearing tracks inside the tunnel, having a little trouble with the dimensions of a train track diminishing into the distance.

"Come on Gramp, help me out," I half joked out loud. I let my inner self flow into the paint, completing the empty train track vanishing into the darkness of the tunnel. Ice cold, good God, I was ice cold. My muscles were cramped from sitting so still on the tiny shelf. My butt was imprinted with the criss-cross shape of my upside down milk crate stool. *A fly must be on the back of my neck*, I thought as I brushed it away. *Wait a minute, it is too cold for flies!* My biological education kicked in. Hummmm... *Was that the breeze and the door again?* I heard a scrape. Definitely a wooden scrape. Like a wooden chair being dragged against the concrete floor. *The guys must be here. They play tricks on me all the time, silently walking in suddenly and scaring me.*

"Hello, I'm in here, " I called out loud, "I know you are there".

No answer. Only the creaking sound of a cold, old building. The fluorescent lights flickered. The sun passed behind a cloud outside the window. The minute additional heat provided by the sun in the windows dissipated.

Alright, now my curiosity is peaked. I'm so cold, my goose pimples may be permanent. I shivered. I knew one of the guys must be sneaking up on me, I felt it. He has done that before. He must get some childish thrill in seeing me jump when he scares me. *I need a break anyway.* I put my paint brush down.

Scraaaaaape. Another wood scraping sound, but longer in duration.

Alright, I am going to find out what is going on. I kneeled off of my milk crate, not trusting my frozen muscles to stand upright on the four foot high shelf. Stretching my leg for the floor, I more rolled than jumped to the concrete floor. Moving slowly on stiff shaky legs, I weaved my way between antique motorcycles towards the metal stanchion gate that would get me out of the display. I walked towards the hallway, tiny tornados stirring up dust ahead of me. *It is a windy day, the entrance doors must of blown open,* I thought.

I walked past the Circus Train, all thoughts of creating a miniature village swept from my mind, as I sought the prankster I knew was around the corner. I stopped one foot from the gray trimmed wide doorway. No one was going to get the best of me. I peered around the doorway, fists clenched, adrenaline ready to not be scared. I would not give the prankster his satisfaction.

I looked to the left. No one there. I looked to the right, no one there. And the entrance doors, twenty feet away, were closed. *Ok, so my brain must be feeling the effect of the cold.* My teeth were chattering. *I must need more hot coffee?* Something caught my eye, a stray dry brown leaf moved out of the corner of my eye. *The entrance doors were closed, yet the breeze was still here? Alright Lori, you ARE cold, exercise will warm you up,* I thought to myself. I walked through the doorway and to the left, intending to do a brisk walk lap around the Museum and back to my painting.

I entered the hallway by the rock exhibit my grandfather had created. Five glass cases gleamed in the afternoon sun, warming the room. Colorful rocks sparkled. Gramp had the rock cases mounted on top of a decorative wooden base with inlaid recesses. I had walked this hallway exhibit countless times. Seen it all before. I stopped, staring like a deer in the headlights. This time I saw something was different....

The inlaid recesses in the base of the rock cases were not purely decorative. They were DOORS. The DOORS were now OPEN, and inside was (and still are) boxes and boxes of miniature train tracks.

At Space Farms the doors in the main building open and close with the breeze. The doors to the offices from the main building opened and closed on their own until my brother, Parker, had locks put on them. We have often joked that Gramp is visiting when the doors opened or closed. I now know that Gramp

Ralph's spirit is still with us, watching, supervising, guiding us along the path he painted for us. I also remember my Gramp loved a good practical joke. So when you come to the Museums, don't sing lullabies by the virginal white child's hearse in the museum. Gramp will rock that hearse, just to scare you. He is always here…, watching…, waiting….

The train tunnel

Photo by Lori Space Day

Chapter 24 And the Little Boy Wet his Pants...

So many people ask me what my day is like. This is a rhetorical question for sure. They want to hear of my frolicking with fawns and llamas, swimming with otters, or cavorting in the grass with lion or tiger cubs. Do they really want to know? Some days are very calm and relaxing, nurturing animals and exercising my creative mind on zoo projects. And then there are days from Hell. This is the story of one of those awful days.

My day started out normal enough. I woke up early wanting to finish up paperwork on daughter Jackie's college financing. Did that. Got dressed and went down to the zoo to feed and care for the infants in the nursery. Not a big job, one fawn, one llama, a baby possum, four assorted alligators and my favorite woodchuck, Jenny. Got that done. I knew we were going to have a number of camp groups, so I was efficient, not playing with my animals or wasting time.

The first busses pulled up at the front of the zoo at 9:30 am, so I knew my parrots would have to wait quite a while to get fed. I greeted the busses, giving my standard speech of where the bathrooms were, don't chase the chickens, ducks, geese, etc. , put your picnic lunches on the picnic tables and so forth. Ok, everything seems normal.

On the second bus, of yellow shirted YMCA campers, was a little Asian boy about hip high. Cute as a button, eyes wide with excitement and wonder. So tiny compared to the hefty kids in our family. And the little boy had wet his pants. His councilor asked if we sold shorts in the gift shop. I replied, "No, but I take home the lost and found clothes and wash them for occasions like this, let me check." The councilor smiled and nodded. I walked to the office to look in the lost and found box and found none. Returning to her I told her such and said I would run home and get a pair of shorts from my daughter to see what we could do. The Councilor went outside with the rest of her clutch, leaving the Camp Director with the little boy standing in the middle of the restaurant in his wet camo cargo pants and bright yellow camp shirt.

I walked to the admissions desk to tell Daisy, a grandmotherly type, but a little hard of hearing, where I was going. Home is only two doors away, and I would only be gone a minute. As I walked back to the entrance door, passing the Asian cutie pie and his Director, a male visitor approached me with crushing words.

" I don't know if you care," *OK that statement means trouble! But he had my complete attention now.* "But one of the gun cases has been jimmied and the glass is goofed up." The spectacled man calmly stated.

"OH SSSS--T" was my native redneck expletive.

On high alert, I sprinted past the yellow shirted boy with councilor and up the landing to the museum steps. Skipping two steps at a time, I covered the balcony steps in record time. The spectacled gentleman followed me up. There, on the right hand side museum case, was obvious evidence of foul play. The locks had been moved and the glass bowed out, pulled past the locking mechanisms. I gently fluffed my fingers behind the bulging glass, I guess to verify what my eyes were telling me. I won't repeat what I said then, but they were not nice words.

I trotted down the stairs, heading to the admission desk, passing the little boy still in wet pants, giving the Director a one finger up 'one minute please' signal. I grabbed the admission phone and called my brother Parker, *(where is he now?)*. I told him the situation and that he should call the State Police. Mere minutes seemed like hours until Parker arrived and the two of us went upstairs where the spectacled man was standing guard. Again, I passed the little boy who had the large wet spot on his pants, below his canary yellow YMCA shirt. The Director could see something was drastically wrong and simply nodded. Parker stayed by the museum case, on his phone. I came back downstairs and walked towards the Director and the uncomfortable boy.

"I might be a minute more," I said, looking out the front windows as another bus arrived. I went out to greet the bus full of campers, Parker went out to greet the State Policeman with Butch, Parker's father in law, who had pictures of all the guns in the cases on his laptop. They went upstairs to the antique gun cases. I went upstairs with them, to confer for a few minutes. I then went back downstairs and outside to the new group that had just arrived. I escorted the new campers into the zoo past the admission doors.

On the way back through the building to go to my house for the dry shorts, I hear "Parker please come to the kitchen", Barb, the kitchen supervisor, was on the public address system. I walked past the Director and the drenched little boy one more time and asked Barb what the problem was.

" Can I help, Parker is upstairs with the policeman?". The word policeman alerted the kitchen staff. Barb explained the cash register was jammed. All eyes were on me, as I viewed the broken cash register. The register belt had slipped and the journal tape was not turning. I barked orders for a flashlight and a screwdriver, since my fingers could not fit in the tiny space. Equipment slapped into my hand like a surgeon, I fixed the darn register.

I walked towards the little boy with wet pants.... and four bus loads of Chasidic kids pulled into the parking lot. I sprinted out the door, met them at the parking lot and told the bus driver how to go around the circle to unload in front of the building. That done, I popped my head in to say I'd probably be a couple of minutes more. The Director patiently nodded.

The two hundred little Chasidic boys lined up in front of the building , the Rabbi shepherding the kids in an unruly mob. The head Rabbi was peering through the gate at the other 400 campers of various ethnicities already in the zoo.

"I was told there would be no one else here. We were to be the only group. We can not stay unless they leave." The Rabbi was adamant in his heavy accent.

"There may have been no other reservations when you called, but we will not discriminate," I explained.

"But I was told we would be the only group here," Rabbi was not pleased.

"Nothing I can do about it, sir. Your only option is to get back on the busses. I can assure you, though that you and your children will not be harmed. We have extra keepers on patrol today," I was sincere, but I had heard the same thing a dozen times over from other Chasidic groups that want the zoo to themselves. I knew none of our staff had said they would be the only ones here. We do not discriminate or refuse anyone entrance.

Doc and some of the staff from the kitchen came out to help. We always need to use a counter on these group. They never seem to have a correct count on the kids they bring. (*Would you send your kids with a teacher who didn't know how many kids he left the school/camp with?)* Once again I walked past the candle flame colored shirt, the little boy with brown eyes and wet pants. I picked up the counter/clicker at admissions and walked back to the gate. The Chasidic kids lined up, I was ready to count them into the zoo.

Doug, my hubby, and Chris, the other zookeeper, drove up simultaneously on their jitneys.

"You better get those kids away from the gate," Doug said.

"Why?" *What now?* I asked.

"The Ambulance is coming and we need to let it in the gate to get it out to the lions?" Doug explained shouting from his jitney.

OH S#!t! "What Happened?" *Oh My God, some kid jumped the fence and a lion got a hold of him?* My mind was racing with the possibilities.

"One of the old ladies with the senior group collapsed, the aid called for an ambulance. They are by the lions." Doug filled me in.

Whew, well almost Whew!

Ok. Deep breath, this all has to end soon, what else can go wrong? I explained the situation to the Rabbi *(or is it Rabbis?)* and that we would take the kids through the building. Sorry about that, I know the Chasidic have religious rules for not being in a building with bones, like we have in the museum. Well, if I don't tell them, they won't know. Getting two hundred kids to do an about face was a cinch for a woman in barking lion mode. Even with my limited Yiddish. *Don't cross me now, my glare will burn you at the stake, or turn you into a pillar of salt. Pick one. Now move!*

Staff assistants lined up beside me, we counted in the two hundred kids, and only ten adult Rabbis. *This is gonna be a messy day on top of everything else.* As I was counting the kids in rapid succession with the clicker, the public address system beeped on again, "Lori, telephone." *Darn, what now.* "Take a message" I shouted to the assistant twenty feet away from me, who relayed it to the next, who relayed it to the admission's desk. (*200 kids between myself and the admission desk telephone. Nothing is ever easy here*) Chasidic kids in the zoo. *Ok, check, that's done.*

"Just one minute more and I am all yours," I smiled at the very patient Director and the little boy, the glowing yellow shirts were a reminding beacon in the dim interior of the building. I followed the last of the Rabbis out towards the Admission counter, handed Daisy the clicker counter with the total number of Chasidics.

Zoo Momma

The phone rang again. Another staff member answered it, cupping the receiver, "Lori it's for you".

"Take a message!"

"It's your Dad and Mira in Colorado."

S#!t, I have time for this now? "OK give me the phone." I glanced at the Director and little boy with a shrug, The Director gave me the ok sign with his fingers. *(could have been worse!).*

"How are my petunias doing?" It was Mira, my step mom. My job while she and Dad were vacationing was to water her plants.

"Ok Mira, We have 400 regular kids, 200 Chasidics now and another 270 coming at any moment, I have a little boy waiting for dry pants, the State Police are upstairs with Parker because one of the gun cases was broken into, the cash register was broken, the ambulance is coming through the gate as we speak because an old lady collapsed in the zoo. And you want to know if I watered your petunias?" I was flabbergasted. I had ecstatic visions of a chain saw cutting through petunias. A shower of petunias! I was Medusa yanking out her snakey hair. But really now, how would they know in Colorado what was happening in Beemerville. "Call me back in an hour." and I hung up. Sorry Mira.

"Lori, just to tell you, that last phone call was the aid for the senior citizen group with the lady that collapsed out by the lions. She wants to know if someone can bring their lunches out to where they are. The aid is alone now because the other one went in the ambulance and she can't come to get the lunches. The old folks are tired and need to rest a while out there on the picnic table," Staffer JoAnn said.

I am an old folk, I need to rest now too! "OK call her back, tell her fifteen minutes". I put blinders on my face and walked out the front door, past the waiting yellow shirts with beautiful Asian eyes (and wet pants), under crime scene police yellow tape, the State Police, Parker, Butch and now, Jill, upstairs by the missing guns, past the ambulance going out the gate, and saw the many regular customers crossing the street anticipating a wonderful day at the zoo. I glanced towards Mira's petunias. *Where is that chain saw?* I got in my car and went home.

Riffling through daughter Jackie's dresser drawers, I came up with a pair of shorts, dashed up to our room, and got a pair of cotton knit boxers from Doug's dresser. (I had visions of Michael Jordon's Hanes commercial when I bought them for Doug. Don't laugh.) I then circled down through our spiral staircase, through the kitchen, and headed out our back door. I glanced at the booze under the cabinet left over from my fiftieth birthday two years ago, *Damn, I've got to start drinking again. Life would be so much easier!.* Got in my car and went back to the zoo.

The Director was actually smiling when I walked into the building. The tiny tyke was eyeing the jumble of clothing in my arm.

"That's not gonna fit me," he whispered, looking sad and still embarrassed. His whole miniature body would fit in one leg of either shorts.

"OH Honey, I know magic," I assured him. I handed the shorts and

106

boxers to the Director with some elastic bands. "Cinch them up together in the back and put a elastic band around the bunched up section. It will work if you pull his yellow shirt back down over it".

"Is every day like this for you?" the Director kindly asked.

"NO, Thank God, or I'd be dead in a week. This is just a really bad day." I told him as they headed for the men's room.

Time for a drink. I asked the young girl at the kitchen counter for a soda and a smile. She obliged. I headed towards admissions once again.

"Lori, the senior citizen lunches?" Joanne was politely helping me remember.

"OH yeah, right now."

I went outside, hailed Zookeeper Chris who was using my quad. I weigh more, (*yeah , Like Double!*) so I drove, as Chris sat on the back deck holding the handle to the wheel barrow type cart with the senior citizen lunches in it. I had one hand on the quad throttle and one hand behind me holding onto Chris's belt on the back of his blue jeans. *Over hill and dale to grandmother's table we go.* It must have been a sight. Doug drove by with a chuckle. After we delivered the lunches, Doug asked if I had eaten. I checked my watch, it was only 1:45 pm. *Darn, the day was only half over.* Chris volunteered to take the second lunch, and stay out in the zoo on patrol. Doug and I went in to have lunch. I fed the llama before I ate. I felt guilty, I had forgotten her 10:30 bottle. By 2:10 Doug and I were done, looking out the restaurant windows when the second group of Chasidics pulled up.

"Nice having lunch with you, babe," Doug said, with his ironic sense of love and sarcasm.

"Right back at ya sweetie." I replied. "Oh, you are on your own for supper. I have that speech to give."

"I remember," Doug said with a wink. And he was off to the zoo to relieve Zookeeper Chris so Chris could eat. I was off to the busses with the counter and two of the kitchen staff I had garnered, again.

The day slowly wound down. Visitors, Campers, State Police, and Chasidics gradually left. Before the Yellow Shirted YMCA group left, the councilor found me and thanked me for the shorts. They wanted my address to send them back. I told them to send them to the zoo. I fed the parrots. By 4:30 the last of the Chasidic busses were lined up out front to leave. I packed up the animals I would need for my speech that night. I fed the llama one more time. The rest of the visitors left by five (with a little coaxing). I locked the front door of the zoo and headed home.

I met Doug at home, intending to put on my bathing suit, go back to Dad and Mira's house by the zoo, jump in the pool and relax for ten minutes before getting dressed for my speech that night.

Our phone rang. Did I mention that our daughter, Jackie, had left for a backpacking trip through Europe with her roommate Lisa? On the Sunday before ? This was Thursday. On Tuesday, Jackie, Doug and I had a long instant message hour. Jackie was upset, sick to her stomach and wanted to come home, aborting the semester abroad at Graz University. Graz Austria. She had planned this since she first found out Rider U. offered this program. We convinced her to stay a few more days and get some rest. All of that had been weighing on my mind and caused two days of sleepless nights.. On the phone was Lisa's Dad letting us know the girls were with Lisa's aunt's friend in London and had gotten some sleep. They were fine now. They were going to see the London Sights tomorrow. Gonna stay the course. Good, Thank God. And nice talking to you Bob. Got to go. Here, talk to Doug.

Fifteen minutes, for me, fifteen minutes is record time to take a shower, get dressed, re-do my make up and be out the door for my speech.

Randolph library is an hour away. I made it with time to spare. The hour sit down ride in the car was a welcome rest. I gave the speech by rote, mayhaps not my best speech ever, but the noisy kids never heard a word anyway. The parents in the back of the room had no control over the kids in the front. Two kids were fighting, another one grabbing the blankie from my precious baby possum, Petunia, (*yeah I know*), who almost bit me. The tortoise behaved, Jenny woodchuck ate her carrot and the snake fascinated the crowd. The hundred or so people gathered seemed to like my speech. I have never ever watched the clock when giving a speech before. I did that night. 60 minutes on the dot. Any questions? No, fine. And I was out of there. Sorry folks. Got to go.

The best part of the day happened at 9 pm. I was arguing with myself as to whether to stop to eat supper. I was getting quite hungry. Amazingly my favorite fast food was coming up on my right, Taco Bell. I don't travel Route 10 enough to know what would be there, so I figured it was a sign. I pulled in, but the drive through was busy. So I said what the heck, I'll go inside.

As I opened the door I heard, "Why it's Miss Lori Space Day" from a familiar voice. It was my friend Lois from Heath Village. I have given speeches at Heath Village retirement village for years. After the day I had it was wonderful to hear Lois's friendly voice and see her smile. Some of Lois's friends wanted to see the animals in my car, so I gave them the quickie tour of the back of the SUV.

I left and enjoyed my supper on the road. I couldn't stop long, because I had animals in the car. Got to the zoo, put the animals away, fed the llama baby one more time, came home, and Doug was waiting up for me at 9:54 pm.

"Tough day, huh babe?" he asked rhetorically. "I left you some ice cream."

The love in his voice made me smile.

So you want to be a zookeeper? Buy lots and lots of ice cream.

Chapter 25 Punkin Head

Doug and I have a wonderful daughter. I know I have referred to her repeatedly while writing my life adventures with animals. I feel like I have written so much on the animals and so little on Jackie and Doug. I guess the easiest way to explain this is to say that Jackie and Doug are part of my private life, even though they also work at the zoo. The animals are my public life, the part the general public can know about. Doug works at the zoo full time but in a different capacity than I do. He is the mechanical genius that can fix anything, and build anything. He is usually in the five bay garage or doing a job that needs tools. I am in the zoo proper with the animals, advising visitors, or in the main building preparing formula in the kitchen or helping with admissions or restaurant visitors. Often I don't see him (unless I need him) until lunch or sometimes not 'till closing time at 5 p.m..

Jackie worked the zoo snack bar, restaurant, and admissions from the time she was fourteen until she went away to college. During her college years she would work the family business in the summers, with all the other college aged kids. I would see Jackie whenever I came in the main building for a drink or to feed babies, which was quite often. She helped me feed baby animals when they were in our house. At the zoo she would let the other kids have the chance to feed. She always had a cheery smile or a joke, or was dancing to a song in the restaurant kitchen. Her blonde hair varied according to her mood, sometimes dishwater blonde, sometimes a bottle blonde. Tight jeans, *she inherited my hips!,* and a Space Farms navy blue polo work shirt, topped by a beautiful freckled face filled with the joy of being a teenager. Like most teenagers she was out with her friends as soon as she got her driver's license. Every mother dreams of having a daughter like mine. We laughed, shopped, fished, sewed, painted, and chatted about everything. When she went away to college, I knew part of my life was over. The intense mommy-ness was no longer needed. Being the mother to an adult child is not easy. Being the mother of a adult child that just backpacked through Europe and turned twenty one far away from home…that was tough. I couldn't even bake her a cake. So I wrote her this:

For Punkin Head on her 21st Birthday

It's your birthday, you're far from home,
So I decided to write you a silly poem.
When you were a baby with no sight of hair,
You wrinkled your punkin head crying in despair.
I called you Punkin Head as a silly game,
'Till Daddy said "No more!, She's answering to that name!"
So in your honor of your special day,
I brought out the pumpkins I had stored away.

Zoo Momma

I thought, "Why bother, she's not here to see",
I realized what pleasure they give to me.
Goofy, smiling faces made me think of you,
the happiness you bring to all that you do.
The house is now grinning with glee,
proof of the love that is between us three.
Things are fine here at the zoo,
there's lots of seasonal things to do.
We're happy and busy, miss you a lot,
But maudlin? We definitely are not.
You've new friends from home and abroad,
Your choices seem great, for which I applaud,
You've expanded your horizons, therefore so have mine.
We miss you, but realize this is your time
So get out there and 'Go Girl!' go have a blast,
But stay safe 'till your home in our arms at last.
Love, Mommy & Poppa October 16, 2007

Our Daughter, Jackie, with Siren and Ed African Lion Cubs
Photo by Lori Space Day

Chapter 26 The Night After Christmas

'Tis the night after your Christmas, But mine's not here yet,
I'm expecting the arrival of my favorite pet,
So twiddling thumbs and worry full too,
I'm writing my annual letter to you.
New babies this year? The same old ones,
Always a challenge, nothing new or fun.
Coons, possums, some chickies, a buck,
Six snappers, but big cats, still just no luck.
Late in the year, my little fawn jumped his fence.
Broke his leg, put him down, just made common sense.
Did some cable TV, lots of PR and talks
Greeted folks, handled crowds, you know, walked the walk.
Started something new, a radio show, once a month, telling all that I know,
On seasonal animal subjects with DJ Steve,
a challenge for me I do believe,
To think in sound, not touch or sight, other than these goofy poems I write.
Of one honor, I was bestowed, it really made my whole heart glow
NJ Herald readers named me best local Author
For my book, "The Zookeeper's Daughter".
That was so sweet, and I got a plaque, gives me a smile, as I look back.
Local Rotary gave me a Vocational Award
For Educational Outreach, spreading the word
About the creatures under my care and carting them with me every where.
Doug has been fine, hale and hearty
But still does not want to go out and party.
He's a treasure to me, my buddy, my pal, and I'm still his favorite gal.
He makes me smile, he makes me think, '
Cause he teases me without the wink.
Doug's mom, Jeanne, she broke her foot, so a long trip to Pa I took.
I helped Doug's Dad, Dan, for only a week,
when Brother Butch took vacation at the beach.
Wow what a challenge , Alzheimer disease,
God, don't give us that, please, oh, please!
April, Dan passed away, mixed blessings sure,
It was hard for Jeanne to endure.
But Jeanne's doing great, new place, new friends,
We go out to see her, now and again.
My mom had her two knees replaced
Best thing she's done, smiles on her face.
I helped Dad with his book for a bit, was a lot of work, but we didn't quit.
"Ralph Space the Legend & Tales of Beemerville"
Complete with the stories of Gramp and his still.

Zoo Momma

Dad's proud as peaches, a feeling I know quite well,
My next book's in progress, when? I can't tell.
Had some trouble with Dad when he picked up dead deer
Dragged it over a bees nest way too near.
He went into anaphylactic shock,
But was quickly brought back with just one shot.
Two weeks ago he took a tumble,
Smacked his tailbone, did you hear the earth rumble?
And hit his head, made quite the lump,
Space heads can't be hurt with one little bump.
I believe there is one energy growth at a time,
Professional, personal, creatively stretching the mind.
This year it's not professional, animals the same,
did nothing fantastic, worthy of fame.
Oh, I did paint bamboo, on a corrugated Aluminum covered loo
Liked it so much I did it again,
on a shed that will be our new peacock den.
I've filled up my time with projects galore,
keeping busy, but I still can't ignore
The empty nest that worries my heart,
because we and Jackie are so far apart.
Jackie backpacked through Europe for 3 whole weeks,
Then U of Graz in Austria, education she seeks.
.I didn't get the traveling gene, I am happy here with the same old scene.
But Jackie, my brave gal, is across the ocean,
which causes me a storm of emotion.
I worry, I fret, in anxiety I pray. five long months since she's been away.
I quit watching the news, more fuel for the fire.
My motherly instincts just won't tire.
But she's doing great, a wonderful trip,
once in a lifetime adventure, she's soooo hip!
Her grades are up there, her German fluent,
what is the reason for this mother's lament?
Safety, simply safety, now she is out of our nest
And that's why our Christmas has not been the best.
Some parents have sick kids, other's have died,
so there is no reason for me to have cried.
A personal growth, I should not complain,
I will thank God when She gets off that plane.
So to all my friends, bear with me a while,
think of us with a prayer and a smile.
Drop me a line, I need to hear from you,
An email, a letter, a call, you know-friendship glue.
And if you hear sleigh bells on that Friday night,

Zoo Momma

Know **OUR** Christmas is here, Santa guiding her flight.

Love Lori Doug and Jackie (Still in Graz)

Zoo Momma

Chapter 27   The Peacock Pen

The previous spring I had finally gotten around to painting the remote bathrooms to look like bamboo. I had seen the technique in practice when I visited Hershey Park Zoo with our daughter Jackie and my sister Renee years before. I must give credit here to the artist that taught me, though I do not know his name. He was painting a small section of corrugated aluminum roofing/siding (the stuff that has ripples in it), at the Hershey Park Zoo. *Yeah a busman's holiday for me!* I stopped to talk to him about the type of paint and his procedure, introducing myself as an artistic zookeeper. The type of paint was very important as some paints are poisonous to animals. The procedure was five basic steps: #1 Paint your base color light beige. #2 Put a dark brown streak in the center of the dips or valley of the corrugated siding. #3 Put a light brown streak to the left or right of the center streak but always on the same side of the dark streak.#4 Put a smile and a frown half circles connecting the two neighboring valley's dark streak at about one foot intervals, varying the vertical spacing, to look like the joints of the bamboo. #5 Splash a little green on and smear it up and down. Add leaves if you want. I don't remember his name, but I would like to say a big thank you for that impromptu lesson.

I painted the remote bathrooms first, since they had always bothered me.Bright, shiny aluminum roofing as siding looked so out of place in our naturally colored zoo. It took me almost a week in between baby feedings to get that job done. But when the paint job was complete, I received the absolute top compliment. I saw multiple visitors walk up to the walls and touch them to see if they were real. Neat-0. Thanks folks. The repetitive motion of painting up and down stripes caused me some repetitive motion injury in my shoulder. *But hey, an artist has to suffer for her work, right?*

The peacocks we had captured in 2006 needed a new pen. I brainstormed with Dad as they would need a decent sized den, due to the length of their tails, to protect them for the winter months. While I was growing up at the zoo,(into the'70s), the zoo grounds were one third the size of the hundred acres it is today. At the far side of the old bar and cement bottom cage zoo was a restroom. When the zoo expanded and the present day remote restrooms built, the interior of the old restrooms were demolished, the now shed being used for storage. I suggested this old shed for the new peacock den.

"Good use of an old building, Lori" complimented Dad. *Wow, write that down compliments from Dad are few and far between! Though, to be honest, Dad is getting better with positive reinforcement as he ages.*

Knowing that I would construct a peacock pen around the den, I painted the faux bamboo on the old aluminum roofing/siding in the fall of 2007. The paint job took me a week, working it around my other chores. I also cleaned out thirty or forty years of junk from the shed.

In the spring of 2008, Dad helped me lay out the design for the peacock enclosure. I dug trenches to lay in the livestock paneling, with Doug and Tommy

114

helping when they could. Dad and I worked on the enclosure and it was up in a week. I dug up variegated green hosta and young lilac trees from my garden at home. I added them to the exhibit. A door was cut into the new den for the peacocks to enter. We put in logs for support, some for the birds to perch on, a few rocks and logs for looks. Voila' we had a new peacock enclosure!

The peahen and peacock loved the new spring grass- they ate every speck of it. They loved the hosta also, in fact they loved those hosta to shreds. I didn't even know hosta were edible! I did manage to learn quickly after the greenery disappeared. I encased the young lilac trees in chicken wire. One survived. My beautifully designed enclosure for spectacularly colored peafowl was quickly reduced to a dusty dirt paddock. Some birds just have no aesthetic appreciation! At least the peafowl like to dust in the dirt bowls they made. I hate to say it but Dad had told me so. Oh WHell!

The peacocks enjoy their new enclosure.
Photo by Michele Mulder

Chapter 28 Roy Mink

Space Farms Zoo has a long history with mink. My grandfather started the farm with trapped wild animals he was keeping until fall when the animal's fur was prime. He also kept a lot of fox, raccoons, a few bobcats, or skunks all in the backyard of the general store. Locals brought in abandoned or injured animals because "Those Spaces know all about animals." Those animals were added to the zoo collection in the early days. Gramp improved his knowledge by observation and experimentation. He expanded the captured wild foxes into a fox farm. When the fox fur fad faded in the forties, *(say that ten times fast!)*, Gramp switched to mink. In it's heyday the Space Farms mink ranch was home to twenty-five-thousand mink. Twenty thousand of those mink were pelted out   every fall, and five thousand were kept for breeding. Space Farms was the largest mink ranch east of the Mississippi. These were mutation mink, so huge compared to the wild mink caught generations of mink ago. The Space Farms mink ranch was renowned and received   many trophies at ranch raised fur shows. Space Farms also had a Fur Shop on premises where the general public came to buy fur coats made from the mink on our farm. So our family knows all about mink. Would I wear a mink coat? Sure would and do. Ranch raised mink is no different than eating beef, chicken, and farm raised fish, etc. And a fur coat is the warmest. Ranch raised fur is a renewable resource. Mink reproduce at only eighteen months old. It takes millions of years to produce the oil from which nylon coats are made. Think about it.

Spring time is baby time for mink. They breed in January through February and have babies in April. My sister, Renee, brother Eric and I spent many hours, days and months over the years working in the Space Farms' mink ranch. My jobs as a child included carrying male mink to their mates, observing and marking down matings, counting babies, and climbing under the cages (yes I crawled through the poopie piles) to rescue and return escaped babies. On many blizzardy cold nights, Dad would wake up my brother, Eric, sister, Renee and myself in the middle of the night to go put the lids on the mink den boxes to prevent the snow from blowing in. I received my farmer's license to drive a truck at age 16. One of the first trips I drove was to pick up fifty five gallon drums of tripe. Tripe was added into the mink's ground-up-oatmeal-consistency gruel. Those were jobs I had all my younger years. The men fed the twenty-five thousand mink on motorized carts, which occasionally I drove also. In the later years of the mink ranch, the water system was automated. Up until I moved to Pittsburgh at twenty two, I often watered the mink. I tested for Aleutian Disease, helped inoculate the entire mink herd for diseases, and helped skin, turn and pin mink after school until I went away to college. All of it was hard work in adverse weather and grimy conditions. I will admit I enjoyed the inoculation procedure. Giving needles to each individual mink was in the medical field, which I was interested in. Testing for Aleutian Disease, involved many hours in our family's travel trailer, with my teenage music blasting from a tiny transistor radio. *Remember them?* So yeah, I have that family experience in my personal history.

As kids we worked wherever the action was at the farm. Fall was pelting season, January inoculation season, then mating season and baby season come April and May. Across the street was our zoo where Eric and Renee and I worked also. I loved the zoo, but put in a lot of time at the mink ranch. Eric and Renee also worked our Dairy farm, which I avoided, but I did like the calves. After high school and college, Eric ran the mink yard with Gramp. That's why the name is Space Farms -plural- because all the three farms ran at the same time: the mink ranch, the dairy farm and the wild animal farm.

Us kids worked right alongside the hired men. In the early forties, my grandfather traveled to Virginia on Native American archeology digs, as a hobby. In Virginia he met and interacted with a number of the locals. When he came back to Beemerville, he brought whole families with him to help work at the farm. They were mountain people that blended in well with our local mountain-country community, the only difference being their deep southern drawl. They were Appalachia poor, transplanted, doing the best they could, and working diligently to better themselves. Hard working, industrious, and loving people, I grew up surrounded by many southern families. We played together as little kids. I ate many snacks at their tables and worked side by side with them as I grew older. My fried green tomato and corn fritter recipes came from those loving southern moms. I can still see their faces and keep in touch with the kids that are my age. The women all wore cotton print housedresses. *It was the fifties and sixties after all.* The ladies' Reuben-esque figures were a testament to their mighty fine cooking.

The Southern men were attired in an assortment of farm clothes. I would have said dirty clothes, but that might give the reader the impression that these folks were dirty, which they were not. Their clothing was soiled and tattered from working with the animals. This difference I know now. Most of the kids I grew up with are upstanding hard working citizens. To be quite honest, we did not look any better? All of us farm kids wore old jeans and T-shirts, or sweatshirts which would get soiled with blood, feces and other gunk. We all smelled the same: Yucky!

I have had many discussions with my Dad on this subject. As the public relations person at the zoo I have had to explain to Dad that today's general public associates dirty, soiled or tattered clothes with ignorance or mental incompetence. My Dad's generation associates dirty, soiled clothes with a hard working person. Hard working is a good thing, a compliment. Therefore being dirty is good. Dad's generation did not have indoor plumbing growing up, nor clothes washing machines. Work for a man was more dirty, or earthy: farming, coal mining, horse shoeing , mechanical or carpentry, for examples. Today's worker is often assembly line, or a computer orientated desk job. I am constantly harping on Dad to clean up especially on weekends or days with large groups of visitors. Dad's trademark blue jean bibs are always speckled with road kill deer blood, guts, axel grease and grime, along with the associated smells. Got to admit, I often loose the battle of getting Dad clean up before meeting the visitors at the zoo.

Roy and Jim Burse were two of the family men that my grandfather transplanted to Beemerville from Virginia. They were wonderful southern gentlemen, good fathers and hard workers. Roy's wife Nina, and Jim's wife Beulah, and all of their children, came with them. Gramp also brought the Olingers, Evelyn and Sam, and their families, up from the South. All of the women were having babies the same years as my Mom, Beverly. I grew up with their children, who are now all good productive citizens.

I remember Roy Burse the most. Tall and slim, his quick hands could catch a mink faster than you could blink. Roy seemed to be all elbows. Maybe that was just my perspective as a shorter, young child standing by his side while he worked the mink. His dark wavy hair was always under a baseball cap. Roy could blow smoke rings from his cigarette. And those cigarettes could burn halfway without the ash falling off, that must have been magic. It seemed he always wore dark green, but I don't know why. Roy worked the mink yard with a passion. He worked six days a week. Sundays he and his family went to the same church we did. He'd learned as much about mink as my gramp, Ralph, could teach him. I can still hear him cursing out numerous unruly mink in his southern drawl. My (more than occasional), cursing does have a decidedly southern touch to it. While Jim, Sam and their families worked the mink for a number of years, Roy worked the mink ranch all his life. A sweet father, Roy treated us Space kids as his own, watching over us when we were new to the yard, cursing us out when need be. He called me Miss Lori, and my sister, Miss Renee, in his southern tradition. We pulled and skinned mink together. Roy Burse tamed midget mink, and let us kids play with them when we were supposed to be working. Roy had a way with mink. He was a whisperer. And I wanted to learn…

When a man came to the zoo in April of '08, he sought out Dad, finding him in his chair by the zoo doors. I was walking towards the admissions desk and caught the tail end of their conversation.

"I think I found a weasel. I was biking up on Crigger and the car ahead of me hit it's mom. She was carrying it in her mouth." the inquisitive man told Dad. "Can you do anything for it?"

"Oh LOOOOORRRRRIIIII," Dad called across the room. I walked towards the two talking men. They were a study in differences, Dad, gray bearded, pudgy, somewhat disheveled, in his stained blue bibs and kaki shirt, the younger Biker in spandex tight bike shorts, tighter black shirt skimming his trim body and aero-dynamic helmet. Both men staring into the upturned open hand of the biker.

"What ya got Pop?" my standard question.

"YOU got a baby wild mink," Dad eye's twinkled as he spoke.

"Oh. It's not a weasel?" the biker asked.

"Nope. For sure it's a mink, and only a couple of days old," Dad replied. "She can raise it." Dad picked up the kit and palmed it.

"You sure it is not a rat pup, Dad? I'm not raising no rat, looks like a rat to me." Tiny, pink, hairless, size of my pinky finger, squirmy, now that it was warming up in Dad's hand. "It's awful small, don't know Dad."

"Oh give it a shot, Lori, you raised those day old chipmunks 'member?", Dad had issued the challenge. He plunked the infant in my outstretched hand. And once again, Abracadabra! Like magic I was the zoo momma, a new baby wigglin' in my palm.

"What ya gonna name him?"

"Are you sure he's a mink?"

"Sure, he's a wild mink. That's why he is so much smaller than you remember mink kits," Dad reassured me.

"Ok, then his name is Roy. Roy Mink," I stated definitively. Dad and I both burst out in happy chuckles, Dad knowing exactly who I was naming the little pitiful excuse for a mink after. Dad slapped his thigh, then wiped the mini mink poo off his hand onto his bib jeans. Dad was explaining the joyous memories of our long dead friend, Roy Burse, to the Biker as I left for the office nursery to warm up and feed Roy Mink.

Roy Mink was tiny. A small basket and a scrap of polar fleece were placed on top of a heating pad. Esbilac was the formula of choice for carnivores. I used the same swizzle stick technology *(OH! I am laughing at those words-swizzle stick technology!)* to feed the tiny mink that I used on Chance, the ring tailed lemur, and the three little chipmunks. Every two hours until midnight blended in well with my other feedings. I already had two of Jenny Woodchuck's babies on a bottle, and a screech owl with a leg problem, so the baby season had begun. Seems once you have one infant on a bottle, one more is no big deal. When you are in baby mode, you automatically think in two hour time chunks. I can be warming up specie number two's bottle while hand feeding specie number one, and wipe baby butts faster than a speeding bullet. *Well, maybe.*

Every night Roy and the Chuckies would come home with me for nighttime and early morning feedings. By mid May, the fawns were born. A calf was delivered and my nursery was getting full. Roy Mink was growing, slowly. He was the size of my pinky finger when he first came to me as a newborn. Three weeks later he was as big as my thumb, doing well, a little chunkier, and after he drank his milk you could see the pea sized puddle of milk through his pink tummy skin. Roy had started to grow fine delicate dark chocolate brown hair on his back, his belly hair coming in white, as is the usual markings for a wild mink. He was small, I knew it. There is no way that an artificial milk and timed feedings can replace the good natural milk and mothering of mom. I do the best I can. I had great faith that Roy was progressing. I thought/knew he would make it. I would have a pet mink, just like Roy Burse did!

Mink are a member of the mustelidae family, like a weasel or a marten. They look so cute and docile to the inexperienced human. Long, cylindrical bodies on short stubby legs with rounded vertebrae for easy spine movement make them look like a furry slinky. They run with a hunch back, in a bounding jump. Teddy Bear ears perch atop an alert face. Their inquisitive minds are as sharp as their teeth. Many a visitor to the Space Farms Mink Ranch has leaned his hand on a mink cage absentmindedly while chatting and felt the quick ferociousness of the deceptively cute mink.

For the purposes of this story I will give information on the wild mink population. A wild mink is much smaller than ranch raised mink. An adult male mink will be about twenty five inches long, the female significantly smaller. A male living within a good feeding range will weigh about four pounds, again, the females are smaller at one to two pounds. Their beady black eyes catch every movement, and are constantly on the lookout for prey or predators. Mink are carnivorous, eating fish, mice, rats, squirrels, and birds etc. Mink are loners except for the breeding season when a male will seek out a female. The musk glands of the mink are put to good communication use during this time. Both sexes excrete musk and mark territory, a flag that says who was where when. After mating each mink goes it's separate way. Female mink have a fascinating reproductive system. The mink breed and have delayed implantation. The fertilized egg does not immediately attach to the uterine wall and begin to grow. The gestation of a mink is between forty and seventy days depending on the weather and food availability. All offspring are born between April and May. When the birth time is near, the mother mink will make a nest under a log, in a woodchuck hole, in a bramble bush, or under rocks. Mink have eight nipples, and will have one to eight offspring. Mink are excellent, protective mothers. The mom mink leaving her den nest only to feed and return to the babies. As the babies grow on her rich milk, they fur out at two weeks. Wild mink are a dark chocolate brown with white markings under their chin and bellies. By four weeks old mom, mink is gathering prey, eating it and regurgitating for the youngsters. The youngsters grow, play fighting, and following mom on hunts. By September of their birth year, at six months old, the mink young strike out on their own. A mink in the wild is lucky to live eight years. A captive raised mink can live up to fourteen years. It is tough out there in the wild. Diseases, predators, weather conditions and food availability all contribute to the life of the wild mink.

Doug and I celebrated twenty five years of marriage that spring. Our anniversary is mid May. I just can't take off lots of time in the height of baby season. Doug has, thankfully, come to understand that fact. Think about it. If a football player's anniversary fell on Super Bowl Sunday, would you expect him to take the days off? Michelle and President Obama's anniversary was on the night of one of the presidential debates. They did not take the night off either. But it was twenty- five years and Doug wanted to go away for "just one night". A surprise trip. It was not a surprise that we were going, but he would not tell me where. He does that for me now and then. I get so caught up in the zoo, the zoo babies, giving speeches at night, and the lack of sleep, wearing me down. Doug will often say, "Ok this day we are going away. Make what plans you have to for the babies." Most times I can find substitute babysitters for the animal infants that are drinking well from a bottle. The kids that work the kitchen are great at filling in. Dad and Hunter always there early in the morning or late at night. And I do have to admit, when Doug takes me on these long car trips, I sleep in the car a lot until we get to our destination.

Roy Mink was still little and a tricky feeder. He was still on a swizzle stick, living in a Nike' shoe box on a heating pad. I didn't ask, didn't have to. I knew Doug would not mind if tiny Roy would come along on our anniversary trip. And Doug knew not to ask me to leave Roy behind. Roy was too delicate. And besides, we would be going right past a mink ranch in New York state. Maybe we could stop in? Dad and Eric knew the guy, I wanted to compare his mink babies to my Roy, and maybe pick up some infant pellets for when Roy got bigger. Roy's eyes were not quite open, mink open their eyes at four weeks old. Wild mink moms eat their prey- mice, squirrels, chipmunks, birds etc, then regurgitate for their babies. There is only so much I am willing to do for my job. The mink pellets would do fine, if I mushed them with formula. But I did not need a fifty pound bag for one little mink. So I planned to ask the mink rancher to sell me a coffee can worth of pellets.

The anniversary trip was wonderful, we drove through upper New York state. I slept in the car on the way up. We would stop every couple of hours for me to feed Roy. I wiped his bottom with a Q-tip and we would be on the road again. I kept Roy warm in my hands on my lap in his polar fleece sleeping bag. When the formula needed warming, I used what God gave me, my body temperature. Roy did fine on the trip. In the motel at night, I plugged in his heating pad, covered him with his camo polar fleece mini blanket and he snoozed.

On the second and last day of our one night trip, we stopped at the mink ranch Dad had told us about. The Spaces had sold the rancher our mink cages and sheds when we went out of the mink business in 1987. The rancher was so sweet and treated us like royalty. His wife was at work, but she had prepared the best butterscotch brownies I've ever had. We took the tour of his mink ranch. The sheds and cages brought back so many memories, some fun, some just hard work. And there was that smell. Oh yeah, I remember that smell. Earthy, biting, yet acrid, like a bad meat burp caught in the back of your throat. That smell grabs at the uppermost part of your lungs and makes you catch your breath.

I asked him to open one of the mink boxes so I could see the size of the kits (baby mink) that were about three weeks old. He opened the den box. I looked in. My heart sank to my toes. Snuggling in the warm nest were five kits. Each the length of a hot dog, and fat. They were round as a southern peach and had chubby, wrinkly folds of skin where their little legs joined their bodies. Their bellies were engorged like they swallowed golf balls. Cutie pies. Eyes just starting to open, their tiny slits were split on the edges. Fully furred, the soft downy fur was fluffier on their tails.

Their condition was a pail of cold water on my head. Rain on my parade. A sucker punch to the guts. The real Mother Nature saying to me, the cheap imitation: "See this is what I can do!" Doug saw the mutant mink also, saw the look on my face and spoke kind words.

"These are farm raised mink, nursing from mom, not a wild kit on a swizzle stick, Lor, you do the best you can," his deep voice reverberated to my heart.

The rancher asked to see my Roy mink. I opened the box.

"Oh," a simple statement of doom from the rancher. "I don't want to take your money for a fifty pound bag of mink kit pellets. Let me see if I have a little Ziplock sandwich baggie."

There it was. We all knew the naked truth. And that truth was crashing on me. My Roy Mink was the size of my thumb. Squiggling, looking for milk, and I hope, happy, but in comparison to the ranch raised mink, pink and puny. The rest of the visit went well enough. The rancher wished us luck and we left.

Doug and I drove home that afternoon. I had a church meeting that night. Roy went with me. I opened the box half way through the meeting to check Roy and he was dead. At least he died at Church, warm and with a full tummy.

The next morning I told Dad about our trip and our visit to the mink farm. I marveled at the size difference between Roy and the mink litter I saw. Then I told Dad that Roy Mink died the night before.

"Lost faith in yourself when you saw those other mink, didn't ya?" Dad stated knowingly. "Don't loose yer faith. It was a tough call , he was tiny. But Roy was a good name."

Yep, it was. So now Roy Burse has Roy Mink, and I still curse with a southern drawl.

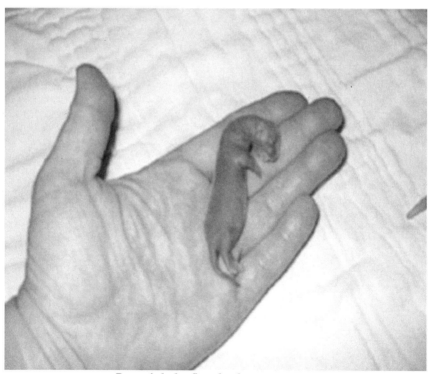

Roy mink the first day he came to me.
Photo by Lori Space Day

Chapter 29 Syrian Sisters

Over the winter of 2007-'08 we lost one of our Syrian grizzly bears due to old age. It happens to us all, if we are lucky enough to just get old. Then some ailment takes us in a snap. The remaining Syrian brother bear was lonely so we wanted to get him a friend. Introducing a new male to an established male bear's territory is a death sentence for one of the bears, usually the oldest bear. A new male bear was not an option.

Parker had been in touch with the Rix family, who are a renowned family of bear breeders. They had two three year old Syrian females. We liked the many bears we had gotten from the Rix family in the past. They hand rear their cubs on bottles and are very involved with their babies, like I am. The cubs are used for educational programs for a few years and then retired. The cubs are deceptively cute when on a bottle, but, kid you not, they attach to only one mom. Bear cubs are amazingly strong. I remember helping my grandmother feed bear cubs. The nursing cubs would shred your shirt or pants trying to get to the bottle. It was hard to get their paws off you. They suck hard and strong.

The bears produced by the Rix family are not handle-able like Teddy Bears. No bears are. The Rixs' raised good, healthy, used to the public, workable bears. A workable bear is a bear that will work with you, come when you call "come" and go away when you holler "get". That is about all we ask from a bear. The Rix daughters, Susan and Jeanette took over the Bear Mountain Ranch when their father Al Rix died a few years back. The ladies are bear experts, taught by their father and learned from years of their personal experience. We never seem to have enough time to talk, their business and our business keeping us, well, busy! Susan and Jeanette raise excellent specimens. So I was glad they had a pair of Syrian females for our zoo.

The two blonde Syrian bear sisters arrived on the back of a trailer, in a steel bar transport cage. Parker had driven to the Bear Mountain Ranch to pick them up. The sisters weighed about four hundred pounds each. The girls were calm in the transport. The grizzlies were used to the transport because they had traveled for educational programs. The men folk and I had gathered to see the new bears and help with the unloading. Yes, they were 'nice' bears, yes they were 'workable' bears, and yes, there was a loaded rifle on the front seat of Parker's truck. Just in case. Hoped we wouldn't need it, but if we needed it, there would be NO time to go get the gun from the office. This is a simple truth in the life of a zookeeper.

Parker had pulled the truck with trailer up parallel to the guard fence on the east side of the acre large bear enclosure. The spring grass and budding trees would add to the invitation for the bears to come out of the transport, Well, at least we hoped. If you want to move a bear, food - Hansel and Gretel style is the best motivation. The earth was moist from the day before's rain. I could smell the poignant exhaust of the diesel truck, mixed with the smell of bear and the damp earth. It was chilly, the men still had their insulated flannel jackets on, and those jackets had their own, hummm... let's just call it fragrance. I mention the smells because bears have very sensitive noses. They have four hundred times the smell receptors in their noses than we humans do. Jeannette Rix had warned me that it may take a while for the bears to settle down. The bears would smell all the other animals at the zoo. The sister bears did not recognize those smells as friendly or good, but as something different, to be wary of. The Syrians did not know. Ignorance begets fear. An afraid animal is a more dangerous animal than usual. And they are all dangerous- everyday.

The transport was six foot by six foot long, black steel bars as thick as my thumb, a solid steel bottom on wheels and an open barred top. It was especially designed to handle Grizzlies, this specie of strong bear. The men, Parker, Doug, and Tommy, (an apprentice zookeeper), climbed up on to the trailer. It was a tight squeeze, the trailer only a foot wider on each side of the transport. The gate doors to the main enclosure were open, the electric fence was turned off and unhooked. Dad manned the gate doors, the old male bear stayed up in the corner. I was there to take pictures and... just in case first aid was needed.

The tailgate of the trailer was lowered. The men pushed on the transport to move it to the rear of the trailer. All the while, the men were very cautious not to put their hands inside the cage. The guys took turns. When one of the bears would put their nose where one guy was pushing, that guy would go hands up and another guy would push from a different spot. A dance of sorts, or maybe more like playing tag on the cage before the bear could be there.

A lot of hollering suddenly happened. I thought someone got bit, but no, the cursing was because the job was not going easy. The guys stopped for a moment and Doug discovered the problem. The transport had a flat tire. *Ok - recalculating...* The easy roll job just got very hard. The transport easily weighed two hundred pounds. Add the weight of the sister Syrians and you have an easy thousand pounds. Parker Dad, and Doug brainstormed ideas. Parker went to get the skid loader from across the street.

The yellow skid loader with the front bucket attached was now in place. The skid loader bucket was placed in front of the transport cage. The skid loader would guide the transport cage to the ground from the sloped tailgate of the trailer. The transport was alternately pushed by Tom and Doug. Under Parker's excellent maneuvering skills the massively heavy transport cage holding the big girl grizzlies was gently received by the skid loader. Tom and Doug stopped pushing, with gravity taking over their task. Parker's skill in manipulating the controls of the skid loader helped him to ease the transport to the ground.

The Grizzly girls were nervous, a little restless, but not greatly upset. How could we tell? The bears were curious, alert, sitting in an upright position, not pacing or snarling. Their eyes were wide open, not in a vicious squint. Their ears were upright and round. They were very aware, but not panicky. They were not fighting the bars of the cage. Grizzly girls' bodies were just swaying with the jostling movement. Occasionally one of the girls would huff, as bears do when they just don't know what is going on. As if to say "HUH?" with a little extra air in it. It was their way of communicating. This is where knowing the history of your animal comes into play. We knew the bears were raised by human hands, female human hands. So just the voice of a female human would help reassure the girls. Dad was talking to the bears, and so was I. Every thing was going just fine. Animals sense when human adrenaline is running high, and can detect the tone of the curse words and conversation. During these events it is important to remain calm. Doing so reassures the animals.

Once the transport was lowered to the ground the guys pushed the cage the additional eight feet to the enclosure gate. That was no easy task. The flat tire sunk into the soft earth, stopping the progress. More curse words. *Whell, it was a heavy push job!* Eventually the transport cage was at the enclosure gate. One side of the double door gate was opened in. Dad was concerned that when we unlocked and opened the transport cage, one of the bears might circle up and out the five foot gap between the top of the transport cage and the top of the open enclosure gate.

"I've seen it happen," Dad's wisdom was still evident.

Tommy was sent to get a piece of livestock paneling, which is a tough fence material. The livestock paneling was placed atop the transport cage to prevent an escape into the zoo. After everything was in place, and double checked twice, Parker opened the transport doors.

The old male Syrian Grizzly had quietly watched the entire procedure from the upper corner of the enclosure. He was by the swimming pool, in the exact opposite corner, as far away from the action as he could get. Bears are curious by nature, but not stupid. He knew something was going on and wanted no part of it. I'm sure he could smell the new ladies on the block, so he would just watch and see what happened. Smart fellow.

The releasing of the lady bears was anticlimactic. They strolled out of the transport cage and into the green grass. They rolled in it. They sniffed the logs and rocks, obviously jubilant in their new lush green acre. Both sisters stood on their hind legs staring at the tree branches above them. Noses sniffing, the sister Syrians explored their new home often rising on their hind legs to see as far as they could see. This acre of paradise was theirs. A natural retirement home for two teaching sister bears.

The old male strolled down from his corner to greet his new neighbors. His hair was more blonde than the ladies, his age showing. Huffs were heard all round, which are greetings in the bear world. The ladies sniffed him, he sniffed them, acknowledging the existence of the other. Noses touched. We held our breath. If there was to be a territorial fight, it would start now. And then…that was it. They each went a separate way in the enclosure. The ladies still exploring, grazing over every tree, rock, log and the grass. Touching, smelling, licking, looking, cocking their heads to the side to see another direction. The old male just sat and watched.

A couple of weeks later, Susan Rix, the Syrian sisters' adopted aunt, came to visit them. Her sister Jeanette had raised these particular bears. She called to them, they came. I saw Susan at the fence and walked over to talk to her. We chatted for a bit about the bears' adjustment. The emotions were still evident. Susan is just a bit older than I and we had both raised and relinquished our babies many times. I put my arms around her for a quick hug.

"The bears are doing well, eatin' good, and playing all day," I reassured Susan. "But I know how you feel."

There was nothing left to say. One mom understanding the other aunt/mom. I've been where she was at, she had been there before too. She knew we would take good care of the Syrian sisters. Susan or Jeanette could come visit whenever they wanted. We've all been at that heartbreaking spot so many times and ya know what? You never get used to it. It does not get any easier.

Parker (left) and Doug (right) fix the electric fence for the sisters.

Photo by Lori Space Day

Chapter 30 The Pilot

I have met the most interesting people at the zoo. Lots of regular folk with an interesting hobby or work. I get to talk to a lot of the visitors during their time at the zoo. I answer their questions. And I ask a few too. Many of our visitors become season pass holders. When a season passer, (the name we call a season pass holder), comes often enough, I recognize them. I often stick a baby bottle in their hands. *Hey, I am not proud. Many hands make light work. I only have two hands, and usually more bottles than two to feed.*

I work a lot of hours. The months of April, May and June are twenty four/seven because of 'my' nursery babies. Most of my friends I have met at the zoo or through the zoo or church. The season passer friends I met at the zoo. I could list many friends here. One of those season passers that became a good friend is Jayne.

Jayne Hinds is a unique photographer. We originally met when she asked me questions about the antique cameras in the museum. Jayne has a collection of antique cameras and specializes in taking pictures with them. She also takes the neatest pictures of bugs. *Bugs, you say? Yes bugs.* Not my first choice of photographic subjects. Bugs are so far down my list, right after every mammal, fish, amphibian, tree and flower. But Jayne takes the most fascinating pictures of bugs. Oh, and of her iguana. Now Jayne has a husband and a son to take photos of also. She takes great pictures of them too, but that is sort of normal.

When I first met Jayne she only wore black. Different textures of black, but only black. I did not see her in any other color for years. Her vibrant wavy red hair cascaded down her back to her waist on cool days. She tied up her Repunzel bounty on hot days. Jayne wore John Lennon type round glasses, but occasionally traded them off for the intense black rims of the 1950's. Why anyone would want to live in Soho, NYC, is a wonderment to me. That's where Jayne lived, her home a studio. But that is where the artsy folk live, in Soho. Maybe that's why. She is a unique individual. Jayne's personality and mine just clicked. We were sisters in another lifetime. Jayne had taken many pictures of my animals and me. She even put some of the pictures in a coffee table book she had published. I had known Jayne a good ten years when I got a phone call.

"Hi Lori, would you consider yourself a leopard expert?" asked Jayne right off. *What? No "Howdy do, how ya doin' what's the weather gonna be?"*

"No not really, I'm much better at lions, African or Mountain, tigers, bears, otter, deer sheep etc." I stammered.

"Well, can you talk about leopards?" Jayne spit out.

"Yeah sure, I've only raised two. Why? What's up?" I wondered out loud.

" I'm going to give your phone number to a friend of mine, actually the fiancé of a friend of mine. She needs a leopard expert for a pilot she is producing for Animal Planet. I'm sitting here with him and his fiancé, Haewon needs a leopard expert in two weeks. He asked where they could get a leopard expert in two weeks short notice and I thought of you." Jayne gushed.

Well that explains everything!

"Sure, have her give me a call," I told Jayne. Jayne and I talked briefly about other friendly type conversation and then Jayne hung up. I got the phone call the next day.

Haewon quizzed me about my knowledge and experience with leopards. I must of passed the quiz, because she invited me to take part in the pilot. She asked me if I had any other leads for experts on impalas, hyena or savanna life in general. I gave her some of the other zoo folk I knew and the names of the zoos in the tri-state area.

"No promises. It's just a pilot. Just come to New York City on December seventeenth," Producer Haewon said.

"Ok," I said, I hoped she had not heard the trepidation in my voice. Haewon said she would email me the particulars. Fine, all I could think of was how do I get to New York City? *Yeah, Right. You might as well have asked me to fly to the moon.* Driving to New York City scares me to death. But I had said yes, so now I needed to figure out how to get to New York City. *How do you call NASA?*

I only knew three friends that were comfortable driving to New York City and two of them were working. My other friend's son was sick. *Ok, Miss Scarlet What to do? What to do? Wait, wait, I think I got it! Daughter Jackie, just traversed, backpacking through Europe. She is a world traveler. She can get me there! She knows how to read a train or subway map and schedules! I can do this, I can do this...*

I called daughter Jackie at Rider University that night and explained the situation. She did not want to drive in New York City either. I knew how to get to the train in Dover. I had gone into the city with my sister-in-law Linda to see Cirque du Soleil. So, I could get us to Dover. That was half way there. I told Jackie that I had a subway map that Jane had given me years before. *Jane actually thought I would drive into the city! Silly girl!* Jackie said she would look up on line the train and subway schedules. *We can do this!* Could her friend, the beau come along? Sure why not? We could use a big handsome guy to be bodyguard. Jackie would take the day off from college and Beau would take off a personal day from work. Entourage complete. *I can do this, I raise lions for a living, I raise lions for a living, I'm going to New York City. I can overcome this driving phobia. We can do this.*

I bought a new navy shirt and sewed a Space Farms patch on it. I took the name tag off my other uniform and put that on my shirt. It was December so I decided to wear a lime green turtle neck under my new uniform shirt. Clean navy pants and my outfit was complete. My hair? Well, my hair has always had a mind of its own. I could hope for the best, *and say a prayer to Gramma Lizzie.* And that is all I can do on hair.

Jackie came home the night before and Beau arrived to escort us early on the morning of December 17th. We left the house at eight fifteen in the morning to catch the 10 a.m. train from Dover, N.J. to Penn Station, NYC. It was cold. We traveled with the commuters that make this trip every day. Wow! I just couldn't do that. Bumper to bumper, the flashes of red tail lights alerted my retinas. I am a country girl for sure. The parking spaces were filling up as we arrived. The walk from the parking lot to the train was chilly and brisk. We stopped for bagels at the nearby deli. I could smell the pungent exhaust from the cars over the warm steamy roast of my coffee.

On the train we passed the mass of suburbia and cities that buffer our little hamlet of Beemerville from New York City. The view was dotted with sporadic winter bare trees and occasional evergreens. The scenery was bleak and depressing, but Jackie's chatter kept me from being nervous about the trip. Speaking in front of a camera didn't bother me at all - just the thought of being lost in the city. But we were doing it. Jackie would guide me.

The train was not too crowded, so we sat next to each other enjoying the excitement. I could smell the coffee from the person sitting across from me, smell the unusual smell of a well used train. Every person on that train had a story. My mind raced at the possibilities.

We arrived in Penn Station and Jackie efficiently guided us to the subway. There were so many of them, each one going somewhere! How Jackie knew which track was which is still a mystery to me. The subway was a whole new experience for me. It was not as bad as I had feared. There were no nasty gang style guys hanging out, no bag ladies or men, no disgusting sleazy looking people, just folks like us. Perfumes occasionally wafted by me, mixed in with the intense smell of the subway tunnels. Earthy, moist, and full of exhaust fumes, the smells bombarded my nose. And the noise! The noise factor was horrendous. Subways whooshing by, doors opening, people talking, whistles, bells, briefcases on wheels, babies, baby strollers, foreign languages, business people clicking their pens, phones ringing their individual ring tones, opening and shutting said phones, high heels on concrete! Wow! What a difference between my country life where the birds tweet, the bees buzz, and the occasional lion roars. Every noise made me jump and pay attention. My brain was on alert overload. Everyone else was just going about their business. We switched subways again and we were almost there. Up a set of iconic subway steps and we were in THE CITY! Walking now, we passed Broome Street where Jayne lived, I waved just for luck, although I knew she was not home.

We walked a little bit until we found the place Haewon said to meet. We had walked past it twice, there were no signs for the Kush Lounge on Christie Street. It was a great location, I could see why she chose it. It was very Moroccan in appearance with sand colored beige on the exterior, dark green doors up a ramp. It almost looked like a 1930's speakeasy. There were no signs to advertise it's existence. We opened the door and took a step back in time. The Kush Lounge looked just like a scene from Casablanca with Humphrey Bogart. Archways, shadows cast by filigreed dividers on sand colored walls, the wooden antique bar, the muted colors of the labels on the bottles on the bar shelves, and the glint of shiny clean glasses all added to the mysterious atmosphere. The antique smell of cigarettes was buffered by exotic spices leftover from the previous night's fare. Cameras and lights were set up. Don from the Beardlsy Zoo in Connecticut was there as an impala expert. He was sitting on a stool in a spotlight as we entered.

We asked for and checked in with Haewon. Haewon was Asian, beautiful, with long black hair, a little shorter than me and tiny compared to my country gal sturdy figure. She was a take charge kind of gal and that I could appreciate. We were early and Haewon said they were running late. Could we come back in an hour? I introduced Jackie as my personal assistant, and Beau as my bodyguard. *Well, they were.*

"Sure, we've been sitting all morning, we can take a walk and get lunch," I responded. *If we're gonna be in the city, we might as well look around.*

We went out to get some lunch. We looked up and down some streets and finally saw a whole bunch of Chinese writing on the buildings. Great, I love Chinese food. I could smell the Chinese food in the air. So we walked down that street. *Well, Dopey country girl me.* We walked a couple of blocks and finally figured out we were in the Chinese food restaurant supply section! Not a restaurant in sight. So we walked some more then saw a place called the Chinese Box Lunch Buffet. It looked clean, had lots of people in it, and we were hungry. Our last meal had been at 7:30 a.m.. It smelled good too, so we went in. Well, it was not like any of the Chinese restaurants I had ever been in. There were no decorations on the walls. Small square tables and folding chairs crowded every corner. No silverware on the tables, heck no empty tables. There were stand up counters around the long narrow room. But I was game. Heck, I eat game. So we got some food and stood until a table became available. We were so hungry. It was now about 1 p.m. The food was good. After we ate, we were sitting there drinking our sodas. I looked around and noticed that we were the only Caucasians in the place. It must have been a really real Chinese restaurant!

After lunch we walked back to the Kush Lounge. Readers: do you know that kush is what camels and llamas do when overwhelmed by the enemy or are tired? They crash down in a heap of fur with legs folded under themselves. They lay down on their chests in an upright position. Trained camels and llamas do this on command. But it happens naturally also. I'm theorizing this activity in the wild would surprise the attacker and shake him off. Anyway, neat name for a lounge. Kush.

Haewon said they were still running late, could we hang out for a few moments. Sure, no problem. It was fun to watch someone else on the hot seat. Don from the Beardlsy Zoo was talking about Impalas. Don was tall, blondish, about my age, and looked relaxed on the seat in the lights. After he was done, Don and I got a chance to chat zoo business. "I have lemurs, do you want some?" That kind of zoo talk. I had brought a package of information, my book, "The Zookeeper's Daughter", Dad's book, "Ralph Space the Legend", and other Space Farms goodies. I gave Don the package to take home.

Then it was my turn. Haewon was so nice, fussed over my hair. I had brought hair spray. She asked if I brought any face powder. Face powder? I don't even own face powder! Haewon was very kind to this country gal. She was nice enough to use her very own face powder, while reassuring me it was good stuff. I would not know good stuff from bad stuff. The only powder I use is baby powder. I had some baby powder in my purse, for nervous heat, but no face powder! Then she hair sprayed and wet down my hair. The production crew were kind enough to call them fly away hairs… but I knew they were those pesky silver kinky kind of hair women my age are prone to have sticking straight up! A gals just gotta love static electricity!

Haewon perched me on the stool in the spotlight. Nice warm lights were shining on me from all directions. I asked for the anti-wrinkle lens, joking with the cameramen. They asked me to take off my name tag, and if it was ok to cut off the Space Farms patch I had so carefully sewn on. I don't know why they asked to do this, Don had his Beardlsy Zoo embroidered shirt on. The hyena expert had his zoo embroidered shirt on also. Oh well. Don't know why.

The lights had dried out my hair again, and again we plastered my helmet with hairspray. *My hair had not gotten that much attention in it's life. I think my hair liked it, it misbehaved all day.*

Haewon proceeded to ask me all the questions we had prepared for by email and some new questions. That part was a breeze. I know my animal facts. I goofed up a couple of times when Haewon asked me to refer to the leopard as "she" instead of "it" or "he". Just nerves. But Haewon emailed me later that I did ok. Jackie said I sounded ok also. So I tried to not stress out over my goof ups. Tape is good, they can edit. Haewon explained again that this was a pilot program that will be presented to the Animal Planet for approval. She would let me know when she knows, and hopefully send me a copy on disk. I hoped I did ok. *Something to tell the grandkids about for sure.*

It was 4:30 p.m. by then and I was mentally drained. I had a lot more leopard facts that I could have told her, but they were running out of time at the Kush lounge. She stopped tape. Haewon covered all the expenses of the day, for myself, my 'personal assistant' and my 'bodyguard'. That was nice.

While I was busy in front of the camera, Jackie and Beau relaxed in the lounge. Their mini couches were covered in dark leather. Afterward Jackie took a bunch of pictures of us there. I gave Haewon a package of books and info while saying good bye and thanks for the experience.

Jackie wanted to see the Christmas tree at Rockefeller Center so we subwayed to the tree. We perused the nearby shop's Christmas windows. Everything was very sparkley. This country girl was craning her neck to see it all. There were trees in cages. *Now why is that? I still don't know.* Wow. The city in winter, at Christmas time was so beautiful, and so decorated. Every inch of the city buildings seemed electrified. Lights were twinkling. There were so many lights twinkling. Part of me, the little girl in me, loved all the twinkley lights. The ecologist in me was baffled by such a waste of fossil fuel. The people trotting by us on the street didn't even seem to notice. Hustle and bustle I guess. The city exhaust smells were still wafting around us but the pretty lights almost made up for it. Jackie snapped a bunch of touristy pictures. We made the 6 p.m. train back to Dover, then I drove us, the three weary travelers, home. We got home at 8:30p.m. Beau left shortly afterwards. He had an hour and half drive home yet to go. In one day we had traveled to an alien universe and made it home, safe and sound.

All in all we had a great day. It was really neat-o to be considered an expert on leopards. I hoped Haewon would get the program approved. I know a lot more on lions, tigers, and cougars than I do on leopards. It was really cool for this country girl to go to the big city and quite an honor to be asked even if nothing came of it.

P.S. for the reader: Haewon did get the show approved. It is called "I, Predator" and it is on the Animal Planet channel. I have not seen the pilot I was on, yet. Maybe they didn't like me. Maybe they did. It's 'out there' somewhere. I had fun, and it was a day quite different from my daily routine. *Face powder? Me? Really?*

Lola the black leopard and her friend King
Photo by Jessie Goble   Photo by Karen Talasco

Zoo Momma

Chapter 31 Let's Chat!

Grab some coffee, soda or mayhaps some tea,
Let's have a chat, just you and me.
So here we are it's two thousand and eight,
And once again my letter is late.
But today, my dear we have the time,
To smile, chat and just unwind.
Our Christmas came late last year,
When Jackie came back from Europe we cheered.
Thank God! She looked so savvy,
You just know Doug and I had missed her badly.
Adventure in her eyes, she left a girl,
Returned all smiles a woman of the world.
Jack was home for only three days,
When college studies whisked her away.
But that's alright, now I don't care,
As long as she's in the States somewhere.
Multiple awards & on the list of the Dean,
A good list, not my list (know what I mean?).
Jack will graduate Rider U. this spring,
Proud Poppa and I will loudly sing.
At the zoo things are quite the same,
Lots of hard work promoting the Space Farms name.
Giving speeches, TV and radio, Seems most of my year is on the go.
Things had gotten staid, my speeches by rote,
So I decided to kick it up a note.
I'd been playing it safe, so to add some spice,
I took a gator, who was not always nice.
It's the challenge I learned, that fuels my drive,
The accomplishment that keeps me alive.
Oh enough of that introspection, this oh so serious contemplation.
Dad and I built that peacock pen, With a faux bamboo metal den.
With lilacs, hostas, landscaping galore,
Looked so much better than it did before.
"Looks great, good job, but the peacocks don't care.
They'll strip all those greens bare!"
Dad grinned, I guess I should of listened to him.
Silly vain birds did not appreciate,
all the improvements I had tried to make.
Jenny woodchuck got married, had three kids,
left her one, raised two on a bottle I did.
Then at 8 weeks, my two started to fight,
And Jenny kicked hers out the very same night.

Zoo Momma

So at 8 weeks I've made the conclusion,
Woodchuck young earn emancipation.
An owl with a bum leg came to me,
Fixed it with time, massage and TLC.
Released him this fall in our yard like I'm supposed to do,
So every night he wakes me with his constant whoooo.
Only two fawns, in the last six moons,
Distemper took out lots of wild raccoons.
Doug's doing fine, always fixing what's broke,
He cusses and swears and says it's a joke
How fast machinery here can get out of wack
He'll pick up a tool and give it a smack.
You name it he'll fix it here at the zoo,
No matter what Dad, Park and Hunter may do.
Doug laughs and says with unabashed certainty
" I just consider it job security!"
We celebrated our 25th Anniversary,
taking a few days off from my nursery.
We kicked back and relaxed,
Like the old days in Pittsburgh, as I think back.
A man brought me a newborn pink mink,
road kill mom was dead in a blink.
So we took "Roy" on our three days, But sadly Roy, he passed away.
I really tried, 'twas an impossible chore,
With cases like that I don't cry much anymore.
The rest of my family are all doing well, hearty, strong and healthy as Hell.
Dad gave us a worry a few weeks ago,
He passed out twice, Doctors still don't know.
A workaholic tried and true, He was off feed and down for a day or two.
After his stay in the hospital they could not diagnose,
He was down and quite morose.
But he perked up just fine to pick up more deer,
I did ride shotgun, more worry than fear.
But Dad's fine, gone hunting again,
With the Beemerville Boys & his old duffer friends.

Hunter, (Parker's son), has grown quite tall,
Doug likes working with him the most of all.
They joke, and work, and joke again,
Then they are both thirteen, my little men!
'Twas a week before Christmas, Jackie and Beau,
Escorted me where I feared to go.
What would make me crawl out of my safe box?
I interviewed for a pilot believe it or not.

Zoo Momma

The Animal Planet is doing a show - on Big cat predators, would I go?
To the Big Apple by car, bus or train,
(the concept of driving just fried my brain).
So Jackie, my assistant, and bodyguard Beau,
Got me on the train and off we did go.
It was a great experience, lots of fun,
With hair and makeup and lights hot as the sun.
I spoke on leopards, their predatory stealth,
Which I found ironic in spite of myself.
I've raised 2 Cougars, 12 tigers, and 36 lions,
and other critters, you know I'm not lying.
Yet only two leopards and not from birth,
So you can see my somewhat snidely mirth
That I spoke on leopards, an expert they said,
I was not worried, only the trip I did dread.
My animal facts were clear and concise,
Make-up, clothes and my hair did look nice.
It's a pilot, so I don't know,
But maybe I'll be on the Animal Planets' "I Predator" show.
If I find out you'll hear me cheer, So friends can watch from far and near.

So that's my year, you know where I'm at,
Come see me anytime, I'd love to chat.
We've had a nice visit, did you finish that tea?
Now it's your turn to write to me.
'Twas the night <u>after</u> Christmas and all through the house,
Not a creature was stirring not even a mouse,
Or a lion or lemur, a fawn or young tiger, you get the idea…
My gracious, you'd think it's a zoo around here!
Love, Lori

Three kids, Hunter, Doug and kid goat!
Photo by Hunter Space

Chapter 32 My Little Pony Daisy Mae

Every little girl of my generation has read <u>Misty of Chincoteague</u>, by Marguerite Henry. It is a story of a little girl and a pony. I did. As a little girl and until I was a teenager, we had horses at the farm. Gramp loved to ride and often took all us grandkids up to Sunrise Mountain on horseback for a picnic. I remember the horses as big and scary. I was young and small. These stories are reflected in <u>The Zookeeper's Daughter</u>, my first book. I have always liked horses and ponies. I don't know anyone who doesn't. It had been many years since I had ridden a horse and I had never raised one. Ponies were just smaller horses. Sort of.

"Do you want to raise a pony?" Dad asked out of the blue one day,.

A pony! A real live baby pony? Oh yes Daddy! Yes Daddy! I want a pony! My little girl brain giggled.

"Sure, I guess, let me get some formula," My reserved adult response, wondering why all of a sudden we were gonna raise ponies by hand.

"They'll be cute, the public will love them. Our herd of Assateague-Chincoteague is getting large and becoming inbred, so we need to take some out," Dad explained. I knew the pony herd was about twelve in number, I counted them every year for inventory. I knew they were a wild herd, that none of them were broken or at the least bit tame. It was not like we could just call one over to the fence, have it trot into the trailer and give it to some one. That was just not gonna happen. Our guys would have to lasso and load up a wild bucking bronco. Someone or the pony, was sure to get hurt. There were two ways to thin the herd. One was to take the foals away when they were newborns, easy to catch and could be tamed easily. So I ordered the milk. I would let Dad know when the milk came in. The local feed store, Farmside, had foal nipples so I bought one when the milk was ordered. I was prepared, or at least that is what I thought.

Assateague Island is a long barrier island off the east coast of Maryland and Virginia and was purchased by the federal government in 1943. The island is divided in half by a fence! The northern Maryland section is managed by the National Park Service as Assateague Island National Seashore and Fish and Wildlife Service. It is home to about 150 wild ponies. The population of horses is controlled by contraceptive vaccine. The herd living there are referred to as Assateague horses.

The southern half of the island is home to the famous Chincoteague herd of wild ponies. Chincoteague is its own island, located in between Assateague Island and the mainland. The town of Chincoteague (the entire island), established a pony swim and auction of horses in 1925 as a fundraiser for the Chincoteague Volunteer Fire Company. The island towns fire department needed equipment. The Chincoteague Fire Company owns the ponies and rents the forage rights from the federal government agencies to keep their herd on the southern half of Assateague Island. Every year the fire department swims the herd from the southern - Virginia side of Assateague Island to the town of Chincoteague. Their annual fair/carnival takes place in July. This is when the herd is inspected by a veterinarian and some are selected to be sold at auction. While this custom started in 1925, it is continued today, as a viable way to control the population on the southern half of the Assateague Island. The horses sold from the Chincoteague Fire Company are called Chincoteague Ponies.

The unique relationship between the federal government and the Chincoteague Fire Company has resulted in a healthy herd. Over the years, new blood was added to the herd to assist with genetic problems incurred by inbreeding. Over population and the resulting illnesses are resolved in two different ways: birth control vaccines and auction.

While only three hundred ponies live on the island, there are over a thousand Chincoteague Island ponies that live on the mainland due to this private auction.

And where did the ponies originally came from? There are three plausible explanations. One theory is that a Spanish galleon ship, a cargo ship, crashed on the shore during the 1750's. The Spanish galleons cargo ponies swam to shore. This theory was given more credibility in 1997 by Mr. John Amrhein's The Hidden Galleon about the wreak of a Spanish cargo ship La Galga in 1750. The second theory involves mainland farmers being taxed on every head of livestock on their farms during colonial times. The farmers, in order to avoid this tax, swam horses to their island 'corral'. The third possibility is the horses were released by pirates. In all three scenarios, the horses/ponies were originally domesticated, escaped and turned feral. All three theories add spice to the mysterious history of this little horse.

According to family lore, Gramp brought ponies up from Virginia. If you recall I have mentioned that Gramp spent a lot of time in Virginia on Native American archeological digs and brought a few whole families back to Beemerville.

Our herd looks a lot like all the Chincoteague ponies I have seen on the internet. We have one stallion (male) and about ten mares. From our original ponies, we've added new blood to our herd by occasionally adding donated pet ponies. One year we took in a blind pony and her pony guide-friend. You would never know that one of the pair was blind. Their bond was amazing to watch.

The Chincoteague pony stallion is about 13.2 hands high (or 54 inches) in the wild. When brought to the main land and given more nutritious food, Chincoteague ponies can grow significantly larger. Ponies on Assateague Island feed on salt marsh cordgrass, bayberry twigs, rosehips and persimmons. It is a tough diet for a tough little pony. Wild ponies graze in herds of five to ten animals, usually one stallion and the rest mares and foals. They look like horses, just smaller versions. (Horses are usually over 14. 2 hands high.) Average weight is eight-hundred and fifty pounds. Stocky and sturdy, rounded ribcages make this type of pony similar to the wild mustangs of western lore. The Chincoteague ponies have straight legs, and a broad chest. Their tails are set low on their rumps but create a feathery cascade when running with tails erect. The ponies can be any solid color, with pinto marking variations. Our herd is chestnut colored, with white pinto markings splattered across their sides and bellies. Our herd has white marks on their foreheads. Our stallion is a dark chestnut brown with a flowing, but coarse, black mane and tail. He has been the daddy of the herd for a number of years. Most of our mares have the black mane and tail also.

Chincoteague ponies are supposed to be easy to train. But first you have to catch them. In any group activity, individuals have their strong points. A good manager uses the individuals to their best ability. I am not the best runner, Hunter, then age 14, was, and still is. I can't carry the weight of the average newborn foal, 35 lbs, while it is kicking or struggling. Doug, Hunter, or Parker can. The guys are just plain old stronger than me. Doug does not run as fast, either, after his broken leg. Neither does Dad. So when it came to catching up a pony foal and all the other foals thereafter (or llama cria, or Scottish Highland Cattle calves for that mater) , everyone had their job.

Dad is gate man. Lori, Doug and other zookeepers are herders, Hunter or Parker are catchers. The ponies established a trail through their one acre paddock, around the shed, the trees and naturally occurring Sussex County rocks and boulders. None of the ponies have been trained. The few ponies donated to us have long since forgotten their training. One thing is for sure. The stallion (male pony) is the king of the herd. His job is to protect the herd from intruders and predators. That would be us humans. The mare (female pony mom), is gonna protect her foal from the same threat. Again, that would be us humans. The rest of the herd would run away, with the exception of the father and mother pony.

I know what my reader is thinking right now. Yeah, I've seen the docile bucolic pictures of folks and their new foals next to the tame mare. Trained horses. From a long line of trained horses that have interacted with humans for generations. Oh that would be so sweet! Our herd is a wild herd. The adult had not been touched by human hands for oh, lets just say four-hundred years. The natural instincts of the stallion and the mare would not be tempered by familiarity with gentle humans. I knew it was not going to be easy to separate a foal from the herd .

"Today we are catching up that newborn pony," Dad said after the newest pony had been nursing off mom for twenty four hours. "It's got enough colostrums, [the important antibody enriched first milk produced by a new mom]. /We'll get the guys around and get this done." This type of dangerous activity is always done before we open the zoo at 9a.m..

We all met at the pony paddock. Dad manned the gate for the quick getaway with the foal. Doug, Hunter, Parker, and I entered the paddock and spread out to entice the ponies to take a certain path in a certain direction. This would enable Parker or Hunter to hide behind the shed and grab the pony foal as it ran past following the mare mom.

The ground in the pony pen is rocky, strewn with so many rocks and boulders it makes one wonder where they all came from. The sturdy Chincoteague ponies have no problem running over the rocks but we humans do. Pony manure dotted the landscape adding to the all natural horsey smell of the paddock. Tufts of grass, greenery, brush and small trees poke up in occasional spots. There is a center section of tall trees and brush. All over the ground are broken twigs and tree limbs. It is not an easy walk let alone run. Doug and I pressed the ponies just by walking behind the herd. We carried sticks and rakes to make ourselves look taller. *Intimidating and scarier? Our redneck selves are scary enough!*

The ponies circled the shed, Parker caught the foal and handed it off to Hunter, the fastest runner. Doug, Parker and my job instantly changed from herder to protectors of the runner- Hunter -with the foal. We swung our rakes and sticks to scare off the parents of the foal, and to keep them from running after Hunter. The stallion challenged once or twice, rearing up on hind feet with hooves pawing the air. Now is when you realize the difference between trained and untrained hoofstock. Those hooves are dangerous. You keep moving towards the gate, but never taking your eye off the ponies. You are half walking backwards over the impossible terrain. Thankfully the stallion soon lost interest in us and was nosing around the mare's backside. The mare followed Hunter and the foal, but was then easily dissuaded by rakes and sticks extended into the air. Hunter's long legs high stepped as he ran with the foal in his arms. As soon as the foal was outside the gate and driven out of sight, the mare and the stallion went back to the rest of the herd.

I hopped in Hunter's mule (a jitney) and drove Hunter, still holding the foal in the back of the vehicle. The foal was ninny-ing, but had stopped kicking and struggling. You can't blame the foal. She was scared. Hunter easily hopped out of the back of his mule, *Oh it would be nice to have young legs again! Mine seem to hurt more every morning.* Releasing my new baby into the nursery gate, Hunter questioned me.

"There's your new baby, Lee," Hunter stated proudly. "She's cute! What ya gonna name 'er?"

"Something country, she's a country pony, how bout Daisy? Daisy Mae? Yeah, I'll give her a couple of hours and try her on a bottle, Thanks kid," I replied. I had other work to do. Hunter drove off to his next chore. I would come back and check on the little pony a couple of times before the two hours were up.

I had never broken a foal to a bottle. I tried to use the special foal nipple that fit over my calf bottle. That nipple seemed way too big. So I tried a regular human baby bottle nipple on the advise of Dr. Parissi, one of the vets at Dr. Spinks' Animal Hospital. That size nipple worked just fine with a single vertical slit. I did have to straddle Daisy Mae between my legs, brining her head up to suck from a bottle. If Daisy Mae were drinking from her natural mom, her head would be pointing down. The little pony's back was at mid thigh on me, so straddling her was not a problem.

When training a foal, cria or calf to drink from a bottle, it is not a pretty sight. I straddle the infant, bringing its head up between my legs. I bend way over covering the infants eyes with my chest. Keeping the bottle in my right hand with the nipple pointing towards my wrist, I gently stoke the infants neck to let it know not to be afraid. I cooo and talk softly all the while. I wiggle the nipple on the front lips. If the infant does not open its mouth for the nipple, then I wiggle a finger from my left hand into the mouth. Often the infant will suck on my finger first.

139

Then it is an easy substitute to slip a finger out and the nipple in. Usually while all that is happening, the foal is backing up, or lunging forward, trying to get away from the nasty thing that has grabbed it. *Yes, that would be ME!* Positioning the infant with it's rear towards a fence or a wall helps here. Often the infant will back up until it hits a wall, then just stop and stand there. Stopping and standing is good! I can't tell you how many times my feet have been stepped on or my legs kicked. *Darn those baby hooves can hurt!*

Once the infant is in position and suckling I gently stroke the neck and blow into its nose while saying soothing baby talk. I also pull the head up to my bent forward body to either cover its eyes, or get the infant close enough to close their eyes. And all for what? A newborn pony will drink maybe four ounces. Every two hours, dawn to dusk. This entire procedure is done every two hours.

I'm sure this process looks strange to the visitors at the zoo. Many a time I have been bottle breaking a cria, pony or calf and the visitors call out to me. I don't mean to be rude, but I do not answer. If I shout while in the nursing position, my mouth, *the loud part,* is right next to the infants ear. That would defeat the calming procedure, and the infant would stop nursing. So if the reader is at the zoo and sees this procedure in process, please be patient, I will speak to you afterwards.

Daisy Mae progressed on the nursing from a bottle very well. She was my first pony ever, so I was maternally proud of her every step. By day three she was coming to me when I called. I would only have to touch the nipple to her lips and she would suckle.

Her big brown eyes with the super long lashes would close. She would lean her body into mine, in a one sided hug, and drink her milk. I use Land- O- Lakes *(yeah the butter people)* Mare's Match, a prepared powder for newborn ponies and horses.

Daisy Mae grew quickly, and bonded with me and the general public. She was a doll baby nudging for a nipple whenever I was around. By the time Daisy was two weeks old, she was drinking six full eight ounce baby bottles a day. Her brown tummy was warm and round. I touched every part of her body daily to prepare her for being touched by our Vet. I washed a lot of butt. I brushed her mane and tail, and fussed over Daisy Mae like I was a giggly ten year old girl again.

At two weeks old Daisy Mae was the hit of the nursery. And then the guys brought me another pony. This one was a colt (boy). Dad wanted to name him Blaze, after one of the horses Dad had in his youth. *Ok well, he's the boss, so Blaze it was*. Now I had two ponies. If you're feeding one, might as well feed two, and ponies are herd animals - they are happier with a friend.

The visitors loved the two ponies. Blaze had a white streak down his forehead, with some pinto white markings on his sides. Daisy Mae was gorgeous, filling out nicely, chocolate brown all over with a beautiful black mane. I would take the ponies out for a walk with the visitors. I did that a couple of times. Then one day the ponies decided to kick up their heels, as ponies do when they are happy, to run. Almost, I said, almost clipped a toddler in the head. I stopped the pony runs with the public after that.

Every night I would let the ponies out to roam the zoo at 5 pm when we closed. I learned Daisy Mae loved to dance. If I wiggled and jumped, she would wiggle and jump. It would crack up any one who saw it. Alice at admissions used to laugh right out loud. Anyhooo…it is a joy to watch the ponies run. The duo would zoom through the zoo, tails held high, flowing with their manes in the created wind. They'd play games and stop short or circle around me like I was the barrel in a barrel racing rodeo. As they tired, the pair would nibble on the zoos fresh, pesticide free grass. I would be back at dusk to feed nursery rounds again. Faithfully the ponies would be waiting for me at the nursery gate. I let them back in and gave them their good night bottles.

The ponies would nip a little when they wanted a bottle. This is not acceptable. Little ponies nip, big ponies bite hard. I consulted with some horse owning friends of mine and they suggested the finger flick on the nose as they were nipping. *Well, darn , I knew that, I do that with the lions and tigers!* A few unknowing visitors commented on my training, but that training has stood with generations of equine specialists. When I explained and educated the visitor ,they seemed to understand.

My summers speed by. There is always a lot to do, and more that I would like to get done. I am never caught up. By September it was time to find new homes for my little colt and filly. I put the word out on the Sussex County Board of Agriculture website and got a great home for Daisy Mae. She would go live with a friend of mine, Glen, who owned a mare who needed a companion. Glen is a horse breeder. Glen came and we led Daisy Mae onto the trailer. Not the easiest lead on but with a tug on her halter she 'pony-ed up'. I talk to Glen quite frequently and check on Daisy Mae. She's fine and enjoying her casual companion pony life in a large pasture with her mare friend.

Blaze was a little tougher to find a home for. No one wanted a male. Stallions can be feisty if you don't castrate them. If they are castrated they are called a gelding. You cannot put two intact males in the same pasture, since they will fight. So placing males can be a problem.

A month later, Blaze had a home. Another friend of mine, living on a farm, had two small kids and wanted a pony. Blaze is doing great, has been saddle broken and treats the growing kids as part of his herd.

I don't really miss them. The little girl in me that was soooo thrilled to get a pony, well, that little girl grew up fast - in about two weeks. I wiped messy poopie off of butts. I shoveled horse apples and forked hay out of sheds once a week if it did not rain. This was done every morning if it did rain. And it rained a lot that summer. I realized how much work horses and ponies are. I've raised other ponies and placed them since. But Daisy Mae, she was special. She was my dancing pony partner. My first little Chincoteague pony.

Chapter 33 Lola the Leopard

As I walked into the office at eight a.m. one morning in April, Dad informed me we were getting a leopard cub. Dad was sitting at his desk. I walked down the hallway to my office. I should say THE office which I share with a secretary and my sister-in-law, Jill. I'm not in the office much, I avoid it to be quite honest. Paperwork, uggghhh! I'd rather be out with the animals. But I do check my desk once a day to check my calendar and see if there are any important messages from the day before. Next on my list was to feed the little ponies their bottles. *Which would you rather do? Paperwork? Or feed bottles to baby ponies? Yeah, I thought so, that is a no brainer!*

"How old?" my standard question.

"Five months, Parker has the particulars," Dad replied.

"Ok, I'll find him and ask," I was on my way to feed the ponies.

I found Parker later that day and found out the leopard cub was coming from New York State. She was a show animal and Parker was not sure exactly what day it would be here. Dad and I had discussed the size of a five month old female leopard figuring she would probably weigh sixty pounds and be about a yard long. I set up a cage on my front porch as a temporary holding spot. The dog corral show cage was in sections, could be assembled in any shape and needed a top. I knew leopards could jump. My front porch was crowded with an eight foot long, three foot wide cage with a litter box and bed inside. The cage was comfy, if not the largest, but would do for one month until the weather warmed up and we could put her outside. April still has cold nights for a little girl leopard that had lived in a mans basement. She needed to be an inside cat for a month or so longer.

The day the little leopard arrived, I was called to Dad's office and closed the doors behind me. Inside the room with Butch, the man who transported her (an animal transporter, former zoo owner and friend of the family), Dad, and Parker, we let the cat out of the dog pet taxi. Our estimates as to weight and size were right on, about the size of an adult greyhound dog. And she was jet black! I did not know she was a melanistic cat, black spots on black fur! *Cool!* I watched her as she explored Dads (messy) office, under desks, and around chairs. Her olive yellow eyes were absorbing every bit of information she could. Her whiskers were twitching double time. Well, to be honest, in Dads office there are lots of smells, not all pleasant ones.

"Want to hold her?" Butch asked as the leopard passed his feet. Butch scooped her up and placed her in my arms. I rubbed her tummy with one hand as I looked her over carefully avoiding direct eye contact. She was a handful, squirming to get down, but she was purring and that was a good sign.

"What's her name? What shots has she had? Last time she was wormed? And what has she been eating?" I asked the standard questions.

"Don't know." Butch's reply. "But I got the guys phone number. You can call him and ask."

Parker and Butch exited the office to take care of the business paperwork.

"Well, you got a new baby," Dad beamed, "She seems nice."

"Yeah, well I'm gonna take her home to my front porch now." I told Pop as I scooted her into her transport dog crate. And I did. I had the porch set up and I dropped the little leopard off on my enclosed front porch, figuring she had had enough excitement for one day. She could rest up and I would play with her after work. After placing her in the cage, she walked right over to the makeshift towel bed, and plopped down in the sunshine and licked the bottom of a paw. The sunshine made her black spots glisten on her black fur. She looked at me with those vertical slit fluorescent yellow-green eyes and purred. I was hooked. *I know, it doesn't take much, just one forlorn look. I'm such a softie.*

I returned the short trip to the zoo and continued my days work. All day I thought about the little leopard. I called the previous owner and after introducing myself, asked the important questions I needed to know.

"What's her name?"

"I called her Cat, you know cats don't answer to a name anyway," the Previous Owner (PO), replied.

"What does she like to eat?" I asked.

"I give her a chicken leg and thigh section a day," he said. *That's it? She is a growing girl, she needs more. No fiber, no extra calcium? But I couldn't say that.*

"Vitamins?"

"Yep, some sprinkle on vitamins."

"When did she have her shots? And which ones?" I asked.

"She hasn't had any." the PO replied curtly. I felt that he and I were not jiving well.

"Has she been kept outside or in?"

"She's been in a cage in my basement. I bought her to use for shows for schools and the like. But now she is too big and New York State law will only let me keep her until she is six months old," he said. Finally the info I needed. Now I knew what I was dealing with as far as the cats personality. She would need a little extra T.L.C. A washed up show girl at six months old. I tried to finish up our conversation on a light note, inviting the PO to come to the zoo to visit.

"A show girl" …rang in my head, … "her name was Lola" and the little girl leopard finally had a name. Everyone deserves a name.

I hung up and called the Animal Hospital of Sussex County to make an appointment for Lola to get shots. Got an appointment for the next day. Dr. Spinks, V.M.D. was away, but Dr. Schott, D.V.M. was there. Schott was new to the Animal Hospital but had years of experience. I worked the rest of the day thinking about all I knew about leopards.

The Felidae (cat) family traces back to a common ancestor eleven million years ago. Panthera pardus, the leopard, evolved around 3.8 million years ago. The leopard is one of the big five of big cats, the leopard, the jaguar, the cougar, the lion and the tiger.

Pliestocene leopard specimens resemble the South American jaguar. The modern leopard evolved around 170 thousand to 300 thousand years ago in Africa and then migrated to Asia. The leopard once roamed Asia and Africa from Korea to South Africa. Now, due to loss of habitat, they are found in sub-Saharan Africa with populations also in India, Indochina, Malaysia and China. In the 18th century, there were determined to be 27 subspecies of leopards. In 1996 the number was revised to 9 subspecies: IndoChinese, Indian, North Chinese, Arabian, Srilanken, Java, Amur, North African, and Persian. The main difference between the types is in the spot formation, density, undercoat color and pattern.

If you think of the continental shift theory, the leopard and jaguars are very similar and inhabit the same type of habitats. South American Jaguars and the African leopard are very similar with the jaguar being stockier than it's svelte cousin the leopard. The jaguar has spots inside of it's spots, called a rosette, whereas leopards just have spots. Melanistic (black) cats appear in both jaguar and leopard species. The darker, black on black cats usually inhabit the jungle areas. The normal beige with dark spots coloration is more common on the savannahs or prairies. The camouflage effect would enhance the survival rate of certain colors in certain habitats.

The leopard species is rated as Near Threatened. Space Farms Zoo and any other zoo or facility must have certain licenses in order to keep leopards in the U.S. Every state has its own laws (that is how PO could have a leopard cub only up to six months old). We have the right licenses to have leopards. And experience. I had raised a set of leopards when I was eighteen years old, but they were off the bottle by the time we received them.

To be sure, the leopard is one of the trickiest cats. Dad says the circus people say they cannot be trusted. A leopard will turn on you in a snap. Leopards are smart and cunning. In India, a legend says that a leopard is so cunning they brush away their tracks with their tails.

The tail of the leopard is three quarters as long as the body of the cat. The tail is used for balance when the leopard leaps from tree to tree, or from ground to tree. After capturing a larger than one meal prey, say like an antelope, leopards have been known to drag the carcass into a tree for future dining. Don't know why I feel the need to stress this, but a carcass hanging in the tree in the hot sun gets ripe quickly, and full of maggots. Guess it all adds to the flavor!

A full grown male leopard is about the size of a German Shepherd dog. Females are about a third smaller, but just as dangerous. The estrus cycle is every 46 days, with individual heats lasting 6 to 7 days. And noisy! Those gals can call in the boys with their whiney cat calls. Gestation is up to 105 days. We've never had leopard cubs born here at Space Farms, but we have had jaguars, lions, tigers, cougars, bobcat and lynx born here.

Leopards love to run, jump, and climb trees. In the wild they spend a fair share of their time in trees if a tree is available. Leopards can easily jump fifteen feet straight up and are known for their leaping kills in the wild. Savannah leopards do not always have that luxury of a tree to lounge in the shade.

The next day I packed Lola up and schlepped her to the Animal Hospital of Sussex County in Augusta, fifteen minutes away. My friend and vet tech, Jennie Beckman was on duty. We let Lola out of the pet taxi and she roamed around the examination room with her jet black whiskers twitching. Dr. Schott, came in the room. Lola paraded around the room, slinking under the examination table. When Dr. Schott was ready I tried to scoop up Lola, but Lola was scared and hissed. Lola disappeared under the examination table again. I pulled her out by her tail. I know it was not the nicest way to get her, but I did not want to deal with the teeth, or biting end of a new-to-me leopard! Jennie and Dr. Schott were side stepping the leopard. We all knew the history of this animal. We could not trust Lola, nor she us. When I saw my chance I grabbed Lola by the scruff of the neck and hoisted her off her feet. *Which by the way was not easy.* I used both hands to hold the squirming forty pound leopard up and away from our bodies. She quickly calmed down. This is called 'scruff-ing'- grabbing an animal by the scruff of the neck. If you can hoist the animal off it's hind feet, it will go limp. This phenomenon reflects back upon the infanthood of the animal. The mother animal would pick up and carry her infant by the neck, without harming the infant.

Dr. Schott, who is more petite than I, positioned herself behind and to the side of me in order to give the resisting leopard a shot in the rump. Hissing teeth and claws were extended. Then came another shot. More hissing, teeth and claws extended. And then just one more. Growling now, with teeth and claws extended. My arms were failing. I put Lola in the taxi, none too easy, since my arms had started to shake. It is so much easier to give shots to a smaller, ten pound, eight week old leopard.

Jennie, Dr. Schott and I discussed Lola's picky eating problem. Dr. Schott had a few ideas to try in order to switch Lola over to venison. I packed Lola up and headed back to the zoo.

The diet of the leopard in the wild is varied between hoofed animals and small birds and game. At Space Farms all the carnivores are fed venison, bone, hair, muscle meat and sinew. Our cats are in great shape, even a little on the fat side.

I had set Lola up on our enclosed front porch. That lasted a couple of days. I noticed Lola looked lonely. I can't tell you exactly how I knew that, but there was a confused, sad aura around the little washed up showgirl. I discussed it with Dad and we decided to set Lola up in Dad's office. I was down at the zoo more in the daytime than at home of course. There was a lot more people traffic, with Dad, the rest of the family, zookeepers and business associates walking through Dad's office. Lola would be happier. So I moved the whole kit and caboodle to Dad's office under the windows. This did also involve a lot of cleaning of Dad's office. *Hummmm… Dad might of got me there, now that I think about it!*

Lola, my showgirl, turned out to be a real problem in the eating department. We have a great supply of venison (deer meat). Space Farms picks up road kill deer from four counties. Some of the spoiled meat or chewed-on-by-wild-creatures meat goes to the landfill, but the fresh kills come to us, and we are able to utilize that completely natural food source for our big cats. So we have lots of venison. It is the basis of all our omnivore and carnivore diets. Our animals do very well on venison. But Lola would not touch it. I let her get hungry for a day and she still would not touch it. I broke down and gave her some chicken legs out of my freezer. She loved those. The next day I chunky cut chicken and venison and mixed the two together, as per Dr. Schott's suggestion. Lola carefully selected and ate the chicken, but did not touch the venison. I minced the chicken finer and used it as a coating on venison. Lola was not outsmarted, she licked the chicken coating off of the venison.

We hung pieces of venison meat on stings, jiggling it like a toy, figuring she would play with it and then realize it tasted good. No go. Dad and I tied fresh deer skin strips in knots for toys. Lola would not touch them. We were scratching our heads.

In the meanwhile we all played with Lola whenever we had a spare moment. We were always conscious that she was a leopard, so we were somewhat wary, you cannot trust a leopard. The family and zookeepers would give her a friendly cheek scratch or rub through the wire as they came through the office. Lola now shared the office with Dad, and Parker. I caught Parker talking to her one day, letting down his macho guard when no one was around. Lola was warming up to us and we her. Visitors could see Lola through the office window. Lola had lots to look at and friends to see. Lola was very aware, always glancing up with those unusual color yellow eyes when anyone came by the windows.

Dad would regularly let Lola out to roam the office. Karen Talasco, my friend and the zoo's photographer, and her beau Brett came up to see our new 'baby'. Karen, Brett, Dad and I were all in the office playing with and holding Lola. Karen took pictures and got a good photo of Dad and Lola. Lola had had many flash pictures taken of her over the weeks she was with us and in her previous showgirl life. Lola jumped down off Dad's lap, trotted around the office, walked back to Dad and without provocation, bit Dad hard in his hand. Dad hollered, and Lola scooted under a desk.

"Damn Cat!," Dad said while his hand was bleeding all over the place. Dad is on blood thinners so he was really pouring out blood. I carefully caught up Lola and put her back in her office cage.

"That's it. Leopards cannot be trusted. She is a cage cat now," Dad decreed. I had to agree. It is well known that leopards cannot be trusted. We all knew that. I knew her time was near up a month before at the vets'. Lola's time with us as a handle-able cat was always limited, and her time had just ran out. *Note to all: Do not bite the boss!*

The weather warmed up and we let Lola into the big, adult leopard enclosure in the zoo. Green grass covers the sixty by forty foot enclosure. Vertical posts support the roof. A horizontal lounging log is five foot off the ground. Our previous leopard had 'aged out', so the expanse of fresh spring grass and the climbing logs were all Lola's. The average person would think that Lola would take off and totally enjoy running and jumping in her new large enclosure. Not true. Lola was scared of unknown territory. It took her a few hours to explore every corner, cowering under the shadow of birds flying overhead, other zoo noises and interesting sights. She had never touched grass or heard birds chirp, let alone been next door neighbors with Kodiak bears and a jaguar. So many new sights, sounds and smells can be overwhelming. She ate chicken that day. I gave her a favorite stuffed animal toy to keep her company during the scary first night.

Next morning, the first thing I did was drive out to see Lola. She was fine, enjoying her new freedom in the large enclosure, climbing and jumping, then rubbing on the fencing for me to pet her. Ok, so all that went well. But she was still eating only chicken.

I raise chickens every year for snake food. We have a lot of roosters. I caught, killed and semi plucked a rooster. I left the intestines intact, and fed it body temperature, still warm. Lola would not touch it. She was one high falutin' cat. Eating just naked store bought chicken legs with thighs attached is not a complete diet for a leopard. Most folks would think so. But no. Leopards need the whole animal. They need the hair/feathers for fiber and calcium, bones for calcium, meat/muscle for protein. In the wild they also eat intestines and organ meats for the nutrients. So she needed more than just chicken legs and thighs. We had so much venison product. We were all scratching our heads as to what to do. In the meanwhile, Parker had purchased a supply of chicken, and we always added the sprinkle on additional vitamins.

One late afternoon, Hunter came to me with a fallow deer fawn with a broken leg. It was a tiny newborn, not much bigger than a football. We have a huge herd of the white, black and spotted fallow deer, so we have a lot of babies every year. The most humane thing to do is to put the fawn down. Under normal circumstances we would have. But I had a finicky leopard that we needed to eat the more wholesome venison diet we feed to all our cats.

It came to me in a flash, one of those light bulb, ah ha moments, *but not exactly the kind that Oprah would brag about.* I would try to use one instinct to kick start another instinct. A leopard kill is fast and humane. Done in a second. Nature's way.

Let it be enough to say that it worked. By using the catch and kill instinct of the leopard, that instinct kicked in the eating instinct. I won't go into the graphic details here, professionals can contact me for the information if needed. I only needed to do that once, which was good since we don't often have fawns with broken legs. Lola eats venison now.

I am writing this three years later and Lola is happy, with a neutered, (also melanistic) male leopard friend. They both enjoy venison for their evening meal. The leopards get turkeys at Thanksgiving, and Christmas, and occasionally veal, beef or goose for a change of pace. Lola eats it all now. Happy and protected, they are carefree leopards, with a medical plan. The pair of jet black leopards look like shadows lounging on their suspended raised logs until they open those huge olive yellow eyes with vertical pupils to stare you down…

Chapter 34 Diego and Chiquita Coati

I had been in touch with Claws and Paws though a friend of mine, Sarah Decker Bachmann. Sarah had shadowed me the previous summer at the zoo. She is really into animals and was thinking about being a Vet. Tech. A dishwater blonde, country gal, (like me), Sarah was an enthusiastic and quick learner. I enjoyed her company. Sarah is the granddaughter of Carol Decker, an internationally famous artist that has been a friend of our family since Mom gave Carol a start selling her artwork in the Space Farms Gift shop in the early 70's. During a summer off of college, Sarah interned at Claws and Paws. Sarah and I kept in touch, and she let me know that Claws and Paws had a litter of Coatimundi born. *Yes, that is networking, old school style.* Vince Hall was the owner. I talked to Vince and told him I wanted the coati at 4 weeks old. Eyes barely open and small enough to still take a bottle and bond with a human.

Kiwi, our previous coatimundi, had aged out, (zoo language for dying of old age). We wanted some more for the zoo, since they are such a unique looking animal. Mountain Coatimundi, or Coati, are members of the Procyonidae family of animals. Other members of the Procyonidae family include the raccoon, kinkajou and the panda. The coati are also called a hog nosed raccoon, snookem bears and Brazilian aardvarks! Their bodies are laterally compressed, or less chubby around than a raccoon. Coati look like a raccoon with an anteater nose. The coati have long snouts that can rotate 60 degrees in any direction, which helps them ferret out insects. Omnivores, the coati diet consists of fruits, vegetables, insects, birds, eggs, and small rodents.

The coloration is a tad more reddish than your typical silver-gray colored raccoon. Their base coloration of the coati coat is a reddish brown with flecks of gold, the tummy is a soft beige and the face has distinctive markings. The tail is striped with beige, and brown, similar to the raccoon, though less fluffy. While traveling in bands of up to twenty five females and young, the tail is held erect and used for signaling other members of the group. Curved at the tip, the tail is not prehensile.

Females deliver their young after an eleven week gestation in July in the wild. Babies are born with sealed eyes and fuzz. At eight weeks, the youngsters are great tree climbers along with their mothers. Their specially adapted feet can rotate beyond 180 degrees at the ankle enabling the agile coatimundi to ascend or descend a tree head first or tail first. They have curved claws and soft leathery foot pads or bottoms, in a smooth chocolate brown color.

In captivity, the coati life span is up to fifteen years. In their wild habitat of South America they live only seven to eight years. There are four separate species of Coatimundi: South American Coati, White Nose Coati, Neilson Coati and the Mountain Coati (also called the Andean Coati). The individual species are differentiated by color markings, size, build and overall body color, developed within geographical niches.

In areas of South America, the coati are kept like tamed outside cats around the homes to help keep down insects and small rodents. Fed table scraps, like an American cat, they are reported to be hard to get rid of.

Claws and Paws is located in eastern Pennsylvania on Route 590 east of Hamlin, It was started by Vince Hall back in the 70's. Vince and my Dad go way back. In the early days, Vince received some animals from us when he was just starting out. Dad and Vince had become friends, visiting each other in the off season. I love it when Vince comes to visit us, I like to sit and listen to all the animal stories Dad and Vince trade. I'm usually in charge of making the lunch when we have guests, amongst my other zoo duties. I learn a lot just listening to Dad's many zoo colleagues, though many of Dad's generation are ageing out also. These men are entrepreneurs having started their private zoos long before the state and federal regulations would of prevented and or restricted it, as they do today. Vince is about fifteen years younger than Dad. Like most men who work outdoors, Vince wears a signature hat, a black Stetson to shade his silver(the color of experience), hair. Cowboy hats work wonderfully for those of us outside all day, offering more shade than the standard baseball cap. Smaller of statue than our family (*but then again I think everybody is!)* Vince has always treated me with kindness and has been a great source of information both on animals and the zoological political world. In short; he knows his stuff.

I set up the pick up date for the two coati to be on a Wednesday. Jennie Beckman, a vet tech for our Vet., Dr. Ted Spinks, had been volunteering at our zoo on her days off from the Animal Hospital. Jennie and I had become friends aside from our professional relationship. Jennie had Wednesdays off and wanted to go along to pick up our two new babies. My nephew Hunter, 15, had been working with us full time in the zoo all summers since he could walk. He wanted to come too. And our daughter, Jackie, 21, had graduated college and was home looking for a professional job. She wanted to come too. *Woooo Whoo a Road trip!! Does not happen often!* I could not fit any more people in my car. Good thing the two coatis would be small!

We set off on our three hour road trip. We stopped for lunch, the 'kids' chatting all the way. This is the road trip where I uttered "Jack, you are not the center of my universe." I meant to say, "you are no longer the center of my universe." Slightly different connotation. I am still living that one down. *Lets face it, when the kid gets to the point of having their own life, you have to refocus your maternal instincts. Empty nest syndrome can be depressing. And me? I focused my attention on the zoo. It would always need me.*

We arrived at Claws and Paws, the "Zoo in the Woods" after 1 pm. We brought our pet taxi for the babies. Vince met us in the main hall. It was great to see him, I had not had much contact with him since I was a young adult. We chatted, and he gave the four of us the grand tour of his zoo. What fun! I loved his African lion exhibit that included a huge glass window. The lion was on the other side of the glass, visitors were THAT close! One detriment to the moat system used by the 'big' zoos is that the animal is so far away it is hard to appreciate the dangerous size and superior strength. Space Farms Zoo has guard fencing six feet from all enclosures. At Claws and Paws, you can get 1 inch away, through the plexi-glass. *I would not want to be the person that has to wash the inside of that window!*

Hunter loved the meerkats exhibit with a buffalo skull in it. I loved the walk-in tortoise and lorry exhibits. I still don't see how he can get away without folks getting bit by the huge tortoises or birds. The four of us on tour were complimenting Vince on certain exhibits, reminding him that imitation is the highest form of flattery! Claws and Paws has a lot of murals, and hand painted artwork to accessorize their exhibits also. My artistic eye caught every one of them. Often when zookeepers go to other zoos we look at more than just the animals- we are looking at exhibits, the structure, design, and plausibility of adapting ideas to our own zoos.

Hunter really loved Twiga, the giraffe. I think everybody does. Giraffes are just so cool. Vince and I discussed the cost of housing a giraffe in winter in snow country. *Maybeeeeee not for us.* At one point Twiga decided she really liked Hunter also. Twiga sloped his head down and gave Hunter a big slurrrrrpy, gooey lick on the cheek. *Ok definitely not for me.* Jackie, Jennie and I had a great knee slapping laugh over that kiss. Hunter's first kiss! Yeah that still makes me smile too.

Claws and Paws location is in the forest, hence his own slogan: "the zoo in the woods". Vince's enclosures have lots of trees inside, and his paths meander through the forest. There is lots of greenery. Our zoo topography is rolling hills, with lots of green grass lawns to mow. Hunter, who has had to sit his share of lawnmower time, remarked at the lack of lawn mower time needed in the woods. Yep, that's true. Claws and Paws had nice enclosures, different from what I remembered going there as a kid with Dad. I marveled at the number of zookeepers Vince had. *Wow, we make due with four.* We finished up our tour and I meandered through the gift shop taking note again of products that we might want to sell in ours.

Vince had called his son Chris to get the coati babies, one male, one female. The little sprouts were about the size of my fist. They looked all legs, tail and nose. Cute, but I could read the apprehension in their eyes. Vince had told me they were handled on a regular basis, so they did not look terrified or afraid. But the little coatis obviously did not know us.

I let Jennie, Jack and Hunter check out the babies while I discussed formula, food and finances with Vince. We said our goodbyes and started for home. The little coatis rode well, not making a peep in the back of the SUV all the way home. Jennie, Jack and Hunter were another story, gabbing up a storm, not a silent moment in the three hour trip. The kids did come up with great names for the coati: Diego and Chiquita.

Upon our arrival at the zoo, I greeted Dad, while the 'kids' dispersed to their jobs. Jackie came home with me to help set up my famous cardboard box with a heating pad brooding box in Jackie's downstairs bathroom. *Good thing she doesn't mind sharing a bathroom with critters. Or maybe I never even asked her, now that I think about it. It was just the way Jackie was raised. What? There are no lions, tigers, otters, raccoons, fawns, skunks or coati in your bathroom?* The downstairs bathroom was a perfect nursery, the warmest room in the house. The tile floor- (*read that easy to clean*), electrical outlet, and enough space on the floor for a decent sized cardboard box is perfect. Coatis safely settled in the loo, I returned to the zoo for my five o'clock feedings. I would be back to the zoo one more time that night, at dusk for the last night feedings.

The coatis were adorable. Pixie faces with wiggly noses, their facial markings are artistically designed by nature. Contrasting dark and light fur on their tails, just soooo cute. At this age they were about the size of my fist, add a striped skinny tail. The little ones were 4 ½ weeks old, old enough to eat moist dog food. I soaked dog food in Esbilac. They ate it but made a horrible mess while doing so. Noses pushed the soaked dog food around the dish, pushing it out, while slurping up the milk. I kept trying them on a bottle, but they did not take it for almost five days. It took them that long to learn that I meant no harm, and to learn the rubber nipple had milk in it. Once they caught on, their was no stopping them. They took the bottle until well, a year old. First as nutrition, then as a positive reward system.

They were both wonderfully tame pets. I could see how the South Americans would tame them as outside house pets. The coati personality could be described as perky, inquisitive, and constantly on the move. A raccoon with ADD. But smelly. Stinky doggy poo in the house in a litter box just does not work for me. But they were to be zoo animals anyway so I did not keep them in the house long. Their inquisitive noses and ½ inch sharp claws were into every crevice in my house. Whenever possible the noses were in our ears, looking for bugs. If we did not pick them up and the coati wanted up they simply scaled our legs with their excellent climbing claws. *Yeeee-owch! And once while I was still in my nightie! A coati climbing up your naked leg is laughable, now.* Coati are natural climbers and jumpers, so were all over the house every night I brought them home. One night I was taking a bath, and Diego jumped in. *Double YEEEE-ouch!* The pair were limited to our bathroom at night.

By the time they were eight weeks old. they stayed in the zoo nursery full time. Every member of the family enjoyed playing with them. Niece Lindsey, 14, was a big help with the coati in the daytime when they were in the zoos office nursery or the outside nursery. She would fill in if I could not be there for a feeding. Her sister Kelsey played with them also.

At eight weeks old the coati took their turn going to the Animal Hospital of Sussex County. On the trip that day also were a pair of serval kittens (see the next chapter). They were all exotic, unique animals not commonly seen in any zoo so I called the newspaper to ask if they wanted to join us for a photo shoot. Dr. Pamela Schott, V.M.D. and Dr. Leslie Parisi handled the visit. What fun we all had. Chiquita did not want to leave my arms, so all her procedures took place on me. I was ok with that. Dr. Schott mentioned how bonded Chiquita and I were. *Yeah, I know. My heart has a warm smile just thinking of Chiquita as I write this, her wiggly nose, smelly BO and all.* The coati and servals made the cover of the newspaper, New Jersey Herald's local section! *Got to admit, they were sooo cute.*

Both coati and the servals (next chapter) accompanied me to "The Pet Stop" on Channel 12. The trip in the car with Dr. Spinks, V.M.D., was noisy. The coatis wanted my constant attention. After the taping of the show, we always stop for lunch at Harolds, a restaurant chain that has the most amazing corned beef sandwiches. Located under a hotel, the hotel staff is always willing to baby sit our exotic animals in an office for an hour or so, while Dr. Spinks and I are eating. Cannot leave animals in the hot car in August, that is for sure. Even though they come from warm climates, the animals would cook in a hot car. You would not believe the inquisitive looks the hotel staff give us and our animals. Well... maybe you would.

Chiquita and Diego stayed in the nursery all summer. Being warm weather animals, the coati were housed in a barn across the street for the winter. Diego and Chiquita were moved to the zoo proper the next spring. They were thriving on the ground venison- dog food mixture, supplemented by the corn and shortbread cookies thrown by visitors. Being human hand raised, Chiquita and Diego responded to our human visitors. They loved to climb the branches in their enclosure. Our nephew Hunter would often go in to play with them, maybe more so than I. I really didn't want their noses in my hair and ears.

All seemed fine. Both animals were happy, making the many chip, chirps and squeaky noises the coati are known for. Two years later, Doug reported to me that he found Chiquita dead on the enclosure grass. *Damn!* I was upset, but knew there was nothing we could do at that point. We work close to death every day. Animals get sick, and die just like we humans do, only they cannot tell us with words when they are not feeling well. We can watch and observe. When Chiquita seemed less chipper one day I figured she was pregnant, it was that time of year. And she was old enough. Dad performed the necropsy, Chiquita's gall bladder was the size of his pinky finger when it should be the size of a pea. It had ruptured. Nothing we could have known or done. Knowing that makes her death a little easier. But not much.

Diego is doing great, and last year Vince brought us another coati female, Hunter named her Selena . Selena is full grown and friendly, but was not hand raised. She is a good companion for Diego, who is definitely more happy with Selena around. Offspring? Selena came to us past the spring breeding season last year. Maybe next year? Maybe not. We can hope. Hope gives us all a reason to wake up and go to work in the morning. *You too? I wish you hope.*

Chapter 35 Savannah and Bush Servals

Dad informed me one day that Parker had spoken to Karl Mogensen from the Natural Bridge Zoo in Virginia. He and his wife Debbie had a pair of Serval kittens she had hand reared. The kittens were for sale. Were we interested? Parker said yes. The kittens would come in a few days when the Mogensens came north on an animal delivery route. Often animal delivery routes are the only way we zoo people get away, not really a vacation, but a break in our routines. Enjoyable, we get to gab with our own 'kind'.

"Got Milk?' Dad grinned, making a silly reference to the famous commercial.

"Always!" my simple reply, as I smiled back. "How big will they be?" I'd not worked with this specie before.

"Smaller than a house cat," Dad laughed. "They are about ten weeks old so they will be slightly smaller than a house cat but with really long legs". Dad is a walking encyclopedia on animals. It is amazing sometimes.

"Yeah, thanks Pop," I responded. "I can set up the dog corral in the office nursery."

"That 'll do for a short time" Dad dropped his head to read papers on his desk, I knew he was done speaking on the subject. I was off to do the rest of the day's morning chores, feeding fawns, and coati, cleaning the barnyard, feeding the calf, answering visitor questions, that kind of stuff. Later that afternoon I set up the transportable dog corral in the nursery office. The dog corral is traditionally used in dog shows, a foldable cage with no top or bottom. Think of a play pen for animals. Each section is 40 inches by 40 inches tall and ingeniously folds upon its self. Set up, the eight sections make a decent sized cage. I put a shower curtain under an old blanket for warm flooring. I added a stiff cardboard box on its side with a fuzzy blue towel for a cozy den and then added a litter box. The door to the corral was easily accessible to change litter box, food and water. I checked my supply of Zoologic 42/25, the feline milk substitute and had plenty on hand. It was August, the kittens would stay inside for a couple of days to a week so we could monitor their adaptation progress. Besides there were alligators in the center nursery enclosure. I would have to move them soon. They could go out with our big gator now that the small gators had grown big enough. (see Chapter 39, GI Gator The Zookeeper's Daughter).

I was set up. Now all I had to do was wait. Most expectant moms have nine months to anticipate and prepare. Luckily this time I had a few days. Often with some species, I have the infant in my arms before I even have a blanket from the nursery shelf!

The scientific name of the Serval is Leptailrus serval. The origin of the name is interesting, Serval is Portuguese for 'wolf deer'. Interesting because servals are African.

Who am I to judge names? My given name is Lorelee, my parents wanted a southern belle for their plantation. They got me, Lori, a somewhat tom-boy nature lover. Like I said, who am I to judge a name!

The servals have the same feline ancestor as the lion. Many different species of cats were worshiped by the Egyptians. The cats were believed to be gods or emissaries of gods. The Serval was one of the species depicted in Egyptian hieroglyphics. You can tell by the distinctive large cone shaped ears! Egyptians first domesticated cats four thousand years ago. The wild cats of Africa were first used to rid their houses and graineries (large buildings used to store grain, such as wheat) of vermin (rats and mice).

Servals have remarkably small heads in comparison to their body size with huge ears. Those large conical ears can hear the noises mice make at levels the human ear cannot. When hunting, servals will stop and close their eyes to listen for prey. The small heads, tawny beige coloration with black spots, help them track prey while camouflaged. The longish tails are striped more than spotted. Melaninistic (black with black spots) colorations occur in the wild, while white mutations have only been seen in captivity.

Servals are 33 to 44 inches long , not including tail. A tall cat, they are up to 26 inches at the shoulder. Females range up to 35 pounds while the heftier males reach up to 55 pounds. Noted for their long legs, they are often called a dwarf cheetah. They have been clocked running up to 50 miles per hour. The long legs are also used for jumping. Servals can jump 16 feet straight up from a standing position. (*Got to admit I did not read that information before I set up the dog corral)* In a long jump they can leap horizontally 20 feet to land on their prey stunning it prior to the kill. The serval can catch birds on the fly. In the wild the serval has often been seen tossing birds in the air. The serval 'plucks' the feathers by tossing the dead bird into the air repeatedly. A quick twist of the servals neck as the bird is re-caught, uses the advantage of gravity in the plucking process.

Maybe our housecats 'playing' with captured killed mice and birds is instinctual, no longer needed in domesticated house cats' process for preparing dinner. Ah hah moment there! Ok back to the kill...

Servals have a 50% kill ratio compared to a 10% kill ratio in the larger cats. Now that is darn good. Birds, small rodents, snakes and young hoofstock all make up the serval's diet.

Servals are sexually mature at three years old and gestation is two and a half months, The average litter is two to three kittens. The young stay with mom for about a year. The spots on the back of the ears signal the young through tall grass while mom is hunting. The kittens catch and kill their own prey by six months old.

In captivity the serval will live up to 25 years in captivity, half that in the wild.

Excellent communicators, the servals have many sounds. They purr, chip, hiss, cackle, growl, meow and grunt. Noises I would soon learn, enjoy and emulate.

Karl and Debbie Mogensen arrived at the zoo a couple of days later just before lunch. I greeted them at the car. Debbie had a pigmy marmoset in her lap, feeding it with a syringe. The tiny creature was so small, brown fuzz with big orange colored eyes. *(Oh I got to get me one of them!)*

Karl jumped out of the car and gave me a huge bear hug, appropriate for the bear sized man that he is. He is tall, and like most zoo folks, strong with silver tipping his short cut hair. I had spoken to Karl on several opportunities when we were getting a new specie with which we had little experience with. He was also helpful while we were constructing our bird/parrot aviary. He has the neatest birds at his zoo! Other big stock also, but a lot of fancy cranes, parrots, and warmer weather exotic birds. *Someday... when we have warm winter quarters for them all...a girl can dream!*

Debbie is much younger than Karl, their love story an endearing, interesting one, but not mine to tell. Debbie is one of the few other multi-specie pediatric specialists, like myself, that I know. I know of three of us east of the Mississippi. I wish I had more time and we were closer in geography, I know we'd be great friends. Younger than Karl, blonde, pretty and petite, in jeans and a t-shirt, Deb had a pigmy marmoset as an accessory. Debbie was feeding the tiniest marmoset with a syringe on her lap and then Debbie put the marmoset back in it's traveling box.

"You should of seen these guys last night," Karl sweetly said about the servals. "Deb and I were on the motel bed and the kittens jumped right up and curled up with us when they were ready to settle down." All zoo people, no matter how big, old, tough or long in the business, have a soft spot for baby animals. *Really now, who wouldn't?*

Karl handed me a crate with the two young servals in it. We all walked into the restaurant where Dad was waiting. I set them all up with coffee and took the servals to the office nursery. Debbie followed along, giving me the details of the servals' care.

"Don't think they are going to stay in that long, [pointing to the dog corral cage]," Debbie said. "They'll be out of that quick." Not having raised servals before, I thought she was referring to their growth rate in a couple of weeks.

The spotted kittens were about twelve inches long nose to base of tail, and boy oh boy, were their legs so out of proportion to the tiny bodies. The ears gave the serval kittens a clownish look. We watched for a minute while both kittens explored the carpet, cardboard box, litter box and toys for all the new smells they could find.

"Yeah, I'm going to move the alligators and then the servals will go in the zoo nursery." I calmly stated. We let the kittens get settled in and left to join the group for coffee, in the restaurant. Parker walked by and said hi to all, returned from the office after he wrote out the check, then was off to his busy schedule. It's always fun to gab with other zoo folk.

Karl and Debbie stayed a short while and then left for the rest of their road trip. With animals in the car, you don't stay anywhere long. I went back to the office nursery to check on our new arrivals. Well... Debbie was right.

Guess I should explain about the office nursery. When I was young, the large room was called the Fur Shop. It is a large room where the mink coats that my grandmother Elinor had designed in NYC were brought to the farm to be sold at our Fur Shop. When we went out of the mink fur business, the room became a stock room for souvenirs and all sorts of junk that we cannot throw away. The office nursery is a section of that larger stock room. I took the curtains off the windows and used them as a divider about ten feet from the windows to make a long rectangular nursery section. This area is reserved for animal infants that need to be inside for one of four reasons: temperature, sun or out of sun, intensity of care, or adjustment period for new arrival infants. Newton Hospital donated an infant warmer when they remodeled their maternity wing. I picked up a baby changing table from alongside the road. A friend donated a baby scale. I created the nursery so visitors could see the animals through the windows but could not touch or breathe on the infants (*germs ya know!*). It is not a separate room. The nursery is part of this large stock room only separated off by that curtain. Back to my story:

Well... Debbie was right. I opened the door to the office nursery to be greeted by two little servals. At first coming towards me, then scooting away. *Ut OH!!* Debbie was right! The little servals did not stay in the dog corral long, maybe a half hour! I really thought Debbie meant they would grow quickly and need more surface area. I had not thought in the vertical! The serval kittens had simply jumped on the cardboard box and out over the top of the 40 inch tall fencing.

"Here kitty kitty.." I called the kitties and they came to me. *(Oh yeah, now how would you call them? Cliché I know! But it worked)*. I gathered the small cats up and put them in a pet taxi, while I went to the barn across the street to get the top of the cage I had used with Lola. They would stay inside for a week. I needed the kittens to bond with me and to observe their behavior and make sure they were eating ok. I would try them on a bottle later, Debbie said they still took a bottle but were eating solid food. One by one inch, dark green plastic coated wire top in place, I then went about my day. The servals did eat their canned cat food very well. I would keep them on canned cat food for a short time and gradually switch them to a new venison diet. When an animals environment and habitat has changed, you do not want to further stress out that animal with a drastic change in diet at the same time. So it was a week before I introduced the ground venison mix we feed the smaller cats.

The servals came home with me every night for those two weeks. They had the freedom of the house while I was awake, staying in the downstairs bathroom while I slept. They were warm and affectionate, like house cat kittens. Bush and Savannah explored the house, enjoying jumping from (what I thought)were impossibly high places. I had thoughts of bringing them home every night forever but decided against it. While the litter box in the bathroom was used, it was only used if the kittens were in that room. After a couple of weeks of cleaning up cat poop in my house, I realized why these cats are not domesticated.

Two weeks after their arrivals, I moved the serval kittens to the outside zoo nursery. The weather was great in August. The kittens needed more room to run and jump, since they were growing quickly. I had named the kittens Bush and Savannah, African habitat names. Bush and Savannah totally enjoyed the larger grass lined enclosure . The center of the enclosure had a platform to climb on and provide shade under. Next to the platform is a tree trunk from ground to ceiling, about six feet tall. The kittens used this as a scratching pole. They were happy. The servals would spend the rest of the summer, and fall, in the nursery. Come winter they would be moved to the warm winter animal room.

About the third day in the outside nursery, I came in first thing in the morning to do my pre-opening chores. I called out to the kittens before I reached the nursery perimeter fence. I saw a flash out of the corner of my eye, then saw Bush greeting me by my feet at the gate! *OH no, an escape! Ok so where is Savannah? God I hope she didn't take off for the hills!*

I scooped up Bush in my arms, then walked the twenty feet to the center enclosure. I called to Savannah, and she came running out of the blue igloo dog house in the enclosure. *Whew!* I scooped her up also and headed for the office. Dad was at his desk, as I walked by. I explained the great escape to Dad, and told him I was putting the small cats in a pet taxi until we could figure out how they escaped.

"OK, I'll join ya," Dad volunteered.

Kittens safely ensconced in the office, Dad and I checked out the possible escape routes. The enclosure is built out of livestock paneling, two inch by four inch sections. We scanned the ground for signs of a dig out, none. The door was securely closed when I came in. So that was not it. Dad's more experienced eyes caught what I did not see.

"Look for bits of hair on the wire," Dad stated. Dads days of tracking and trapping gave him far more knowledge in the field than I have. "Here it is!" Dad pointed. And there it was- a tiny tuft of beige colored hair on a corner piece of the two by four   flimsy livestock wire stretched across the top of the enclosure. The wire had been cut to accommodate the center tree trunk. Obviously the young serval kitten had climbed the trunk, which was the purpose of the trunk, and shimmied out, pushing the wire aside. The mystery of the great escape was solved and repaired.

Both the servals and the two coatis accompanied me on the speaking circuit that summer. The unusual looks of the two species captivated the audiences. The coatis would seek out bugs in my hair and ears as I spoke about them. The servals would turn their heads with the huge clownish ears to capture the noises of the children's squeals and giggles.

The little servals grew, and as they grew, needed me less. As winter approached, I knew they would need an enclosure in the warm winter animal room. Years before, in '98, Doug, Dad and I had built a section for the tiger cubs, Tara and Khyber in the winter quarters barn. That room had not been used, and had accumulated an amazing amount of , oh lets just call it junk. This is stuff that is too good to throw away, but you don't know what you're gonna do with it. I took on the job and cleaned the room. Got to admit, I looked like an alien, with face mask, head phones and my worst garb. That winter the kittens spent the cold days in the modified enclosure built for them in the old tiger cub room. Safe and warm and out of the storm, they did well.

The next spring they joined the other older female serval we had in the adult zoo. After they graduated from the nursery to the adult zoo, I had less time to interact with Bush and Savannah. They do remember me, but have reverted to a wild state, no longer wanting to cuddle with their old zoo momma. It's ok. It is natures way.

The serval kittens loved the sink in our bathroom.

Photo by Lori Space Day

Chapter 36 Escaped!

"Escaped!" The one word that will stop a zookeeper in his tracks at the bat of an eyelash, is "Escaped!". You never want to hear that word while visiting a zoo, even less if you are a zookeeper.

In order to move the recently arrived young serval cats into the nursery center enclosure, I first had to move the small alligators I had raised. Two had been confiscated by the New Jersey Division of Fish and Wildlife and brought to us. Folks just don't seem to check with state laws before buying an exotic pet. It is illegal for Joe Q. Public to have an alligator in the state of New Jersey. When the state finds out, they send a conservation officer to confiscate the animal. The state then has to find a home for the animal. And that is how I got two youngish gators, which were about two feet long when I received them. Gators grow fast - about a foot a year if fed well. I agreed to take them in because I already had young gators brought to me by the parents of U.S. Servicemen. After I took in G.I. Gator, (See the Zookeeper's Daughter Chapter 93), the word spread through the barracks in Colorado that I would take in their mascots when the guys shipped out. I felt it was my duty to the servicemen. They were, after all, fighting for our nation. Grand total after two years, I had three youngish gators, with the largest about three and a half feet long, and G.I. Gator, our big boy who came to us in 2002, maybe eight feet long (he doesn't stand still for measuring).

The young gators were kept in the center nursery enclosure. I had a small blue kiddy pool for them, which I replaced after a year with a larger green fiberglass pool as the gators grew. The alligators were a big hit at nursery feeding time. I do have a quirky sense of humor, for those of you who do not know me personally. I noticed early in their rearing the alligators had started to respond to my voice. I decided (*with a touch of my grandfather Ralph and father Fred's showmanship genes),*to train them to come to my voice for food. The phase I used consistently was "Come to Momma, baby!" Right out of Lake Placid movie, where Betty White was feeding the giant gator. *Hysterical right?* So after a year of saying "Come to Momma, Baby" every time I fed the small gators, they were pretty well trained and very responsive. At nursery feeding times, usually 2 p.m. every day, I would ask for volunteers to help bottle feed the floppy eared kid goats and fuzzy Mouflon lambs I always seem to have in the nursery. Little kids can do that job. I would also scope out the gathered crowd of visitors for young teen age boys. You know that age group, with the 'I am too cool to care' attitude. I would ask them to help me feed the young gators. The teenagers loved it. I would hold their one hand in mine. Their predominate hand held a two foot tong grasping a venison chunk. That hand would also have my hand on their hand. I had a strangle hold on both the kid's hands, just for safety sake. I would explain to the crowd how I had trained them to the special words, "Come to Momma, Baby".

Disclaimer: for those who might get concerned here, the kids were never closer than two feet length of the grilling tongs and a fence was between the gators and the children. With my hands guiding the process, everyone was safe.

It was a hoot to see the young teens get so excited feeding the little gators. The crowd would roar with laughter as the boys said, "Come to Momma, Baby!" The gators would come running right over to the side of the enclosure to eat. The gators would grab their chunk of meat through the fencing rather aggressively. Gators flip the meat to the back of their throat and gulp the meat down in one chunk. Gators don't chew. The crowd would laugh and ohhhh and ahhhh *Ok, so maybe you had to be there.*

The big gator enclosure for G.I. Gator was made out of two by four livestock paneling and was located in a half land, half water position in the two acre water fowl pond. We needed to make sure the little gators could not get through the paneling. I tried to shove the gators through an experimental piece of two by four livestock paneling and could not get them through. Gators can be tricky, flattening themselves to exit or enter small crevices. *(Yeah, so how would you check if they could escape through that size fencing?)* They could not escape. *Ok fine,* They can graduate to the big enclosure with G.I. Gator. I packed them into a couple of pet taxis and hauled them over to G.I. Gators enclosure. I unlocked the enclosure and placed the taxis inside and opened the doors. The gators would eventually walk out. They joined the big eight foot G.I. Gator swimming in the water section. I let the guys know at lunch that the little gators had graduated to the big zoo, so the zookeepers would feed more in the big gator pen that afternoon. All went well. I moved the servals outside that afternoon after spiffing up the enclosure for cats instead of gators.

A month or so passed. Everyone was adjusting well to their new enclosures. One afternoon in September, Alice called me to the admission desk.

"A lady just told me she saw a baby alligator by the pond," Alice was excited. The electricity from her eyes seemed to shoot out her snow white hair.

" Yeah, the little gators are in the pond now, with G.I. Gator," I explained. "I thought I told you I had moved them. It is not a new hatch."

"No. You didn't," Alice replied. "You better check, the lady said it was IN the pond." Our conversation ensued as to where in the pond.

"Yes the Gator pen is IN the pond."

When Alice gets excited it is hard to understand her sometimes. Ok, never mind, it is easier to just go check. I walked out the zoo doors and the two hundred feet up the dirt path to the alligator enclosure. I saw G.I. *(he was easy to spot - he was eight foot long),* and two little gator noses poking out of the water. The other one must be under water. *Alice, she can make ya crazy.* I brushed it off as a miscommunication. Yes the gators are IN the pond IN the enclosure.

A couple of days passed and I was walking in the zoo. A gentleman came up to me and said,

"Hey, ya know ya have a little alligator escaped in the pond?" he half whispered.

Escape! The one word that makes any zookeeper in the world stop and pay attention. NOW!

Zoo Momma

"Where did you see him?" I asked as we walked towards the two acre pond.

"There he is, swimming by the island!" the visitor responded. I looked, and by golly there he was. I saw him gliding under the water. His nostrils and eye bumps barely visible above the brownish green water line.

"Damn!" I sated. "Whoops, sorry!" I replied over my shoulder. I turned on my heel and sought out my Dad. It was early September, the nights were chilly, the water warm. I knew the gator would not leave the safety of the warm water and wander off. I also knew he would stay by his food source: fish, frogs, ducks and other waterfowl. The zoo visitors were in zero danger, the zoo fencing around the pond preventing further escape. But that algae filled pond was growing in size... It was awful big to catch a four foot gator out of. And I didn't want to swim in it, too much goose poop for me. *A girl has to draw the line somewhere!*

After explaining to Dad what had happened, he and I decided to wait until the cooler nights prevailed and the gator came to the shallow, warmer sections of the pond. I/we would be able to scoop the little gator out of the water just like I did when G.I. Gator was small. It appeared to be my smallest gator, he must of slipped out through the 2 by 4 fencing. The reports of little gator sightings continued for the next few weeks. Each time I had to explain we had to wait for the water temperature to drop below the sunny afternoon air temperatures.

In October, Dad and Doug were fixing the yellow and red tire swing set by the pond. I decided I would go out and weed the pond islands picker bushes. There is an official name for the small reddish colored bushes I planted there, but for the life of me I cannot remember it. They were the only bushes the landscape professionals said our visiting Canada geese would not eat. However, scrawny tall bright fluorescent green weeds grow up through the bushes, which is very unsightly. I loaded up the fourteen foot jon boat with heavy gloves and brush nippers. Rowing out to the island was not a problem, but dismounting the boat onto the island, well, now that was a bit of a challenge. I am not as limber as I was in my youth. I left my cell phone on shore just incase I ended up in the greenish drink. I did manage however to scale the one foot height difference from the water level to the rock ledge on the island without incident.

Columbus Days weather was warm, t-shirt weather. I was happily weeding the prickly bushes with heavy welding gloves protecting my arms from the elbow to finger tips. It was a beautiful day, I was singing, not so loud as folks fifty feet away on shore could hear, but merrily I weeded along. Doug and Dad were still on shore fixing the swing set when Dad called out:

"Oh Lori, you have company!"

I looked around, on shore was only Dad, smiling and Doug. There was no one on shore by the nursery area where I had pushed the boat off.

"Yeah? Who?" I shouted, still looking. *Guess a friend stopped by for an impromptu visit.*

"In the water," Dad was laughing. I looked around the island. And there they were!! All three small alligators were circling the island.

161

"Holy S#!T, I see 'em Pop!" I was amazed they still remembered me after a couple of months passed. Alligators' brains are very small, the size of a walnut, so they do not have emotions or higher thinking, just instinct. They must of heard my singing. And 'came to momma'. My heart chuckled.

Dad and Doug continued to fix that tire swing. I do not know what possessed me to try, but I took off the elbow long brown leather welding glove and slapped it on the top side of the rock retaining wall of the island.

"Come to Momma, Baby, come to Momma," I called. *Hey it was worth a shot.*

Oh my God, you would not believe it! One of the little gators crawled right up on the island, coming towards me. Mouth open, snapping its jaws for food. Shiny white teeth glistened with water drops. Naturally, I backed up. The four foot gator followed me! I was in the middle of the island, and the gator was following me!!! *What to do? What to do?* I did not have any catching equipment with me. Only the gloves. I could catch him, but then I could not hold him AND row the boat to shore. No one could come and row the boat for me, I had the *only* boat out by the island! If I put him in the bottom of the jon boat he would scurry out quick as a wink. Humm!!! *Think, Lori. Think!. Ok I can take off my t-shirt and tie him up in it. I'd seen my Dad do that with snakes. Oh wait, there are people in the zoo and kids in the pre-school on the hill in direct line of sight. Can't take off my t-shirt in that much public. Ok, think, girl, think. I need a rope to tie him up. Belt? Nope, didn't wear one. Hat band, no too short. Ah hah, I'll use my bra! Long stretchy, it will wrap around him, hog tie him so to speak so I can row to shore.*

"What are ya gonna do now, girl?" I could hear the laughter in Dad's voice. Doug had stopped his work to watch his crazy wife. Big grin on his face too, I imagined. I didn't have time to look. *Why do these things happen to me?*

I shimmied one arm out of my t-shirt, slowly so as not to alarm the waiting, *yes still snapping his mouth open and closed, food wanting* young gator. I kept talking to him in a calm voice that belied my truth. I reached to my back to unhook my green flowered bra. A slight breeze brushed by and my red t-shirt sleeve flapped in the wind. The young gator saw the movement and scurried quickly back into the water.

Full belly laughs were heard from shore.

"Knew you wouldn't catch 'im!" said Dad, with knee slapping laughter. Doug, smart man that he is, just went back to working on the tire swing. Doug was grinning, I could tell by the negative shake of his head.

"Oh Well, I tried," I hollered and went back to my weeding job. The gators were still circling the island a half hour later when I had finished. Well, maybe if...... When I got into the boat they had disappeared.

I rowed back to shore, collected THE plastic bucket I had fed the gators with for the past year. I found the tongs. I went to the feed house and cut some chunks of venison. I gathered my biggest fish net, (maybe two foot in diameter), and a large pet taxi. Might as well try. I had nothing else on my agenda for the

162

afternoon. *What the heck.* I rowed back to the island.

Dad and Doug saw me unload my supplies, and laboriously climb back onto the island from the rocking jon boat. I do want to say here that the pond water is not the cleanest, home to hundreds of migratory -read that messy pooping - waterfowl.

"Forget it, you've spooked 'em, you'll never get 'em now!" Dad laughed as he shouted. I ignored him.

"Just tell me where they are," I hollered back. Sometimes you just have to run on faith.

"They went down by the windmill," Doug said encouragingly.

The windmill is/was way down the other end of the pond, maybe two hundred feet from the island. I could not see the gators in the water. When a gator swims, the nostrils and eyes are all you see above the water. The ripple the tail creates below water is gently reproduced on the top of the water. I didn't see a sign. So on pure faith, I called:

"Here big boys, are you hungry?, Come to momma!, I got your food, come on big boys, come to momma!". I repeated variations of the familiar phrases over and over while tapping the tongs on the side of the plastic bucket full of venison strips. Years of talking loudly to school kids had trained my loud, not quite opera quality, voice. I called as loud as I could without shouting. I was ready. Knowing that the gators were top water swimmers, I had placed the net underwater and stepped on the three foot handle to secure it. I called and tapped, then called and tapped again.

"By Golly, Here comes one," I heard Dad holler. I did not look Dad's way, I was searching for the gator. All the commotion had alerted the zoo visitors. Doug and Dad had stopped working, lining the fence by the pond with the rest of the spectators. I heard the people cheer me on, or maybe they were cheering for the alligator. I kept callin' and tappin', tappin' and callin'. My adrenaline peaking. I was ready. I saw him. He was swimming right for me and the submerged green net. His beady green eyes twinkled above the water level. His tail creating a swirl on the surface of the water.

"Are you hungry big boy? Come to Momma. Oh, big boy come to Momma!" in my best alligator enticing voice.

The not so little gator made one heck of a big splash when he found out he was scooped into a net. I hauled him up on land, flipping the net over on the ground so he could not climb out. I stepped on the net with both feet to give myself time to think and catch my breath.

"Ya get 'im? Did ya get 'im? Dad hollered across the pond. I looked up and saw Dad, Doug and about fifty visitors lined up at the fence by the side of the pond. My adrenaline was still surging. I gave the thumbs up sign. The crowd roared with cheers and laughter. *Ok so the laughter was from Dad and Doug.* I had caught the darn gator. Now I just had to get him in the pet taxi.

Prior to catching the gator I had set the pet taxi up on end, figuring I would easily drop the gator into the taxi. The pet taxi looked plenty big enough when I was on shore. I carefully flipped the net over with my hand grabbing on the not so little gator's tail. He had certainly grown. Seemed he was growing as I tried to pick him up out of the net! I had both hands on his tail trying to keep the snapping gator away from my body. I didn't want him to clamp onto my leg or any other body part for that matter. The gator's toenails were grasping the net. I was having a tough time. I proceeded to tap dance. Two hands in front of me with the four foot gator curving towards me. Its mouth was still snapping open and closed. Only now the gator was beyond angry and in defense mode. I placed one foot on the net pushing it down and off his toenails. I tapped with my foot, and withdrew it, avoiding the snapping mouth and row of needle sharp teeth. I repeated the dance until all four alligator feet were free. The crowd cheered again. Such encouragement from afar. *Yeah, it was safe where they were!* I carried the gator a couple of steps to the pet taxi. None too delicately, head first, he was dumped into the crate. Door slammed and locked. Done.

"Got you, You son of a …" well you know, I had to release all that pent up tension somehow. Don't think the folks on shore heard. Then I did the happy dance. You know, that happy dance that Snoopy does, when the joy is just so great, you have to let it out. More laughing and cheering from shore.

As I am dancing I look up. Dad is holding up his cell phone. Pointing at me.

"I left my cell phone on shore, Pop," I hollered, thinking he wanted to talk to me on my phone. "In case I fell in the drink."

"It's the State Police," Dad said loud enough for all to hear. "They said the pre-school next door just called. Some wacko lady is trying to call the little boys to come out for food! Do we know anything about it?"

Good one, Dad, very funny. But I got the gator.

Photo by Donna Traylor

Zoo Momma

Chapter 37 Believe Me!

Catching the one little gator out of the pond gave me hope that I could catch the other two small alligators also. In winter the pond would freeze over and they would suffocate and die if I did not catch them. Alligators can take cold weather, and cold water, they just go into brumation. Brumation is like hibernation, only the animal does not go 'under' mentally, they are still awake. But like all animals, alligators need to breathe. They would not survive under the ice.

I rowed the jon boat around the pond daily chasing the two elusive alligators. I brought along the plastic bucket with venison, the tongs, my faithful two foot wide green net, and a pet taxi. We still hadn't figured out how they had escaped. The men in the family just figured I messed up on calculating their size and the size of the paneling in the alligator pen. *Yep, egg on my face!* I caught one, and was giving a Rosie the Riveter 'I can do it!" try to catch the other two. I must admit, I enjoyed rowing the boat slowly around the pond on sunny afternoons. With my other work chores done, it was relaxing. The crisp fall weather, colorful trees and calm waters made rowing easy. I was trying to catch the elusive two, really yes I was. I would spot them under the fallen tree in the pond and row over. I came close a couple of times, but as soon as I picked up my net, they would submerge and be gone. In ten minutes I would spot them down the other end of the pond. It was a cat and mouse game that I lost repeatedly. But I did try for a couple of weeks. Really.

I kept seeing their eye brow ridges and nostrils above water. The gators had really grown while loose in the pond. No Canada geese stopped by on their normal migration path that year. There were no little ducks on the pond. Our visiting herons ceased stopping in for a quick fish. Top of the food chain in the pond, the little alligators enjoyed their royal status.

The brow ridge on one gator seemed a little big. And the distance between the brow ridge and the nostrils was longer. Hummmm..... Could it be the big alligator, G.I. Gator? I hadn't seen him in the alligator enclosure, but then again, he could have been under the water IN his enclosure. Could be my perspective. I mentioned this question to Dad one morning at coffee.

"You think it is the big gator?" Dad dipped his cookie into his coffee. "Naw, I saw him just the yesterday in his cage. It is just your perspective. On the water things look different."

"I don't know, Dad. We'll have to keep our eyes out," I said, angry that Dad did not take me seriously. "The distance between the nostril and the brow ridge is almost a foot."

"Naw, he can't get out of that cage," Dad insisted. "It's gotta be one of the smaller gators, just grown a lot this summer."

I left the restaurant, somewhat aggravated at my Dad for not believing in me and my judgment. I tootled around the pond again that afternoon.

The next morning my older brother Eric stopped in at coffee time. Again I brought up the subject. I mentioned it to Eric because he brings his little grandchildren to the pond to fish evenings after supper. If it was the big G. I. Gator, his grandkids would be an easy fast food meal. Grab and go before anyone could believe what happened. It just so happened that Eric had been at the pond fishing with his grandkids the night before.

"Yeah, I saw him last night." Eric confirmed.

"The big gator?" Dad questioned.

"Yeah, there was at least a foot between his nostrils and eyes," Eric confirmed.

Parker walked by at that moment and joined the conversation.

"I was up on the porch the other day," Parker contributed, looking at me. "It is the big gator. I thought you knew."

"I told Pop," I replied. "But he didn't believe me."

With both his precious sons confirming what his 'what does she know' daughter had said, Dad finally believed. *Does that sound sarcastic? Keep in mind my Dad is from a male chauvinist generation. The frustration of that fact taints my daily life. If I let it. Most of the time, I can laugh it off, knowing that I am the more intelligent sex. Somehow this time it really bothered me. Anyhooo....*

A roundtable coffee fueled discussion followed. All agreed we would have to wait until the water cooled and the air temp was warmer, warming up the shallow waters. The cold blooded alligators would seek out the warmer waters near shore. In the shallows we could net them or noose 'em. So we would wait and watch.

The zoo nursery is right next to the pond. The back wall of the main building is the back wall of the zoo nursery. The side of the main building faced the pond. I had collected pet rabbits and set up "Lori's Bunny Ranch". I breed the rabbits that we use to feed the large snakes. The Bunny Ranch is on the side of the main building, near the shallow end of the pond. Under a massive willow tree the water was strewn with wind washed willow tree twigs. I checked daily to see if the gators, any of the three still loose in the pond, had come to the warmer shallow water, where I had caught G. I. years before. I would peek through the fence before I opened the gate. I did not see anything.

Parker had constructed a gator trap out of livestock paneling. We would have to pull a rope attached to a fence to pull up a section of paneling and close the trap. Meat was used as a bait up on shore. The trap was in place.

Then one day, I noticed a flash as I came into the nursery from the zoo proper. Looked again, nothing there. We were still seeing gators in the water, but always too far away to do anything about.

As fall progressed the leaves fell from the giant willow and the weeds surrounding the pond turned brown. The grasses died off. We kept looking. One day I noticed a half circle of crushed grasses on the far side of the pond past the big rusty gate. Looking closer, there was a big old log there. *Wait a minute.... That's no log, it's the BIG gator, G.I. Gator! Found him!* I knew he was too big for me to tackle alone. But I had found his sunning spot, his lair. The half circle gave it away. Unless an alligator is under immense danger, an alligator does not walk backwards. Don't know where I got that tidbit of information. But I know it. Hence the half circle of up and out on the shore and back down into the safety of the water. G.I. Gator's trail.

I told Dad. I set up a long thick hemp rope noose snare trap right where G.I. would walk through it. The noose should catch him behind the head in front of his shoulders. Hemp would not be shiny, it would blend in with the brown dead weeds. The thickness would be strong enough. I left and waited. One end of the thick hemp rope was tied to a cement filled tire with a two inch diameter pipe sticking up through it. We used this type of tire/pipe for temporary fencing in the zoo if needed. If the snare worked, I hoped the heavy tire/pipe would hold. That tire/pipe was certainly heavy enough, I had trouble just moving it to the grass by the pond. So we waited.

Well, ya know that was not going to be good enough for Dad and Eric. My noose had been set up for less than 12 hours overnight (read that no sun to bathe in) when Eric came to set up an official snare. Alright, I will admit, Eric and Dad have lots more trapping experience than I do. My brother Eric is a renowned trapper east of the Mississippi. We needed a plastic jug with a screw on top for a bobber. So I helped by finding an almost empty plastic jug of windshield washer fluid. I emptied the last of the fluid into my car. Eric set the metal snare noose with the plastic jug bobber attached to one end in the same exact spot I had my hemp noose the night before. And we waited again. The theory was to snare the gator with the wire cable attached to the gator with the plastic jug acting like a bobber. The plastic jug bobber would float above the huge gator on the snare leash. We would be able to reel him in to shore with a the jon boat. So we waited.

The next morning I informed Dad that the gator had been snared, the jug was floating above the tannic tainted pond water.

"Ok, we'll get the men around after they clean the zoo," Dad took command. "I'll get the huge transport case I use on the back of my car. You know, the insulated gray one I bring back the elk meat in from Colorado."

"Is that gonna be big enough?" I asked.

"Gonna have to be," And Dad took off in the direction of his car and transport case. I left to finish cleaning up in the nursery so I would be ready.

Hunter was still in school, Parker had gone to a political meeting, so that left Dad, at 81 years old, Doug, Kyle Banta (that year's extra zookeeper) and myself. Kyle was young, maybe 25, local farm boy strong, and cute, sort of impish. Kyle's eyes often twinkled when the guys were carrying on. Kyle was a little on the shy side, but very polite. He had only been working for us for a couple of weeks and had never seen the big gator out on dry land.

The four of us gathered by the side of the pond a couple of hours later. Dad had the car loaded with the transport case which was as wide as the back of his Explorer, about six feet. Three feet high and two feet from front to back, the six foot case was going to be a tight squeeze.

Dad headed up the team as we discussed the plan. Simple enough, one person rows, one person grabs the snare cable turned leash under the plastic bobber jug and we haul/row G.I. Gator back to shore where the other two would be waiting.

"I'll row Dad, I'm the weakest, " I volunteered. "That will leave Doug and you to help haul the gator up on shore when we get there. I'm a strong rower, but Doug will be stronger on the rabies pole."

"Ok, Kyle you get in the boat with Lori," Dad, instructed, "Doug and I will stay on shore to grab him." So that was the plan. Dad and Doug had the rabies pole, a four feet long cable snare encased in a pvc pipe, and more heavy rope. Kyle and I unloaded our cell phones, placing them on the rock retaining wall.

The gator's bobber was only twenty five feet from shore. I kept my eye on him and jumped into the boat. Kyle joined me.

"Can you swim, Kyle?" I asked half jokingly.

"No, I can't." Kyle replied. I was surprised. All farm kids learned how to swim in the local farm ponds.

"Don't worry about it, If Kyle falls in, he won't have to worry about swimming," Doug laughed. "He'll be running on top of the water with that gator chasing him! Or he's supper." *Yeah, funny one Doug.*

The flat bottom boat had a square stern and a pointed bow. Kyle and I switched places, putting Kyle on the seat closest to the flat back on the boat. The boat rocked and I could see Kyle's eyes go wide. But to his credit, Kyle was game. I put the oars in the water and quietly paddled out into the pond. Since the gator was only twenty five feet away from the access area on shore, this should be easy, right? Out in the middle of the pond, I positioned the boat so Kyle would be closest to the plastic jug bobber, rowing backwards.

"Do you have gloves on you?" I asked Kyle.

"No. I'm not cold, I'll be ok," Kyle responded.

"You are going to be grabbing a wire cable. That gator is gonna pull hard. The wire will cut through your hand," I explained in a whisper. *Why didn't we think of that while on shore?* "Pull your jacket down over the palm of your hand to protect it." Zoo Momma I am.

Kyle did as instructed. Kyle's dark brown cow eyes were round with excitement. One final big row with the oars and we silently glided over the sunken big gator. The moment of truth had arrived. Kyle grabbed the wet cable line. And….. Nothing. Kyle looked at me.

"Is he on the cable line?" I asked. "Did he get out of the snare?"

"There is weight on it," Kyle stated.

"Ok, here goes," I nodded to Dad and Doug on shore as I started to row. Well… that was too easy. I rowed, Kyle held the cable leash with the eight foot gator on the other end. We glided fifteen feet towards shore. This is way too easy, I remember thinking.

Maybe six feet from Dad and Doug waiting on shore, either G.I. Gator woke up, or his feet hit the bottom of the lake.

"Son of a !***#," Kyle shouted. I could see Kyle's hand and arm swinging around the end of the ten foot jon boat. He had his jacket protecting his hand while his arm and hand were swinging vigorously! He looked like he was conducting an imaginary symphony. Up and down, left to right, right to left, down and up again. G.I. had figured out that he was caught. And boy oh boy was he angry! G.I. was swimming back and forth under the boat from side to side. Now that we were in the shallows, the gator wanted to go back out to the safety of the deep. I rowed hard. I rowed harder. I learned real quick that I was not going to row stronger than that alligator could swim. *$#! +!*

Dad and Doug were shouting encouragement from shore. We were so close. One final big shove with an oar against the bottom of the pond brought the boat, Kyle and the gator just close enough to one tree that had a piece of livestock paneling attached to it. I grabbed the livestock paneling.

While I was maneuvering the boat, Kyle, to his credit, still had the cable with the eight foot, maybe three hundred pound, really scared and angry gator on the other end. *You know the phrase holding a tiger by the tail? Tigers might be easier.*

Doug and Dad were still six feet away on shore. The angry gator was between them and the boat. G.I. Gator pulled a breach, he leapt straight up and out of the water flailing. The alligator's full body was out of the water, with the exception of his tail. Kyle held on. Doug would tell me later, that Kyle's eyes were the size of dinner plates. Remember, I did mention that Kyle had never seen the whole gator on land. Well, now he had that huge (and growing bigger by the second) gator on a thin metal string! And that gator didn't want to do what we were trying to get him to do.

I worked our way hand over hand up the livestock paneling. I got the boat close enough for Doug to walk into the water and grab the boat. With Doug's help we got the boat closer to shore. The gator was still in the shallow water, on the side of the jon boat. His huge mouth was flashing white sharp teeth. I don't remember who got the rabies poll snare over his mouth, but we did. The scared gator kept trying to roll over. The small diameter of the snare cable with the jug would cut the alligators skin and kill it. The rabies poll had thicker cable with a clear plastic coating over it. The men hauled the flailing alligator on shore. With the men on shore and the eight foot long gator, there was no place to park the jon boat on the action side of the abandoned paneling alligator trap that Parker had constructed. I docked the boat on the other side of the huge trap, then ran up the steps from the pond, around the little 'Humble' house, and inside the rusty pond gate to help the guys.

Doug held the four foot rabies poll and the front half of the angry gator away from our bodies. Kyle and Dad picked up a hind leg each. I got the tail. We slugged and slogged the waterlogged gator towards the transport case on the back of Dad's car. It was only a couple of feet, but seemed like miles.

"On a count of three," Dad instructed. We hauled up, placing the glistening gator none to gently into the transport case. Doug held the neck of the gator down with the rabies poll.

"Lori, fold his tail in," Dad commanded. I grabbed the mucky bottom of his tail and folded him in. G.I. Gator's tail was two foot longer than the six foot case. Eight feet of angry alligator.

Dad closed the lid on the gray wooden transport case and flipped the lock. The cheers and relief could be heard for miles I am sure. We had a huge surge of adrenaline going through all of our bodies. That high can't be beat. We chuckled, we laughed and relived the action for a couple of minutes. We were happy that we were all unhurt, including G.I..

After a couple of minutes, the guys drove the gator to Dad's basement, and unceremoniously dumped the defeated G.I. Gator in the winter eight feet by eight feet water semi-filled holding tank. He had one companion that winter. G.I Gator and the 'come to Momma', smaller 4 ft gator, spent the winter in Dad's basement. Much to my step-mother Mira's dismay.

Just a note: Huge G.I. Gator's escape told the men folk that the enclosure had a fault in it. The men pulled up the entire enclosure onto shore with a tractor that fall. They found the wires holding the sides together had rotted away under water. That was remedied the next spring. The other two small gators never came to my call. I tried until the pond froze over. So just remember folks, always come to momma when she calls.

Chapter 38 Ode to Jenny Woodchuck

Jenny Woodchuck was very special to me. Yes, I have raised lions, tigers and bears, *OH MY!* and many other exotic animals, but I have to admit, a simple woodchuck won my heart. Jenny accompanied me on more educational outreach speeches then I can count. She would always sit upright on my hand chomping down her bright orange carrot while I spoke. Her back nestled against my chest, she was quite the show animal. When she finished her carrot Jenny would lay in my arms like a baby, belly side up waiting for another carrot or tummy tickles.

My affection for Jenny Woodchuck was well known. Our Vet, Dr. Ted Spinks, V.M.D. and his veterinarian friends could never understand it. To every one of them, woodchucks were vermin, a danger to the hooves and legs of horses and cattle. The woodchucks would dig their burrows, and the horse or cow would step in the hole breaking their legs. The local farmers also could not understand my affection for Jenny. I took a lot of ribbing on the subject. My Dad was the only one that understood.

I did arrange Jenny's marriage to a special black woodchuck. Jenny produced black and normal colored offspring, three years in a row. Jenny was a little feisty during nursing, but I could always distract her with a fresh carrot while I inspected her babies. After her nursing time was over, she once again became my handle-able woodchuck.

Just for the reader's information: We placed one of Jenny's offspring with The Staten Island Zoo, I called him Elvis. The Staten Island Zoo renamed him Chuck E. (for Elvis) Groundhog. Chuck E. Groundhog was the groundhog that bit Mayor Bloomburg! Just Saying.

Sad part about any pet animal, they do not live as long as we humans. Woodchuck, also called groundhogs, or whistle pigs only live about six years. Jenny came to us in 2004, as I have written earlier in this book.

In the summer of 2009, when the coatis Diego and Chiquita came to us, the coati needed someplace to stay in the nursery. I moved Jenny Woodchuck to the Bunny Ranch around the corner from the nursery. I still saw her and worked with her every day. Jenny would whistle when she heard my voice, especially if she could not see me. The coati were displayed in the red enclosure on the side by the pond, Jenny's previous home for the past five years.

One morning that fall, I reported to the nursery for my morning chores. Jenny's cage was open. I don't know what happened, but the cage was open and Jenny was gone. I looked around half heartedly, knowing in my heart that she could be anywhere. If she showed up, I could recapture her. She posed no germ threat to any wild woodchuck, Jenny never had any shots and had never been exposed to any sick animals. However I never found her again. Jenny was free, loose somewhere on the zoo grounds. I don't consider Jenny 'escaped', more rather like retired. She had worked/ performed hard during her time as a working woodchuck, entertaining, educating and having cutie pie woodchuck babies.

I still miss her almond shaped eyes, her strawberry blonde tipped , silvery layered fur coat and little grasping hands. Her soft round ears were the size of half a nickel. Chubby tummy and wispy tail, what was not to love? I have raised many woodchucks, none of them had Jenny's personality. Maybe one will be born this year. with Jenny's genes in our gene pool….. I hope so.

Jenny Woodchuck
Photo by Jackie Day

Chapter 39 Christmas '09 Feelin' Fine

My letter is not late, Oh dear friends of mine,
I planned it for now, so we would have time.
The holidays come in a hurry, everything in a blur
Getting ready for Christmas, bedding down those with fur.
Gale winds are now blowing outside
And finite snowflakes have no place to hide,
But our Christmas tree is still shining bright
So we're warm and cozy while I write tonight.
There's so much that happened with us this year
I'll try to express for friends far and near.
Or Jackie, sweet Jackie, she graduated
Suma Cum Laude she matriculated.
Proud parents we watched, mixed sadness with glee
She received her diploma at Rider University.
Then Jack came home for about twelve weeks,
Diploma with laptop and jobs she did seek.
Never rains but it pours, she was offered three
And had to decide what she wanted to be.
Planned Parenthood won, her passion at heart
To help other women, August 3rd she did start.
Assistant Administrator of a very nice clinic
Learning while helping everyone in it.
The staff have adopted her, think she is divine,
I'd expect nothing less from a daughter of mine.
Her roommate from college is her apartment mate now
Two gals with jobs, boyfriends and apartment, Oh Wow!
They are living the Mary Tyler Moore life that's true…
But I've got to admit sometimes I'm blue.
She grew up so fast, seems like just yesterday
That "Mommy" and "Daddy" was all she could say.
The boyfriend is still on the scene,
"No questions, no pressure!", says my little queen.
He is a great guy, fits in our family well
What the future holds only time will tell.
At the zoo I raised new species, some quite unique
two little ponies from Assateague.
My first equine experience since I was thirteen
If you don't count some zebras in-between.
Blaze, a stallion, and Daisy Mae the little filly,
And I've got to admit I felt quite silly,
When folks would ask " hey Lor what's new?"
My response, "Two little ponies at the zoo!"

173

Zoo Momma

But my inner child was shouting with glee
"My daddy gave me two newborn ponies!"
Raised 'em on bottles, became quite the chore
With all the rain, wet hay and yucky manure
(I don't want ponies any more)
In April a five month old black leopard cub
Skittish, but likes her belly rubbed.
Lola, a former showgirl, a picky eater
If I'd had her younger, she would be sweeter.
In July we received two coatimundi
Diego and Chiquita, so sweet to me.
Their long noses will check out your ears
And any other orifice that they can get near (Yuck!)
They are tucked in quite snuggly down at the zoo
Though they litter trained well- but oh stinky poo.
Two young Servals were more challenge in August,
African Cats, a new cage a must.
They can jump sixteen feet high and long twenty feet
Interesting specie, affectionate and neat.
Servals in my nursery, so the little gators had to go
Out to the big cage with 'ole GI Joe
GI Gator, the last chapter in my first book
Whom had since grown to over seven foot!
My three little gators- maybe five foot in length
Good swimmers, good eaters, unbelievable strength.
That lasted a month, well, maybe by week three
When in our pond visitors started to see
Free ranging gators- Oh God what do we do now?
The story too long to tell you all how.
Wait for the next book, or better yet-
Come visit, I'll explain, we didn't even get wet!
Jenny Woodchuck escaped again last fall
Hope to find her in the Spring, if at all.
Speeches, Publicity, writing some more,
Next summer has the same in store.
I've done TV with Dr. Brian and Dr. Ted
Talked so much, can't remember what I've said.
I'm still doing the monthly radio show
On any animal subject under the rainbow.
So much to do, my world in a whirl,
I've free lanced some writing, you go, country girl!
Doug's still my hero his talents diverse
To many to name, can't put them in verse.
He works so hard all day at the zoo

Zoo Momma

Then at night helps friends with computers too.
That's my guy, an amazing man
And he puts up with my family the best that he can.
We fished in Canada, Spent time with Doug's sister
It was nice to see how much he had missed her.
Dad is doing well, very set in his ways
Hunting or hay takes up most of his days.
He's full of advice, animal advice I treasure,
But Dad's political views, I give them full measure.
The Beemerville High Holidays, a redneck delight
Shot enough deer for us to eat plenty alright.
Last winter I wrote our Beemerville Church History
With original session minutes from Presbytery.
Wow! What a process- I touched history for sure
Those books were hand written in 1834!
My Mom helped me a lot with all the research,
In the end I felt way 'over churched'.
We celebrated in costume, made it come alive
For our Church's anniversary - One Hundred Seventy Five!
My "Zoo Momma" Book, I've got chapters to compose
When it will be done, God only Knows.
I'm writing and painting, and sewing some too
But I'd really love to hear from YOU.
Send me an email, drop me a line,
I love to hear from friends of mine.
Love from us all, Lori and Doug Day
and Jackie (from two hours away□).

Hunter and Diego the Coatimundi
Photo by Lori Space Day

Zoo Momma

Chapter 40 The Seasons

Hunter jokingly explained to me one day that here at Space Farms we only have two seasons, open and closed. And that is about right. The toughest work times of the year are the weeks after we close for the season on October 31st. Those weeks are a race to get the animals bedded down before snow flies.

The warm weather animals are moved to the warm animal room in one of the old barns. Stands to reason, the rhesus monkeys, crab eating macaques, ring tailed lemurs, baboons, ostrich, emus, serval and gennets come inside to the barn's warm room.

The woodchucks, prairie dogs and skunks come into the barn also. Why ? Yes, those animals are used to the cold, the woodchucks dig burrows in their enclosures. The prairie dogs do the same. The skunks toddle into those burrows also, just like they would do in the wild. The animals in the wild would cuddle up and hibernate (woodchucks) or sleep (prairie dogs and skunks) through the cold snowy winter months. The woodchucks, prairie dogs and skunks at Space Farms are all exhibited in open top enclosures for the public to view. Their burrow system is extensive in their earthy bottomed exhibits. In the mid winter warm up that happens here during January or February the local hawks, owls, black vultures and even eagles swarm the skies looking for lunch. Lunch is the rodent critters that wake up to enjoy the temporary warm sun shine. The local birds of prey found out real quick that it is easier to sit on the railing around our enclosures waiting for the rodent critters to wake up. When those rodents sunbathe in the warm sun, the birds of prey would pick them off. It is easier to sit at the buffet table and wait for lunch than to fly through the thick forest of tree branches or brambly bushes to hunt elusive wild prey. So the woodchucks, prairie dogs and skunks come inside.

There is a benefit to bringing the woodchucks inside. Kept all winter in a huge ball of hay to hibernate, when we bring them out in the spring we are able to find the new babies and hand rear them to make them tame. If we don't hand rear the offspring, the local birds of prey come and get 'em before the woodchuck mothers can make a new nest. Soo.... sometimes we place the chuckies at other zoos. Or we keep the really cute ones!

The big cats are another story. The lions and tigers here at Space Farms have large concrete dens. Those dens are stuffed with hay and stay plenty warm. The African lions we have are Atlas lions aka Barbary Coast lions These are the lions that used to roam the southern parts of Europe, the Middle East and the northern parts of Africa. The last wild Atlas lion was killed in Europe in 80 A.D. As we all know the southern part of Europe has the Alps mountain range, which gets snow. The tigers roam Siberia, where snow is the norm in the winter. The lower Asian continent has mountain ranges with snow also. Leopards roam the southern Asian continent also, not only Africa! All of those cats, - and lets throw in the Mountain Lion, Lynx and Bobcat of North America - are capable of living in cold habitats. All of the animals develop a secondary warm coat of fur as long as they can experience the slow decline in the temperature. If we were to take a leopard out of Florida in January, and put it outside in New Jersey, the cat would be dead in a week. But if that same cat is given time to experience the slow decline in temperature, it will grow a secondary coat. All of these animals need a good food/energy source and a den to get out of the wind, rain and snow of winter. They do just fine.

The African lions and tigers at Space Farms have large concrete dens available to them all year. All of the other felines also have dens available to them year round. Oh and the hyenas also. In the summer months the dens are open. In the late fall, after we close for the winter season, Doug, Hunter, and John, Tommy, Bruce, Keith, Kyle, Andy or Mike (auxiliary zookeepers) put on the outside covers on the face of the dens. All summer long people can look into the dens. In the winter, there is only a doggy door type entrance so the cats can get indoors out of the elements. In the winter the hay in the dens is changed religiously once a week. This is back breaking work with a pitch fork, no big machines are used because the noise would scare the animals.

Elk, buffalo, yak, deer all do just fine outside in the winter. Zoological historians have a chuckle about certain U.S.D.A. laws that insist we have buildings for these animals to use in case of bad rain or snowy weather. I mean really? The elk, buffalo, yak and deer do not use the sheds for shelter. And a fish needs a bicycle? There are no buildings for the wild buffalo or elk in Yellowstone to shelter in.

If you think about it for a minute, my father's generation lived with only a central stove for heat. My Dad talks about the chamber pot freezing under the bed. It's got to be really cold for urine to freeze! The Native Americans lived in this area with just a campfire in a tepee. We humans have become very spoiled with our central heat and air conditioning. Think about that and stop whining about the weather.

The month before we open is just the opposite. The 100 acres of green grassy grounds need to be raked. All the winters hay piles have to be removed. This is dirty hay that was taken weekly out of the dens. The winters frozen-to-the-ground-poop has to be cleaned up. If you need to fix any animal damage to an enclosure, it is easier without the animals in it. So that gets done before the animals from the barns animal warm room are moved. The process is reversed- the warm room animals are transported outside to the zoo. Informational signs have to be put back up, and the water reconnected in the zoo. Locks on guard fencing, that were removed for easy entrance, have to be oiled and replaced. This year we have a lot of snow storm damage to fix also. Want to hear a zookeeper moan? Mention March or November!

Zoo Momma

Chapter 41 Siren

One day I was driving past the zoo on my way home from the A&P grocery store in Sussex. I noticed my Dad trying to drag a huge brown bookcase into the main building from the front porch. *Why was Dad doing that? He's 82 years old. I better help.* I pulled over in front of the seasonally defunct flower pot feed bunkers.

"Hold up, Pop," I needed to speak loudly so Dad could hear. " I'll help."

"OK," Replied Dad, as he stopped dragging the bookshelf. I hooked the double glass doors to the building open. I grabbed the bottom end of the awkward bookcase and we proceeded to lug the bookcase inside. We stopped just short of the steps in front of the overseeing Goliath. Dad seemed to need a breath.

"Have you seen Doug," Dad asked. "Have you been home?"

"No?" I replied.

"You better go find him," Dad was being evasive. And I didn't like that at all.

"Is he alright? Did he get hurt? Or one of the guys?" I fired off in rapid questions. I must have been obviously worried, because Dad decided to 'let the cat out of the bag'.

"No, everything is ok, but you better go home," Dad insisted.

"Tell me what's going on, now!" I insisted, still worried.

"Ok, I didn't want to ruin the surprise," Dad chuckled. "There are two little lion cubs waiting for you in a cardboard box."

"Woooooo Whooooooo!" I jumped up and down in literal glee. Happy Dance!!

"Mom's not taking care of them," Dad explained further. "So they're all yours."

"Them? How many?" I asked Dad.

"Two as of now, Doug will check back later," Dad was grinning. "Got milk?"

"Yep," I said over my shoulder half way out the front door in a trot.

This was the first litter of lion cubs that this particular lioness had given birth too. Not taking care of the first litter is nothing unusual. Missy had been breeding through repetitive cycles but we had never seen any cubs. So I had stopped counting the days. The older moms had aged out, that left us with lioness Missy, and Attila the Hunk. They were born in 2002, eight years before. I loved the new little lions before I even saw them.

I didn't even put my seat belt on for the quarter mile car trip home. Not even sure I closed the car door! Dad must of moved the bookshelf into position by himself, I guess.

Our living room is full of sun. On that day, the cubs would not survive if Mom Missy did not keep them warm in the lions' den. I rushed into the house leaving groceries to melt in the warm car, baking in the sun . Who cared? My hubby was so smart. He had placed the two cubs on an old flannel shirt inside a

178

cardboard box and put them in the sunny room to be warm until I got home. The box top was open, and I peered inside. Two nice fat healthy cubs, umbilical cords still long, wet and attached. I zoomed back to the office nursery and picked up the supplies I would need, including an aluminum table to set up for a feeding and cleaning station in the corner of my living room. With that equipment came my baby scale. Old fashioned and baby yellow, it cradled the cubs while I weighed them. Missy had cleaned one but not the other. I cleaned them up and weighed them, 3 lbs each. A three pound birth weight is really good and large for newborn African lions. I was thrilled. Having smaller numbers of cubs in the litter is also the norm for first time mothers. I spent the next hours setting the cubs up with heating pads under towels in their cardboard box. I would keep them together for a week then separate them into separate boxes. I mixed up the Zoologic 42/25 that I always kept on hand. They both drank vigorously. The cubs were in great condition.

The phone rang. It was Doug.

"Saw our car pull in," he said in his happy voice. "Did you find your surprise?"

"Yeah, hon, I did. What's the scoop?" Doug knew I was asking what Mom Missy did that he brought the cubs to me.

" Well, we opened the den door to do our weekly clean out, and Missy just split," Doug explained. "It was cold, and she should of defended her cubs. How are they?"

"They're fine honey, ate well and are sleeping," I replied.

"I bet you're happy now," Doug laughed. "I'll leave you to 'em."

I took care of the cubs and settled them in to life at my house. Their cardboard box was set up in the living room, so I could hear and see them in the daytime. After all the commotion, I settled down, too. Oh and I brought in the semi-thawed frozen groceries from the car sitting in the warm sun. We ate 'em any way.

While the cubs were napping I notified Dr. Ted that the cubs were born, in good shape and that I had them. I knew I could call him day or night for help if I needed it. And there was always Jennie Beckman, Dr. Ted's vet tech, who had become my friend.

Doug was right. The lionesses we had in the past had always vigorously defended the den. And not only the den, but the entire area around the concrete section of the enclosure would be defended. Zookeepers walk behind the guard fence daily to clean the concrete section where we feed, because the food can be messy. When a lioness is near term to deliver, they get 'barky'. Barky is my word for a female lion defending her territory. The lioness will actually charge the fence of the enclosure, growling, barking and challenging the intruder to back off. On a daily basis when not pregnant, the lioness and lion will come get their food and run off with it. If it is not feeding time and we are mowing grass, cleaning cage or putting up a sign, the lions will just glance in our direction, never even bothering to move. Like we are peon ants to them. When a female is barky, she is snarling at

179

you as soon as you are inside that guard fence. Barky. Yes, But I've been that too.

The cubs did great. It had been eight years since I raised a cub, so I was happy. I knew they would go to other zoos, so I steeled my heart to love them for a while. I had forgotten how noisy the cubs can be in the first two weeks. These babies were born hungry, sometimes crying for food every forty-five minutes or so. No breaks for me.

"God knows these cubs are noisy!," I mentioned to Doug that night between feedings.

"You just don't remember, they are always noisy!" Doug replied. "But yeah, these are particularly loud."

I named the female cub Siren, and her brother Ed Growley. Siren was a play on words for a beautiful female and the noise of a fire siren. Ed Growley, because he was constantly growley and one of my Dad's old hunting buddies was named Ed Growley. I remember Ed Growley, the human hunter, fondly. He was a kind man to me as a child. So Ed Growley and Siren would spout off loudly whenever they were hungry. And that was often. The bags under my eyes grew heavy, my age was showing, but I was happy, and constantly tired. I could sleep on a moments notice.

A week later I received bad news that actually made me happy. I know that does not make sense but here goes. That morning the men folk had found the female lioness, Missy, dead in the den. Parker performed an unofficial necropsy and found two more large cubs stuck inside the mother. We had no clue. Other than being a bad first time mother, which is not unusual, Missy showed no symptoms. Everyone was appropriately saddened. We have had so many lions born here and never had a problem with a breech birth before. It happens. It happens with humans, but humans can talk and say something is wrong. Missy showed no symptoms.

I, however, was not sad. I was not gleeful at Missy's death, but I was not sad. Missy's death meant that we could keep the female cub. We had not kept one of our home grown, hand raised lions since Mosses of 1974. I knew I could keep her when her mother passed away. Now that made me gleeful! I would not have to place her at another zoo. Yahoo! No trip to the airport, no departure- post partum blues, no sad eyes questioning as I walk away. Double yahoo!! I would have to place Ed in a few weeks, but I could keep Siren. Not that I played favorites, but well, maybe I did. I would pour all my years of pent up love on Siren, the love that I had to turn off with other cubs when I sent them to other zoos.

I don't play much with the cubs in the first two weeks, they need their energy to grow. And grow they did, right according to schedule. They doubled their weight in the first week. And they were noisy, particularly noisy. I fed, burped and stimulated for urine and bowel movements. Often during this process my hand gets peed on. After a couple of days the urine on your hands really starts to sting. I wash my hands so much, but that is part of the job. I love to pat round little bellies and the cubs sure enjoyed it.

Siren's first eye opened at 4 days, same as Ed's. They looked like stuffed toy animals that an imaginative child had played pirate with. The second eyes opened on day five. The fur is not soft and silky like your house cat, they have fur that feels like the fur of a stuffed fake toy animal. Very deceptive to the eye.

It was so much fun to watch Doug play with the lion cubs. Dougs favorite was Ed Growley. Ed Growley was barely toddling along, and would always gravitate towards Doug in his Lazy Boy chair. (I really think they should rename that chair for all of us working folks - maybe Hard Working Guy's Chair.) At two weeks, the cubs pulled themselves up on their legs, chubby tummies barely off the carpet. Toddling along at three weeks old, they half wobbled, half walked like drunken old men. By three weeks old, Doug had Ed Growley shaking paws on voice command. It was so cute to see.

Jackie came home from her job in Lawrenceville to see the cubs. I'm not sure who was happier that the cubs had arrived. I'm sure the cubs were happy. There is no lack of food or affection in my world.

Dr. Ted made arrangements for us to take the two lion cubs down to News 12 NJ for Dr Brian Voynick V.M.D's show, "The Pet Stop". I always enjoyed the day away from the zoo. I did get all my animal work done in the morning and set up sitters and feeders for the critter infants I had left behind. The show is filmed at the studio in Edison, N.J. about an hour and a half from Dr. Ted's Animal Hospital of Sussex County in Augusta. I fed and pottied the cubs before we set off. One of Dr. Ted's associates went with us. The cubs slept most of the way. Most animal babies sleep in a moving car, just like human babies. Upon our arrival, I asked for a room to let the cubs walk around. An assistant let us into an office room. I let the cubs walk around a vacant office. Or should I say an office who's human inhabitant was out that day. Imagine his/her surprise the next day when neighboring officemates talked about the cubs!

Ed and Siren did great on the show. Dr. Ted talked about the medical necessities of captive lions, I filled in on the day to day nursing care. Dr. Brian asked all the questions. Dr. Ted and I dutifully answered. The cubs had their third bottle of the morning on the show. Lion cubs really guzzle down the formula, then need to be burped. Siren seemed a little off and I started to worry.

After the show's taping we always go to Harold's on the bottom floor of the Marriott Hotel nearby. The huge corned beef sandwiches are our positive reward for a job well done. The Marriott Hotel is so nice. The folks at the desk always have an office for us to put our animals in for the hour plus lunch. I could not leave Siren and Ed in the car, the sun was warm and internal car temperatures heat up fast.

Chatting with Dr. Ted and Dr. Brian is so much fun. The guys are light hearted and cheerful and I learn so much just by listening to them. Occasionally other colleagues would join us. I am not so nervous before a TV show, it is on tape, and you can ask to re-take it, (but it is frowned upon, time is always tight in the studio). Naw, I'm not so nervous before. My mind races with the information that I know and that we need to give out. And I must not forget to give the daily hours of operations, and how people can get more information on Space Farms

Zoo and Museum. Let's face it, that is why we are on TV, it helps to promote our businesses. But after the tapings, I fall apart, am almost giddy with relief, very chatty. More so than usual. Dr. Ted is the exact opposite, he gets nervous before a show. So all the way down to the show, we go over facts that we need to say. Afterward, at lunch, with those eight inch high corned beef on rye bread sandwiches, we unwind. You should see the deserts at Harold's! The cakes are so huge, but I've never had any, between the corned beef and the pickle bar, I'm usually full up.

Anyway, Siren and Ed slept through lunch. Again many thanks to the folks at the Marriott. They have put up snakes, servals, raccoons, fawns, tigers, skunks, *(yeah, they were deodorized)*, Ed and Siren and any animal I had taken with us. Though when we took a calf and Timmy the llama, (next chapter), the animals stayed in the car with open windows. Dr. Ted brought us a picnic lunch outside.

All the way home, Dr. Ted and I tell each other how wonderful we were on TV, then chat about hunting, fishing, traveling, our spouses, kids, and work related issues. Being in the animal business, we never seem to lack interesting conversation. Or maybe it's because I am just gabby and letting out my nervousness on the way home.

Our home was a revolving door of family at night. Everyone would come and babysit, read that play with the cubs for a while so Doug and I could go out to dinner. Hunter came quite frequently, laying on the floor letting the cubs climb the mountain that is Hunter. Our nieces Lindsey and Kelsey would stop by now and then too. Everybody loved getting their picture taken with the cubs. But I had to restrict flashes into the infant eye, or at least directly into the eye. Doug's sister, Jackie and her husband Bill came to visit for two weeks, with their two dogs. *You know the kind of dogs - big cats call them 'dental floss'!* They all had a good time playing together. *Yeah, now when Siren and Ed are so small. Another week or so and those toy dogs would be ummm… toys.*

Ed and Siren grew right on schedule. I knew Ed would have to leave us and go to another zoo. No way would our male Attila accept another male in his territory, not even his own son. Dad mentioned to me again that I needed to put the word out. I had delayed, like I always do. So I did. I put the word out and got an instant reply…

I took Siren and Ed to Dr. Ted for his stamp of approval (the required veterinary health certificate) and inoculations. The technicians at the Animal Hospital of Sussex Co. know me well. Don't tell the folks at the zoo, but when I go to the vet with animals, I schedule my time to give me an extra fifteen minutes at the office. You never know, the animals may poop in the crate and I may need to clean them up before Dr. Ted can work/check on them. Yeah, that is my excuse for that extra fifteen to thirty minutes I am gone. Here's my secret, at baby time of the year, I am so exhausted I can use a couple of extra winks. I trust the techs at the clinic, and my friend Jennie Beckman would always greet us upon arrival, shepherding us into a special room for exotic animals. If we wait in the main waiting room and other dog patients come in, well… those dogs have not always seen what I have in my crate and can put up quite a noisy scene. Which scares me and my babies. So in our private examination room, I turn off the lights, sit on the floor, lean my head against the wall, the cubs crawl on my lap, and we take a snooze. Dr. Ted or the staff, gently knock on the door when it is our turn. This is a little different definition of a cat nap, but it serves the same purpose! The cubs did fine, Dr. Ted drew blood for testing for unseen, non-symptomatic diseases. Neither Siren or Ed had any problems. Afterwards, the staff get their pictures taken with my babies. In a world of cats and dogs, the exotics I deal with are a change of pace at the vets office. My babies are never boring, no insult to regular cats and dogs intended.

I needed to have my gall bladder removed and would be an outpatient. I needed a sitter for a day. Jennie Beckman volunteered for the job. She spent the morning and afternoon at my house, watching and feeding Siren and Ed. Thanks Jennie.

We found Ed a wonderful home with Jim Jablon in Florida. Jim runs the Wildlife Rehabilitation Center of Hernando. Jim had a slightly older female cub that he was looking for a playmate/ mate for. It seemed like a good match for Ed. Jim asked all the right questions in his phone interview, showing me that he had the experience, knowledge and concern that I would look for in a new daddy for Ed. My Dad built the crate and I drove the horrible drive to the airport. I really hate that drive. It's the traffic, and of coarse, the upcoming separation of myself and Ed. The cub's eyes follow you as you walk away…. It hurts, every time.

Dad and Mira went to Florida on their yearly vacation a month or so later. Dad stopped in at Jim's invitation and was very happy with the conditions that Ed was being raised under. Ed was running around the home compound with two enormous dogs, happily playing according to Dad.

"Don't know how long that'll last,' Dad remarked. "But when we got there, and Jim called Ed, Ed came running out of Jim's house with the two huge dogs, right behind him through a doggie door!" Dad had a chuckle in his voice and a twinkle in his eye when he told me that story.

"You picked Ed a great home," Dad patted me on the back. "Good job"
Wow did he just say that? Damn where is that recorder when I need it!

You can look up Jim Jablon on Google and see video of him and Ed and Ed's girlfriend. Neat-O. Jim lived with his teenage lions for a whole month and made national news. Ed looked happy and healthy. Not much more a mom can ask for. Happy and Healthy.

Meanwhile, I had Siren all to myself. She traveled with me to the zoo in the daytime, and home with me when the work day was done. I spent a lot of special extra time with her since I knew we could keep her. It was still cold outside when Ed left for Florida, so Siren stayed home at night. She stayed by my feet or sat by me in my chair every minute of the evenings. At bedtime, which is midnight by the way, she would get a good night bottle and go in her large refrigerator box with towels and stuffed animals to cuddle with. Daytimes, she was in her enclosure in the zoo nursery.

She was the best little lioness. Siren would go to the back door and sit. She would not make a sound, so you needed to keep an eye on her, but when she was at the back door she needed to go potty. An animal that you have had since birth and had to stimulate to produce urine and bowel movements, is easier to potty train. When the weather was good enough, even as a small cub, I would take her outside and put her feet in the grass and stimulate her. Eventually she came to know the feel of the grass meant I wanted her to void. Not rocket science, just conditioning. Doug had his job to do also, he left a taller patch of grass outside our mud room door. As soon as Siren had her leash on and walked to where the tall grass tickled her bottom (the same tickley stimulation I did with a paper towel), she would do her business. On nice nights she and I would go for a walk around our house on the zoo property. When I planted my flower gardens I would put her on the longer lead and attach it to my foot. She did not like being restrained, she would rather walk. So I planted my colorful gardens a little faster that year. She was precious to me. Jackie would laugh at me and all the goofy doggy clothes I would dress her in. Not Jackie, but the little lioness. But soon Siren didn't want to wear such frivolous outfits. You really can't argue with a lion, even a little one.

As she grew, Siren needed a larger enclosure than her refrigerator box in the nursery office. I set up a transportable dog corral, the kind you see at dog shows, with a blanket on the floor for my pretty girl. A medium sized cardboard box made a great den with fluffy towels in it. It was also a great toy. Siren had a number of stuffed animal toys, she loved them and played whenever she was not sleeping. Visitors to the zoo that spring saw Siren through the nursery office windows. There was usually quite a crowd.

I took Siren to see Dr. Ted and get her booster shots. By then she was getting fairly large, a good twenty-five pounds of playful kitten. I had taught Siren certain commands: NO Bite, NO Claws, come, sit, stay, and I would sing to her when she was outside to do business. There is a song that has a line in it "Party Party Parrrrrrty!" I changed it a little and when it was time would sing "Potty, Potty, Potttttttty!". *Ok so maybe I am the only one who thinks that is funny.* By eight weeks old she was peeing and pooping on her own. Siren understood NO Bite, and NO Claws, and Come, but the sit and stay is a foreign language to any cat anyway.

Siren outgrew her refrigerator box in my mudroom, so I set her up in the downstairs bathroom, next to Jackie's room. She was getting bigger, frisker and I had other babies to attend to. So, by late April I started to try to leave her at the zoo at night.

This took me a week. Every night I would tell Doug my good intentions. He would just smile and say "We'll see" and go back to whatever he was doing. For a week I would leave Siren down at the zoo until dark, and my last feedings of infants at the zoo. Then I would look at those huge honey colored eyes peering at me, imploring and bring her home. She was still living in Jackie's bathroom, (it had tiling in case of accidents). She had gotten quite destructive in the house. So first thing in the morning, (still in my PJs) I would take Siren back down to the zoo at 6 a.m. and feed the other babies their bottles. Then I would come home to get coffee and dressed for my day. I left Siren at the zoo at night when I realized I was waking her up to take a bottle. It took me a week to realize that my car engine noise was waking her up. One night I walked into the zoo and found Siren fast asleep After that I knew she didn't need to come home.. *Daaaahhh!*

Siren was a big hit at the zoo and on the lecture circuit. I would give daily speeches on Siren in the nursery. Her playful nature, cutie pie looks and inquisitive eyes made everyone fall in love with her. Being hand raised, Siren was very interested in the general public. No one, except staff, got to work with her. She was dangerous and the germs from the general public could possibly kill her. Plus the State of NJ laws on zoos says there is to be no contact between the general public and exotic cats. That law works for me. I don't have to explain my germ phobia to everyone or explain asymptomatic cat diseases. I just need to say it's NJ state Law. It's easier. For those who persist I explain the asymptomatic diseases. Other states have different laws, but Jersey laws work just fine for me with my big cat cubs. That being said, Siren was very interactive with visitors to the zoo, vocally and reacting physically, by waving, jumping and playing.

And boy oh boy did she grow. Siren consumed a hind leg of a road kill deer a day by the time she was five months old. For your information, that is what a full grown lion eats in one day. She still loved her bottle. I had set up her nursery enclosure with the same large wooden box den that I had used for Tara and Khyber tigers when I had hand raised them twelve years before. The den was attached to the outside of the nursery enclosure, and had two bottle sized holes in the outside door. I could trap Siren in the box, calling her in for a bottle though the holes, then drop the vertical door slide between the den and the enclosure. By six months old, I didn't go in with Siren any more. She was just too big, too strong, and too affectionate for me to handle. She was stronger than I. I was becoming her rag doll. She often did not want me to leave when the time came to exit her enclosure. That's when she would grab on tight, sometimes using claws. She was a lion, my sweetheart, but I was not going to train her to be a circus lion. It was time for me to stop going in with her. The den with the bottle holes became more important. I locked her in the den on a daily basis when I cleaned her grassy compound.

Siren would call to me whenever she saw me. She would demand pets and loves through the fencing. She would rub the fence and I would sink my fingers in her fur, giving her those favorite scratches. The oil and smell of a lion is distinct. There is a brownish oil which is sticky and coats your finger tips. The smell is sort of like rancid butter, a little bittersweet. It washes off easily, although you have to use soap.

I discussed with all the guys, what to do with her. Siren was the size of a German shepherd dog. She needed more room, but could not be put in with the larger lion pride yet. She had to be bigger to hold her own against the big cats in case of a squabble .

We decided to move Siren to the auxiliary enclosure, adapting the enclosure so we would be able to clean it easily with her inside.

Hunter, my brother Parker's son, had become a intrical part of our zookeeping work force. After his day at high school, he would change clothes and come to the zoo. He would shadow Doug helping and learning. He assisted me with parts of the new enclosure as I set it up. I wanted a log scratching post/perch. Hunter was good with a chain saw and cut a huge eight foot log and braced it across the enclosure. Thirty feet long by eight foot wide, with a house in one end, and her bark covered log perch on the other.

Dad and I had many discussions on how to move Siren. At six months old and probably a hundred twenty five pounds, she was going to be heavy and scared. Dad wanted me to lock her in her den and have the guys move the entire heavy wooden den with Siren in it to the new location. I told Dad I could probably get her into a large plastic crate if he thought the plastic crate could hold her. We discussed it over a couple of days. I was confident I could get her into a large plastic dog crate, but a dog crate with lion would be lighter and easier to carry, than the wooden den.

Early on the appointed day, right after the guys had finished cleaning the zoo and before the general public was allowed in, I told Alice at the admission desk not to open the zoo until I came back and said ok. If Siren managed to escape I did not want to deal with the general public being in the zoo. Doug and I set up the dog crate on the end of Siren's den. I enticed Siren in the den with her usual morning bottle. For all she knew I was just going to clean her cage again. Once Siren was in the den, Doug and I aligned the opened plastic dog crate with the outside den door. Dad waited by the nursery fence, with Hunter and Kyle, just in case. I kneeled down and put my face by the back of the dog crate so Siren could see me and her unfinished baby bottle of magic milk. *No drugs in that milk, Siren just loved her bottles.*

On my command, Doug lifted the sliding vertical door on the back of the den. I expected Siren to come bounding to me. But no go. It took a couple of minutes of baby talk and my waving of the bottle to get her to move into the crate. When she did, Doug took the slide and moved it out of the tract and placed it in front of the plastic crate door. Doug had realized it, but I had not, that we were going to have to move the crate back at least two feet in order to close the horizontally hinged door on the crate. I stayed by my now hissing lion, talking incessantly to calm her.

"Talk to her, Lori, talk to her," Dad kept saying from the nursery fence. He had grown hard of hearing and could not hear that I was already talking.

Doug, Kyle and Hunter worked as a team, two sliding the crate towards me, the other holding the wooden slide over the open door. Then at the right moment, the slide was slid quickly over to the side as the crate door swung closed in one fell swoop. And Latched. Then double checked that it was latched. Then as a precaution, we also wired the door shut. I stopped talking to hissing Siren. But to her credit, she had never swiped aclawed paw. Whew!! Worst part over, the hard part still to come.

Siren weighed lots more than just her number. When carrying a crate with a moving animal, when the animal moves to one end, or side the entire animals weight is on that side. Upset animals move a lot more than calm ones. Siren remembered the crates that she traveled in back and forth to our home at night so she was not totally undone. But she was still on the move. She was crying constantly, but not fighting or screaming. Her short yips let me know she was upset. I talked to her more. We struggled to carry the crate out the gate and to the back of the jitney. Siren was scared, hissy and she defecated in the crate. There is a phrase for that - scared s#!tless. A scared animal is a dangerous animal. Hand raised or not, we had to keep in mind that she was a frightened lion and very strong, with a full set of four inch fangs and three inch claws.

As soon as we got to the auxiliary enclosure, we all sprang into action again getting the plastic dog crate into the narrow hallway at the door. Hunter hopped over the crate and was on the inside. Instead of carrying the crate down the hallway, the guys started to slide the crate along the concrete floor. The noise of scraping plastic on the concrete set Siren's last nerve off. She started to growl and hiss, with bared fangs.

"Hey, guys, can we pick the crate up? The noise of sliding is scaring her," I asked. The men started to pick up the crate for the last ten feet of the trip. Suddenly Parker was there, asking what was the holdup, and when we were going to open the zoo.

"Let's get this done!" he stated as he gave the crate a final big push to the door of the enclosure. And the job was done. The crate was inside, we closed the gate to the enclosure. I quickly opened Sirens plastic prison and darted out the enclosure door into the hallway. And....

Siren sat in the plastic dog crate. She had stopped making any noise, her large honey eyes looking out through the open slats on the side of the pet crate. She was looking at me. She was afraid of her new environment. Constant eye contact. I could read her eyes.

"Yeah, so what do you want me to do now, MOM?", she seemed to say. The auxiliary enclosure had two gates on the inside four foot wide hallway chain link fencing. The bark covered log was half way down the enclosure, the second door past the log. I left the rectangular building and walked to the outside, where Siren could see me and the bottle, through the open front door of the dog transport crate. I called her out. She bolted out of the dog crate and came running to me. She would not take the bottle, but rubbed on the fencing. I reassured her with pets and scratches as Doug unlatched the inside chain link door and quickly removed the crate.

Siren looked so small in her new larger enclosure. Siren would need to adjust. The guys cleared out and we all went back to our other work. I let the admission desk know we could open the zoo. I checked on Siren a couple of times that day. She had not moved from the corner to where I had called her. Each time I would walk the outside of the enclosure enticing her to follow me. Eventually, I figured out what it was. Siren was afraid of the one foot diameter bark covered log. Her eyes were constantly averting to it before retreating again to her corner. Ok. So I learned something new that day. Just because I knew what it was and was not afraid, did not mean that Siren knew also. So, I put my hands through the fencing and patted and stroked the log. Do you have any idea how stupid I felt, talking to and petting a log?? *If my college mates could see me now!*

"Pretty log, oh what a nice log, Pretty Log, Nice girl log," I repeated, while stroking the dead, eight foot long log. I used the same tone of voice which I used for Siren. A visitor asked me what I was doing. I explained that I was showing Siren that it was a nice log and she didn't need to be afraid. Those folks walked away rather quickly, glancing back over their shoulders. *Yeah, ok, I must be nuts.* But it worked. Siren cautiously came to me, sniffed my hand, then sniffed the giant log. I kept talking to the log, slowly inching towards the other side of the log in the enclosure, (I was on the outside of the fencing), moving in the direction I wanted Siren to go. Why all this bother about which side of the log a little scaredy cat lion cub was on? Siren's den and water dish were set up on the other side. It took a couple of tries, but finally Siren darted under the log and ran to the large hayed den and water dish. It took her a solid two weeks to walk past that log again. Soon enough she would bound past it, and was jumping over and on it, but to begin with, she was afraid of that log.

Even lions have obstacles in life. So if you visit the zoo and see someone doing something really strange, there is always a good reason.

Zoo Momma talking to Siren
Photo by Karen Talasco

Zoo Momma

Chapter 42 Tiny Tim

During the April clean up in 2010, Hunter sought me out. He is six feet tall, thin as a bean pole, but jam packed with wiry muscles He has a lupine walk. Hunter is a typical teenage kid, his dark hair shaved close as is the style. He looks and acts like a hard ass redneck. But I know better. Hunter has a fantastic sense of humor and a soft heart. But don't tell anybody - it would ruin the image he wants to portray.

Siren was a few months old at this time and still in the zoo nursery. (I know the last chapter took the reader to the fall of 2010.But we need to back up here.).

"Got something for you to look at Lee," He told me. "A little llama might need you."

"Ok, let's go see," was my simple reply. I hopped on his jitney and we rode up to the llama paddock and over to the back of the llama shed.

Hunter unlocked the fencing gate and slowly unlatched the back of the white wooden shed. Upon opening the door, two adult llamas quickly exited the front of the shed heading out to the green grass pasture. Laying curled up in the hay was the smallest little llama I had ever seen. The white puff ball attempted to stand, but Hunter caught him up in his strong arms first. We exited the shed, latched it, exited the paddock and locked that gate also. It surprised me that the cria did not make a fuss or try to escape Hunter's gentle grip. I drove and Hunter held the llama until we reached the barnyard. It looked like Hunter had a small swan on his lap. The little llama's legs were tucked underneath itself, its long neck holding its head held upright (a good sign). Oversized pink ears were flying in the gentle breeze.

Siren was in the center enclosure by then so the petite llama was going into the smaller gated section. I didn't want the tiny cotton ball to sit down by the side of Siren's cage and maybe be played with, (read that - injured) by Siren's claws. Oh yeah, Siren would love to play with a ball of fluff.

Hunter carried his charge to the smaller section and tenderly placed it down. We checked its sex, a boy. Inspecting the minute llama we discovered he had a turned out leg, and was about half the size of a normal cria (baby llama). With normal sized llama cria the newborn's back is about three feet high. This little cripple was only up to my knee. White and fuzzy, llama mom had cleaned him off. But Hunter was right, we were not sure this baby could reach his mother's nipples. His name came easy, tiny and crippled: Tiny Tim. And, oh my gosh, did I mention how adorable he was?

If we are taking a cria away from the parent, we usually leave it with them for the first week to get the colostrums, or first milk. Colostrum has antibodies from the mother that help initiate the immune system and helps the infant digest milk. When the guys bring me a llama that has suckled off of mom, the process to get that cria on a bottle is arduous. I straddle the cria and hold the bottle towards my inner palm as I pry open the mouth and insert the bottle tip. I don't sit on the baby, but just restrain them with my legs while my hands work on the bottle section. It is not easy. I am often kicked by hind feet trying to get away until the baby learns that I have milk. It may take two days before the little llamas drink from the bottle readily. Even then I have to be a little pushy with the nipple on their gums.

Tiny Tim was so hungry, he immediately sucked on my fingers as I examined him. That was a good sign, #1 that he was hungry, #2 that we did the right thing by bringing him in . I was right he had not drank from his mom. Hoofstock should be up on its feet and nursing within the first hour of birth. His pale pink llama ears flickered in the breeze. 'A Boy named Sue' I thought to myself as I checked his pink ears, pink legs and snout. His snow white fur was soft. His mother had cleaned him well. His little silky tail was curled in the upward position, curving over his back. His tail was chocolate brown. The rest of Tiny Tim was Clorox white, with the exception of his fore legs, ears and snout that had a strange pink cast to it. Tiny's two little toes on each foot had jet black toenails. Jet black eyes with long lush lashes coordinated his God given outfit. He had eyes like the Moppet paintings popular in my youth. As I examined his feet, his little head nestled in the curve of my neck, and he closed his eyes. He had a rough birth and a scary morning. I was in love. Tiny Tim needed me AND he was adorable.

Hunter went about his chores and left me with my tiny charge. Dad came by to see the mini cria (news travels fast through the zoo). I mentioned to Dad about the pink cast to Tiny Tim, and did he think I should bathe the rest of the blood off so Tim would be all white.

"He's not bloody. He just doesn't have enough hair yet, his skin is showing through," Dad explained. "He sure is a tiny mite."

"I named him Tiny Tim," I grinned at Dad, "Oh and look at his leg, it turns out."

"Don't worry about that. I've seen it a mess of times with calves in the barn," Dad explained. "That is a birth injury. He will walk it off. Have fun."

I made up the goats milk formula that we use on llama cria. Tiny Tim sucked down four whole ounces! Wow, did that surprise me. #1 that he drank so soon and #2 that he drank so much. I am lucky to get that much in a full sized cria.

I went about the rest of my day, with the interruptions of a baby on a bottle again. That is not a complaint. It is the reason I was put on this earth, I know it.

Come evening, I had a problem. Who to take home? I only had one large refrigerator box that would hold the little llama, and it was Siren's box. Well, let me think... Siren could sleep in the downstairs bathroom. Siren did for a week, then I successfully left her at the zoo. Until the next bad lightning rainstorm. I was also raising two baby farm goats that needed my help. They fit in a smaller box in my mud room every night. The big fridge box was moved to the corner of our great room by an electrical outlet. I taped *(donchya just love Duct Tape)* , a heating pad to the side of the box so Tiny Tim could lay against it if he got cold. He found it that first night and leaned on it like he was leaning against his natural mom. Not that he was in his box all night, everyone took turns running at my feet, two goats, Siren and Tiny Tim. Siren would make a quick game of the goats and the midget llama so everyone took turns being out of their boxes!

Last bottles are given at my house at eleven p.m.. After that it is lights out. I fed Tiny Tim first, then the goats, then Siren got her treat bottle for the night. Then I would circle back around quietly and put a towel on top of Tiny Tim's little back. Just for some extra warmth in case he needed it. Then it is bedtime, until six a.m. OR somebody cries loud enough to wake me up.

Tiny Tim was the hit of the nursery. Right up there with Siren the lion cub. In the afternoons I would take Tiny Tim out for a walk around the zoo with the kids that wanted to walk with him. Tim stayed so small, I worried that he would never grow. But slowly he did. I brushed him daily. My nieces and friends brushed him too. Tim came to love the affection. Llamas groom each other as part of the herd affection, so he was instinctually programmed for brushing.

Llamas are a member of the Camel family which originated in North America, according to fossil records. The smallest were the size of rabbits, the largest fifteen feet at the shoulder. As the species grew and diversified, they spread across the Bering Straits land bridge into Asia, south to Africa and some went due south to South America. Many of the different species died out, leaving the two humped bactrain camel (from which the one humped dromedary camel was domesticated), in Africa and the South American Llamas.

The South American llama lives in the high mountain plateaus of the Andes Mountains , usually between 13,000 and 16,000 feet above sea level. There are three subspecies of the llama family, Llama vicungua, Llama gunaco, and Llama llama. Space Farms Zoo had Llama llamas, which are about the size of a small horse. Llamas are shy and possess exceptionally good eyesight and hearing. The eyes of the llama are huge rounded orbs with luxurious long lashes. The protruding eyeballs enable the llama to see one hundred and thirty degrees from the front center, an obvious advantage against predators. The long lashes protect the eyeball itself. The combination of large eyes and long lashes give the llama an appealing, doe-eyed, sweet and innocent appearance. Llamas come in colors of black, brown, white, chestnut, pumpkin, and/or any combination thereof. The abundant thick fur is an insulating factor in the winter and the summer, enabling the llama to endure extreme temperature variations. The fur is shed naturally, giving the llama a natural clumpy Rastafarian look if they are not brushed.

The main defense of a llama is to run, fast. Or, if they think they can intimidate the foe, llamas will belly bump (like a sumo wrestler), kick or spit. The spit is actually chewed cud, the llama being a bovine. That fact does not make it any nicer if a llama spits on you. Green slimy spit does not accessorize any outfit well. We always know who is behaving in the zoo and who is teasing the animals. The visitors that tease the animals always come in to buy a clean T-shirt from the gift shop!

Llamas are herbivores, feeding on grasses and grains, browsing constantly during the day. Llamas are herd animals. A herd consisting of one male, a harem of females and young. When young male llamas mature they join a teenage male herd, jousting and practice fighting, waiting for their chance to fight for supremacy of a herd. Mother Nature has equipped the male llamas with slightly bucked bottom teeth. Llamas have no top teeth, only a hard palate. The head honcho (alpha) male of a herd will attempt to castrate the younger males that challenge his supremacy. It is not a pleasant sight. We always remove the young males before sexual maturity. The South American natives domestically breed llamas as pack animals. The natives use the llamas as pack animals, comb out their fur for yarn, milk them for dairy products, and on occasion, while stuck in an Andes snowstorm, eat them.

Cria (the Spanish word for llama babies) are born after an eleven-month gestation and walk within an hour of birth. By five hours old they can run with the herd. The neat thing about llamas (that we keepers and the vets appreciate) is that the cria are always born during daytime. Dad explained it to me. The babies could be born year round but any baby born in the cold winter months would be doomed to freeze to death if it was born (and stayed wet from birth fluids) at night. Cria born in the daytime have the warm sun to help them dry off and get the thick coat ready to insulate them for warmth through the night. Here is an evolutionary survival trait of being born in the daytime. Makes sense if you think about it. Another interesting fact of llama husbandry is that llamas always pee and poop in one spot, making them easier to clean up after than, say, horses or cows, that leave patties all over the pasture. The alpha male will mark this territory with his own urine.

The Space Farms Zoo had purchased a pair of llamas in the early nineteen eighties. The herd increased naturally as time progressed. In the mid eighties the llamas became a fad species for gentleman farmers looking for unique animals to add to their farms. The natural territorialism of the males and females made them a safe alternative to guard dogs. Llamas are used to this day as protection for sheep herds and other herd animals. Llamas challenge intruders, belly bumping, kicking and spitting, but rarely doing any permanent harm, while intimidating their foe.

The price of a female llama in the late eighties was $10,000 for a newborn. The fancy purebred breeder llamas were selling for upwards of $50,000. It was easy money for gentleman farmers. By the nineteen nineties the cost for a pet quality llama had dropped to $500. The fad had played itself out, a classic case of supply and demand, but the popularity of llamas had not.

Space Farms Zoo has a standing herd of fourteen females and one male. Training a llama cria to drink from a bottle is no easy task. Newborns are easier to break to a bottle than a cria that has been with mama for a couple of weeks. Nipple confusion happens to animals too. Of course the baby is frightened of you, you are a strange creature to them. They can run fast. I leave them alone for about six hours to get used to their new environment; even chickens can be scary if you've never seen them before. After being away from mama for about six hours they get hungry. That's when I first try them on a bottle. We use the kid goat milk replacer and a standard human baby bottle with an elongated nipple. Llamas cush (or koosh), which means to kneel quickly into a sitting position on the ground. One member of the herd will cush under duress of predators, sacrificing themselves if need be. Llamas will also cush individually under pressure. I use this natural phenomenon while training the infant. I slowly approach the baby and wait till the last possible moment to reach out and grab a hold of them. There is no use running or trying to chase young llamas down, they run faster than I. I use both hands to settle him down and swing one leg over its back. I seem to be just the right height so I am not riding them with my body weight, but gently corralling the cria between my legs. One hand rubs the neck while the other hand slowly comes up with the bottle between the thumb and forefinger, nipple towards the palm. Using the middle or ring finger of the bottle hand I ever so gently pry open the jaw behind the front teeth (cria are born with teeth) and insert the nipple. If the cria does not suck right away, I rub the neck area. I often cover the baby's eyes to eliminate distractions. If they were drinking from mama, the eyes would be closed, chin resting between mama's back legs. As soon as they figure out that the milk flows when they suck, they drink greedily. I remain as quiet as possible so as not to scare the cria with a strange voice.

I learned a trick from a llama herder, Cathy the Llama Lady. I gently blow on the nose of the llama baby to 'scent' him. The mama llama would nuzzle and breathe on her baby while nursing. This helps with the bonding process between the cria and myself. So here I am straddling a tiny llama, bending close to shade his eyes with my chest and arms, blowing on the nose, all the while holding a bottle in reverse position with one hand, rubbing the little llama's neck with the other.

Tiny Tim got all the affection he needed and I blew on his wiggly nose every time I could. He still likes me to 'give kisses' today! Llamas have almost prehensile lips, and Tiny Tim's rubbery lips love to give me kisses back. When you see Tim all you have to say is "Kisses Timmy, Kisses" and make the kissy noise with your lips. Smack, smack, smack and he will come right up to you and kiss your lips. But don't do it right after he has had a mouth full of food. Sometimes Timmy does not like to be disturbed while he is eating.

Dr. Ted came and neutered Timmy one afternoon. It needed to be done, as Timmy was maturing, and I did not want the constant 'Timmy and Lori Show'! Male llamas that are hand raised need to be neutered to avoid berserk llama syndrome, where the llama is much too familiar with humans. We also had him sheared the first year. I had the shearers leave Timmy a mane, like a horse. It was a rough procedure, for Tim, having the shearers manipulate Timmy professionally. For me, the mom, it was rough too. Now I just brush him, and that will have to be good enough.

Timmy stayed in the nursery for two years. He was our giant mascot greeting visitors right outside the zoo doors. I would take Timmy out for walks every so often, in his bright blue halter. We would go for a jog around the Syrian bear enclosure. Timmy's long white hair would stream out behind him like the best of the Baywatch Babes. As Timmy got older, he did not want to go back into his nursery gate, even though he had the whole run of the nursery area.

Tiny Tim only had one flaw. He hated our daughter Jackie. Every time the llama saw/sees Jackie, he'd come running to spit on her. If Jackie was home visiting me and in 'Timmy's' barnyard, Tim would hold his head high and glare at Jackie out of the corner of his eye. At every opportunity, Tim would sneak up on Jackie and try to bite her rump or push her with his body. Once Timmy was almost successful in bumping Jackie into the murky green pond by the nursery! I could not believe my eyes, but he did try to belly bump our daughter. It was obvious and intentional. Jackie avoided Tiny Tim after that and a sibling rivalry developed between the two. I have a white llama Christmas tree ornament on my tree. It has 'pooped' on Jackie's baby picture ornament. *And Jackie did not think that was funny?* I mention this because any blonde, tallish, thin female visiting the zoo may have a problem. Sierra, my current assistant has a problem with Timmy. Sierra looks a lot like Jackie. *Oh well, what is a mom to do? Kids!*

Tim had grown quite large, maybe hip high at his back. His luxurious fluffy white fur makes him appear larger. One day, Timmy escaped the nursery (with some help from Alice from admissions!), and was running loose in the zoo unsupervised. Timmy gracefully grazed on the lush green grass of the zoo grounds... until he saw a visitor coming through the zoo doors. Then Tim bee lined for that visitor, knowing that the visitor most likely had a bag of corn. Well, the lady and her daughter came running back inside petrified. In Timmy's defense, the lady saw big Tim, and started running, with two bags of corn in her hand, jiggling the bags as she ran. Timmy must of thought, "This is good fun, food and a run!" and ran right up to her backside, trying to nip at the clear plastic corn bags in her hand. The lady started screaming as she ran, which got my attention. Any animal on the run with it's head down is scary for sure. I saw what was happening, grabbed a bag of corn and went out to solve the situation. The lady was quite shook up, even after I explained she and her daughter were in no danger. I could understand that. She and I have since become friends.

And Timmy was put into a larger paddock in the back of the zoo with lots more grass to eat and room to run. I see him often if not daily to brush him. He has a spot on his back where if you rub him, he will move his lips like Mr. Ed the horse. Every year he gets a few little goats to befriend when the male goats come off of the bottle and start butting heads. Tim is the king of the hoofstock. If you go to visit Tiny Tim, do not wear sunglasses that reflect. If you do, Tim sees the male llama in the reflection and will spit on you. He has become very territorial and protective of his paddock. Other than that, he greets everyone looking for affection or food.

I had a local farm lady offer to buy Timmy. I thought about it. I discussed it with Hunter, Doug and Dad.

"Naw, we gotta keep Timmy, everybody loves him! He gives kisses!" Hunter said. Good enough for me. Timmy stays. As I am writing this Tim is now four years old and has quite a zoo visitor following. The visitors bring him treats and goodies. When I need a minute's peace, I go brush Timmy. And Timmy still hugs me back, curving his neck around mine.

Tiny Tim gives Zoo Momma a smooch.
Photo by Leonard Rue III

Chapter 43 Lynx

Sometimes animals come to us by word of mouth. A gentleman that owns horses in New York State also had a home in Florida. Florida animal laws are very lax compared to New Jersey animal laws. In Florida, anyone can own just about any animal. You need to get a permit, but there are no laws prohibiting Joe Q. Public from owning exotic animals. The equine gentleman owned lynx he kept in his home in Florida. His vet talked to our vet and the equine gentleman gave me a call. The equine gentleman said the two parents had been rescued from a fur farm in Colorado. The adult pair had offspring, and would I take three of the offspring off his hands? Why not? And I became the adoptive mom to three twelve week old lynx kittens. He wanted to keep a one year old kitten he had hand raised, but did not have the time to care for three more. The parents were non-handleable.

The lynx (plural of lynx is lynx) arrived in August. Siren was in the middle enclosure in the nursery. Timmy was roaming the entire nursery with three little goats and a couple of Mouflon sheep. I set a dog cage up in Dad's basement to keep the kittens in quarantine away from the rest of the zoo for a couple of weeks. Feline diseases are very communicable. (The lynx kittens did well by the way)

When the kittens arrived they hissed at me, not a good sign. Their adoptive mom picked them up and put them in the dog crate. Got to admit they were adorable. They were about the size of a eight week old house cat - only on stilts! Their legs seemed so long. We did the paperwork and they said goodbyes. I figured I'd better read up on lynx.

The lynx is the Canadian cousin of the bobcat. The lynx is the third largest cat in North America after the cougar and the jaguar. It is larger of frame than a bobcat, as far as height, but stays streamlined even in areas of abundant food. Up to twenty four inches tall at the shoulder, the body weight rarely exceeds thirty pounds. The most distinctive characteristic difference is the extended black hair tuft on tip of each of the ears and a facial ruff, like muttonchop sideburns on the side of the face. The ears have black tips and there are dark vertical lines in the ruff next to the face. The color of the fur is tawny reddish in the spring and summer, turning into a silvery color in the winter. In the winter their fur is longer and of course helps to keep the animal warm. The warm winter fur coat of the lynx is shed out in the spring. Without his thick winter fur, the lynx looks scrawny. The distinct rings on the tail of the young fade over time to be barely visible.

Lynx eyes can see exceptionally well in the nighttime. They almost glow with the reflection of the light on their retinas. Peering into the eyes of a lynx is like peering into a pool of honeyed lemon. The fluorescent yellow gold will stare you down, the deep yellow of the iris somehow has an evil taint with his vertical pupils.

The front legs of the lynx are shorter than the rear legs. The long rear legs gives the lynx a distinct advantage in jumping. Lynx will tree, jumping in and out of the tree. Their spine is very supple, enabling the cat to twist in amazing ways. If you have ever seen the videos of lynx chasing snowshoe rabbits (their main source of food) in the wild, you will notice this feature. With the front legs shorter, the walking lynx looks stooped over, like an old man. The muttonchops contribute to this image. Those long jumping legs help the lynx to run ten to twelve miles per hour and leap forward, up to fifteen feet according to Dr. Leonard Lee Rue III's book, Furbearing Animals of North America.

The feet of the lynx are amazing. The front paws of the adult lynx are about four inches in diameter. The retractable claws are covered in fur. The paw itself serves as a snowshoe. Now here is the part that I discovered and I had not seen in any lynx literature or information. This was true for all the lynx I raised and observed. Our lynx were all from the same family line, so whether or not this is a genetic trait with only this family I don't know. But here goes: The lynx toes are webbed with furry skin up to the first knuckle. That makes the snowshoe effect even more advantageous. *Remember that, you heard it from me first!*

I discovered this by accident. An accident. The kittens never really bonded with me. They had each other and were eating solid canned cat food when they came to me. After a couple of weeks of quarantine in Dad's basement, I set up a portable dog corral in the nursery. Stretched out long ways, it was eight feet long and three feet wide, with a top on it. The kittens enjoyed being outside. Sand and grass and a large wooden den completed their enclosure. The kittens loved toys which they were supplied with constantly. The lynx would tear up the average housecat toy, so we went through quite a few stuffed animal toys. The visiting public could see them but not touch. The lynx avoided me whenever I changed their litter box. These were to be exhibit animals only. But that was ok. Wild animal babies revert very quickly if not constantly handled and worked with. The kittens stayed in that enclosure until after Labor Day.

After Labor Day we moved Siren, my big girl lion cub to the auxiliary enclosure that would be Siren's winter home. The auxiliary enclosure was much larger for Siren. That left the center enclosure in the nursery available for the lynx kittens.

I had to make a few adaptations. Siren had walked/packed down the grass in the enclosure. So all the soil was removed. Dad always said to put new animals on clean soil. New soil was added and grass seed was planted. I replaced the rusty chicken wire I had put over the top of the enclosure when the servals escaped. I in no way want the reader to think I did all this work by myself. I did a lot of it, but I had help. I would plan my weeks to do this labor on the weekends when Jennie Beckman would stop by and help. I also had assistance from Sierra, a season pass local kid that always seemed willing. Hunter and Lindsey were always around too. So weekends were a good work time for the nursery. I had a platform to create shade in the enclosure when Siren was little. When Siren grew, she would sit on top of it, princess that she had become. The platform had become quite worn, and wobbly. I took that down and removed it. After the quick growing grass seed had sprouted, we carefully moved the little lynx the six foot distance to their 'new' enclosure. They enjoyed the new space, running and jumping around as young kids would do.

Every time I walked past the back of the den the naturally skittish lynx would rocket out of the den. One morning as I first walked in the nursery, I noticed one of the little lynx had its paw stuck on the turned up fencing where the den door was. I knew this was going to be a two man job. I called Hunter and he met me at the nursery. I explained the problem. All three not so little lynx were hissing and barring their teeth, obviously upset. I'm sure the reader is thinking house cat sized kittens. At three months old the lynx were eighteen inches high at the shoulder, with carnasial (canine) teeth at least two inches long. So figure twice the size of a large house cat. Handled just enough so the lynx knew we could be frightened of them if they hissed and showed teeth. AND that we humans would back off if bitten.

First we tried using a shovel to lift the stuck lynx off the ground, loosening up the body weight of the lynx on its paw, so the lynx could pull free. Well, between the panicked little lynx and the slipperiness of the shovel, that did not work. Hunter and I decided we needed 'the gloves'. The gloves are a set of leather welder's gloves that we keep in the office on top of my file cabinet. We have three pair. We always return them to the same spot, so everyone knows where they are in case of an emergency, just like this. The gloves are well used, a quicker solution than knocking an animal out with drugs, (which we would have to call Dr. Ted and arrange a visit, which would take more time). A quick discussion ensued. Hunter's arms were longer than mine, and longer than the lynx's legs. Keep in mind the lynx also has razor sharp claws, four sets on four paws, and a great set of fangs. Hunter would be able to grab the lynx by the belly, behind the front legs, and lift the kitten off the pointed fencing, without the lynx being able to get claws on Hunter's body core. Or maneuver to bite his hand (we hoped). The gloves go to the elbow, so his arms would be protected. I grabbed a snake hook and we were set.

Fifteen year old Hunter grabbed the long slinky lynx and lifted it upward taking the gravity pressure off the trapped foot. Do not for a minute think that the lynx was passively enjoying this attention. Hunter had his gloved hands on a wild lynx kitten, panicked, hissing and snarling. The lynx was fighting for its life, not realizing we were trying to help. The upset lynx's other three paws were extended, slashing with wicked curved claws. As Hunter lifted the wild cat, the lynx kept fighting us, not realizing the foot could be released. So I took the snake hook and pried the paw upwards releasing it. As I did so, I noticed exactly how the paw was impaled on the fencing. The paw was impaled through the webbing between the toes. Through that accident is how I first came to know that the lynx have webbed toes.

I contacted Dr. Ted and we chatted about the lynx. She was prescribed antibiotics, which I placed in small meatballs to administer. The other lynx kittens were in that enclosure also, so I made some dud meatballs for them, and medicated meatballs for Twinkletoes. Liverwurst is the best meatball ingredient, as it smells stronger than almost any medicine. Twinkletoes limped for a day or two and recuperated just fine from her paw puncture wound

I bent the exposed prong of the fencing over so that type of accident could not happen again. I checked the rest of the enclosure for any other potential problems and fixed what needed to be done. The baby bottle holes in the back of the den were covered over, giving the young skittish lynx a place to hide comfortably without being scared by what was moving behind them.

The end of the next winter season the little lynx had grown to full size, and they were moved into the adult zoo.

Lori and Lynx kittens

Photo by Karen Talasco

Zoo Momma

Chapter 44 Juggling

In October, the same equine gentleman called and wanted to bring the parent lynx. I set up a section of the auxiliary enclosure for the lynx parents. Diego and Chiquita Coatimundi would share a common fence wall and I did not want the lynx grabbing them through the nine gauge chain link for fun and games. Doug and I installed some one by one fencing over the chain link between the two species.

After the zoo closed for the season, the coati would be moved to winter quarters. I scrubbed clean the section before opening the connecting door and letting the lynx into the vacated cage. I anticipated problems and was quite surprised when the lynx seemed to know what I wanted and padded softly on their huge furry paws over to the new section. Or maybe it was the very nice new wooden den full of hay that attracted them. Whatever it was, the short move was much easier than I anticipated.

Moving the adult lynx was part of a larger plan to give Siren more room and a place to go while we cleaned her section of the enclosure. Siren had the long section all by herself but that would be a problem when snow flew. We could hay down her side and den but needed to remove the dirty hay when she pooed and peed on it. A tunnel was created through the end of the hallway to the halved section where the adult lynx had been. By using a horizontal slide through the tunnel section, we could trap Siren into the smaller half section. This allowed us to clean the full side of the auxiliary enclosure, safely, without Siren (the adult German Shepard sized, and very frisky), lion cub. When no cleaning procedures were in process, Siren had the full run of both the full side and the half side of the auxiliary enclosure. Once while cleaning Siren's enclosure I left my cotton garden gloves stuffed in the chain link fence. You guessed it, Siren ate one. I called Dr. Spinks just for the reassurance that they would pass through her intestinal tract. And it did, undigested, but I did not want to use that glove again! Cheap lesson learned.

When the adult lynx needed to be cleaned, we reversed the process. Siren was locked into her full side The door between the two half sides was opened. The parent lynx would slowly trot into the other half side of the enclosure. It was quite the dance going on once a week. Everybody knew the steps, and they all got dry hay to cuddle in and clean homes.

By the next spring we had a larger natural turf enclosure available for the lynx as the fifteen year old fishers had 'aged out'. We moved the adult lynx. They must of liked the new natural turf, because they had offspring . Dad and I watched the babies for two weeks, twice peeking into the mother lynx's specially designed den. That mom lynx was all hiss, fangs and claws when Dad very quickly peeked. She charged at him. At two weeks old we could see through the den door that the kittens were beginning to crawl. We knew it was time. We live trapped the mom out with food, and then took the young away to bottle feed. Later that day Jennie Beckman and I were surprised when the tiny, two fists long, kittens drank formula at first offering. That was extremely unusual for young that had nursed off of mom for two weeks. The kittens thrived, and did well, but I must admit I never truly bonded with the clown faced kittens. I knew we would place them at another zoo.

Bernadette (Bunny) Hoffman, an animal handler from New York state came to us and chose first. She named her kitten Max. I could not have asked for a better home for Max. Bunny works on the positive reward and communication method with Max. He is well trained and an absolutely fabulous specimen. Bunny used the Syn Alia Training System with Max from an early age. Syn Alia Training Systems foster synergistic alliances with people or animals. This training recognizes and respects the intelligence, ability and sovereignty of every being, focusing on partnership. Max is still a wild animal but with training he is much easier to handle in public. And Max is more relaxed, less skittish. Bunny says he behaves on command, if he feels like it! Such a diva! Max is a wonderful animal ambassador, educating the public he meets. He posed for Bunny and let her take a picture of his webbed feet. Max is just gorgeous.

The second kitten stayed with us until Doug and my vacation in July. We met folks from a zoo in Buffalo, N.Y. at a restaurant stop off of the N.Y. State Thruway. Once again I was doing paperwork on top of our car, while the new keepers were cuddling the little male lynx. After a quick but sad goodbye, Doug and I continued on to our Canadian vacation.

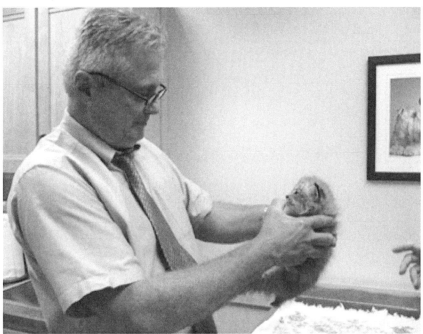

Ted Spinks V.M.D. holds lynx kitten.
Photo by Lori Space Day

Chapter 45 Bobcats

Claws and Paws Zoo out in Pennsylvania gave us a call. Vince Hall, first generation owner, said he had a litter of baby bobcats. Were we interested? Dad decided to take in two as our resident bobcat was getting older. Bobcats are protected in New Jersey as an endangered specie. Bobcats live eighteen to twenty-two years in captivity but are lucky to reach twelve in the wild. My Grandfather, Ralph Space, raised a bobcat and had it at our zoo for thirty two years!

We wanted a male and a female. Claws and Paws thought they had two males. I say that because on small, mother raised (-read that wild) kittens, the examinations are quick, the genitals are tiny. The youngsters were wiggly, clawing, hissy and bitey. At ten weeks old they would be a handful, but I did not feel the need to hand tame them anyway. The kittens had received their first set of shots. My hands were full with other infants. But we needed the bobcats and they were young. To make sure that the small cats would adapt ok to our food system, the youngster bobcats spent the summer in the nursery.

The bobcats adapted well to ground venison, my special mix with dry cat food mixed in. In the wild the cats do not eat just the meat of the prey animal. The majority of their diet is rabbit. However Bobcats will prey upon any small mammals, birds, bird eggs, frogs and fish. They also eat the intestines, small bones, (we are talking bobcats here, not lions), some hide and hair, and the offal. Offal is organ meat. Each part of the prey animal has its own special nutrients. The scat of the wild bobcat has told keen observers all these edible facts. So just straight ground venison meat would not be the proper diet for the young bobcats.

The little ones were about ten inches tall and just about that long when we received them. Their facial markings made the kittens look like fuzzy clowns. Black stripes across the muzzle and immature white ruffs sat below shoe button round gold iris eyes. The eye liner applied by nature made their round eyes appear almost Asian. I've only seen beige colored base coated bobcats in our area. In winter, the natural fur coats become more silvery and much fluffier. Bobcats do come in beige to reddish brown to more silver colors due to geographical differences. The young are spotted, but most gradually loose those spots upon maturity. Southwestern Bobcats keep their spots throughout their lives. The tail is notable because it is short, hence the name 'bobbed'. That name eventually became bob cat. They are also called a wildcat. *I don't use that name as it is too easily confused with a feral, wild cat - a housecat gone wild.* The tail has a white tip, is short (or bob-ed, hence the name) and distinct black rings as youngsters. As adults the rings fade slightly. The kittens' fluffy fur was so inviting to the touch, however I knew better. Soon enough they became used to my voice, and less afraid of their new environment. They never calmed down enough to come to my hand. *Always offer your non-dominate hand by the way!*

Bobcats are protected in New Jersey, and seldom seen. The bobcat is a medium sized cat, with a body as big as a bread box and add long legs. The larger bobcat males may weigh up to fifty pounds in a prey rich environment. The average male bobcat weighs in about twenty five pounds; the females a little less. If the snow is deep, a bobcat can take down a white tailed deer by jumping on its back and biting the neck. So these are not a small housecat gone wild. Bobcats are natural predators.

A wild bobcat can make a frightful noise. The scream is loud and guttural. The little kittens did not scream. They had nothing to be afraid of, but I did hear chufs, snorts, trills, a lot of hissing and gentle meows. Snarling was only heard when we needed to move them to the adult zoo in the fall.

The loud scream of the bobcat is often made during the breeding season as a territorial marker, along with urinating as a sign of ownership. The males will follow the scent of the female to find her to breed. A female will make a den wherever she finds a good spot - under a fallen tree, in a rocky crevice, a hollow tree, or in another animals abandoned burrow. Gestation is about sixty-five days and a litter average is three. Kittens are born weighing about half a pound, with closed eyes that open on day 14. Like other cats, the bobcat kittens are fairly mobile at three weeks, and mom bobcat starts to bring home prey for the youngsters to chew on. Up until the kittens are two months old, mom only leaves them long enough to hunt and drink. Good babies sleep while mom is gone. Bad, noisy babies are killed off by predators. Mom bobcat is their only source of protection as father bobcat has no family role.

Our little bobcats grew up and are doing well at the zoo. Even though they have been on public display for five years as of this writing, they have not warmed up to the general public. The bobcats are often hiding in the long grass in their enclosure. They are bobcats, beautiful yet elusive, just like their wild cousins.

One of the bobcat kittens
Photo by Karen Talasco

Chapter 46 Dasari

With the death of Siren's mom, Parker had put the word out that we were in need of an adult lioness. Attila the Hunk was forth generation born at the zoo. He needed a companion to keep him happy. Some animals are just as happy solitary, like lynx, tigers, leopards, and bears. Those species are innately geared to live alone. In the wild those types of species would be alone except during courtship and breeding. African lions are a different story. They have been genetically wired to be a social animal living in a pride. So Attila needed a friend. It would take a year to eighteen months until Siren would be big enough to be reunited with Attila. So Parker had put the word out.

Animal people are always very colorful personalities. And boy did our new lioness come with an outstanding character! Shortly after we closed for the season, I was caring for the six exotic parrots by the large picture windows in our now closed restaurant. A double cab pick-up truck pulled up in front of the feed bunker flower pots in front of the main building. The flowers in the beds always look their best just before our first frost. *Wouldntcha know!* A large blue tarp was covered over a huge box shape weighing down the bed of the truck. Out of the back seats on each side, came two burly men, dressed like us... Slightly unkempt looking, but obviously hard working guys. From the passenger side of the truck spilled out a tiny young woman, blonde, and cute, also dressed as if she knew what kind of work we would be doing. The driver exited the side of the truck closest to the large windows I was working behind. Tall, well built and wearing... a kilt. *I must admit, I stifled a snicker and tried not to roll my eyes. Oh my God, another God's gift to women!* The kilt was made of faded olive green canvas, with brass rivets and had obviously been worn quite a bit. Muscular legs strode beneath the knee length kilt. *Wonder if he is a true Scotsman?* They walked towards the locked double front doors as I arrived at the door with my zoo keys in hand to unlock it. My other hand was on my phone.

"Hi guys, what can I help you with?" I queried.

"We're here to see Parker, we have the lioness," the tall kilted driver stated.

"Ok, I'll get him, Hi, I'm Lori, Parker's sister, want some coffee? Or the rest rooms? They're over there," I pointed out as I extended my hand for a shake. I didn't know the lioness was coming that day but that didn't matter. My days after we close are very flexible. At least my momentary fear of letting a strange guy in a kilt into the building abated. If he was an animal person, I knew I had nothing to fear. I called Parker and let him know the unusual crew was here.

Parker magically appeared and shook hands with the Kilted Driver. Hunter and Doug showed up at the same time, Hunter had been assisting Doug when they got the call. I could not see a change in the look on Doug's face when he saw the kilt, but having been married to Doug for close to thirty years, I could read the chuckle in his eyes. *Oh yeah, Hon, this ones a gem!* Hunter, being young and unsophisticated literally stopped in his tracks for one moment, then said nothing and continued. The chuckle in his eyes mimicked Doug's. Introductions were made all round. After everyone's rest room and coffee break, we headed out to the lion's den.

Parker, Kilted Driver and Doug discussed the logistics of the truck, the lioness in the cage and our lion enclosure. It was decided to get the skid loader and lift the guard fencing posts out of the way. Hunter was sent to retrieve the skid loader with the large forks attached. Doug and the two burly guys from the truck took down what they needed to of the chain link guard fencing. Attila was locked up onto the concrete section.

I chatted with the young woman. She was new in the business, and we both listened in on Parker's conversation with the Kilted Driver. I had questions concerning the lioness. Was she de-clawed or de-fanged? No. Neither. *Good, in case of a fight, she would have a chance.* When were her last shots and worming? *Good answers.* Is she friendly, what is her name, and was she hand reared. Yes, she is friendly, her name is Dasari , and she was hand reared. Did the lioness ever have young? No. How old is she? Nine. Has she been socialized with other lions? Yes.

The young woman, maybe twenty years old, was obviously besotted with the Kilted Driver. Her eyes traveled to him constantly, body contact, not PDA, was exhibited. Kilted Driver was/is about Parker's age, forty-ish, with thinning long mousy brown hair in a pony tail down his back. By any standards he was a handsome man, if you were not put off by the hair and outfit that screamed for attention. His clothing, while unique, was not my concern. I mention it only as a chuckle to my reader. Animal people can be, hummm… let's say different. *And I just cut out a pair of wild jungle and animal print capris last night! So I really have nothing to say.*

Hunter arrived with the skid loader and pressed the forks right up to the uprights of the gate posts on the guard fence. Doug was on his knees wrapping chain around the lower cement encased fence posts. Kilted Driver walked by with more chain for the other side. *Just look Doug, Oh just look up and let me know later! Is Kilted Driver a true Scotsman?* Doug never even glanced upwards. *Darn! I asked Doug later and Doug said the thought never even crossed his mind. Ok so I am a curious female.* Doug moved to the other side and fixed the chain in place around the opposite cement bottom fence post. On Doug's hand signal, Hunter slowly raised the fence posts out of the ground. The men grabbed them and pushed them out of the way.

The next part was tricky. The wheeled cage with Dasari, a 500 lb. lioness, in it was rolled to the edge of the truck. The long two inch diameter metal fence poles were utilized and slid through the transport cage to the other side, where the men could grab a hold of each side to lift, safely away from the lioness. They lifted and slid the large cage with lioness to the ground. The grass impeded the movement of the wheels as they sunk into the soft earth. More lifting and groaning.

With the final "On Three! One, two, three," the huge eight foot by five foot by five foot cage was at the lion's enclosure gate to the grassy section. More discussion ensued. A piece of paneling fencing was brought to place over the gaping difference between the top of the transport cage and the top opening of the door. All of us with enough experience have seen animals try to exit the transport and circle right back up and over the transport cage to get back to the safety of the truck's inside. The animal was safe inside the truck but the new enclosure territory can be scary. The paneling was temporarily wired into place.

More discussion and inspection took place. Dad drove out in his car and observed. No one could think of any precaution that had not been taken. There was a loaded gun in Dad's car, just in case. When we move an animal we think of the procedure for weeks, brainstorming, going over safety protocols etc. That was done, the thoughts were thought, safety taken into account and the animal in place and all we had to do was open the horizontal slide on the red transport cage.

On Parker's signal, the slide was opened. Attila had been sitting by the chute door calmly, quietly watching every move. When the slide was opened, Dasari just sat in the transport cage. The swinging chain link door of the enclosure had swung closed in the breeze.

Not thinking twice, Kilted Driver signaled to the young woman and held his hands in a stirrup position. The young woman placed a foot in Kilted Driver's hands and was boosted into the air. She landed acrobatically on the edge of the top of the transport cage. Dasari looked up, but still did not move.

" Stay on the edge, and walk the cage to the door," Kilted Driver confidently instructed. "She won't bother you." Snug faded jeans clad petite legs that walked the narrow three inch edge of the cage. Almost like she was walking an acrobatic barre. The bars on the cage were wide enough for the lioness to reach out easily and grab the graceful, agile girl. The young lady swung the enclosure door open.

"Shoo!" said Kilted Driver as he waved his hand.

Dasari stood and moseyed out of the transport onto the November brown grass.

Attila stood up, much more interested now that a strange female lioness was in HIS territory.

Ok so only one hitch so far. That was pretty good. The girl held the chain link door open and quickly closed it so it could be latched and locked. The transport cage, a lot lighter now, was placed back in the truck. Dasari had circled the grassy section and was standing next to the chute with Attila.

Since there was no hissing, snarling, or baring of teeth, things were going well. The chute door was open and Attila strutted, literally strutted out. Sniffing the air, giving the Flehman response, he strode confidently over to Dasari. The Flehman response is when a cat opens its mouth wide, almost looking like it has a nasty taste in its mouth, rubbing the top/back of the tongue on the roof of the mouth. This takes minute molecules of surrounding air to the Jacobian organs located on the roof of the cat's mouth. Jacobian organs are super sensitive scent organs.

Attila was certainly strutting his stuff! This is the same strut I see on human body builders pumped full of themselves. Dasari stood her ground, but did not show teeth. Attila sniffed her, and they walked side by side over to the center of the enclosure and lay in the sun covered greenish fading-to-brown grass. And that was that. We were prepared for a rough house round of friskiness that never happened. Or a nasty lion fight. Once a lion fight happens, there is nothing you can do to stop it. Hosing the fighters down with water will temporarily work, but not forever. We were all very, very relieved.

Everyone packed up and Dad covered lunch at the Mountain View Country Store. Yep, our hometown deli full of local lunchtime rednecks and we brought in a man in a kilt, a twenty something gorgeous gal, and two more redneck types. No comments were said out loud... But I could hear our neighbor's thoughts, though.

We all ate and said good bye. I wished the young woman well, and hope she learned all she needed to learn about the animals she worked with. I never did learn what was up with the kilt.

Hunter Space feeds Attila and Dasari
Photo by Lori Space Day

Chapter 47 Peggy Roo

Dear Peggy Roo,   October 18, 2010

I am so sorry Peggy Roo, we tried, we really tried. We had waited in anticipation after you first played peek-a-boo at five months old. When we first saw you two months ago, we were all so excited to have a little girl. After your three brothers, we had hoped for a little girl. When you sunbathed next to your mom, you were the cutest little thing. All that was missing was a pair of flashy sunglasses to make you a star. Then the worst thing happened to your long beautiful legs. I'm sure the kids that spooked your brothers had no idea of the consequences, and your brothers did not mean to break your foot. Good thing I did not see it happen, or I'd be in jail for assault.

You were so cute that we decided to give you the best care possible. So we called Dr. Ted Spinks V.M.D. and you went for your first car ride to his hospital. Mom was waiting for you in the warm hay lined barn room when you came home with your amputated foot covered in massive bandages. When you woke up, Mom welcomed you and let you nurse again. We were worried that she would not accept you, with your snow white bandages, but maternal instincts are amazing. So we waited for your stubby foot to heal. Dr. Ted and Technician Jennie came to clean, re-bandage, and give you antibiotics every couple of days. Parker and the guys chased you down and Parker would hold you while Dr. Ted worked. We were all amazed at how fast you could run with an amputated foot. You had admirable spunk.

After a hard rain the bandage needed to be changed again. Hunter my nephew volunteered. He knew the bandage needed to be changed and Hunter was the fastest runner to catch you, fifteen year old humans are fast. *Darn! You were faster on that stump!* After a few misses and nose dives, Hunter caught you. Kneeling on the ground, Hunter simply held you and turned his head to the side. Hunter held you safe and secure in his arms while I changed the dressing. Doug was there to hand me the equipment and bandages you needed. I commend Hunter because it took a major effort for him to hold you. Not that you struggled so much, you were small, docile and barely moved in his arms. Hunter, you see, is afraid of needles and medical procedures. He passes out. Cold. Just so you know what a trial it was for him. Hunter did well.

I unwrapped the bandages and knew what I saw was not healing well. Oh your foot stub had started to heal, but then your constant jumping and walking on it caused the skin to break the stitches and peel up your leg, exposing the bones of your foot stub and lower leg. Good thing Hunter did not look, it was not a pretty sight. And your foot smelled.

I called Dr. Ted and set up a time for you to be checked out. Another ride in the car to the hospital. You were a wonderful patient, having become accustomed to the constant care and attention. Watchful, perky shoe button brown eyes looked around as they removed bandages. Ears alert to every sound, and your nose still twitching with the unusual smell of the atmosphere at the hospital. We discussed the progress of your healing, or lack thereof. After the exam, Dr. Ted said we needed to take off your damaged leg before it caused infection to seep into your body. If he did not take the whole leg, you would instinctually use the stub and break the stitches again, causing repeated infections once you were off antibiotics. The exposed bone would wick infections into your delicate little body. We knew you could use your tail and one leg to hop. So to save your life, Dr. Ted decided to amputate your left leg at the hip.

Marge the office manager came by the examination room. I asked her to please get my car keys from my purse in the waiting room, and hand the keys to my visiting friends, Meredith and Keith Standish. They had accompanied us to the hospital. Marge sent the young couple to Newton to shop. We should be done in two hours, my friends could pick us up and take us home to the zoo.

I watched Jennie in the preparations. I love Dr. Ted's new hospital, with a large glass window on the operating suite doors. Jennie skillfully, with the gentle strokes of an artist, shaved off your cottony fur while the tiny face mask connected by clear tubes pumped invisible anesthesia. Jennie was assisting Dr. Ted at the state of the art, glistening surgical steel operating pod. All the necessary equipment was at easy reach. Dr. Ted's and Jennie's hands crisscrossed in an experienced choreography of operating technique. Dr. Ted made the first cut, and I admit I cringed. I was glad Hunter was in school. Disarticulated muscles, blood and bone saw, working around your femoral artery and nerve, I admired Dr. Ted's experience, knowledge and confidence. I was there for you, doing my very minor part, hoping and praying. Jennie holding the face mask and monitoring your heart beat with her fingers. I hoped the touch of my positive thoughts gave you encouragement to hang in there. Dr. Ted was finished with the worst part of the amputation, then rinsed the area with saline. Dr. Ted began to stitch your baby body back together. Amazing. The banter in the operating center was cheery and hopeful. Gordon Lightfoot was playing in the background, Dr. Ted's favorite band from his college years. Jennie turned down the anesthesia to start your wake up.

Then we lost your heart beat. I looked at Jenny and Dr. Ted. The blur of activity that followed could not be scripted better in a television medical drama. The staff was efficiency in motion. Jennie circled the table, flipped switches to put you on full oxygen. She pushed on your chest, tiny, furry and white, and told Dr. Ted to finish the stitching. Dr. Lesley Parisi D.V.M., was on a computer nearby and jumped up to help. Dr. Lesley whipped off your face mask and stuck a needle in your upper lip, midline under your now motionless nose. *What was she was doing? To intubate? But isn't that the wrong kind of equipment?* I found out later that midline under the nose above the lip is an acupuncture site for the heart. Dr. Ted finished up his stitch work, and helped with the resuscitation. You were "bagged", *given breaths with a large plastic balloon piece of equipment,* and an injection was given directly into your heart. *OUCH !* Heat was applied to your tiny comatose body. We waited, held our collective breath, while we were all waiting for you to take one, just one breath. Please, just one breath. Then you came back to us. One heart beat, one breath at a time. Slowly, so slowly. Patiently we all waited for you to wake up. Dr. Ted later explained to me that the shock of the operation caused you to go under.

Jennie wrapped you in a towel, holding you snuggly in her arms. We knew you would be comforted by the suggestion of being in a pouch. I felt so helpless, so ignorant and so grateful all at the same time. I had only known you for such a short time, and I cared so much. I try to guard my heart. I try not to get too attached to an animal that will leave me. I try not to love lost causes. And I try to realize sometimes it is more humane to put an animal down. But you were back. Your personality and perseverance under duress had won me over and everyone else who knew you. Jennie stood there holding you wrapped in a towel, bouncing you ever so gently, every new parent knows that motion. Dr. Ted and Dr. Lesley hovered over you, taking your temperature and touching your eye lashes waiting for the anesthesia to wear off. Dr. Lesley assured me that the blink response was the last to wear off of anesthesia.

Ever so slowly, but in God's own time, you came around. What seemed a lifetime later, we were in the car going home to my house. We left with high hopes and the operating room littered with your useless leg. I said thank you to the entire staff for all their heroic efforts. Meredith and Keith assisted me setting you up in an upright half of a refrigerator box in the corner of our living room. Heat pad and towels, you weren't moving much. Water and food, with a healthy sprinkling of fresh dampened clover. I knew you needed more friction for gripping with your one good leg and tail. My mind raced over possibilities. The carpeting I had placed in the box was not giving you enough grip to stand, so I piled in more towels for the time being.

Doug, my friends, and I left to go out to Chinese dinner. I picked the Chinese restaurant because it was halfway to the store that would have just what you needed. Door mats, the bristly kind that scrape mud automatically off dirty shoes. Dinner was nice, the conversation lively and fun, but my mind was on door mats. We made a quick stop at Wal-Mart, where we picked up two doormats for the bottom of the refrigerator box and headed home.

Keith and Meredith helped me put the "Wipe your Paws" , *(ah yes! How appropriate!),* bristly door mats in the bottom of your box and halleluiah you stood successfully and easily. My hopes soared. You were going to be fine. A one legged kangaroo, but functional and fine.

You stayed home in our house for the next few days, in the corner of our living room. I was able to check on you, and our house is quiet and safe. Our friends left, knowing that all was well. On the fourth day, I moved you to Dad's office, quiet, close and able to hold a refrigerator box on it's side to give you more room to exercise. Dr. Ted had explained you needed to learn how to hop/walk/run on your one leg and tail. Dogs and cats and humans learn, so would you. We all wanted you to get better as quickly as possible, before your Mom's milk dried up. You had a lot of growing to do to become a full grown Kangaroo and you would need the calcium from mom's perfect milk for your bones. I supplemented your food with dried milk, but was not sure that would be enough.

I cleaned your box daily - you and I crammed into a giant refrigerator box. I'm sure we appeared quite funny, you so tiny and me... well, not so tiny! We became accustomed to the dance, Peggy, you move here, I clean there, and repeat. I scared my dad once when he walked into his office and I poked my head out of the top of the box. A blonde jack in the box. I would give you loving scratches and pets on your cotton soft fur. All of us were amazed at your recovery. You were eating well, snarking down all the clover I could pull. I don't think you were eating the dried milk powder though. But you sure could chow down on the kangaroo feed. Seems I put in the full dish, light cookie color brown and dime shaped, and would scrape it out of the bottom of the box the next day, like dark brown raisins.

Dr. Ted and I had discussed putting you back in with the kangaroo mob and your mom. We were worried that after ten days your mother's milk would dry up. You needed that milk to grow, the calcium so necessary for your growing bones. So after seven days, I took you home to your mom. She immediately nursed you, I was so relieved, but still so worried. I left you with her for the afternoon, brought you back into the office before closing and/or the coming rain. We repeated this time with mom for the next couple of days, due to the rainy forecast. The rain makes the grass slick and in the dark....?

I knew you could not make the big jump of one vertical foot literally on one foot into the warm den. Doug had built a warm room in the barn adjacent to the Kangaroo run. It was full of hay and had a heat lamp. October was getting colder. So the next day I scoured the woodshop for the materials to make you a handicap ramp. Imagine my surprise when I spotted a piece of plywood painted hot pink. Just the right size, and perfect color for a little girl. I knew it was an good omen. I mean really now, who keeps a piece of four foot by four foot pink plywood hanging around? I screwed strips of one by two onto the hot pink plywood. Four strips ought to do it. I took it to the kangaroo run and screwed it to the barn step.

The weather forecast was clear of rain for the next couple of days. I did not know what your learning curve would be for using the pink handicap ramp. I did know that you would follow your mom. Things were looking up. This was doable.

You were a pitiful sight, a kangaroo with one leg, so tiny, maybe two feet tall, but full of sparkle and spunk. I came to appreciate your life sparkle. Between Dad, Dr. Ted and myself, we decided it was time to let you stay outside with your mom and the mob.

Dr. Pam Schott, D.V.M., an associate of Dr. Spinks', stopped by in the afternoon to take out your stitches. Hunter assisted again, since he was home from school. This part of the procedure did not involve blood, so I figured it was good experience for Hunter when he climbed in the horizontal refrigerator box. Hunter cradled you in his arms as Dr. Schott deftly removed your stitches and examined the incision site. Clean and free of infection, you were pronounced 'good to go'. One more night inside, away from mom and you would have the entire warm, sunny next day to learn how to use the bright pink handicap ramp attached to the big red barn.

The October night was warm, darkness coming early. At seven o'clock I was down at the zoo to close in the exotic parrots, feed my last bottles and check on you. I had hoped you had hopped into the warm barn room following your mom. As I swung my car on the grass to close up the parrots, I noticed you laying next to your mom in the grass. Mom was standing (*was she beaconing?*), looking at the headlights. *Hummm... good mom staying by her infant or was there another problem?* I decided to check you out. Leaving the car on the grass for the headlight illumination, I walked to the opposite end of the grassy paddock with my zoo keys in hand. Unlocking the gate, I kept my eye on you and mom. Mom moved away from you and you struggled to stand. *Peggy Roo get up, please get up and hobble away with mom!* You dragged your hind section with your front legs. I knew this was a problem. I apologized to your mom and scooped you up in my arms. I inspected your incision site, and it was clean, still closed. When I gently felt your last leg, I knew that was where the problem was. I don't know what happened, whether it was broken, dislocated or what. But I did know one thing: your future was gone.

As I walked you towards the gate, you gazed at me with those big shoe button brown eyes, then laid your head on my arm, and heaved a big sigh. I knew you were done, your sparkle diminished, your will to live vanished. It was a tough life for you, with the constant attention, and the stress of multiple operations. I knew I had to make the tough decision. For all our efforts it was time to make the final call.

I drove to Dad's house with you cradled in one arm, your limp hind section in my lap. The lights were on, Dad and Uncle Milton, my dad's lifetime friend, were still awake and watching TV. I didn't drive into the driveway but right up onto the lawn to the front door. Knocking was out of the question, I could barely turn the knob on the marroon door. I walked in and stood in front of the orange plaid couch.

"Uh oh, we have a problem?" Dad queried. He saw the look on my face before I had a chance to speak. I explained what had happened to Dad sitting in his easy chair. I put you on the floor to show Dad the problem. It was so hard for me to come to the decision that had to be made, I wanted the reassurance from the man. *Why wasn't my Dad putting his shoes on?*

"Come on Dad, put your shoes on, you have to do this for me", I spoke in short jabs. "We have to put Peggy down."

"Not yet, put her in the nest box in our basement, turn on the heat lamp, let's see what happens by morning. She'll be warm and safe" Dad's basement is also set up for animals.

I must admit I was a little miffed that Dad did not jump when I told him to. I stared at Dad pleading with my eyes for a moment, then turned on my heel, my 'tail tucked between my legs', for the basement. The basement was warm, next to the furnace, so I put you in a box of hay and turned off the lights. You were warm, your tummy full of mom's milk and fall grass. It was dark, you would sleep until morning. With no noises to bother you, your stress level would be less. I closed the garage door and sat in my car for a moment until I was able to drive the block home to our house.

Doug knew by the look on my face that something was wrong during the night visit to the zoo. I had taken too long. I explained to him what had happened.

"You O.K.?" he sympathized.

"Part of the job," I stammered, as silence ruled our house. Sometimes you need the silence.

Knowledge is weighed in time. Dad knew, I didn't want to acknowledge, but other hands were at work here. It was time, I knew, but did not want the responsibility of the decision or the action to put Peggy Roo down. She had taught me to appreciate the sparkle and spunk, the tenaciousness of her spirit, even though she did not fit the perfect body conformation of the specie that I had previously valued. This was the lesson I learned from you. Thank you.

My decision racked my mind all night. Sleep was elusive. Somehow I fell asleep and was awakened at 2 a.m. My first waking thought in the middle of the night was of you, Peggy Roo. I fought the idea of checking on you. By the next morning, I realized the wisdom of Dad's delay. God made the same decision I had. You were gone.

I am sorry, Peggy Roo, we tried, we really tried. All of us, Parker, Hunter, Doug, Vet Tech Jennie, Dr. Ted, Dr. Lesley, Dr. Pam, the rest of the Animal Hospital of Sussex County staff and myself. A heroic group effort full of care. We really tried.

I wish for you the expanses of green clover covered fields above the blue skies.

Love, Your adopted human Mom.

Dear Reader, I wrote this the night after Peggy Roo died. I usually write an animal's story months or even years later, the emotional memory is tempered with time. Heartfelt and raw, writing Peggy Roo's story helped me at the time. You may have experienced the death of a beloved pet a few times in your lifetime. Zookeepers keep larger numbers of animals, all of which have lesser life spans than we humans. So we experience more death, more births, more life changing events with our animals. It is a numbers game, but that does not mean we don't get attached and death hurts us less. We accept death as part of a life's process, but it still hurts. A quiet dull ache in the core of our memory.

Chapter 48 Hello Again in 2010

Hello Once Again in 2010
Our hamlet is festooned with holiday lights,
Animals at the zoo bedded warm for the night.
It's time for my friends around the nation,
to sit with me for a conversation.
Where shall we start, well, guess I can…
Best to start where the year began.
Last year driving past the zoo,
Stopped to help Dad as a good daughter would do.
Dad surprised me, asked if I'd been home
"Did Doug call you on the phone?"
I said "No, But what is the problem? Is Doug ok, is it one of the men?"
"No he's fine, but you're in for a surprise
Doug brought in two lion cubs with very blue eyes.
So go home zoo momma, you've got work to do
Cubs are in your living room, starting to mew."
So I raised Siren and Ed Growley, little lion cubs
With bottles to wash and bellies to rub.
Sadly their mother passed away in four days,
But gladly that meant that Siren gets to stay.
Now she's big, maybe hundred fifty pounds
Siren's still noisy- always making her sounds.
Last time we kept a little lion here to mature
Was young Mosses, I raised in 'seventy four.
Cub Ed went to Florida and is living the life
Romping with doggies, a pampered pet with no strife.
Tiny Tim the midget has won my heart
A white fuzzy llama with which I won't part.
I had two kid goats in my mud room, like I had nothing to do,
Tiny Tim in my living room, Siren in my loo!
Raised fawns, two lynx, ponies and two bobcat
A challenging year thinking of that.
Decided I don't like raising little ponies,
Sure is a whole lot of labor for ME.
I've shoveled and forked out mountains of hay,
My biceps would keep a lumberjack at bay.
But we have more orders for babies next year,
So I'll be feeding all hours, oh jolly good cheer.
Our littlest kangaroo broke her big toes,
Dr. Spinks operated, amputated - oh no!
Then four weeks later took off her leg, So we decided to call her Peg.
Peggy Roo taught me to love outside the norm

Zoo Momma

A great spirit in a body that did not conform.
Peggy Roo did well, recouped in our home
Size of a jackrabbit, she looked like a gnome.
I made her a handicap ramp -it was pink, She'd do ok, we really did think.
Peggy Roo only made it one day with the mob,
It was soooo hard not to sob.
Days like that are really rough, we really tried-but she'd had enough.
This roller coaster ride that is my life,
Is challenging, rewarding, littered with strife.
That's it on animals down at the zoo, did some TV, radio and writing too,
Speeches, and lots of public relations,
With visitors that often give me consternation.
I love my work, my challenge is time, and once a year to put it in rhyme.
I awake each morning with projects galore,
And go till I just can't go anymore.
We have new staff and old staff that are truly great,
Which brings me to my very own mate:
Doug's beard's turning gray, which is very distinguished,
though not quite as short as I would have wished.
But it nicely keeps him toasty warm, on cold days like the previous storm.
After twenty seven years (!) he still cracks me up-
Even with all the conventions that we continue to buck.
That's fine, I know I'm not the norm either,
So we just smile and go play with the tigers.
Our daughter is working down Trenton way
Wish she was closer, but what can I say?
Jack's received promotions at her work,
With a workaholic mom, she's learned not to shirk.
We tell her to relax and have some fun,
Something I'm still learning when the day is done.
My next book's in the computer- a constant beckoning
I hope to write quite a bit by spring
Dad's doing fine, Out hunting today
At eighty two he continues to work and play.
Mom's doing great, and the rest of the fam-damn-ily,
Hunter is a big help to both Doug and me.
So that's been my year now how about you?
A call, a letter, an email will do.
I don't have a face page I'm working on it,
I just haven't had that much time to sit.
I certainly don't have time to twitter,
And often leave my cell phone with a sitter.
But I am one with the universe, my animals and me,
Becoming whatever I'm supposed to be.

Zoo Momma

I miss my friends both near and far,
Would love to hear just how you are.
As I look out upon twinkling holiday lights,
I wish you challenging days and warm cozy nights.
Love, Me.

Sierra Walsh receives fawn kisses.
Photo by Lori Space Day

Chapter 49 My Siren Song

Siren had grown quite a bit in her first year - from a two and a half pound lion cub to at least two hundred pounds of tawny playful muscle. She had lived in the nursery for the previous summer. By fall, if you recall, we had moved her to the auxiliary enclosure. We knew she needed to grow before we re-introduced her to our pride now consisting of Dasari, an unrelated adult female and Attila the Hunk, her father. And grow she had.

Siren was very affectionate, constantly rubbing against the chain link fencing whenever I was near. Her juvenile spots had faded except for those on her rump and hind legs. Her tawny new fur was still fluffy from growing over the winter, but she would shed that heavy coat soon. Siren loved her scratches and the pets I could give her through the fencing. I could not go in with her because she would bowl me over with affection and I would simply be her toy rag doll. She loved the public and would play 'chase' with he small kids that ran up and down the side of the auxiliary enclosure. You would think that was cruel - the kids teasing this huge cub. But if you studied Siren's body language, you would see she enjoyed the chase. Ears relaxed, paws flexibly extended, tail flicking back and forth, and soft chortling told me that Siren loved the game.

Siren was good at listening to command sand she quickly learned what to do when we were cleaning her enclosure. "Siren, go here, come here, up , down, patty cake," etc. "Sit," was not in her vocabulary though. Siren was always on the move when I was near. I could see her napping if I stayed farther away, so I only visited when I had time to play and love.

Siren was eighteen months old and looking quite large in her auxiliary enclosure. Six feet long and four feet tall when standing on all fours, Siren had grown into a wonderful lioness. Of coarse she had maximum natural nutrition and medical care - not that she had needed more than her shots. Dad and I discussed moving the large cat and acclimating her to the larger lions enclosure and the lions themselves. A lot of lion pride psychology was included in those discussions. Attila had accepted Dasari without incident. That was a good sign. When a new male lion takes over a pride in the wild, he will kill all the young cubs fathered by the previous king. Siren was Attila's daughter, so that should not be a problem. Siren was a loving lion and did not have an overly aggressive character. *Don't laugh, I've raised some cubs that were much more antagonistic and hostile.* Siren had a great personality. So the plans were made.

On Maundy Thursday, we kept the zoo closed until we had the move completed. The day was bright and sunny and we expected a large Chasidic crowd since it was their holiday. The adult lions were locked onto the grassy section of their enclosure. They would stay out there for a couple of days since the forecast was for five sunny days in a row. The time was right.

Our men gathered. Siren was locked on the far side of the enclosure. She sensed something was up, but was her jolly inquisitive self, happy to see all her friends first thing in the morning. The guard rail was dismantled by the end of the enclosure. A large six feet by four feet by four feet transport made out of livestock paneling was moved into place on the pond side of the auxiliary enclosure. The chain link on the exterior of the cage was unhooked from the support vertical pipes and pinned back. The men lifted the transport cage and slid it into place on the concrete floor. It was placed in front of the connecting tunnel with which Siren was familiar. She had used the tunnel daily to go from one side of the enclosure to the other. Pipes were handy to help with the move, portage style.

The pick up truck was moved into place so the guys would not have to carry the heavy huge feline far. And yes, there was a shotgun on the driver's seat just in case. Doug was in the four foot wide hallway inside the auxiliary enclosure. On cue, the slide door was opened to let Siren into the tunnel. The tunnel was extended now with the transport cage. Siren trotted right in with a few encouraging calls from me. Once she was close enough to give me kisses, Doug closed the tunnel slide, and closed the slide on the transport cage. Now the muscle part would begin.

Parker, Doug, Dad and Mike slid the poles though the top of the transport cage. Siren hissed, and moved from side to side. Mike Courtwright had been the manager of the kitchen for a year. When a position in the zoo was open, he asked for it. Dark, curly hair, and a set of bright twinkley eyes anticipated his first 'big' zoo adventure. Good thing he had muscles, we would need everybody's.

"Talk to her Lori, keep talking," Dad gently commanded. So I did.

"Good girl, Siren, what a good girl, easy girl, what a good girl, pretty girl, oh what a good girl," I constantly encouraged Siren for the next half hour. I am strong for a woman, but my skill right now was to keep my voice calm and reassuring for Siren, to let her know not to get tensed up or overly frightened. Frightened lions are dangerous, tensed up stress can cause a number of both physical and psychological problems. So I talked to Siren., a broken record of mommy soothing sounds. Siren did not bark or growl, she chortled, and was constantly watching me.

The transport cage was heavy with the almost full grown lion. A full grown lioness can weigh five hundred pounds. Dad estimated Siren's weight at three hundred to three hundred fifty pounds. So the guys had no easy chore lifting the transport first to the ground, and then over the bottom rail of the guard fence, which had not been disconnected. The early morning dew caused Mike to slip, his muddy workboot skidding under the bottom guard rail. Men cursed, and yelled. *We zookeepers do that a lot under stress.* Siren barked once loud, crisp and sharp, her ears back. I kept talking, soothing the frightened overgrown lion cub and maybe the men. *Well, maybe not the men folk. They ignore me most of the time anyway.* My focus, all of our focus was on Siren. One slip, -a hand on the transport to steady oneself -and she could grab that hand or any other body part for that matter. She was not a mean cat, but a frightened lion is unpredictable. I kept coooing.

Muscles flexed, grown muscular men groaned. Siren was being so good, all considering. The men folk lifted and slid the transport cage on the back of the beat up navy blue pickup truck. That zoo truck had seen many battles in the zoo, from Yak ramming the sides to elk climbing in the back for faster food delivery. It had carried many a hay bale, tools, feed buckets, picnic tables, garbage cans, loads of wood, dead road kill deer etc. The old blue pickup showed every battle scar with pride. The tailgate had been tied on with baler twine for years and then had given up the ghost, lost on the road somewhere. A redneck jalopy, now in its fading days of glory, carrying a princess lioness. our Siren.

Dad and I walked behind the beat up pickup truck as it slowly drove down the hill to the backside of the lion's den. The lions and tigers had been locked onto the grassy section. I was still chatting for/with Siren. When the men backed the pick up to the den door, I knew my job had changed. I unlocked the guard gate and walked to the pond side of the concrete section of the lions' enclosure. Siren would be released into the back den, I was to call her out of the transport cage.

"OK, Lori, call her out!" I heard my Dad say. So I did.

"Hey pretty girl, look here I am, come see me, oh Siren, pretty girl, come see me," I called in my calmest mommy voice. It took a few moments, then suddenly Siren sprinted towards me, furtively glancing left to right, paws extended rigidly, eyes piercing, ears erect and fixed. She was scared. She came to me. One of the guys (I could not see who from my vantage point) lowered the vertical slide on the den with a heavy metal thunk. Siren visibly tensed with the noise. They needed to maneuver the transport cage out of the back gate and doorway. I reassured Siren with more conversation and rubbing her back, front and whatever section she presented to me. I was kissing and purring my lips off. She seemed to be calming down. After the men folk got the transport cage out of the way, the back gate was locked and the slide door opened again, so Siren would have access to the den.

I walked past the water dish, putting my hand inside and splashing the water so Siren would know where it was in her new digs. She followed me, not interested in the water, but she knew it was there. I walked to the back of the long rectangular enclosure to the cement block twenty by ten feet den. The guys were packing up the equipment, Dad stood by me.

"Call her in, so she knows where her bed is, and she can hide out if she wants," Dad gently reminded me. I knew all that, but it was reassuring for me to have my Dad reinforce my thoughts.

"Here, Here, Pretty Kitty," I softly called, Siren found her way in. The guys had put down fresh hay in the corner, Siren walked over and plopped down. A golden beige princess on her golden hay throne.

"Now she just needs, time, Lori," Dad's voice was also calm and reassuring, for me or Siren, who knows, probably both.

"Let's let her be to rest and explore. Later, bring her out a bottle or two and get her to walk the enclosure all the way down the chute to the grassy area where the gate is closed. She needs to see the adult lions." Dad explained again. I knew that was the plan. Dad and I had discussed it many times. Siren would be called back into the den and the vertical door slid shut when the adult lions needed to come up on the concrete section, for cleaning or a big drink. But for now, Siren needed to see her family. She needed to get to know them, and they her.

Dad and I locked up the back den door. I walked to the front and called Siren out of the den, just so she knew she could go out of the den at will. I slowly walked over the zoo path hill with Dad. I noticed Dad glancing at me. Siren was watching me also, calling in short high pitched mews.

" Yeah, Dad, I hear her, but she has to learn for herself. If I stay she will only stay by me. She has to stay there," I said, "so I am ignoring her."

"That worked out ok" Dad responded. "Make sure you visit her and walk her down the ramp a couple of times today."

"Every hour ok?" I asked.

"We should be busy," Dad looked towards the filling parking lot from the top of the hill. "As much as you can."

And I did. I walked out to the lions' frequently that day, Maundy Thursday. I took bottles a couple of times. Siren hadn't had that much milk in over a year, so I skipped some times and just petted her. If she was nervous in her new home, and with a radical change in her diet (read that me spoiling her with a lot of bottles of milk!), she would get diarrhea. I walked her down the ramp through the chute to the closed fenced slide/ gate. Every time I did, Dasari, the female, would come over to the gate and greet Siren. Siren would hiss and back away for the first few times but then her curiosity would take over. Attila just continued his sunbathing. After we closed the zoo that night I walked down to the lions again. I found if I walked, Siren would not hear me coming on my four wheel quad, so I could observe from a distance to see what was happening. On my final visit that night, it was late dusk and I could barely see. Siren was laying at the end of the chute, leaning up against the fenced gate/slide. Dasari was laying against it on the other side. That was such a good sign. I went back home to my bed, happy with silent, thankful prayers.

The next morning was Good Friday. The Chasidic holidays were also in full swing, and the Christian school kids had off for the Easter weekend. I knew we would be busy. The moment my eyes opened my first thought was of Siren in the big lion's den. Well, actually my first thought every morning is *Oh it is morning*. The lions awaken me every day at dawn, with sexual territorial marking roars. Attila is always greeting the dawn, announcing to all the lions within earshot, "I am the king as far as my voice will travel." And yes, Attila was. So my second thought was of Siren.

I hurried through my morning coffee, dressed rapidly and was applying my make-up in the upstairs bathroom mirror. The bathroom window was cracked to let in April's sweet morning fresh air. Our house is located on zoo property. The large pond, full of geese, ducks and swans is in between the lion's enclosure and my house. The expanse of water carries sounds from the zoo. I am not a master of acoustics but the sounds travel well across water. I know the normal sounds of the zoo. There is a symphony at any given moment, I know the tune well.

And then there was Siren's frantic, fearful bark. *OH S#!t! I gotta get to the zoo!* I knew something had gone wrong. One eye mascara-ed, I put on my sneakers and was out the door into my car. I did not park, waiting for the remote controlled gate to open was torture. Once the gate opened I sped through the gate, hit the remote button to close, not waiting to see if it did. I drove directly out to the lions' enclosure. I immediately saw the problem. I don't know how it happened, I was not there, and there was no use asking the questions right now.

The two adult lions were up on the concrete section, Siren was cowering in the corner. Why Siren was not in the den as planned I did not know. The two adult lions were drinking from the water dish. I parked the car on the grass in front of the chute. Siren saw me and ran towards me. Using my zoo keys I opened the guard fence gate and let myself in by the enclosure. Parker was filling up the water dish keeping the lions busy. Doug walked down towards me and passed me. Siren walked with me to the grassy section. Doug was going to lock Siren on the grassy section, since the two adult lions were on the concrete. But he did not get there fast enough.

Siren was three feet away from me, on the other side of the nine gauge chain link fence. She was frightened, she had not been in that section before. And the two bossy big lions… Dasari came down the chute first. She walked to Siren. Siren bared her teeth and hissed. Dasari, being the older more experienced lioness, simply sniffed and sauntered away, as if to say "Yeah, hi new kid on the block, talk to you later, I am late for my nap."
Siren stuck my me. Hissing, but then calmed down a bit.

Next Attila came down the chute to the grassy section. Parker was yelling instructions to Doug, Doug was yelling back, I didn't hear a word. I was calming Siren. My big beautiful three hundred pound tawny baby was scared. Attila came to Siren and sniffed and snarled. Siren bared teeth and snarled back. And that was it. You do not sass a man in his own house, and you do not sass a male lion in his home territory. Not without really pissing them off. Siren was scared and did not know the proper lion etiquette. Her merely human mother had not taught her. Siren hissed, snarled and then swatted at Attila. Then ran. And the chase was on. The fat lazy lion basking in yesterday's sun became an agile killing machine in a flash. Attila's muscles were tense. You could see the outline of the strength in his rear flanks. Clods of grass were spewed up behind his hind feet as he ran. His claws were extended. Attila chased Siren to the two hundred foot end of the grassy section, and pinned her. Doug had grabbed a metal pole used for cleaning and tried to separate the fighting lions with it. Louder fighting ensued. Snarling, hissing, baring of teeth and roaring reverberated the air. Every lions' hair stood on end. Attila's black mane seemed double in size, spiked out punk rock style. Siren escaped Attila's grasp and ran back towards me. Parker was near me by then and said to try to get Siren back up the ramp. So I called to her, waving my arm in the corner where the ramp was hoping she would see the ramp and get to the den. Siren ran towards me. Siren had a chance if she could just get up the ramp to

221

safety. She was not marked or bleeding.

Siren ran towards me and hesitated, not being able to determine where the chute was. She was lost. Siren glanced back at the approaching Attila. I could see the fear in her eyes and I'm sure she could see the fear in mine. Siren ran to the opposite corner thirty feet in front of me. Attila followed, determined, creating the hypotenuse of the triangle Siren had just ran. Parker, not taking time to care for his own safety, scaled over the lion's chute like a superhero. He climbed down into the three foot gap between the concrete cage section and the grassy section's chain link fence. He grabbed another metal pole. Before he could poke Attila, Attila had grabbed Siren by the neck and hoisted her off the ground with one fell jerk.

Parker looked over at me. I can still see him somehow propped in mid air, one foot on the edge of the concrete tiger section, one foot propped on the chain link fence, with the long metal pole half in the fencing, above Parker's head.

"She's gone," Parker simply said.

We all seemed frozen in time for a while there. Attila posed proud with his prize, Parker magically suspended in mid air on the ten feet tall fence and Doug holding his metal pole staff. I stood there for a minute, stunned.

"Well, there is nothing I can do now," I mumbled, speaking to no one in particular. I turned to walk to my car. *Funny thing, my legs are not working well. Hummm... hard to walk. One foot, Lori, one foot in front of the other. Whoa, knees where are you going? I felt like I was walking stiff, like a robot. My mind having to remind my body what to do. One foot, one foot in front of the other, three more feet to the car...*

I should not have driven, but I could not walk either. The zoo was still closed. All of this happened at eight o'clock in the morning of what was to be a glorious, sunny, busy day. I pulled my car through the zoo gate and saw Dad unlocking the front door. I parked in front of the office and went to tell Dad the sad news.

"Pop," I said. "He killed her." was all I could get out before heaving sobs broke my spirit and the quiet morning air. Tears streaming down my face, my body finally gave way to the flood of emotions I had held back. With shaking tremors, I could hardly stand. I leaned on Dad and he caught me up with his fatherly arm around my waist. My caterwauling echoed through the hollow between the main building and the feed house complex across the street, reverberating my pain. I'm sure the entire hamlet of Beemerville could hear me.

"That Bastard!" Dad exclaimed. Hunter had come from across the street and Mike appeared out of nowhere. Everyone was consoling me. Hunter would tell me later that I was crying so hard, he thought my mom, his grandmother, had died. Or Doug.

Dad took me inside the main building and told me to sit down which was good since I was not sure how much longer I could stand. I sobbed, I heaved heavy breath and cried. My arm cradled my head on the table, tears dripped to the floor. Dad cried too. Hunter and Mike went on their way with tear laden eyes. Everyone felt the loss. And then it was nine am, time to open the zoo for the busy day ahead. One foot in front of the other, we opened the zoo.

When I could gather my wits about me, I stepped to the back porch and called Dr. Ted.

"I need a favor," I started to sob again.

"Sure Lor, what's up?" Dr. Ted must of figured we needed some new medicines or a office visit, his uninformed tone was casual.

" I need you to tell Jennie, (*sob, sob, crying, pause to gather myself),* that Siren is dead. Attila killed her," I stammered between sobs. I gave him a nutshell account of the early morning events.

"I will," Dr. Ted said, "You ok?"

"No, not really, I'll talk to you later." More crying.

I meandered around by the back of the building for a minute trying to compose myself again. Parker pulled up with the dirty old blue pick up truck. People were starting to come across the street from the parking lot. I saw Siren's beautiful body in the back of the truck. I petted her paw, noting her perfection. No blood or puncture wounds. Attila's snap of her neck was mercifully quick. Her vacant eyes were glazed over. Her spark of life, her twinkle was gone. I prayed as I closed them. I petted her huge paw.

"So sorry baby girl, go be with Mosses and Gramma. Run Free."

Parker put the four foot by six foot dirt catching carpet from outside the back porch door over Siren to drive her across the street. No use ruining any of the visitors' day.

"Time to go, Lor," Parkers sympathetic words were soft. He drove through the gate.

I opened the back kitchen door and told whoever was listening, that I was going home for a while. I went home, and called Jackie at work in Hamilton, and let her know, blubbering all over the phone. I took some Tylenol and went back to work. I know I was not the best public relations person that day. My face was reddened, eyes puffy and with obvious tears spewing at any given point that day.

Doug checked in with me a number of times that day. He was attached to Siren too. Doug's eyes were bloodshot next time I saw him. I knew he had shed his tears privately. He had worked with Siren daily. She was a good cat. His hugs only made me cry again. Hunter also came by and gave me a big bear hug. We were all hurting. I felt like everyone was watching me that day. The entire family and staff was. I had to be strong.

Parker would ask me later what we should tell the visitor folks that ask. I told him to spread the word that Siren went to another zoo. I didn't want Siren's fan club of little children to be upset. I was not lying, Siren did go to another zoo. The BIG ZOO. You know, the one on the other side of the pastel rainbow, where the fluffy clouds are. I'll be a keeper there someday. *(Gotta stop here for a while.)*

Ninety seconds. It took Attila ninety seconds to kill my Siren. It had been forty years since we kept one of our own hand raised lions here at the zoo. All that love, all that devotion, all the hours of training, cleaning, hard work - was gone in ninety seconds. For months, I relived those ninety seconds every night before I slept.. Every morning it was the first thing I saw before I opened my eyes to Attila's territorial roar. The sight felt burned into the backside of my eyelids. And my baby died afraid. I have relived it, rehashed it, and hopefully we have all learned from it. I can understand it, but I am so dreadfully heartbroken that Siren was afraid when she died.

I have to stop now. I can no longer see the page. I need some time and Tylenol. Sorry reader.

I hated Attila for quite a while, looking at him from a different perspective. After about six months my feelings eased. A few conversations with Dr. Ted and more with Rev. Charlie Jenkins helped me understand. I could accept Attila for what he is- an African lion, a wild animal. You cannot predict what they will do. You may think you can, but we inevitably attribute human characteristics to them and that is just not correct. In literature they call it personification. In the scientific world it is anthropomorphism. My mistake was thinking that Attila would recognize Siren as his daughter. He did not. She was a strange lioness, who had sassed him, introduced into HIS territory . That was all it took to set Attila on his instinctual path to eliminate any threat to his superiority.

Two years later an incident occurred in the Dallas Zoo. Five African Lions had lived together for three years. One day out of the blue, a male turned on a female and grabbed her by the throat and killed her. It happens. And we tougher than nails zookeepers… we cry.

This is the hardest chapter I have ever lived.

Siren
Photo by Brian Jenkins

Zoo Momma

Chapter 50 On a Lighter Note

After the last Chapter and knowing that 2011 was a tough year, I thought this would be a good time to inject a little levity. We are constantly asked some really dumb questions here at the zoo. I thought we might share a good chuckle.

We answer the phones with the greeting: "Hello, or Good morning/afternoon Space Farms." Each of these questions were from different phone calls. **We did give each caller nice answers over the phone** but here is what we really wanted to say. Enjoy!

Question: "Can I get there from here?"

A: " No"

Q: "Do you have live animals?"

A: "No we have a zoo full of animal-tronic figures, no feeding, watering or poop scooping needed! And at 5 pm we turn off the lights, unplug the animals, and go home!" Dream on.

Q: "Is your place appropriate for children?"

A: "Yes, The animals would love to have them over for dinner!"

Q: "Can we borrow a monkey for a day?"

A: "No, we don't rent out monkeys. I'll loan you my nephew though!"

Q: "Can I bring my parrot in my backpack?"

A: "Yes you can, but no you **may** not!"

And always on April Fool's day the numerous calls:

Q: " Is Mr. Fox (or Bear or Lyon, or High Ena, or take your pick of an animal) there?"

A: " You've been played a trick on, this is a zoo. Here is your response. Leave a note on the note-giver's desk and here is what it says: Mr. Mann Nor says you are full of it."

And people ask great questions at the admission desk also:

Q: " Did my husband come through here?"

A: "Yes with about a hundred other husbands, which one was yours?"

Q: "Are the snakes alive? They would not eat the corn I threw in, they didn't even move towards it."

A: "Snakes don't eat corn, do you want to go into the den and retrieve it? I'll open the gate."

Q: "Can you hand feed the bears?"

A: "NO you cannot feed the bears your hand. We prefer you throw the food into them."

Q: "When I walk out the door, what do I do?"

A: " Put one foot in front of the other, and repeat!"

Q: " If I bring the receipt back, will I get in free next time?"

A: "No, next time we will charge you double."

Q: " Do you know your chickens are fighting?"

A: "No Sir, that is a rooster and a hen...ahem... get it?"

And the questions working zookeepers get:

I was in full uniform, painting a white building with a fresh coat of white paint. Paint roller in hand, while on the upstroke a lady taps me on my embroidered uniform that says Space Farms Zoo on it and says:

Q: "Do you work here?"

A: " Shuuusssh, 'Mam, don't tell anybody! I regularly break into zoos and paint white buildings white."

Kids with bird egg in hand:

Q: " What kind of egg is this?"

A: "WOW that is a Dinosaur Egg, Lucky you. Where did you find it?"

Q: " Do your monkeys (or pick any animal) have water? I didn't see any."

A: This one I don't like to joke about, of course every animal has water, or else they would be dead in seven days! The answer involves an in depth explanation of a plumbing fixture called a pig nipple. Sometimes I think we should eliminate the natural color scheme we try to employ, and should paint all water fixtures bright red. Or paint bright red arrows pointing to the water apparatus. I mean really now, not give an animal water? How dumb do people think we are?

Q: "I have a question…"

A: "I have an answer, Tomatoes! Was that right?" Usually met with puzzled laughter.

Q: "Do you know the sheep and her two lambs by the lake?

A: "Yessss?"

Questioner: "They have no water!"

My hubby Doug is the king of dry wit at the zoo. He has such a dead pan face that sometimes even I cannot tell if he is kidding. One particularly inquisitive lady asked Doug a number of questions. And then the final question: "What's your name, you've been so helpful?" Doug's reply: "George." Five years later and that lady is still calling him George. And his correct name is printed on the name tag of his uniform!

Depending upon the day, Doug is very busy with jobs around the zoo. Since this is a working zoo, we pretty much have something to do every minute of the day. If Doug is involved in a project, he doesn't like to be interrupted. He considers it my job if someone has questions. And it is. But I am not at Doug's side every second. So if a visitor asks Doug a question, sometimes they get the correct answer. Doug does have a standard statement that to this day cracks me up. He will look the inquisitive visitor straight in the eye and say:

"I don't know, I just started here today! Go ask Lori!" I guess it is funnier if you know, that as of this writing, my husband Doug has worked here for twenty one years.

Often when we are feeding the large carnivores, like the lions, people ask:

Q: "Raw meat? Shouldn't that be cooked?"

A: "God doesn't send a lightning bolt to cook every lion's (insert animal in question here) food!"

Q: "When are the tigers being fed?"

A: "12:45 with the rest of the carnivores."

Q: "You only feed them once a day?" Shocked and puzzled look on visitor.

A: "Yes. How often do you feed your tigers?" (Thanks Hunter!)

It may be hard to believe, but people really have asked those questions. And often the same question by multiple people. Common sense goes on vacation too I guess. You have to laugh and enjoy each day. You never know what tomorrow will bring.

Just Smile!
Photo by Karen Talasco

Zoo Momma

Chapter 51 Khyber Tiger

Zookeepers each have their section of the zoo to clean first thing in the morning. My hunky husband, Doug, cleans and feed the monkeys. His next stop with his jitney is the lions and tigers. Locking the lions and tigers out onto the morning dewy grass section of the enclosure, he is then able to wash the concrete patio and den section. Everyday, it is the same routine. If you do the procedure the same every day the animals become aware, and cooperate most of the time. Doug is the first to see those animals in the morning. Good zookeepers are trained to spot any problems with the animals in their care. By listening and observing their walking cadence, eyes, ears, mouth, and yes, (!), the poop, you can figure out if anyone is ill.

"Hey Babe, Khyber has a bloody nose. You may want to look at him." Doug surprised me one August morning as I was cleaning the nursery. Khyber, our male tiger, the baby I had raised in 1998, was now thirteen years old. Tigers in the wild are lucky to live to fifteen years old, in captivity eighteen to twenty two years is achievable.

"Ok, I'll check on him." I replied, finished up what I was doing before heading out to see Khyber. I was not alarmed. Tara the female tiger and Khyber had gotten into a few tussles in the past. Minor scratches from their squabbles were not uncommon. Once I had to pull a toenail sheath out of Khyber's nose when Tara had said a definite "NO!"

I rode out on my quad and the tigers heard me coming. The animals have learned the sound that goes with the machinery driven by each zookeeper. The tigers were at the chain link gate to greet me. Chuffing happy noises were my greetings. Tara and Khyber each vying for the position closest to me on the other side of the chain link. The August grass had just started to brown out a little due to the hot summer sun. The dirt trail that the tigers used to patrol their territory circled just inside of the fencing. Other trails meandered through the high grass. Right next to the chain link gate I had a great view of Khyber and the slight trickle of blood by his nostril. The trickle looked minor, as thick as a pencil line. I would keep an eye on it. I told the other zookeepers to keep an eye on his nose also.

"Maybe Tara, just said NO!" Doug joked at lunch when I explained.

"Let me know if it gets worse today, instead of better, or less blood!" I reminded Hunter, Mike and Doug.

"OH, how much blood?" Hunter said. And the conversation veered off into the bloody world of exaggeration, Doug obviously teasing young Hunter about his aversion to blood, needles and 'nuttin' pigs (farmer style castration of piglets). Hunter passes out, cold.

Khyber's nosebleed would heal up for a couple of days then reappear - evident to those who knew to look. Khyber, being a member of the feline family kept licking his nose clean. Then the nosebleed was back big time. I put a call in to Dr. Ted. My friend and zoo photographer Karen Talasco was able to catch the nosebleed in a photo in between Khyber's personal hygiene lickings. I sent that photo along to Dr. Ted and his staff.

Dr. Ted called and we set up a time for Khyber to be examined. Now this is not an easy thing to do. We all coordinated on what we would need for the exam the next day. Dr. Ted, Dr. Pam Schott, certified veterinary technicians Pam Fagersten, and Jennie Beckman came with two vehicles. Dr. Ted's white Veterinary Porta Vet Unit and SUV were stocked out with medical supplies and tools. Our stretcher, a study table, warm blankets, quilts, a side table, a generator for electricity to run the medical equipment, and extra clean hay for afterwards loaded up the zoo trucks and jitneys. And, as usual, there was a loaded gun on the old blue pick up truck's seat, just in case. Parker, Hunter, Doug, Mike, Tommy, Dad and myself were all present. This was an 'all hands on deck' situation.

Tara Tiger had been locked out of the den into the grassy section early that morning when Doug was first on the scene. Khyber was locked into the den.

Dr. Ted and Dr. Pam prepared the syringe with anesthesia. An extension handle was duct taped onto the end of the punch pole we keep at the zoo. A punch pole, also called a jab stick, is a syringe on a long stick, used to give shots to animals you cannot get close to safely. I had a stuffed animal to keep Khyber's attention and draw him to our side of the den for an easier jab. The tiger's den is six feet wide by twenty feet long, and stuffed with hay bedding. There is a four foot human walkway between the inside fencing and the exterior wall. Everyone waited outside the den except Parker, Dr. Ted and I. Parker handled the jab stick, being the strongest and having the longest reach. Khyber roared. His bloody nose was visible again. After the jab of the needle, Khyber was pacing the inside of the den, obviously upset. *Well, wouldn't you be?* Now it was my turn.

It is difficult to correctly guess the exact weight of an animal on the hoof. Dr. Ted and Dr. Pam were working on our estimate of Khyber's weight, a good estimate, but tricky because you do not want to overdose an animal on anesthesia, because that will kill them. So a margin of error on weight is calculated. But, and this is a big but, if the dangerous animal is not completely 'out' you risk the lives and limbs of the staff. Or the panicked animal hurting himself. So it is much better to under-dose the anesthesia, then give the animal a little more. To do that, it would be helpful if Khyber relaxed and lay down to sleep by the fencing, not by the concrete block wall six feet away. So my job with the stuffed animal was to draw Khyber to the fence to sleep. I called to him, hopefully calming him, and he lay down by the fence to sleep. And we waited for the full effect of the anesthesia.

Outside the den the chatting was casual about other animals at the zoo, hunting season was around the corner, and Dad's cabin in Colorado. Dr. Ted and Dad had lots to chat about. The ladies and I gabbed about our kids and other pets. It takes up to forty minutes to get the full effect of the anesthesia.

"Not yet," Dr. Ted checked a number of times on his huge striped patient. Finally after about forty five minutes, the anesthesia took a good hold of Khyber. Dr. Ted gently brushed his fingers across Khyber's eyelashes.

"The blink reflex is the last to go under," Dr. Ted explained, his teaching method was truly appreciated. It always fills me in and reassures me that things were going as expected. With his word, our well rehearsed dance began. Most of us knew the choreography, we had fixed Tara's tail and the Lion's tooth in this den, (see "The Zookeeper's Daughter"). Senior staff members were giving instructions to the newer members.

The den cage door was opened, the WWI army olive green stretcher was brought in. Our daughter's old childhood sleeping bag was placed over the stretcher, for warmth from the underside. The sturdy wooden table was handed into the den cage and set up.

Parker, Hunter, Mike and Doug helped Dr. Ted get Khyber on the stretcher. "On Three, -one, two, three," Parker, gave the traditional order. There were groans from the brawny men involved. Khyber was lifted up onto the top of the wooden table and plunked down still laying stretched out on the hot pink blanketed stretcher. Khyber was an easy eight feet from the nose to extended back feet and paws. What a huge cat! Six hundred pounds at least. Khyber had recently been off feed a little due to the illness we were investigating. He had lost weight. With the huge orange and black striped cat on the table it was time for the initial exam. All the muscle men came outside the den enclosure except for Parker, Dad and myself, who stood, watched and waited in the walkway.

The anesthesia machine was carried in and Dr. Ted, Dr. Pam, and vet techs Pam and Jennie started the exam. Part of Khyber's paw was shaved of fur for better access to a vein. Khyber's huge head, about double the size of a basketball sat regally, eyes glassed over. Jennie applied jell to Khyber's eyes so they would not dry out, without the blinking process. Then she taped Khyber's eyes shut. Dr. Ted and Dr. Pam were examining the giant feline. I heard a lot of mumbling but could not make out the words. The examination continued. I moved so I could see what was going on. Hanging lights gave the whole scene an other worldly glow. *Maybe it was just me.* Dr. Ted's blue surgical scrubs and the colorful prints of Dr. Pam and the vet tech smocks were a bright contrast to the concrete block den. Everything above the table was bright and colorful, shirts, hot pink blanket, tiger, and lights. Everything below was drab, gray concrete block, hay, dark jeans and work boots. The smell of the tiger's den permeated my nose. It was the strong smell of urine marked territory.

Hovering over the colorful tiger, the team of veterinarians were looking up inside Khyber's nose. White latex gloved hands were investigating with shiny metal probes. Dr. Pam glanced in our direction. They all knew my history with the big cat. They had been there for each step of his infant, toddler and teen development. And we had all just lost Siren a few months before. I caught Dr. Ted glancing my way. Worry consumed me. I waited to hear, "Oh he'll be fine he just has …maybe a splinter?".

Dr. Ted's eyes met mine at the next glance. The slightest negative shake of his head gave away Dr. Ted's diagnosis.

"We've seen this a lot in house cats," Dr. Ted explained. " He has a nasal carcinoma, it's big, and has progressed…" He said more, but don't ask me what he said.

Zoo Momma

My heart sank. *A simple nose bleed? Guess not.* The words were repeated to Dad who did not hear Dr. Ted due to Dad's hearing loss. The word cancer was whispered. *Keep it together Lori, not in front of the men, again.* I wiped a single tear and walked outside. I simply shook my head in the negative for the gathered men. We all hung our heads for a moment as green sod was kicked.

Khyber was unhooked from his medical apparatuses. A new bed of clean, dry fresh hay was fluffed for a bed. The men were called in to put the stretcher back down next to the hay. The guys each lifted one huge paw, each the size of a dinner plate, and rolled Khyber off the stretcher. He was gently placed in an upright position. Our daughter Jackie's childhood sleeping bag, vibrant hot pink and denim was draped over Khyber to help keep him warm until he awoke. Dr. Ted was concerned with hypothermia, (Khyber getting too cold). The heavy wooden table was dismantled, folded and removed out the four by four gate of the den. Our guys gathered up all the equipment putting some in the beat up blue pick up truck. The Animal Hospital of Sussex County's equipment was put in the back of their clean and pristine full sized Veterinary Porta Vet truck. Our guys left to go back to their assorted chores. Hearts were heavy. Work never ends here at the zoo.

Dad, Parker, the two vets and I discussed the options. There was no cure. Only prolonging life. Hopefully without pain. Chemotherapy was a possibility, but again no cure. The antibiotic shot Khyber had received while he was under should help for a while. I felt like the decision rested on me. No one wanted to say the words, especially to me after loosing Siren. But we had to let Khyber go when the time came. We decided to keep him comfortable. We would let nature take it's course as long as he was in no pain, until we would have to put him down.

It took Khyber a while to awake from his anesthesia. Once he was sitting up with his head erect on his own we let Tara back into the den. The reunion was happy, Tara rubbing her head on Khyber's in affection.

Dr. Ted told me there was nothing we could have done to prevent this nasal carcinoma, and it was no one's fault. His big brother attitude with me was not condescending but very consoling. *Wonder if they teach that in Vet School?*
I held it together until Dr. Pam gave me a hug and said "I'm sorry".

"Thank you," I cried a little at that hug. It was ok to cry now, our guys had gone. The vets, vet techs and I cleaned up the last of the equipment, and rode down to the gate. I let the vet crew out of the zoo, waving goodbye.

Khyber lived only three weeks after that diagnosis. He ate, drank and he sat outside in the grassy sunshine, watching the world go by. A few visitors noticed the occasional trickle of blood. He was sluggish some days but did not show signs of being in any pain.

I was feeding the fawns their first bottle of the morning when Hunter drove up. Waiting patiently for me to finish, he wrapped his long arms around me in a giant bear hug, just like the teddy bear he is. *But don't tell anybody he is a teddy bear!*

"Khyber is dead," he gently whispered, "Died in his sleep last night."

231

"I knew it," I teared up. "I could read it on your face. It was not our fault, and there was nothing we could have done to prevent it. It's ok. I'm ok. " Khyber had a lovely life at the zoo, ate every day, fathered cubs and enjoyed the afternoon suns with Tara. And we were all ok with Khyber's death.

Tara and Khyber Tigers holding paws.

Photo by Karen Talasco

Chapter 52 Hurricane Irene

In the weeks between the Veterinarians' diagnosis of Khyber and his death, zoo life continued as usual. Life moves on even in stasis. We keep a constant awareness of the weather forecast. If bad weather is coming, we need to know. It is a lot easier now that smart cell phones have been invented. Parker and Hunter are constantly checking. Doug checks every morning and evening. We need to know. So when the forecast was for Hurricane Irene to come up the coast and hit us, we were ready.

Hunter had outfitted one of the zoo trucks with everything we would need. If one of the trees came down over a fence in the zoo it could be a problem. If a tree comes down, say, on the elk or llama fence, that is not such a big problem. Elk and llama do not climb trees, and don't eat people. If a tree comes down across the fencing of the lions, tigers, cougars, leopards or jag, now that is a problem, because those animals climb trees, and could eat you. So prior to the hurricane's arrival, all the big cats were locked in their secure dens. The bear enclosures were a different story. The bear enclosures are open top, natural grass and weed turf, with tall leafy trees inside and right outside the enclosures. Bears climb trees. So do raccoons, but let's face a few facts, bears are more dangerous than raccoons.

As the rain and the wind increased, Hunter and Tommy patrolled the zoo. They were not only looking for trees down on the interior cages, but also on the outside rim of the zoo, where the hoof stock paddocks are. It is not dangerous if elk or llama, even buffalo, get out, but it is very embarrassing, and hard to get them back. So if a tree went down over that fencing, we would need to fix it fast so the animal could not escape. But again those animals do not climb trees.

The water level was coming up fast in the zoo pond that feeds into the stream which meanders through the zoo. The first area that floods out in a heavy rain storm is the land bridge between the fallow deer and the elk or the fallow and sika deer. So the trucks and jitneys had to swash through those spots. It was work, but you could see the youthful enthusiasm in Hunter's eyes as he barreled through the huge washouts, creating six foot high fans of muddy brown water. The men folk were patrolling and I was inside the main building watching out through the zoo entrance doors as the weather worsened.

Winds had picked up, coming from the west with force. I first heard a crack, like lightning, but with no flash of light. Then I realized that a large tree had cracked and came down across the Syrian bear enclosure fence. I got on my cell phone immediately to Parker.

"Yes, we know. Hunter's on his way" Parker stated. "Grab the bear bucket and meet us there" I saw Hunter and Tommy coming from the back of the zoo. Doug came on his jitney. I turned off the breaker for the electric fence at the breaker box in the rear of the gift shop before running for the bear bucket. We all met at the bear gate.

It was a bizarre sight. Think of a Chinese fire drill, *(hope that is not*

233

politically incorrect), or maybe a swarm of ants each with a purpose as the menfolk very quickly gathered their supplies from the vehicles. Tommy was at the gate, Parker with pitchfork, Doug and Hunter each manned a chain saw. The coordination of the team was remarkable. Each had a job to do. Parker unlocked the gate. Doug dismantled the electric fencing. The old blue pick up was driven in. Just in case the guys needed a place to get away from the bears, (and the shotgun was on the seat). The men folk hopped out and quickly spread out into position. The bears, seeing all the commotion, retreated to the other side of the one hundred-twenty foot by one hundred-twenty foot natural turf enclosure. My job was to stand outside the enclosure on the far side, farthest away from the men, chainsaws and downed tree, to distract the bears with food. It was August 27th so the trees were in full leaf, bushy and green. I had grabbed the bear bucket. *(That is what we call the bucket we kept in the restaurant cooler, filled with scrap food, that need not be wasted)* I threw four packages of a dozen ice cream sandwiches each on top of discarded hamburgers and French fries. Hard rain pelted my yellow longshoreman raincoat as I stood inside the guard fence throwing food.

"Here, bear, come on, Bear," I repeated, keeping one eye on the bears and the other watching all my loved ones in that enclosure with loud chainsaws and only one pitchfork. Doug and Hunter, with the chainsaws, could defend themselves if need be, but they were not looking at the two five hundred pound Syrian Grizzly bears. Parker stood guard ten feet away from the screaming chainsaws, with pitchfork in hand. Doug and Hunter concentrated on cutting the fallen bridge of the tree.

"Here bear, come on bears," I repeated again and again. I have quite a loud voice, trained by many years of speaking over the gleeful noises of school kids. I never realized how loud my voice was until after the storm. Dad told me he had stepped out on his front porch a quarter mile away across the pond from the bears. He explained he had heard me calling the bears. *Say what you want, having a loud voice comes in handy now and then.*

I had run out of hamburger and French fry scraps from the bear bucket. I broke into the first package of ice cream sandwiches, which had started to melt in the warm August air. The noise from the wind, my own loud voice, the crackle of my yellow rubber rain coat and the buzzing of chainsaws was deafening. I broke off quarter sized pieces and tossed them over the fence in different spots, playing a seek and find with the bears. This spread out the time each bear would eat, making the ice cream sandwiches last longer. I was still calling the bears every time I threw the ice cream. *Oh by the way did I mention that ice cream is a bears favorite food?* I was down to the last two dozen ice cream sandwiches when Parker's wife, Jill, came out to help. We were both throwing ice cream bites to keep the bears distracted. My knarly calloused and cracked fingers were in extreme contrast with Jill's beautifully manicured acrylic fingernails. *Like I said, in times like these, it is all hands on deck.* Our men were in that cage with two five hundred pound frightened grizzly bears. Ok, so maybe that is an exaggeration. The bears were not all that frightened They were happily slurping up chunks of ice cream sandwiches from the grass at our feet on the other side of the chain link fence. We threw the small pieces of soggy ice cream sandwich with purposed gusto as the men chainsawed on.

Dad arrived on the scene and took over the gate position. It may seem like a lesser job, but if you need that gate open to get the men out fast in case of rampaging bears, that becomes such an important lifesaving job. Tommy came into the enclosure with another pitch fork. The bears were getting full, slowing down on their chow down. The guys were just about finished with the tree cutting, pulling the broken trunk off the fence so the bears could not climb out. I hollered that the bears were on the move. Finally the men gathered the equipment and exited the enclosure. The two light brown fuzzy grizzly females immediately explored the downed tree sections on the ground. Oh Boy new Toys!

Standing around the outside gate of the Syrian bear enclosure, the guys were reliving the excitement to dissipate adrenaline. Hunter asked if I would mind taking a spin around the zoo while the men fixed the fence from the outside. Not a problem. Now it was my turn to splash through flooded out sections of the zoo. I looked for more downed trees over outside fencing. Another tree had come down over the fence between the elk and the pigs, but was of no concern. I rounded the zoo in Parker's Kabota ending up again at the path beside the bent fencing by the Syrians. There was a lull in the storm, thank God, hopefully it was over…? It was not.

I had parked the Kabota on the blacktopped path between the Syrians and the wooded picnic area. Some of the trees in the picnic area are large oaks, over two hundred years old. Large majestic trees were swaying as the wind started to pick up again.

We all heard the cracking sound at the same time. I was still sitting in the Kabota, when Dad, Doug, Parker and Hunter's synchronized yells reverberated:

"Let's get out of here!"

The brief lull we had experienced was the eye of the storm. Now the wind had switched directions and was coming from the east. The cracking was the beginning of the trees crashing down in the picnic area. We could hear the swoosh of leafy trees falling towards the ground. I started up the Kabota and jammed it into reverse. Gears screeched. I backed up fast, hoping the men were not in the way. I couldn't see, the back window is so obtuse. *Wouldn't it be ironic to have the guys survive the episode in the grizzly bear's enclosure to be hit by me with the Kabota?* We all cleared ground safely, getting to the treeless blacktop right outside the glass zoo doors. Four huge, two-hundred-years-old-plus oak trees crashed over, down in two minutes in the picnic area. None hit fencing.

All in all, twelve trees went down on the zoo property. The most dangerous was the tree in the Syrian Grizzly bears. We, like all our neighbors, were cutting wood for weeks. Some neighbors stopped by to help cut wood and took it home for the oncoming winter.

The electric here goes out with the first slight breeze! With the hurricane hitting the east coast, everyone was out of electric for almost a week. Because of hurricane Irene we lost quite a bit of frozen road kill deer when the freezer went out. I also lost all the frozen rabbits, (for snake food), that I had bred up, harvested and frozen over the year. Way life goes sometime. We would get more road kill and the rabbits… well you know what they do.

A week later, Jeff Little of Wantage Excavating came into the zoo with a Caterpillar 311 excavator, a huge-o machine, with a large scoop bucket on a giant arm. The familiar bright yellow and black coloring of the Caterpillar brand stood out vividly against the natural greens and browns of the zoo. One of the trees felled by hurricane Irene was a huge three foot in diameter oak and (darn it!) fell right next to my wonderfully artistically faux bamboo painted peacock pen. Though I must admit, we were lucky. The bulk of the tree fell on the flat section of land between the peacock pen and the Syrian Grizzlies. However, one six inch diameter branch fell on top and bent the support poles of the peacock pen. Humph! Hurricane Irene had no aesthetic appreciation.

I watched as Jeff Little, a six foot something hunky son of a school chum of mine, worked on the trees. Jeff was the bachelor of the town, every gal had their eye on him, and he knew it. For such a large young man, proud of his redneck heritage, Jeff was a master of that colossal Caterpillar machine. I was fascinated watching Jeff maneuver the bulky swinging arm. It looked like a giant yellow swan, using its head and beak to gently nuzzle cygnets onto it's back. Only this was a enormous Caterpillar machine, nuzzling giant ton chunks of tree trunks into a 427 HP Mack tandem dump truck. Jeff's touch was so gentle on the controls. Only the thunk of the humungous tree chunks being dropped into the Mack truck gave evidence to the dangerous equipment and job he was performing. Receiving each section of trunk, the massive Mack truck shook, dipped and rumbled. Jeff was able to turn a mammoth Caterpillar machine on tracks into a graceful Swan Lake ballet artist. Jeff has a very impressive skill set.

And under the learn something new every day category: Syrian Grizzly bears stomach capacity is twenty four ice cream sandwiches - each- after a full five pound bucket meal of leftover hamburgers and French fries! Who Knew? Now you do.

Zoo Momma

Chapter 53 Maggots and Decomposition

The following is a presentation I did on Maggots and Decomposition for Hopatcong High School Forensic Class. It was a fun day, out of my ordinary daily routine. *If you could ever call my life ordinary?*

Summer: In the summer it takes 10 days to 2 weeks for a carcass to deteriorate to bone. You might find some hide, since the hide dries out fast in the sun. Insect pests will not feast on dry pelt. Blow Fly Maggots only eat moist dead meat. Other bugs and grubs also help in decomp. Ticks and fleas leave the carcass as soon as the body is cold, in search of their next warm live body who's heart pumps blood, (their food). Fermentative and putrefactive bacteria in the intestinal tract help digest food when the animal is alive. That process is carried on by those bacteria in the gut after death. You have heard of pro-biotics? Those are the microbes, one celled organisms that help digest food. They do not die with the death of the animal, only with the drying out of their environment (the inside of the gut). Those microbes produce gas, microbe farts so to speak. Gas formed in the dead animal's intestinal tract blows the carcass up to the point of exploding, stretching the skin covering to the max This build up of gas causes bloat: a microbial proliferation of anaerobic metabolism within the intestine. Then it explodes. Hopefully you are not standing nearby! In life, this gas is expelled by chewing cud, burping, and flatulence.

In this area of New Jersey, dead carcasses are fed upon by coyotes, foxes, skunks, raccoons, opossums, hawks, owls, crows, eagles, mice, rats and bears. And an entire host of insects and nematodes, (worms). They dine on the soft tissues of muscles, intestines and offal. Bones, hooves and antlers are eventually used as a calcium source by rodents. But this is about maggots. Lovely, wiggly, squirmy maggots.

Often in the summer our dead deer truck drivers pick up what they call a 'self crawler'. That is a dead deer so loaded with maggots the maggots ripple under the skin, making the deer look like it is moving.. Yuck.

Fall and Winter: Heat is needed for good maggot infestation. Compost pit maggots live year round, due to methane produced heat/ lack of freezing. Maggots will grow to the size of your pinky, but never develop into a fly with out warmth.

Below ground: Decomp is microbial and slower. The environment is less warm, with no predators, no maggots, and more nematodes.

On ground: Decomp is faster, lots of maggots, animals that eat carrion: bears, possum, raccoons, fox coyotes, hawks and vultures, occasionally owls and eagles. Evidence of

Bears: large bites located on the chest for entry to the vital organs rich in blood and therefore vitamins. Liver is a great source of Vitamin B. Intestinal tract with pre-digested food is a good source of vitamins especially C - Inuit Americans and Russians eat this delicacy- it is called Nerrock.

Coyotes & Foxes go for the stomach first, and then intestinal tract.

Turkey Vultures: Eat from the soft orifices first, eyes, mouth rectum, or wound, the easiest access to the rest of the body. Black Vultures: are predatory birds, not specifically carrion eaters, but will join the T. Vultures in a feast. T. & Black Vultures are classified as migratory birds but resident birds are now in NJ.

Above ground: Decomp is faster with maggots, slower due to less mammalian feasting. The larger predators or climbing ones may be able to reach and feast. YUMMMY!

Water: Decomp is microbial, if there is anything left after fishes, invertebrates, turtles, etc. Nothing is left in alligator infested waters. By the way, alligators will tuck food under muddy outcrops or logs underwater and wait for it's meal to be tenderized by microbial action, then rip off bite sized chunks.

Maggots are considered ugly, dirty and disgusting in today's society, because they feed on the dead. However modern science and medicine is returning to using maggots. Maggot Debridement therapy is the intentional introduction of live disinfected maggots into the non healing skin and soft tissue wounds of humans or animals to clean out necrotic, (dead), tissue. Maggots were used medicinally by Mayans, and Aboriginal tribes in Australia. Records of the medical use of Maggots were also found in the Renaissance, Napoleon's time, and the Civil War.

Dr. J.F. Zacharis of the Civil War said " Maggots in a single day would clean a wound much better than any agents we had at our command". Maggot flatulence, (farts) help heal the wound and create an environment unsympathetic to bacteria. In 1929 John Hopkins University produced more than 100 papers were written on the subject. American Hospitals used maggot therapy until 1940 when penicillin was invented and maggots were deemed outdated.

In 2007 medical trials, maggots were used successfully to treat MRSA (staphylococcus aureus) Today 800 healthcare facilities still use maggot therapy. 50 thousand maggot treatments were used in 2006.

So next time you see a maggot infested carcass, take a moment and appreciate the wiggling wonders of decomposition.

Lori Space Day for Hopatcong HS. Oct 21,2011

Chapter 54 Weltschmercz!

Weltschmercz!
Two days before New Years, so sorry I'm late,
Like Alice in Wonderland, for our "important date".
So Hello, how-ya-doin'? to all my friends,
Let's have this chat before the year ends.
This year has been a real roller coaster ride,
good and bad times that still hurt inside.
On the uphill:
I raised two baby lynx a first for me,
Another addition to my list of new species.
And a little Scottish Highland bull,
Looked like a buffalo- sure could push and pull.
Did speeches, radio, and some TV,
With my favorite Vets, Dr. Ted, Dr. Brian, and me.
On the downhill:
Seemed it rained nearly all summer long,
Bad weather-poor cash flow, same old song.
Rain and floods plagued the zoo. Oh what trouble with a hurricane too!
A tree came down on the grizzly bear gate,
We worried about a great escape.
The men brought chainsaws and I ice cream,
Kept the bears busy, you know what I mean.
Amidst the storm the men cut branches,
While I gave bears ice cream sandwiches.
Guys got the fence fixed while I fed,
Cut back the tree while the wind swirled and sped.
We were done as the eye of the storm whipped around,
Then more trees in the picnic area fell to the ground.
A lesson learned in Nature's great feat, 24 sandwiches all a bear can eat!
On the subject of the weather, a blizzard in October was a bummer.
Winterized the zoo in just three days, to keep the critters warmer.
Got it done and hunkered down, while a foot of snow covered the town.
Lesson learned on the downhill:
Sometimes there's nothing you can do, to prevent heartache at the zoo.
Savannah, the serval kitten I raised, died,
And Chiquita my coati for whom I cried.
Lost my big baby Siren in a lion fight,
Still gives me nightmares every other night.
The mistake was not made by me, but I will remember for eternity.
She deserves more than four lines in this silly rhyme,
But I still can't write it at this time.
I bawled like a baby, was quite a wreak,

Zoo Momma

But fate was not quite done with me yet
So Khyber my tiger he passed away too,
It's been a tough year for me here at the zoo..
My tiger developed cancer in his nose, how or why, nobody knows.
My religion helps me greatly with this, and I wish upon Karma's Kiss.
I keep plodding on here at the farm, trying to keep all others from harm.
On a the uphill:
I was asked to give a demonstration, a forensic class on decomposition!
My power point on the life of the maggot,
Something those high school kids won't forget.
Tummies were held, eyes rolled for sure, but no one headed out the door!
Wrote History of The Beemerville Fire Department,
Took lots of time, and energy spent.
My Grandfather would be proud of me,
so involved is my family in the BFD.
Taught a class for Rutgers to farm folk,
on publicity, free advertising, really-no joke.
Quite an honor to be asked, Seems I'm a self taught example of that class.
On the downhill:
Another decision, not made by me, I stopped writing Space Farms publicity.
On the uphill:
Oh well gives me lots more time, to write in that next book of mine.
Hope to get it up to date this year, if I do - you'll know, don't fear!
Doug's doing great, my hubby and friend,
keeps me guessing and laughing to no end.
He's the zoo's mechanical miracle man for sure,
fixing the wagon for manure.
Carpentry, plumbing, electric, or the dead deer truck,
and anything else that runs amuck,
His wise guy humor and dark countenance,
lets him keep his reserved distance.
But I know he's a softy (though he would object),
He fascinates me, still and yet.
On the downhill:
Doug's brother Don passed on, to be with his dad and mom.
They'd been out of touch for quite a while,
just didn't seem to be Don's style.
On the uphill:
Daughter Jackie's my angel, my buddy and pal,
I'm just so proud of our grown up gal.
She's dropped weight, but still a beauty is she,
and always a great comfort to me.
I miss her terribly, she's two hours away,
but I'll see her in just a couple of days.

Zoo Momma

Spunky and perky, with her dad's great sense of wit,
she's a young gal that has all "it".
She's still working, but sending out resume,
fine as long as she does not go farther away.
Dad's doin' fine, up and out hunting every day,
enjoys his tractor and making the hay.
Or collecting dead deer across the land,
knows these roads like the back of his hand.
He gives advice, a great teacher is he,
on animals, life and a touch of history.
I see my mom once a week for lunch,
A grand 'ole gal, she loves me a bunch.
A greater cheerleader for me could not be found,
her ambition for me has no bounds.
We went to Canada and then Black Lake,
fishing, reading, painting, two nice breaks.
I love the calm, no people, just Doug and me,
and the wilderness is so beautiful to see.
W-hell, that's been my year, a roller coaster ride,
Which I could not stand without friends by my side.
And that brings me back to my date with you,
Please write or call, tell me how you do.
With out my friends I'd be so much worse,
Sometimes I just need to laugh, cry, or curse.
Weltschmercz!, but this is my life,
great joys, deep sorrows with a big dash of strife.
Don't worry I'm tough, or pretend to be,
I've got to be strong in this family.
So happy New Year! I hope next year is great,
'Till we chat again on our annual date.
To all my friends across the nation:
A toast to you in celebration
Of loved ones.
Love, Lori

Chapter 55 Mary Queen of Scots

Do you have a bucket list? I do. I want to raise certain animals that I have not done before. Like a baby buffalo. Trouble is, they grow up big, as I have discussed before. It' still on my list. Maybe someday…

Word came to me on a Saturday morning that we had a new Scottish Highland calf born. I rode up to check on it. It was cute, an auburn ball of fuzz, chubby baby legs folded up underneath itself. Looked fine, Mom Scottish Highland was cleaning it off, things seemed to be going well. The baby stood and was nursing within the ½ hour time frame. I noted the birth and went about my day. It looked like a red baby buffalo.

The next day, Hunter comes to me and asked if I had checked out the calf. I told him I had, why? Seems mom was not cleaning off the bum. There was a substantial amount of honey gold poo sticking to the backside of the calf. If not kept clean flies and soon maggots, *(oh yuck)*, would be a problem. If I raised it by hand, and it was a male, it would have to go to another farm. It looked like it was a male under all that ewwwy poop. A female we could put back in with the herd. But a sick or dead baby goes nowhere. Ok so we decided to bring the calf in.

We conscripted Dad as a driver, he would drive his Explorer in the paddock after Hunter opened and closed the gate, Hunter would hop back into the protective car. Mom Scottish Highland was a one thousand pound first time mom, with, *oh by the way did I mention,* two foot long pointy horns on each side of her head? The bull, two other females and a young bull were all part of the protective herd. Game plan was Dad would drive the Explorer as close as possible to the calf. Hunter would jump out grab the calf and hand it off to me in the car. Then Hunter would jump back into the car. We would drive off and repeat our exit. The unknown here was how protective the neglectful first time mother and herd bull would be…

Dad drove right up to the calf that was conveniently sleeping in the hay next to the building that edged the paddock. As we drove in the entire herd followed the car. Not angrily, seemingly curious. There was maybe six feet between the white explorer and the wall. Scottish Highland Mom's horns were just about six foot wide. *OK, make the play Hunter.*

Hunter jumped out of the driver's side back seat door and circled the car to the calf, still cuddled in the hay. I opened my door , prepared to receive the calf. Mom Scottish Highland was the first to clear the corner of the building. Before Mom Scottish Highland could get to the car, Hunter had swooped up the calf and handed it off to me in the car. There was a mish mash of our bodies, the fuzzy auburn calf across my lap with it's legs down on both sides. Hunter urged me to scoot over as the Scottish Highland Mom was approaching almost breathing down his back. There was no time for Hunter to run back to the driver's side of the car. Urgently, I lifted myself with the calf, now struggling on my lap, moving to the middle of the back seat as fast as I could. Now I am not a small woman, and Hunter has grown to six foot easy. The adorable calf that looked so tiny in the huge field, was actually a good four foot long, three foot high, most of which was legs, with sharp little black hooves. The calf was floundering, and bellowed. Hunter slammed the door shut, cramming the three of us in one half of the back seat of the Explorer. Luckily I had the head end of the calf. Hunter tucked his long legs under the back legs of the calf. We drove out of the paddock, Hunter quickly opening and closing the gate to the half acre green paddock and snuggling back into the backseat with the struggling calf.

The little auburn calf had a messy poopy backside where mom had not licked it clean. The poo was good consistency, and a healthy honey gold color. *(Yeah I am a Poopolgist!)* And now the calf was upset, and let go a good stream of yucky poop. Yep, right down the side of Hunter's kacki pants, decorating the beige inside of Dad's Explorer!

" Oh Yuck!" Hunter's two words as he rolled his eyes.

"Well, It's bio-degradeable?" I replied, a half hearted joke.

We drove down to the nursery and Hunter carried the youngster to the smaller section of the paddock. Hunter left to go about his work. Later that day he would help me move a beige plastic calf hutch to the smaller section. But first we had a yucky job to do.

Jennie Beckman had come to volunteer for the day. Jenny often came on Wednesdays and Sundays. We had become great friends. Jenny has a fun, perky personality, and is my daughter, Jackie's age. Her knowledge of animal medicine is extensive, with Dr. Spinks as her tutor, she has surpassed my humble teachings.

Jennie and I gathered up what we would need. A bucket of warm water from the restaurant kitchen, clean rags, and scissors. We joked about who was going to do what job, who's turn it was this time. You can only ask a volunteer to do so much, but I knew Jennie would do the yucky part if I asked her. But that was my job. Jennie and I are both stronger than your average woman, so I had no hesitation to ask Jennie to hold the head end of the calf.

We had to maneuver the calf around the paddock a couple of times until I grabbed the fuzzy broad nosed cutie by the neck. Jennie came and took over the hold. I washed the fuzzy backside of the calf, removing the yucky gold poop. After a few moments with Jennie cooing to the calf and me gently wiping it's butt, the reddish brown calf settled down. Some ewwwy sections were dried on, encased in the auburn fuzz of the newborn calf. That is what the scissors were for. I trimmed the entire backside, because the mess would happen in the future. I had no intention of licking the backside like its natural mom should of. So trimming the entire backside was the easiest way for future cleanliness.

"Well, surprise Jennie, it's a girl!" I exclaimed, after I had cleaned down to the 'basics'. We both smiled, knowing that we could keep her. "Now we need a name? Know any Scottish ladies?" We tossed a few back and forth. And that is how we got her name. Mary Queen of Scots was the only Scottish lady we could come up with.

We mixed up formula and tried Mary a couple of times that day. It took a couple of days, but eventually she drank cow's milk out of (what else?) a calf bottle. We had to clean her up a couple of times before the poops solided up enough to not stay attached. Oh and afterwards I cleaned out the back of my Dad's car too. Zoo keeping involves many chores your just wouldn't think of.

Mary quickly became the hit of the nursery. She answered to her name, bellowing in response Her huge brown eyes were surrounded by long chocolate colored lashes. Fuzzy, fluffy, longish bright auburn hair was naturally tousled, going this way and that. She looked like a baby buffalo, and I had always wanted to raise one. Later in the fall we would move her to the adult pen to reunite with her family. But for the summer, Mary Queen of Scots and Timmy the llama became great friends in the nursery.

Hello!

Photo by Lori Space Day

Chapter 56 Do you Emu?

Word came to us that emu chicks had hatched at Catoctin Wildlife Preserve and Zoo. Dad and Mira love to travel. For years Dad had been devoted and therefore grounded to the zoo. Now that we kids had 'taken over', he was free. Mira, just because she loves to travel. *I find that travel bug fascinating because I don't have it. I think it may be genetic! There are three places I wanted to see on my bucket list but that is another chapter! I do like to visit other zoos though.* Emu chicks would be a nice addition to the zoo. We had them years before, when I was growing up as a child, but I did not know a lot about them. Dad and Mira would bring them back in a couple of days so I studied up:

Official classification by the Australian government is Aves Casuariiformes Dromaiidae, Dromaius novaehollandiae. Which to our non Latin speaking ears sounds just as strange as the native Australian names for the bird: barrimal, myoure, courn, murawung or birabay. I like the name emu, and it is easy to spell!

Emu are the second largest bird in existence, second to the African ostrich. The average emu is five to six ft high and weighs up to one-hundred-thirty pounds. They are classified along with the Ostrich, rhea, and cassowary as Ratites- large flightless birds.

Emu are native to Australia. Full grown they are giant flightless birds, similar in shape and behavior to the ostrich of Africa. Before the European settlers arrived on the Australian island continent full of unusual species, there were several species of emu. All but one have been wiped out. The extinct species of emu fell prey to humans, as they were an easy food source.

Emu inhabit desert, plains and forests and are diurnal. Seen in flocks along the Australian countryside, they eat fruit, grains grasses insects, caterpillars according to what I had read and heard from other keepers. *Remember that.* Emus also eat small pebbles and stones to help aid digestion, the pebbles jiggle along in their system to help break up food.

 Emu are great runners, with long legs. Running, jumping and kicking are their main defenses. They can sprint at thirty-one miles per hour, reaching long strides of nine feet. Emu have three toes, making their feet look like dinosaur feet we have seen in museums. The center toe is larger than the two on either side. The underside of the foot has thick pads, which undoubtedly helps the emu traverse hot desert sand or prickly brush substrate. The end of the toes have very sharp thick claws which are used for fighting. Emus have been seen tearing down metal fencing with those strong legs and claws. The emu leg may look funny to us, because the knees appear to be put on backwards.

Emu eyesight is sharp. Their eyes are located on the sides of their pyramid shaped head and beak. This enables the emu to see danger coming from a wide range of peripheral vision. Nictitating membranes, or an extra eyelid act as a visor against dust protecting the eye itself while running. Large round brown irises give the emu a cute look if you can ignore the blue tinged bumpy skin covered neck and head. Ear orifice are visible on the adults, with tufts of 'old man' feathers guarding the opening itself. The emu has a mane of small spiky feathers extending from the beak over the top of the head and down the neck. This gives the emu a punk rock look.

The feather coloration is a mottled gray/brown, in sharp contrast to the blue and , a touch of red bumpy skin on its neck during the mating season. Each feather is actually a double feather, two feathers branching out of the same shaft. The feathers are barb-less, and fluffy. This is great insulation, protecting the emu from both extreme heat and cold. Emus do also pant on hot days. Emu wings are tiny and vestigial, their purpose vanished over eons of evolution. When an emu flock is laying on the ground, with feet folded underneath, and heads tucked down, they look like giant boulders. So the camouflage of the gray brown coloration works well.

Emu are not sexually dimorphic, you can not distinguish the difference of the sexes from the outside of the body. The males are a little smaller. Males make a guttural sound. The females makes a big boomy kettle drum sound. The difference in vocalization is drastic.

Emus breed at two years old, laying eggs in February or March. The male builds a nest, three foot wide, made up of grass, twigs and weeds. The nests are usually located in open areas where the emu dad can have a clear view. After courting the male, the female will lay eggs in the nest her male has prepared. The female lays dark teal green eggs weighing one and half pounds each., seven inches long, by five inches in diameter. She will lay an egg every two days and up to twenty in the clutch. Interestingly, the number of eggs produced varies with the amount of rainfall. One emu egg equals twelve chicken eggs. Funny thing is after the initial intense possessive courtship the female is not faithful and will lay eggs in other local male's nests. The MALE incubates the nest for eight weeks. During that time the male does not leave the nest to eat, sleep or poop! He will stand up about ten times a day to turn eggs. Occasionally he will leave the nest at night to get a quick drink nearby. After fifty six days of incubation, the male will loose one third of his body weight. His defense while setting is to lay low, look like a boulder, then at the last moment, jump up and scare the predator with his height and chase them away. Sort of a pop goes the weasel defense. *Boo! Go away.*

The chicks are hatched out at five inches tall and weigh about one pound. They have distinctive stripe pattern, of gray and beige colors. The infants grow rapidly and are their full height by six months old. The father guards the chicks for up to eighteen months, Sometimes the females stick around to help, often not. Interesting note: the young eat lots of insects. There is a legend that emus lay a sterile egg for the chicks to eat or to support a colony of fly maggots and insects for the chicks to eat! *YUMMY! Here kids, lunch!*

The emu does have a few natural predators. Dingoes, (Australia's wild dogs), eagles and hawks all prey upon the emu. The chicks of coarse being the easiest prey. Emu adults and chicks have been and still are a food source for the Aborigines. The Aborigines use every part of the emu, wasting nothing. They also have a tradition that you only kill what you can use, leaving the rest of the flock for the future. This is very similar to the Native American's culture of co- existing with nature.

In 1932 Australia emus were considered vermin. A war was declared on them, one hundred twenty thousand adults and over one hundred thousand eggs were destroyed. The government set up machine guns to kill large flocks. The flocks outsmarted and outflanked the machine guns by splitting up and running helter skelter about. Next the government decided to herd large flocks towards the machine guns, waiting until the last minute to shoot. Well, the first batch of emus killed collapsed onto the machine guns jamming them up. *Ya just can't mess with mother nature!* Today the kangaroo and the emu are still considered vermin in Australia, especially to farmers. The ultimate irony is the emu and kangaroo are on the official Australian crest.

Today, the USDA has taken the Emu, ostrich, llama and yak off the exotic specie list and lists them as an agricultural specie in the US. The emu's meat is considered a red meat and is low fat. I have eaten emu hot dogs, they tasted the same as the beef hot dogs. Emu farms also harvest oil for use in medicines, perfumes and make up. The oil is rendered from the subcutaneous (under the skin) and the retro peritoneal fat. The emu oil is supposed to have anti-inflammatory and antioxidant properties. Creams, potions and pills are all available.

Ok so that is what I learned gleaning the internet, and books in the Space Farms Library in three days. In three days, after all my other work at the zoo, feeding babies at night, and taking care of my husband, and house. *Ok get real, I don't do housework during baby season.* I felt I was ready for the three emus chicks to arrive.

I had set up our chicken brooder cage, a one by one inch wire cage on top of a wooden tray. The wire top had a hole in it to suspend a heat lamp. I put the brooder cage on the back porch by the kitchen window so I could thread the cord form the red heat lamp through the window to the socket in the kitchen. I used ground corn as a substrate and bedding. I set up a water dish, feed dish and a bunch of hay in the corner for a nest. We were feeding emu pellets *(yes they do make those)* and grasses. I thought I was prepared. I was not.

When Dad and Mira pulled in three days after they had left, I met them at the chain link gate next to the kitchen. The largest pet taxi we had was in the back of Dad's white Explorer. I saw that and said, ut oh, I underestimated the size of these baby emus. My fears were allayed however when I peeked in. Three adorable emu chicks, half the size of a foot ball, stared at me with huge googley eyes peeking over blue black beaks. Baby tufts of shiny spiky feathers topped their noggins. Instant love on my part. Sooooo ugly that you have to adore them, like baby possums or troll dolls. They cowered in the corner when I reached in for them. Dad by my side, I handed him one, Mira another and I took one. Their pencil thin navy blue/black legs flailed the air, not being used to being handled. We put them in the brooder cage to let them settle. Dad suggested I cover two corner sides of the cage to give them a place to hide. I had to move the heat lamp. A heat lamp should be located eighteen inches from the top of the standing head of the infant (of any specie). If the heat lamp is too close you risk inadvertently burning the animal. The baby emu chicks were already a foot tall and could easily stretch to eighteen inches. Those adjustments made, I went about my day.

The chicks settled down after a little while and their curious nature had them exploring the new four foot square territory. I would talk to my new charges every time I passed them. The emu became accustomed to my voice. After a few days they would come to my hand. Spikey feathers, distinctive stripes, googgley eyes and inquisitive natures quickly won my heart.

Note to reader, as I am writing this, Hunter called on my cell. Tara the tiger won't come out of the den and her belly has been very rounded. It is February, twenty degrees out. We are on baby watch. Lily the twenty month old tiger cub (future chapter) is the unknown. We don't know what Lily will do if there are cubs. She may eat them, she may ignore them, but it is cold out, anyway so those cubs will come in to me. So we wait and watch. By the way, there were no offspring. Tara is old and was just resting. Ok back to the emus story.

All went well for the first week. Then one morning, Parker saw one chick was down dead on the brooder floor. It had a long string of grass protruding out it's backside. I called Natural Bridge zoo and they informed me this was not uncommon. So for the future, I would cut all the grass I gave them into one inch pieces. I also added parakeet gravel and grit in a bowl to help with their digestion process.

The remaining two I named Ozzie and Harriet. They certainly looked strange, but they love me too now. I was amazed at the growth they exhibited. By two months old they were an easy three foot tall. I had moved them to a grassy paddock next to the fawn paddock. By three months old they were shedding their original baby downy stripped feathers and were growing in the traditional drab gray/ brown coloration. And boy oh boy did they grow. By November they were as tall as I, five foot six! It was all I could do to get them into a crate to take across the street to the warm animal barn for the winter. Cajoling, pushing and shoving got the job done. Did I mention that the emus had learned how to kick? Ouch!

The next spring the emu were full grown, easy six foot tall when neck stretched out. We decided to put them in the white tail deer paddock. Two different species with the same requirements. Both eat corn, grasses and grains. The acre large white tail pen would give the emus lots of room to run. The white tails were used to the emus being next door, so they would not be afraid of the emu or vice versa. Everything went well for a while…

Later in the spring, I was taking care of one white tail fawn that needed help. As I was in the white tail fawn paddock right next to the adult white tail deer paddock, I saw one emu go darting across the pen, not being chased, but chasing something. The grass was tall, we let it grow tall to protect the fawns as nature would do. The grass was moving just ahead of the emu's path. The emu was chasing a fawn, out ran it and stomped on it. *HOLY Mackeral!* I had done my research and never read anything about emus eating anything more than a lizzard or a snake. I rode my quad to the other side of the zoo where the entrance to the white tail paddock was. Unlocking the gate, the emus spotted me and came running for the affectionate neck rubs that Ozzie and Harriet had come to love. I pushed them away. They trotted behind me, curious. I scanned the spot where the emu was chasing the frightened fawn. Camouflaged in the grass, the spotted fawn cowered. I scooped up the fawn, bringing it down to the office nursery. I watched the white tail paddock that year, bringing in all the fawns I saw. Only three escaped the emus sharp eyesight. I mention this because after speaking to all the keepers I knew and one Australian Aboriginal Forest Ranger none had ever heard of this behavior or of emus eating fawns. *Whodathunk? Learn something new every day.*

The white tails did have their revenge however. That fall when the white tail males came into rut, one of the emus was found dead in the morning. It had been gored by a rutting white tail deer male. Whodathunk that also?

At this writing we do have Ozzie, warm and safe in the barn. Next spring we will be getting a couple more emu chicks. I look forward to the challenge. Love the challenge mater of fact.

Talking to the animals, again!
Photo by Karen Talasco

Chapter 57 Good Time Charlie Tiger

Since Khyber's death the year before, we were keeping an eye on Tara. We were interacting with her more often. We gave her toys and a jolly ball to keep her busy. The jolly ball, made for bears, only lasted about a week. Tara had torn it apart! She did have her down days, when she just laid around the den. We knew she was lonely, Khyber had been her play mate for 13years and he was gone. Parker got word that a young tiger cub male was available at Catoctin Wildlife Preserve and Zoo, in Thurmont Maryland. The tiger cub was 18 months old and a male. We were not looking to breed Tara, just perk up her spirits. Parker told me he was going to pick up the tiger cub on Feb 2ndso I notified the state. We are required to report to the state every time we transport a dangerous animal on N.J. roads. *Oh and by the way, every animal at the zoo is considered dangerous.*

Parker drove to Maryland, and picked up the cub in a steel bar transport cage in the back of his white Space Farms pick up truck. When Parker came home, the steel bar transport cage was put in the five bay garage across the street from the zoo. We would keep the cub quarantined for a week, and the five bay garage was warmer. We could make sure the cub was eating our food, venison and in general make sure that he was ok from the trip. We also needed Dr. Ted to come and micro chip the tiger cub. The new law requiring chips having been recently passed. I anticipated the tiger cub at 18 months old to be about half Tara's size. Well, I was wrong.

Dr. Ted came and Jennie, my friend the vet tech. We maneuvered the large two- hundred pound, five foot long (not counting tail)'cub' in the steel transport cage to give him updates on his shots and to micro chip him. We did not anesthetize him, a couple of quick jabs and we would be done. It took a couple of tries, but I grabbed the tail and Dr. Ted jabbed quick for the inoculations. Micro chips are a little trickier. Micro chips are supposed to go on the neck behind the shoulder. Well, the cub was chipped on his left hind hip. It was not an easy process, working through the bars, trying to stay safe. We all decided if the state did not like the placement of the chip, the state folks could come and move the darn chip themselves! But we got the job done.

The whole concept of micro chipping the tigers is supposed to save the tiger from the possibility of being sold on the black market, or to trace him if he gets out and gets lost. If a tiger gets sold into the black market, for sure someone is going to cut out the micro chip which is about the size of a grain of rice. Not that I know anything about the supposed black market for tiger parts for Asian folk lore medicine. I've only heard the rumors. So that was not going to apply to our tigers anyway. And if he did get out, *(knock on wood for me now!)*, he would not leave the zoo grounds...alive. Something all zookeepers have to acknowledge and accept. Micro-chipping is just another senseless law from bureaucrats. *Sorry I'll get off my soapbox now.*

We named the cub Charlie, Good time Charlie to be exact. He had the playful goofy attitude of a good time Charlie, and he was to be Tara's friend. Tara was fourteen years old, tigers are lucky to live fifteen years in the wild, but often do reach eighteen to twenty -two years old in captivity. In the wild, tigers have to hunt hard to eat, fight off diseases, endure parasites, find shelter from the elements, avoid poachers and hopefully find a mate. In a zoo setting, none of that applies, and most zoos like us have a Vet on call. So Tara was healthy but older. No one knows when reproduction senescence, (menopause in humans) is for tigers. There is just not any research out there. So Good Time Charlie was to be just a friend, and maybe a friend with benefits if Tara felt so inclined.

After the trauma I faced during the introduction of Siren to the African lions I did not want to be around when the slightly-smaller-but-younger-and-stronger-than-Tara cub was released into the cage. I was not attached to Charlie, though he had been hand reared, and was through the fence/bars friendly. He did enjoy the distracting pets we gave him before the inoculations. But I was attached to Tara. I had raised her in 1998, and nursed her through a couple of bad injuries, and hand raised some her offspring. So I did not want to be there to see all that could possibly go wrong, if it went wrong. *Does that make sense?* I am the weakest on staff so my muscles were not needed. Again, my worrying is what makes me a good zoo momma.

Nothing went wrong. *Halleluiah!* Charlie was introduced through the den door into the back of the den with Tara in the grassy section. After a while the slide in the chute was opened and the two massive orange cats could interact. And they did in a joyous fashion. Charlie, being a youngster had all the goofy vigor of a Irish Setter puppy. He was frolicking and jumping around chasing after the inquisitive but sedate older woman, Tara.

They got along very well. Very well indeed. Matter of fact, before long, two year old Goodtime Charlie the tiger made magic with Tara the tiger and turned fifteen year old Tara into a Cougar!

And I started counting the days. And I counted days again, and again, until I gave up counting and hoping, and was just happy that Tara and Charlie were happy. Tara had a friend.

Chapter 58 Tonto, Vixen and Ralph

Now readers, I know that I have written about foxes in chapters before, so this chapter is about three little foxes that came my way for a purpose. After our silver fox aged out, *(zoo talk for dying of old age)*, we decided to get some more for the exhibit of North American Red foxes. I contacted Gary Sunderland once again and arranged to pick up three little babies. One silver, one cross fox and I hoped for one platinum fox also. On the appointed day Gary and I met, again at a truck stop, I examined the babies and was thrilled to see a platinum baby.

The jet black baby was a silver fox, I named him Tonto, for Jay Silverheals, the actor who was the side kick of The Lone Ranger. The cross fox baby was charcoal grey, Gary assured me of the genetic stock it came from that she would be the typical cross fox that looks like red fox on the legs and belly, silver fox on the cross of it's back when looking from above. I named her Vixen, the word for a female fox. And the little platinum fox was pure white, with pale beige eye patches. His color would not change. I named the platinum fox Ralph, after my Grandfather Ralph Space. Grampa brought the first platinum fox into his fox farm in 1937 from Canada. This was the first platinum colored fox in the United States. Grampa became well known for his excellent genetics in his fox farm and won many trophies from fur breeding associations. We have a picture of Gramp holding his first platinum fox. So twenty five years after my grandfather's death, I was raising a platinum fox in his honor. Though this fox would essentially win the lottery, having free food, shelter, medical care and friends for life.

I love foxes, they are warm, affectionate, intelligent, and medium sized. They are peppy like a Jack Russell Terrier. The soft fur is just sensational to immerse your hands into. Every time I raise foxes, I want to keep them in the house as a pet. Until their natural body odor comes up at about eight weeks old. Then it is "peeeeee ewe, - you go down to the zoo". The smell is almost skunky, the musky odor is very strong, you could smell it the moment you opened my mudroom door.

Ralph, Tonto and Vixen grew up in the nursery in the center enclosure for most of the summer. They accompanied me on every promotional speech I had that summer. They were hand tamed, as bottle babies become. I could pick them up, cuddle them and flip them over on their backs for belly rubs.

When I had constructed the center enclosure at the nursery, I had made it for lions not foxes. The bottom of the fencing had a two foot in on a 45$\square$ angle under ground. Lions and tigers try to paw at the ground but are not smart enough to dig back further from the fencing. Well, not foxes. Foxes are well known for their digging abilities. Their dens are elaborate, second only to the woodchuck hole dens. I knew they were digging out, but had not seen the exit hole. Figured when I saw that exit hole I would loose a couple of chickens before I could call the foxes to me and catch them up. Well that was my plan. Not their plan.

All summer into September the foxes played and entertained the public in the nursery center. Dad had decided that the fox trio would be a great hit in with the Syrian Bears right outside the entrance door of the zoo. The foxes were peppy and responsive to the visitors. The current movement in the zoological world was to common house compatible species that would cohabitate in the wild. Foxes and bears are compatible species. The foxes follow the bear trails in the wild and clean up the scraps as bears are messy eaters. The day came and we went out to catch up my pet foxes. The foxes had a different plan. I swear they knew we were coming for them and dashed under the ground into their den. The underground they had not made an outside exit for, (yet).

Tommy Williamson was the new keeper for the summer. Tommy was just out of high school, tall, dark and strong. He was/is a good kid. I enjoyed working with him that summer. Tommy enjoyed visiting in the Nursery and would sit and play with the foxes on his breaks or after work.

Tommy, Dad and I chatted about the possibilities. We decided to dig the foxes out. Playful and teasing us, the foxes were always just one shovel away, sticking their noses out as we exited the shovel full of dirt. Eventually Tommy had dug them back far enough the foxes had no escape. Tom reached in with bare hands, grabbed first one, then the others and put the frisky foxes into a travel case. After the hour long job, the foxes were caught up. We looked around and had dug out the fox den, fifteen feet under and outside of the center nursery enclosure. When you are at the zoo, check it out, the den went from the center of the nursery enclosure to the blacktop section under the baby strollers. WOW! Those babies really dug an escape route! But had never dug up to make their escape. Guess they liked the nursery.

We transferred the foxes to the Syrian Bear enclosure. Tonto, Ralph and Vixen loved their new enclosure with an acre's room to run and play. The next spring the trio had babies, seven in all, that came up above the ground from the new den their parents had dug. Interesting colors on those babies, we had one platinum baby, two chocolate colored babies, two cross colored, and two silver colored fox babies.

I was worried for the safety of the fox kits, and discussed the possibilities the Syrian Bears would eat them with Dad.

"Don't fret, there is nothing we can do and those foxes will be protective," Dad explained. "Remember in the wild, both parents feed and protect the young, and here we have a trio of fox parents."

I kept an eye on the situation. When the parent foxes brought the babies above ground the kits did not move far from the den for the first couple of weeks. It was a delight just to see them. Our friend, Leonard Rue III came with wife, Ushi to photograph them. One day I saw the astonishing parental courage of foxes. The two huge cumbersome Syrian bears approached the sunbathing offspring. The Syrians started up from the bottom of the hill and sniffed the air. Like magic, on cue the parent trio of foxes charged down the hill, barking at the two four-hundred pound bears. The vocal intent of the foxes was clear, "stay away!" To my amazement, the Syrians backed down the hill. One swift swat and those bears could of eliminated the foxes. But no, the Syrians backed down the hill and ran away. Those foxes were intense in their command.

Later that fall I took Gary Sunderland into the zoo and showed him our babies. He loved seeing the foxes skipper and run though the enclosure. Gary explained to me the chocolate colored foxes are called merlot in the fur trade. Well, that is just dumb, women crave chocolate over merlot! At least I do. I also found out that Tonto in Native American means slow or stupid one. Did not know that when I named him, and it certainly does not apply

I still interact with the foxes, and now their offspring. I regularly go out and call them, "Tonto, Vixen, Ralph!" The visiting public is amazed to see the foxes appear from the dense greenery in the large Syrian bear enclosure. Our season pass folk know the call. And the reward is the zoo cookies, sold at admissions desk. Just call, and watch the foxes magically appear!

"Tonto, Vixen, Raaalphhhhh!" And my grandfather smiles.

Lori and Ralph the Platinum Fox
Photo by Jackie Day

Zoo Momma

Chapter 59 "Ut Oh!, Lor, He's got me!"

"Ut oh Lor, he's got me!" Dad barely whispered. "Quick, hold the door shut so he doesn't get out and..." Dad was so still, like a statue, it took me a minute to register that he was speaking to me at all. It was just a whisper, spoken out the side of his mouth. I followed orders and put two hands on the back of the case door and slammed the door shut on Dad's left forearm, scraping his forearm. *Ok maybe I should start from the beginning:*

My Dad, Fred, is getting older, aren't we all? I assist dad whenever the snake cases need be cleaned or the snakes in those cases need be fed. It is standard zoological protocol for two people to do the job. The first person's job is to get the job done. The second person's job is to get help in case of trouble, not to jump in and help. If the job is dangerous and goes wrong, you are going to need more than two people in a zoo scenario. It is a good rule for safe zookeeping.

Years before a group of young men came strolling across the parking lot with an eight foot Burmese python. A nice, big, healthy snake. The snake's browns, rusty brown, gray and black patterned skin glistened in the sunlight. The wonderful specimen was draped across the shoulders of three burly young men. The young owner was looking for a home for his pet. My Dad loves snakes and had said yes, over the phone. And so we had a large python. Dad built him a special case, eight foot long, six foot tall, and three feet wide. Dad built it, I painted it with jungle plants on the inside. The front side had a large plexi glass window for viewing the snake. The back of the case had doors on either end. One end of the case had an imbedded large gray tub for a water dish, right inside the door. Originally the case had a thermostat for it's heat lamp, but the snake made quick work of destroying that. So the python has been here for a good ten maybe fifteen years. The python had graduated from eating large rats, to medium rabbits to large rabbits or chickens. He will eat a large rabbit or chicken once a week in the summer, less often in the winter. Originally we bought the rats and frozen rabbits. Soon we decided to grow our own. All in all he is a good snake, not snippy like his next door neighbor the albino python. (Hisssss!)

Dad and I were set up to feed the snake, one day in August. I had filled a bucket with clean water to change the python's water while he was eating the rabbit. That is the safest time, when the snake is committed to eating, with a rabbit in his jaws, he can not bite ME. That works for me!

I brought the appropriate sized rabbit over to Dad who was waiting behind the python case by the kitchen's back door. We feed a freshly killed rabbit to the python. A live rabbit will fight for it's life and possibly injure the snake. An injured snake needs medication, and that is just not easy. Did I mention that over the years we had the snake the python had now grown to sixteen feet long? A good twelve inches in diameter at his thickest, the python's head the size of a man's hand. Rubbing medicine on an injury would not be easy at all.

Dad had the rabbit in his hand. I was stationed in front of the case so I could see and call out to Dad where the snake's head was at any given time. We wanted the snake's head away from the door when Dad first opened it so he would have time to toss the rabbit in. I told Dad where the snake's head was and Dad threw the rabbit. The large oval python head moved toward the light brown rabbit with intent. I started to walk the three feet to the back of the case to help with the clean up of the poo that was by the door of the case. I was two steps away. Then I hear the words, whispered words that still haunt me:

"Ut oh Lor, he's got me!" Dad barely whispered. "Quick hold the door shut so he doesn't get out and..." Dad was so still, like a statue, it took me a minute to register that he was speaking to me at all. It was a whisper, out the side of his mouth. I followed orders and put two hands on the back of the case door and slammed the door shut on Dad's left forearm.

I knew my next job was to get some help. I could not let the door go, or the mighty python might come out and wrap around my Dad, crushing his ribs. I had heard of it happening to other people. And my dad was 85 years old. The door handle on the kitchen door is lever style. I held the case door shut with my hands, balanced on one foot and kicked the lever down. The door opened with the force. There, standing wide eyed, startled that the door opened so forcefully, was Mason Pheil, Parker's nephew, Hunter's cousin, fourteen years old, first day on the job-in the kitchen. Tall for his age, schoolboy good looks that will grow into a handsome man, Mason sported a flattop butch.

"Get me some help!" I demanded.

"Sure," Mason replied and started towards me and the door, obviously volunteering his services.

"NO! Get Parker and Doug here, NOW!", I hollered. "The big snake's got Pop".

I had the entire kitchen's attention at that moment. Mason and JoAnn, the kitchen manager snapped to it and called both Doug, and Parker. JoAnn came out to me and asked what I needed.

"Get me the knife we keep behind the door," I commanded. We always kept a large hunting knife behind the kitchen door, close to the snake enclosures just for this purpose. I was prepared to cut the snake's head off. And the knife was not in the sheath. JoAnn reported to me. *Damn! Double Damn!*

Dad was still as a statue the whole time, I thought he was in shock. He did not jerk his hand back, he did not make a painful sound. Absolute silence. I anticipated Dad having a heart attack. Dad was a sculpture of himself. His face was solemn and gray.

"OK, Dad," I encouraged. "Help is on the way."

"Good," Dad once again whispered. "Now open the door just enough for me to get my other hand in."

In my mind I questioned the action. However I had total faith in my Dad's call. There must be a reason.

"Ok, Dad, you ready?" I questioned.

"Yep" his solitary reply.

"On Three!" and I counted.

I opened the 2 foot by 2 foot case door just a crack. Dad stuck his right hand in, zipping under the python's mouth and put his right hand fingers into the lower jaw. Dad pried the lower jaw open enough to stick his fingers over the front edge, *Yes that is where the teeth are!* of the huge snake's jaw. Dad's blood was flowing freely now. The python immediately threw another coil around Dad's two hands, in effect handcuffing him. All in maybe ten seconds.

"Ok, close 'er up tight now," Dad was in charge, but still mostly silent. I slammed the door shut on Dad's arm once again with force. The hungry snake had two coils around Dad's hands. The last movement of Dad with his right hand told the giagunda reptile that it's prey (MY DAD!) was not dead. Instinct made the snake coil tighter. The entire snake's body was writhing now, but still inside the case. The snake wanted out to finish the job on his prey. I used my whole body weight via my arms pushing against that door. I could feel, but not see, the snake pushing hard against the other side of the door. I listened for the snap of Dad's arm bones that I thought was inevitable.

It seemed like hours but only seconds, maybe two minutes max, went by, when Doug and Parker showed up. They had been working somewhere else on the farm.

"I need the gloves," Parker stated after he quickly surveyed the situation.

"OK, you hold the door, I'll get them," I replied, "You're stronger, and he is pushing hard."

Parker took over the door holding job. I ran, *(yes I can run when I need to),* through the kitchen, slamming through the swinging doors that separated the kitchen from the busy-with-customers restaurant. I felt all eyes on me as I sprinted to the museum steps. Some season passers called out to me but I ignored them, *Sorry.* I took the steps two at a time in my hurry. Rushing to the office door I swung it open not bothering to close it. Three little steps were skipped as I ran to my desk, slinging my black and chrome chair into position. I jumped up on the chair to reach the leather welding gloves always kept on the top of my gray file cabinet, *(so we know where they are- yeah just like that hunting knife).* Retrieving my now treasured gloves, I jumped the three office steps, ran back to the museum steps and skipped all four of them in a leap of faith that my stocky legs would not break. I could hear the buzz of the customers in the restaurant sensing something was up. When you see a fifty something year old woman run like lightning, something must be up! I dashed through the restaurant to the swinging doors, slamming through them once again. *"Who was that masked woman"* I heard in my head. *Lol!* I was really making time.

Jill, Hunter and the rest of the staff were coagulated at the kitchen's back door.

"You don't want to see this," I hollered to Hunter. I did not want to have to deal with him passing out also. Everyone backed off and got out of my way. Which was good, I tend to bulldozer in an emergency.

"Jill, we are going to need a chair," I spoke sharply to Jill, "And the medical kit." *(Sorry, it was the stress of the moment).* Jill went to get a restaurant chair and kit.

Outside the kitchen door we spoke with out words. Parker extended one hand from holding the door and I put the mustard colored leather elbow length welding glove on that hand. Parker was like a surgeon receiving a latex sterilized glove. Doug was on the other side of Dad to catch him if Dad went down. When Parker was ready, he opened the door, and grabbed the snake's neck with his other ungloved hand. Parker's strength came to play as he pulled the snake, still coiled on Dad's hand, quickly into position. Faster than you could see, Parker took his gloved hand and inserted it into the mouth of the python, with the coils still around Dad's hand, and pulled down. Dad, still conscious, and very much aware of what needed to be done, slipped his hand out of the coils of the snake. His own slippery blood lubricating the extraction. The snake came undone at the opening pressure on his jaw.

"AAAAAWWWWHHHH!" my Dad finally raised his voice to holler.

My immediate attention was on Dad. Dad staggered back the two or three steps to lean against the stone wall of the building. There was a cascade of blood when Dad first pulled his hand back, it splattered all over the wall now holding Dad up. Blood was pouring out of his hand, Dad at 85 years old, is on blood thinners. The color contrast of the bright red spots fanned out on the gray stone is etched in my memory. We all knew Dad was going to pass out, or have a heart attack. We were wrong. Doug had ashen Dad by one arm, I held the other. We were all intently focused on Dad.

"Hey, Darn it! Can I get some help with this snake?," Parker hollered. *Darn was not really the word. It is so funny now, but at the time...* Doug and I left drooping and pale Dad leaning up against the strong stone wall. Parker still had the snake by the neck with his bare hand. The rest of the huge reptile was coiled around Parker's legs on the ground at his feet.

"On three!" Parker instructed. Doug and I bent down in unison with Parker to help pick up the two-hundred-fifty pound snake. Adrenaline laced strength helped the three of us to lift the shiny snake back into it's case. Parker kept a hold on the reptilian head until its entire body was in the eight foot long case. With a jerk of his wrist, Parker flung the head into the case and slammed the door. Then Parker, also splattered with our father's blood, gracefully scooped up the dead rabbit. He opened the case door one more time and threw in the discarded, forgotten rabbit, slamming the door. The snake got fed.

I looked around and saw people videoing us from outside the fence by the cannon. *Huh? I've got other things to do.* Dad was visibly shaking.

Dad was still leaning up against the wall. Jill came out with a chair and placed it by Dad.

"Sit down," we all commanded Dad.

"No." Dad argued. "Take the chair over by Gramma's house." So we did. Dad ambled over to the chair by the hose at Gramma's house. I hollered for a clean bucket, Don't remember who brought it, but it appeared. I placed Dad's still profusely bleeding hand into the bucket and filled it with cold water from the hose.

After a few moments the bleeding slowed.

"Dad, you ought to go to the hospital and get some antibiotics," I gently suggested.

"Naw, I'm a farmer, I don't need no antibiotics," Dad argued.

"Yes you do, this is a snake bite, and not just a scratch," I admonished.

"NO Darn it! I don't need no antibiotics, I'm not going to no hospital," Dad raised his voice. I could see he was under stress and did not want to add to his aggravations.

I bandaged Dad's hand up with the first aid kit. Dad had forty two puncture wounds from the needle sharp teeth of the python. Most on one hand and the fingertips of the other. One tooth had broken off and was imbedded in Dad's knuckle, but we wouldn't know that for a couple of days. The needle sharp teeth created the minor but bleeding wounds. The worst wound Dad had was from where I slammed the door on his arm, scraping his delicate old man skin right off. That is the only scar he has today. The adrenaline in Dad's body was fully functioning, and he started to talk.

"I knew I couldn't move, or that python would think I was still alive," Dad explained to me.

"You were very brave, Dad," I was trying to help him calm down as I bandaged his hand. "I gotta hand it to ya, I would of jerked my hand back!"

"You did just what you were supposed to do, but don't blame the snake, it was my fault, I was in a hurry and moved poop before the snake was solid on the rabbit," he explained. "Don't kill the snake, it was my fault," Dad pleaded for the snake's life. Dad was getting gabby, the after effects of the excitement. But I did want to kill the snake.

"You want to go to the hospital now?" I gently questioned.

"No, I want to sit in my chair by the door," Dad simply stated.

And after all that trauma, Dad got his wish. The rest of his entourage and I followed Dad around the outside of the building, holding the door open so he could sit in his chair by admissions. I got him a drink of water.

"I don't need that?" Dad questioned.

"You've lost a lot of blood," I stated, "Drink the water."

I left Dad in his chair, gabbing to all the excited visitors about what had just happened. I was shaky also as I walked out on the front porch of the main building, around the corner and dry heaved into the grass. I called our Vet. I knew Dad would listen to Dr. Ted on a medical issue. More so than a human doctor. And definitely more than he would listen to me! And I knew darn well Dad needed antibiotics. After a brief description of events to Dr. Ted, he and I concurred.

"Yes, Fred needs some antibiotics. Snakes have gram negative and gram positive bacteria in their mouths, a bite can get nasty," Dr. Ted told me. I re-entered the building, walked right over to my Dad, repeated verbatim what Dr. Ted had said.

"Ok, I'll go get some antibiotics, now stop bothering me," Dad smiled. "I'm a tough old bird."

Yes, Dad you are, a tough old bird with nerves of steel. I looked at my aging father a lot different after that day. His body may have arthritis, his hearing poor, his walking stiff and obviously painful and his attitude is very old school, but his animal knowledge and knowledge of zoo work still astounds me.

The Burmese python's open mouth!

Photo by Lori Space Day

260

Chapter 60 Alaska!

The Christmas of 2011 Dad gave Doug and I a trip to Alaska. Wow! What a gift. It had always been my dream to go to Alaska. I had watched my Dad and brothers go off on hunting trips and so wanted to go. I didn't want to hunt, just a photo excursion to see all the animals in the wild, especially those animals we do not have here in New Jersey. Dad and Mira had gone to Alaska on a Dunn's Tour when my Aunt Loretta still had the tour business. So I chatted with my cousin Irish on what to do and where to go. Irish suggested Holland American tours. Great choice.

We arrived in Vancouver, Canada headed for Alaska in the middle two weeks of August, which is Alaska's autumn. The cruise ship was beautiful, state of the art, the staff wonderfully attentive. The cruise was smooth sailing, which was good because I get horrible motion sickness. I was not the slightest bit ill. On days at sea we saw all species of whales, seals, sea birds, and eagles. The whales were a first for me. The cities we ported at were fantastic examples of Alaskan culture. I can not praise enough the clockwork precision of the Holland American Cruise company. I work in the zoo which is also a people service business, so I can appreciate the behind the scenes work involved. The artist in me loved the artwork on the ship, the fruit carvings in the dinning areas, and the simply fascinating bath towels rolled into animal sculptures left on our bed. Shipboard entertainment was great, and the ocean cruise was very relaxing.

I wanted to see the animals of the area so the whale watching was big for me. The second week of the trip was even more fascinating than the first. The land tour took us through The upper section of Alaska. The scenery was breathtaking, I don't know how to express it other than to say the expanse of natural views was astounding. Every view was photo worthy.

I do a lot of gardening at Space Farms so I paid special attention to the beautiful flowers in full bloom at every hotel. I remarked on the gorgeous colors, especially the chrysanthemums, which had grown to dinner plate size. The gardens looked like God took buckets of vibrant paint and just had a rain dance. I told Doug they must have a fantastic gardener. Second night, second hotel, same thing, great gardeners, fantastic plants.

The third hotel, Doug and I were walking next to another woman, we mentioned the fabulous gardens. We all were chatting about the effort on the gardeners part when the hotel's concierge decided to chip in.

"We do have fantastic gardeners, but also keep in mind, we have twenty four hours of sunlight also!" she smiled. "That's why the plants are so large." Then I understood!. *Dummy me.*

When Doug and I travel on vacation we don't tell people that we are zookeepers. If you tell people our professions then all the conversation becomes around the zoo and zoo keeping. There is no vacation 'down' time then for us. When people ask a question you can't say "Sorry, I'm on vacation, I don't want to talk to you." Well, I can't, Doug would, no doubt in my mind. But it is just bad public relations, so it is easier to just not say anything. So we don't. If anybody asks then Doug says he does maintenance for a company , and I say I work in public relations. Which truthfully are parts of our jobs at Space Farms. Those are boring professions, so no one engages in more conversation.

The people of Alaska were warm and cordial. Most of the folks we talked to were not native Alaskans, but summer migrants for the tourist industry. We did visit a number of Native Alaskan villages as part of the tour package, and found the native inhabitants to be great ambassadors for their culture. It was especially neat to see a hand made fur parka coat that had the same unique diamond pattern that my grandfather had commissioned a mink parka made from Space Farms Mink Ranch fur in the 1950's. That Parka coat is on display in our museum. I have never seen another pattern like that in the fur industry.

Doug particularly liked the 'Ghosts and Goodtime Girls' Tour in Skagway. If you go to Alaska, don't miss that one either, Doug says with a twinkle in his eye!

The best part of the trip for me was a bus trip through Denali National Park. I had focused on the bus trip, wanting to see all the animals I could possibly see. I prayed the night before for good weather, that the animals would be hale and hearty, and come to where we could see them. I'm sure everybody on the trip did the same. I was excited, and so was Doug. Moose, caribou, Dall sheep and eagles, were all species we did not work with, and had not seen in the wild. Wolves, grizzly and black bears, even though we work with them daily, yeah- we wanted to see them also. It would be a treat to see them in their natural habitat.

The day of the bus tour the weather was cooperative, scattered sunshine, a high of 60°, and we were off. The driver/tour guide told us we would not be let off the bus, but could let the windows of the bus down for better pictures. The bus was an old style school bus repainted in olive green and drab beige colors of the National Park system. The bench seats denoted the bus's age. Did I care? NO! The guide gave us a run down of his qualifications while we were on the way. He seemed to have knowledgeable credentials.

Well, let me tell you, what a ride! We saw more caribou than I could count. So many I stopped taking pictures. Tall and graceful the caribou antlers were still in velvet. Their white rumps stood out amongst the colors of fall.

Dall sheep, they look more like a white shaggy goat clung to the side of a mountain. Their footing is noteworthy. The Dall sheep are able to navigate the rock strewn narrow self made paths on the steep inclines of their home terrain. Ptarmigans, are a grouse like bird, but size of a basketball on stilts. These birds sprinkled the sides of the dirt road we traversed, pecking at seeds. Their speckled backs were great camouflage. As the old bus growled up the rolling hills we could see the autumn colors of the native plants around us for miles. The purples, greens, reds and oranges stretched out until the base of the next mountain, where the scrub brush line showed a distinct color stop.

We saw three grizzly bears enjoying the last of summer's sun, sleeping right out in the open. Another one was perusing a river mud flat for food or what ever. The guide explained to us: if you hold your thumb up and see some bear on either side of your thumb, you are too close to that bear. Grizzlies can and do charge and they charge fast. Grizzlies don't always bluff charge first, like a black bear. They looked large, in full fur for the upcoming winter season. Rounded, but not fat, the bears were preparing for winter.

Around another corner and there, to my amazement, my life long bucket list animal to see in the wild, was a magnificent bull moose. He was browsing on multi-hued bushes not twenty feet from our bus. The guide slowly stopped and then courteously backed up some so we could all see and photograph this mighty monster. The moose was huge, much larger than I had anticipated. He was twenty feet away and downhill from the bus but his head was tall enough to be on level with the bus windows. Everyone rushed to the left side of the bus, jockeying for the best photo spot. The guide reminded everyone to keep their cameras and arms inside the bus as the moose was so close. Moose have been known to charge a bus that gave them 'grief'! Everyone complied. That moose was huge, if I a 5 ' 7" woman like me, stood on tippy toes, held my hands above my head, and bent my hands at my wrists, I might have reached the top of his shoulders. The closest thing I had ever seen was a Clydesdale horse. I'm talking big. Mr. Moose's antlers were an easy six foot spread of horned crown on the top of his head. A shaggy beard and munching lips continued their eating chores as if we were so insignificant and caused him no alarm. *Good, I didn't want him mad at me!* Bountiful colorful leaves disappeared at the flick of his tongue. We were close enough to hear the moose chomping and break twigs and the swish of the leaves going into his mouth. His lush brown coat was luxurious. Moose eyes with saggy bags nary gave us a glance. This moose was two times the size of the other wild moose I had seen in Canada. I was impressed. What a creature! Photos were snapped, including mine. And we continued on.

We were in Denali park for hours, but the trip sped by. Around every turn was another sight to see, gorgeous mountains, rivers, plants and of course the animals. We saw marmosets, the northern cousin to the woodchuck, and all sorts of other animals. The only thing we did not see was a wolf. Oh well, got to leave something for next time.

As the tour wound to a close, the guide was giving us his usual spiel. I could tell, because I have a few of those also. *Sorry, now you know.* At the end of his speech, he added:

" You folks don't know how lucky you are, we saw more animals today than I've ever seen in one trip through Denali ," the guide gushed, then added: "Somebody here must have a real touch for animals." Maybe it was just part of his spiel. Maybe not.

I looked at Doug and smiled. Doug winked at me. He knew how important this trip was to me, and how long I had dreamed of seeing these animals in the wilds of Alaska. A life time of wondering, and wishing had come true. We loved Alaska, and will go back again before we can't.

Chapter 61 Blue Cowgirl Love

Blue Cowgirl Love
She was twenty six years old with a fire in her eyes
Some bitch named Sandy had just whupped her guy.
Oh no sirreee!! This just wouldn't do,
She put on her big girl panties and cowboy boots too.
Tied up her Rapunzels, a peacock feather for luck,
And set out on her mission through the destruction and muck.
A singular thought, no hesitation had she,
Jumped in her blue horse and turned the darn key.
Northeast was her heading, she was on her way
To rescue her sweetheart, Yeah, this was the day.
The trail was lonely, strewn with debris
Of others who suffered the attack of Sandy.
She didn't tell her mama, didn't want her to worry
Peddle to the mettle, determined she hurried.
She'd told him she'd come, "Meet me somewhere,
I've got my boots on, peacock feather in my hair.
Don't know how long but I will be there!"
His phone had crackled, the battery low,
He shouted the Target, and off they did go.
The highway almost deserted, she traversed on,
Other travelers, intimidated, were simply gone.
Blue Cowgirl Love, knew no time or fear
She swerved to the left, and shifted gears.
Road law was absent, cowgirl driving ensued,
Wrong way down a one way, this cowgirl was blue.
Passed gas lines, and downed lines, on a singular mission
To rescue her man, and get some good kissin'.

Stranded in Hoboken, in his apartment building,
Food and water had run out, electric missing.
He packed his belongings, his laptop, his dead phone,
Said good bye and hiked out of his Hoboken home.
He spoke to his Cowgirl gave her the Target,
Then set out on an epic journey, he'd never forget.
Down the flights of his apartment, the elevator was broke,
He traveled with two friends, Sandy'd been no joke.
They hiked two miles, poisonous water swirled at their feet,
Determined his blue cowgirl he was going to meet.
Rivers of debris, rats running hither and yon,
Backpacks full of hope, the trio traveled on.
Smoke in the air, sewer fumes stung their eyes.

Zoo Momma

Nothing would keep this blue cowgirl from her guy.
A truck passed the trio, splashed them with toxic goo,
They lumbered on, simply nothing else would do.
After their noxious journey, they hit the Target,
But what of his blue cowgirl, she wasn't there yet?
What happened, oh please, where could she be?
He fretted, They waited, for what they could not see.

She saw him first, across the parking lot
Gunk splashed and dirty, it mattered not..
She geared down her blue horse, parked not far away,
Her heart sung with courage for what she did that day.
He was so proud of his brave blue cowgirl whom nothing could deter
He knew in that second, the honor it was to be loved by her.
Nothing mattered more in that moment of time,
An instant of joy, the reunion divine
Greeting hugs and kisses a matter of course,
Emotional detox, next to her blue horse.
They packed up their gear on the back of that old blue,
Rode off into the sunset, as young lovers do.
With two extra friends in back, headed north, then south,
All joyful and satisfied smiles on their mouths.
Dropped off the friends, then headed home,
Where the Old Blue is parked but the Cowgirl still roams.
The power came on, and after all this drama,
 The delighted brave Cowgirl finally called her momma.

This is the story of the man from Hoboken,
And his blue Cowgirl's love that could not be broken.
Lori S. Day 11/3/2012 5am- 7am.

Note to my readers:
       Hurricane Sandy did not do a lot of damage at the zoo. We had a lot of
wind, and rain, which knocked out the electric for a week. We were out of the loop
of information from the world, not knowing how bad other parts of New Jersey
had been hit.
       Jackie and I have had an agreement ever since she went to Austria and
was out of my control. If you see imminent danger, like a tsunami, get safe and call
me later. Don't call me and say "I see the tsunami coming…" That will only add
hours to my worry time when there is nothing I can do. Because as soon as I hear
on the news I am going to worry. So concentrate on getting safe, and call me as
soon as you can. Jackie called me at home at night on 11/2/2012 and gave me the
verbal story of her rescue of her boyfriend Mark the day before. I slept on that
story, woke up at 5 am and wrote this poem.

Zoo Momma

And that is what happened when the delighted brave Cowgirl finally called her Momma !

Chapter 62 Silent Snowy Nights of Christmas

The Silent Snowy Nights of Christmas '12
"Tis Christmas night, the tree's still lit,
I know we've not chatted in quite a bit.
Starlight so peaceful, ground covered in snow,
the zoo is asleep, gentle silence bestowed.
So I'll seize this time… for my holiday rhyme.
Raised animals all spring, keeps me quite busy,
my multitasking could make anyone dizzy!
Let's see-my nursery was quite full,
with a Scottish Highland cattle calf bull.
They are very frisky in case you don't know,
and hairy so their parts don't show.
Bathed it one day and believe it or not,
She's a girl, now named Mary Queen of Scots!
4 fawns, 2 ponies, 2 turtles that snap, chickies, duckies and bunnies galore
Seems there's always room for one more.
Raised two emu chicks, WOW! They really grew up quick!
Or Three - a platinum, cross and sliver foxes,
that came to me in cardboard boxes.
My Gramp, he sure would be beamin',
Watching over me with 'lil foxes screamin'
For bottles and playing we had so much fun,
now they are all in the adult zoo run.
I painted, cleaned and shoved my fair share,
all while enjoying the fresh country air.
Covered for lunches, and answered visitor questions,
To myriads of people from around the nation.
Tara'd been lonely since the death of Khyber,
So we got her a companion, an 18 month old tiger.
I named him Charlie, a real good time sugar,
Then Charlie made magic, turned Tara into a cougar!
No offspring yet, maybe, I'll surely let you know,
Tara's making kissy faces with our lion, sooooo…?
Some days are same day, but from my work you can't pry me away.
I had articles published, was on TV, even a cover girl, yeah, that's me!
The joy of my animals a wonder to behold, no matter that I'm getting old.
Last Christmas Dad gave us a trip to Alaska,
WOW, what a trip, I just got to tell ya.
On the cruise we saw pods of Orcas and humpback whales,
Sea lions, dolphins and belugas, (well, only their tails).
The cruise was fantastic, the food top notch,
we enjoyed the entertainment, quite a lot.

Zoo Momma

Denali was just unbelievable, everything so big,
including a moose chomping on twigs.
And grizzlies, Dall sheep, so many caribou,
a lifetime dream trip come true.
Alaska in August is in it's fall, Such vibrant colors, God painted it all.
Saw salmon climb ladders, then we panned for gold,
24 hours of daylight makes flowers big and bold.
And Doug he loved the Ghost and Goodtime Girls tour,
Tipped that gal once, then tipped her some more!
So special thanks to Dad that really was quite the gift.
A zookeeper's dream trip, we might of missed.
Speaking of Dad:
Almost lost Dad, again this year, with a snake bite that put us all in fear.
I was the assistant as is protocol, feeding a 250 pound python, 18 foot tall.
Snake passed the rabbit, got Dad's hand,
He knew to survive he would just have to stand,
Still and quiet, while I did my assistant chore,
not to help- but to holler and get lots more.
Python wrapped around his hand tight twice,
with 32 teeth marks, not so nice.
I shouted to the kitchen , sent out the alarm,
and held the door shut on Dad's arm.
If the python got out he would of coiled,
a death grip on Dad's body, destroying my world.
Parker and Doug were on the scene quick,
Park held the door while I ran for mitts.
Delivered: then Park grabbed the neck of the snake,
Park's mitt hand in it's mouth, the snake's grip to break.
Dad hollered in pain for the first time,
then stepped back so the snake could not wind.
We worried, Dad had started to shake,
but we still had to deal with that dastardly snake.
Doug , Parker and I put the snake back in,
I patched up dad with 32 puncture wounds on his skin.
Dad wouldn't listen to me, to get some meds,
(the old coot with such a stubborn head.)
So I called Dr. Ted , our Vet, So Ted said, then Dad said, "Ok yep".
Dad saw his Doctor and that's about it.
You can see it on youtube: space farms snake bit!
Hurricane Sandy blew through the scene,
We had more damage from Hurricane Irene.
Doug's had some adventures here at the zoo,
There's never a lack of things to do.
He figures he's earned job security,

Zoo Momma

fixing things broken by Dad, Hunter and me.
He's a local reputation as a computer geek,
helping folks when info they seek.
An amazing man, my hubby and best friend,
with wit and humor that just doesn't end.
He's shy and elusive, the opposite of me,
sometimes I wonder just how we can be.
It's now New Years Eve and I'm back to you,
after Christmas and shoveling at the zoo.
While all lies quiet in the moon's gentle light,
it gives me more time, for me to write.
Jackie's doing great with a major life change,
Moved in with two gal pals, life re-arranged.
Still managing Planned Parenthood, her motive strong,
Applied to Grad schools, we'll know before long.
She's become quite the cook, much better than me-
(I'm bored with that, cooked since I was three.)
She's dropped eighty pounds, looking quite sharp.
An angel with blonde hair, minus the harp.
Well… maybe not an angel, but certainly like no other,
Would expect nothing less, because I am her mother!
Hunter, our nephew, has grown to a man,
where the time flew, I don't understand.
Hunter helps me with projects 'round the farm,
when I need a bit more muscular arm.
A good sense of humor gets us though rough times,
glad to say Hunter is a friend of mine.
And Sam his girlfriend, is so sweet, a cuter couple you could not meet.
Lindsey, our niece, a personality gem,
I've helped with sewing projects and will do again.
She's a joy in our lives, a sharp sense of wit,
And an artistic spirit that just won't quit.

So to all my friends on this New Year's Eve, one simple wish I would like to leave:
Please remember this heartfelt refrain:
I wish you the joy of young fawns dancing in the rain.

Love, Lori, Jackie and Doug

Chapter 63 "Honey, Just Walk it Off!"

Zookeeping is hard physical labor. I will admit, I have the least of the hard labor jobs, but the animal infant care is round the clock sometimes. Doug, Hunter and the guys get the worst of it. Dad is out by age, and me, well, I'm usually busy with babies or visitors, or staff issues. *My good excuse anyway!* Winter is terribly cold, and the guys are shoveling snow, hauling buckets of water and chipping ice out of water dishes all the time. Summers are hot enough to fry an egg on a rock some days, and you know darn well that will be the day the guys have to put away hay in the mow. I worry about our guys constantly.

In January of 2012 I was just visiting and feeding the parrots treats and goodies. The parrots were located inside our main building, the restaurant being closed with the zoo for the season. *The birds love me, the guys hate the birds because the birds hate them. I give the goodies and treats therefore the birds like me. You would think the guys would catch on to that, but no.* The back kitchen door slammed shut and I looked up from inside the large macaw parrot cage to see my hubby Doug plod in from the outside cold. He was dressed in his olive green camouflage army coat. His ski cap was pulled down to the top of his dark reflective sunglasses. His Carhart black canvas pants, insulated Bean boots, and thick gloves, showed Doug was dressed for working outside. Doug's long, thick, silver skunk stripped winter beard protected his face. He had no skin exposed to the elements. Ok, so maybe his nose.

"Hi Hon," my greeting.

"I'm having a heart attack," Doug so calmly stated. "Take me to the hospital."

Now I never heard of any one having a heart attack standing up. I took the CPR class at the Beemerville Fire House across the street with the rest of the firemen. The victim was always on the floor. And in my defense, Doug does tend to be overly melodramatic about every little scratch. *Yeah, women readers are understanding me here.* Doug was so serene, I thought he was joking.

"What did you just do?" my query.

"I just emptied the pig water dish," he replied, grumpy. "Take me to the hospital."

Again in my defense, I should inform the reader that the pig's water dish is a human bathtub full of water, that was mostly ice and I could see Doug tipping it over and pulling a muscle or something. That would be an extremely heavy lifting job, and he was working by himself.

"Oh, you probably just pulled a muscle," I stated. " Just go like this and walk it off." I demonstrated a shoulder shake to relax the strained muscles in his shoulders and upper back. The parrots squawked in the background, some imitated my dance.

"Take me to the hospital," Again he replied. "I'm having a !@**#! heart attack.

"Ok," I could see he was getting upset. "Just let me close up the parrots."

"NO, NOW!" Urgency became the message. I got it.

Doug was walking up towards the office via the steps to the museum. I followed. Doug walked through the office doors. Jill was on the computer and Parker was sitting reading a newspaper.

"I'm having a heart attack," Doug's calmness was eerie. "Lor's gonna take me to the hospital." Doug told Jill and Parker. There was a long pause in action at that point. Stunned deer in the headlights comes to mind. I grabbed my coat from my chair to follow Doug.

"We need to stop at the house so I can get my purse and our medical cards," I prattled after Doug as I walked behind him.

"Don't go home, go straight to the Sussex hospital," Parker advised, "You can straighten the paperwork out afterwards. I had a friend who died last week, he didn't make it to the hospital. I'll call the hospital and tell 'em you are coming." Parker had followed me following Doug out the door.

"OOOOKKKKay," I stammered. Still not believing.

Doug got in our blue Tucson Hyundai parked in front of the building. I started to drive past the zoo, and got as far as the Firehouse when now ashen colored Doug spoke.

"Where the @#$%@ are you going?" He asked

"I'm taking you to the hospital," I calmly replied. *Was this a bad joke?* "You are having a heart attack."

"I can't go to the hospital," Doug declared. "I have pig shit on my boots. Take me home, I'll change shoes then you can take me." Doug was now sweating profusely.

My brother's words echoed in my brain as I turned the car around in the firehouse parking lot and drove the block to our house. A quick boot change, I did grab my purse with the medical cards, and we were on our way to Sussex Hospital. Six miles, I told myself. The concept of calling an ambulance did not enter my mind. I could have Doug to the hospital before the ambulance could get out of its garage. At least that is what I told myself until my speeding brought us to the light at McCoys corner. The light was red. I had kept an eye on Doug, he had been phasing in and out. I stopped for the light, looking both ways and then at Doug. I saw him lean his head back to the head rest and his eyes rolled to the back of his head. Now I was angry.

"Don't you die on me now, You @#$%@#$!" and I gave him a hard backhanded punch in the chest to wake him up. "Stay with me buddy, don't go to sleep." Doug abruptly woke up and was paying better attention as he noted out loud that I had just run a red light. *Yeah, thanks for that Hon! Don't mention it.*

"Yeah, so where are the cops when you need one!" I shouted my appropriate cliché. Doug started to empty out his jacket of cigarettes and handed his wallet to me. *Yeah, like they won't smell the smoke on your clothes, Oh well at least he won't smell like pig shit. Sorry reader, that is what I thought at the time.* We were less than a mile from the hospital.

"Ok," Again Doug was amazingly composed, "Just let me off at the emergency door, then go park the car." His wish was my command. I remember thinking this is all very surreal. I was close enough to the automatic glass doors to hear Doug announce as HE WALKED through the doors:

"I'm having a heart attack!" And I am sure that Doug was relieved that someone finally believed him. I saw staff swing into action like a Chinese fire drill. *(Sorry don't mean to be politically incorrect but you have the concept-)* Or how about like ants on a honey hill? Anyway, I pulled the car away and parked it.

When I walked into the Emergency Room the nurse at the desk showed me to the room where Doug was on the stretcher/gurney/ bed. I walked in just in time to see Doug go under again. Tubes had been attached while I was parking, and they gave Doug more medicine. Doug came to. Then they gave him a nitro pill under the tongue and Doug was out again. This time they told me to step back, I did, I stepped into the corner, just trying to become small. I wanted to become so small I would disappear. To be anywhere but there. The doctors and nurses were working on Doug. I'm sure I looked thunder struck. One nurse came to me and asked if I needed anything.

"I need a ladies room, I'm gonna be sick" I replied, as soon as I saw Doug had come back to us again.

On my return from the ladies room, Doug was a little better looking, not quite the ash gray color he had come in with. His eyes were glazed and drugged looking. A nurse was gathering up his dirty work clothes with a wrinkled nose. *She was lucky he changed his boots!* The clothes were put in a plastic bag and handed to me.

"We are sending him to Denville Hospital, he needs more than we can do here," the Doctor told me. "Do you want to drive him? Or do you want the ambulance to take him?" *Now what kind of a question is that? Really , the man is in the process of having a heart attack and they think I want to drive him to the city? I'll be having the heart attack. Or Doug will have another on the way! Now I believe, I believe., I believe him.*

"Let the ambulance take him," I felt so small, embarrassed to be so chicken, and unknowing of what to do. "I'll follow."

"Don't try to follow, they will go to fast, the procedure will be over by the time you get there," I was advised.

"What procedure?" I asked, worried.

"Whatever needs to be done," was the answer. "You may want to go home and get organized, then go to the hospital." Good thing someone was thinking. I was on another planet. *Planet what do I do now? Deer in the headlights look.*

They packed Doug up on the gurney, I took the clothes. As they wheeled Doug away, I touched his hand and said, "Don't leave me now honey, I don't know how to pay the bills online." *What senseless prattle. I kicked myself for the next two hours for that stupid sentence. What if Doug died and those were my last words to him? Not 'I love You' or 'Babe, don't leave me, I can't live without you' Or 'Jackie and I love you, stay strong,' but some dumb prattle about paying bills on line? I'm a writer for God's sake, and that was all I could come up with? He better live, I can't leave those to be our last words.*

I watched the ambulance pull away, speeding down the hill with the lights on. I got in my car, leaning my head against the steering wheel for a moment. I prayed. I cried, I bargained, I prayed again. Then I started the car and drove a silent six miles to Beemerville. I saw Dad's car at the Mountain View Country Store, owned by my childhood friend John Nataro. Nice country deli, great ambiance, stop in sometime, but this is not the point of my story. I had stopped to give Dad the update. I had not eaten breakfast and lunch was no where on the horizon. *Not to focus on food, but I was going to have a busy afternoon.* So I got a roast beef sandwich to go and told Dad and Aunt Loretta the update while it was being prepared. Grabbed my goods, and told Dad to cover my bill.

Next stop at the zoo, I double checked I had closed up the parrots, whom had finished all their treats. I bumped into Jill in the office. I gave her the update on Doug.

"Don't call Jackie, no use her worrying until we know what is happening," I asked. "I don't want her driving a couple of hours all upset."

"Yeah, we're not telling Hunter either," Jill explained. "He'd rush home from High School. So let us know when you know." Everyone knew that Hunter and Doug were very close, work buddies.

Everyone was couching their words. We all knew Doug was a two pack a day smoker, and overweight. What he had in his favor was that he was physically active, and he 'caught it' early. And maybe my prayers.

The trip to St. Claire's in Denville was tedious. I did not know what I would encounter when I got there. And that was another hour's worth of worry.

When I got to the hospital they showed me to the waiting area, told me Doug was in surgery, for angioplasty, that they had found two blocked arteries on the front of his heart. And so I waited, and prayed some more.

Dr. Paul DeRenzi from Lakeland Cardiology Center was Doug's cardiologist. We lucked out, that he was there when Doug needed him. When Dr. DeRenzi delivered the good news that Doug was going to be fine, and there was no damage to his heart, I fell apart and cried all over the nurse.

After gathering what little wits I had left, I texted Jackie: "Tsunami over, call A.S.A.P." She called within the minute. I explained all that had happened. Jackie took the afternoon off and met me at the hospital within an hour. We saw her daddy together when he was out of the recovery room. We stayed most of that day at the hospital, Jackie came home with me that night. The next day we went back to the hospital, Jackie visited with her Daddy and then left to go back to her home in Hamilton, N.J.. The next few days are a blur of a giant learning curve, visits to Doug and keeping the families informed. We had some life changes to make.

Two weeks later we were at Morristown Hospital with Dr. DeRenzi again, for a scheduled angioplasty for a blockage on the backside of Doug's heart that the Dr. had found. The constant trips to the hospital were stressful. But Doug was alive and going to be fine.

I had raised an Assateague pony the previous summer and placed it with a local family, the Walshes. Their daughter Sierra was the recipient of the pony the prior Christmas. Even though Christmas was only a couple of weeks before, it seemed a lifetime ago. The Walshes were not yet prepared for the pony, their barn had not been delivered yet. So whenever possible, Sierra, her mom, Karen, or dad, Terry, would come and walk Duchess the pony on a lead, brush her etc. The Walshes were very patient with me when Doug had his heart attack. Karen, Sierra and I would become good friends. I remember the first time I saw them after Doug's heart attack. Sierra and her Mom Karen came and we brushed Duchess and then I wanted to go see Timmy the Llama. So we did. While I was brushing him, Timmy knew I was unsettled. Timmy leaned into me and gave me the biggest neck hug. His static-y white hair, sparking me. I cried all over Timmy. Don't know why. Just did. Guess I really needed that llama hug.

I know that this is not an animal related narrative. I included it in this book because of the importance of the health issue in our lives. We all realized, as sudden as that heart attack, how valuable Doug was to the zoo/farm with his mechanical, plumbing, electric and carpentry expertise. He is an un-sung hero at the zoo. I had the sudden jolt of how much I loved and depended on Doug to cover certain aspects of our lives, so I could continue with my passion: the zoo. And yes, I know how to pay bills on line. I have a better phrase at the ready, but really hope I don't have to use it soon. .

After a two month recovery Doug was back at the zoo in 'limited capacity, light duty' work. *Yeah, like there is such a thing.* Oh and never ever use the phrase:

"Honey, just walk it off!" I'll never live that one down. Lesson learned.

My hubby, Doug and I
Photo by Kelly Little

Chapter 64 Tiger Lily

You know when my phone rings before eight a.m. , it's either really good news, or really bad news. It was 7:15 and the phone rang. Doug was on the other end according to my caller id.

" Hi Hon," Doug's voice was cheery so it must be good news. "Listen to this, recognize this sound?"

'Weeeahhh, Weeeahh" was the call.

"Lion cubs?" I responded. I had figured Tara tiger was too old, she and Charlie had been breeding for the past year with no resulting progeny.

"No, a tiger!" Doug's voice was almost gleeful. *'Almost ', got to protect his macho image!* "You coming down?" was a rhetorical question.

"Be there in five," was my reply. *Who needs make-up? Messy hair, who cares!* I grabbed towels, a cardboard box, and I was out the door as soon as my sneakers were on.

I drove directly to the tiger enclosure. Tara and Charlie were locked up on the concrete section. Doug and Ed, one of the other zookeepers, were walking in the outside grassy section of the enclosure when I pulled up. I had grabbed a box and towels during my hasty exit from our home. It was May 17th so the weather was not too chilly, but why did Tara have the cubs outside? She was an experienced mother, always having her cubs previously in the cozy hay filled den.

"Ed heard it, Tara had it outside," Doug spoke as he strode towards me. "So I figured she didn't want it." Doug and Ed were checking the grass tufts, pushing back the tall grass with the silver snake grabbing tongs we also use to pick up litter. "OH! Here's another one!" That baby was under a different tuft of tall grass. Both guys strode towards me.

The first cub was found by the fence, by the litter pile, and looked fine. Ed had picked it up and kept it warm inside his jacket, next to his body. Ed is a distant cousin, of ours, his great grandfather and my grandmother were brother and sister. Ed had a farming background, and also was a new daddy himself. A happy natured guy, Ed was a good set of strong hands when needed. Ed pulled the limp cub out of his jacket and handed it to me.

The second cub, under the tall grass tuft was in bad shape. It's tail had been ripped off, taking part of it's spinal cord. The rectum was in tact but the skin around it had been pealed back. There were puncture wounds in front of it's hips. And of course there was dirt and debris stuck on the wounds. Not a pretty sight, but the cub was alive. This damage obviously was the result of what is commonly called a breach birth. Breach birth happens with animals just like it happens every now and then with human mothers. Dystocia is the official term meaning slow or difficult birth. The cub had been stuck in the birth canal, backwards, tail end born first. Tara assisted her cub's birth in the middle of the night with her teeth. Not to be too graphic, but you can figure the actions out by the wound pattern.

"I'll take these two back with me, bring me in any others you find," I stated. "Tara has had up to five cubs in the past so check everywhere."

"I know, Hon," Doug grinned. He knew. I knew he knew, and it was the excitement of the moment that made me barky.

The nursery at the zoo is always prepared for imminent birth or medical problems. I took the abandoned cubs to the nursery and plugged in the heating pad. The first cub was fine, Tara had obviously cleaned her (!) off, but the umbilical was still attached and long. A quick tie off with dental floss, a trim of the extra length and I put the cub on the heating pad to warm up. It was May, their umbilical cords were still wet, so I estimated the cubs to be only an hour or so old. The weather was warm so I was not concerned with pneumonia, or hypothermia. The cub was robust, weighed 2 lbs 13 oz. It started to snuggle against the warm towel on the heating pad. She would be fine.

The damaged cub was dirty, and in bad shape. The cub's ears were cold. She had lost lots of blood, not to mention the open gaping wound of the ripped off tail and the surrounding skin and fur. The puncture wounds in front of the hips were a sure sign of breach birth, I'd seen that before with lion cubs. The missing tail also told the same story, but also was a tale of woe.

While the first cub warmed resting comfortably, I took the wounded 2 lb. cub to the kitchen sink. Good thing the restaurant was not open yet. *Ya know those board of health rules!* The kitchen was the only place with warm water, I used the mop sink. *Someday in my dream nursery....* I ran the water until it became warm to the touch. I up-ended the wounded cub and thoroughly rinsed the cubs bottom side. It was worse than I thought under the leaves and debris. The cub was responding to the warm water, I'm sure it felt good for the warm, but stung in the open wound. A gentle pat dry and I placed her next to her sister on the heating pad.

I prepped formula, Zoologic 42/25, (42% protein, 25% fat), cut a bottle nipple to my specifications and offered it to the cubs. The first cub drank/sucked ravenously, the whole two ounces I offered her. She would be satisfied for at least two hours. The damaged cub sucked also, but half heartedly. Didn't matter, as long as she got some fluids to replace the blood she lost. The warmth of the formula would help also. I knew she was a lost cause, but I had to try. The worst thing in the world is to die cold and hungry. I settled the cubs down on the heating pad and made a phone call to the vet. I reached my friend Jennie Beckman, .

Dr. Ted was out of town , Dr. Pam Schott was in and so was Dr. Lauren Gross, they would see the little cub. I had hope, but not much for the little tigress. I drove the fifteen minute trip to the Animal Hospital of Sussex County in Augusta.

The two Doctors checked out the cub. The rectum itself was intact, the tail missing along with part of the last inch of spine. I could tell by the look on their faces they thought she was a lost cause also. Between all of us, we held the skin together and the Drs. put staples in her tiny butt to hold the skin in place. No harm in trying. Many thanks to the Vets for giving it a try. When finished Jennie asked for the pitiful little cub's name, for their records. I was not prepared for that. I hadn't thought that far in the future for this cub. I looked at the cub, saw the staples in her backside and thought metal bolts and rivets. She needed a strong name to get though this. And that is how Rosie the Riveter got her name.

Rosie's name is how Lily got her name. Rose is a flower, so after talking to Jackie that night, Tiger Lily got her name. Tiger Lilies are my favorite flower, *yeah, go figure.* Lily and even Rosie suckled just fine for the next twenty-four hours, which were the usual blur of new babies. Feedings, cleanings, and worry mixed in with my usual work. I had other babies on a bottle in the nursery, the usual assortment of hoof stock and fawns.

At two days old, Rosie the Riveter died. Warm, with her tummy full, she died in her sleep. Sometimes that is the best you can hope for.

So I still had Tiger Lily. I discussed it with Dad and Parker, we decided we could keep Lily, as Tara was getting older. *I would have to face the possibility that Siren's fate would be Lily's also. That was constantly on my mind.* Tiger Lily, my little orange flower that bloomed in the spring. Lily became a delight to me and all those around her.

I took on my first intern that year, Victoria Ciccolelle. Vicky had written requesting an internship, so I set up an interview with her. I figured I had enough knowledge to pass on to someone willing to learn. Dad and I were sitting down for lunch and interviewed her. She would come in from eight am till noon, then head out to her paying job. The intern job was non paying, but would be fantastic experience for her. That interview had taken place a few weeks before Lily's surprise birth. And my new intern was surprised also! Vicky became an integral part of the zoo nursery staff that year and was a fantastic help. Young, beautiful and full of fun spirit, Vicky blended right in. She was petite and had trouble carrying a bucket of water when she started the summer with us. By the end of that summer she had help raise Tiger Lily, fawns, sheep, goats, a calf, chickens, rabbits, alligators and some woodchucks. Vicky helped with whatever jobs I was working on, be it gators, snakes, or greeting school busses and children. She had raked and shoveled and cleaned more yuck than you'd think. By summer's end she could carry two buckets of water at the same time! And young Sierra was there almost every morning also, her activities limited by safety and her age. So I had good staffing.

But now, back to Lily: Lily was doing just fine, growing right on schedule, eyes open at two weeks, wobble-ly walking at two weeks, running at three, carnasial teeth at four weeks, and special ground venison starting at four weeks. Tiger Lily was tiger number thirteen in my life, but I have to say, it never gets old. I treasured every moment especially at the end of my busy days at ten p.m. when I would just lay down and watch TV with Lily. We would cuddle and I was at peace with the universe.

Hunter and Sam, Hunter's girlfriend, would come up to our house and play with Lily after work and supper. Lindsey, my niece, and her boyfriend Dominic would stop by also. Lindsey would baby sit the little tiger whenever I needed her to. And sometimes a mom just has to go grocery shopping or get away for a few hours. So many thanks to Vicky and Lindsey, it was so nice to have an occasional break.

Lily's bright orange color did not develop right away, not till about ten weeks. She also developed a ruff, a section of fur that sticks out on the sides of her face, sort of like the old fashioned muttonchops sideburns. Lily was/is gorgeous and the apple of my eye. *Shuuusssh! Don't tell Jackie! Or actually, just like Jackie!* All this time I was taking Tiger Lily wherever I went. She was a hit on the lecture circuit that year. She stayed home at our house longer than she needed to, once again I had trouble leaving a baby down at the zoo.

Lily did have one residual birth issue. I noticed when she started to walk that she constantly carried her head to the right. I was worried, spoke to Dr. Ted about it. We figured that she may have a stiff neck from possibly having her head in the birth canal smacking up against Rosie's head during contractions. Lily is the only tiger I ever raised that did not like to be carried in arms or ride in a car. That lasted the entire time she was with me, either at home or in the zoo nursery. The ride from our house to the zoo is short maybe a city block, but Lily would scream bloody murder the whole trip. Going out to give a speech with her was the same. I discussed it with Dr. Ted many times, but did not feel the need for a sedative for Lily, I don't go all that far away for speeches.

Lily and I were invited down to The Pet Stop on Channel 12, with Dr. Brian Voynick. Dr. Ted and Vicky would come with us. Now that is an hour and a half trip there, not including the twenty minutes to get to Dr. Ted's contemporary Animal Hospital of Sussex County. Dr. Ted and I decided to give Lily a sedative for the ride. A quick shot in the rear and we packed up Lily and hit the road. I was prepared for the show, had a full baby bottle and extra towels. Dr. Ted drives when we go on these trips, I hate city driving. I was in the passenger seat, Vicky in the backseat and Lily in her crate where Lily could see Vicky and myself. After a ten minute screaming ride, Lily was asleep. Good, I could not stand her crying for me.

We arrived at the studio after the long trip, I unpacked Lily. Dr. Ted went off to chat with his buddy, Dr. Brian. Vicky and I walked Lily up and down the hallway trying to wake her up a little more. She was like a drunken sailor, the sedative just starting to wear off. Lily was hungry, it had been three hours since her last bottle. At only three weeks old Lily was about twelve pounds. Vicky and I kept walking the swaggering tiger in the hallway.

When it was Lily's turn on TV, Dr. Brian, Dr. Ted and I were on stage with her. We chatted about the tiger from the notes that I had emailed. We played with little Lily for a few moments, rubbing her tummy etc. Then I gave Lily the baby bottle. Lily drank the eight ounces vigorously. The bottle in my right hand pointing down to Lily, her striped body curled on my lap, cuddled by my left hand. Lily rested her chin on my right palm, just as I had taught her to nurse. Lily finished the bottle. The veterinarians were talking, keep in mind this is all on video. Lily finished the bottle and her head dropped down. Like she was dead. Clunk, her head hit my thigh. I shot a look to Vicky who was standing off stage out of camera range. Vicky said my eyes were like saucers. So were hers! I really thought Lily had died right on my lap in front of the TV camera. Vicky had seen the unusual behavior also. And the guys weren't even paying attention to Lily, they were just chatting along! I quickly arranged Lily's comatose head into a sleeping position on my lap. Then I took her pulse. She still had one. Phewwwh! As soon as the camera man said cut I elbowed Dr. Ted to get his attention. He spun towards Lily took her pulse also. Lily was fine, just sleeping off her sedative after her full bottle. Phewwwwh! Scared me to death!

After taping the show we all went out to lunch at Harold's, their corned beef sandwiches are the positive reward for us doing a great job. The Marriott located at the same spot is always great about watching our animals while we eat. That night the staff got to go home and tell every one that they baby sat a sleeping tiger cub! *Well, now, wouldn't you?* Lily slept the whole ride home. Multiple times I would glance back at Vicky in the backseat of our car. I didn't even have to ask, Vicky's simple reply:

"She's fine I see her breathing."

And we all gabbed all the way home.

Tiger Lily was housebroken. She would go to the back door of our farmhouse mud room and sit, waiting to have her pink *,(of course),* leash put on. One day I hadn't had my coffee so I let her out the back door with out me. She was on the spring grass doing her business. I left the door open, I could see her as I was pouring my coffee. She never went far, barely left my side when we were outside. I glanced away to look at the white milk swirling in my coffee mug and heard a terrible tiny tiger scream. I quickly walked the three steps to the back door and to my panic saw Lily limping back to me, whimpering. She was shaking her paw. *OH My God what could of happened?* Lily was holding up her front right paw, walking towards me as quick as she could on the other three paws. I scanned the horizon for an animal that may have bitten Lily and the sky for a predatory bird. Nothing. I bent down to see the beagle sized tiger's paw as she whimpered. Lily even held it up for me. There in the middle of the top of her orangey brown paw was .... A slug. Ahhh the moments a mother tiger treasures! Vicky and I had a good laugh on that one.

Time rolled on as it always does and babies grow bigger. Lily was getting to be a handful at six months old. I had the same four foot square by three foot high den box on the center nursery enclosure that I had raised Tara and Khyber in years before. The specially designed den had bottle sized holes in the back gate. Lily would walk in to suck her bottle and I would close her in the den in order to clean her cage. I stopped going in to play with Lily when she was bout seven months old, as big as a German Shepherd dog. Not that she was mean, Lily just played hard, like a tiger. She would be a zoo cat, so she did not need to jump through hoops for me. She could just be a tiger.

Always in the back of my mind was Lily's re-introduction to her parents in the adult enclosure. I did my research. I asked Dad his opinions. I knew what to do if they were dogs or pussy cats from my time studying those species in the pet stop. Heck, I even know how to introduce piranha to each other! I went over and over the mistakes that were made with Siren. I consulted Dr. Ted and all the vets at his clinic. I consulted every vet I knew, (*Sorry Dr. Ted, not that I didn't have faith in you, I was just super concerned*). I consulted all the zoo folks I knew. Dad and I hashed out a plan. The plan took into account the fact that Tara and Charlie were used to seeing other tigers. Lily was not. Tara and Charlie knew their home territory, Lily did not. I typed up a plan, circulated it by email to all the zoo folks I knew, and again to all the vets I knew. When I didn't get any nay-sayers, or additions, I printed up the plan and handed it out to everybody on staff, just so everyone was on the same page with the same information. It was a five step process:

Tiger Introductions

End Purpose: To re- introduce Tiger Lily (10 month old female tiger cub-½ to 3/4 adult size) to her adult parents Tara (15years old) and Charlie (3 years old). Both adults and cub were hand raised by humans. All involved have full teeth and claws and are in excellent health.

Phase 1: Introductions- temporary auxiliary enclosure is (was) placed on the far side of the outside enclosure for the tigers. Tiger cub in temporary enclosure. The placement of the enclosure enables all tigers to have face to face contact with fencing separating the cub from the two parents in the large enclosure.

Purpose: to introduce tigers and teach cub by familiarization not to be afraid of adults and/or show fear, signs of defensive aggression: teeth baring, etc.

Time: two months

Phase 2: Familiarization of territory for cub- Locking the male and female parent on the concrete section of the enclosure, the cub will be released into outside grassy compound of enclosure. Cub will learn territory and learn her way back to temporary enclosure/den.

Time: Approximately one week.

Purpose: to give cub a retreat area when eventual release of tiger adults into grassy enclosure.

Phase 3: Introduction of female to cub. Releasing female only into outside grassy compound with cub.

Purpose: face to face contact with mother/female, the lesser aggressive, less spunky of tigers. One on one so cub is not chased/played with to exhaustion by two superior adult tigers. To win the mother over to help guide/ protect the cub?

Time: One Week

Phase 4: Introduction of male to cub. Releasing male to join the female and cub into outside grassy compound.

Purpose: to have all tigers live together in enclosure.

Time: Two weeks, or Until prayers are no longer needed.

Phase 5: Remove temporary enclosure. **Time:** Complete by April 1st

The day of the big move was a week after we closed the zoo. Lily had seriously outgrown the nursery. Lily was trained to go into her den box for a bottle. In order to remove the den box with the skid loader, Hunter and Doug removed the chain link fence from the blacktop side of the barnyard. Doug and

Hunter had previously reinforced a sliding gate on the far side of the tiger enclosure, and removed the guard fencing. The removal of the guard fencing was why we had to wait until after we closed and no visitors would be allowed into the park. They had also moved an auxiliary enclosure to the back side of the tiger enclosure. The same auxiliary enclosure/den that we had used years before when Tara and Khyber were afraid of the lions and would not go up into the den on the concrete pad. Everything in place, and a shotgun on the backseat of Dad's car just in case something went terribly wrong, we were ready.

On cue Lily went into her barn red den box for a bottle. I let the slide down to lock her inside just like I had done every day to clean her enclosure. I knew the rumbling noise of the old yellow skid loader would frighten her, so I was prepared to walk beside Lily who was in the den box on the skid loader and talk to her. My Dad had also suggested the same thing.

"Just keep talking to her, Lori," Pop told me repeatedly. "It will reassure her that you are near."

Hunter, now eighteen and graduated high school, was working full time at the zoo. Hunter and Doug nailed the slides down on both sides of the tunnel shaped wooden den, locking Lily in. Hunter expertly maneuvered the forks of the skid loader under the den box and gently lifted it from the ground. The red wooden box wiggled and swayed, as Lily moved inside of it. pacing. I started to worry after I calculated that the specially designed oversized wooden crate was built in 1998, fifteen years before. However the crate held.

Hunter slowly moved down the path by the side of the lake towards the back of the zoo. I walked alongside talking and chuffing to Lily constantly. Doug and Parker sped by on his jitney and Dad was not far behind us in his car. I talked the whole way trying to keep Lily calm. If I talked, she stopped crying. But she was still pacing, not happy in the moving wooden crate. It was a very long five minute drive.

The hillside on the back of the tiger's enclosure is steep, and it caught the bottom of the slide on the wooden crate. Wood cracked, and Dad hollered for Hunter to slow down. A few sharp words were exchanged, *Yeah so what is new with that? Everyone was tense, a lot of things could go wrong.* After that minor problem the wooden crate was eased onto a platform built on to the back of the temporary little tiger's enclosure. The den was secured with wire and checked once again for sturdiness. Lily's den slide door was open. Lily sat inside her hay filled den and peered out. Like the queen of Sheba, she sat with her orangey paws crossed in front of her, her head erect and shoulders squared. Her face was framed in the ruff she inherited from her father Charlie. I called her out, and she bounded to the side of the temporary enclosure to get some pets and loves. That was to be Lily's home for a couple of months.

After all was secure, and Lily seemed content in her new digs, we opened the chute door for Tara and Charlie to come face to fence to face with Lily. At first Lily was frightened and showed obvious signs of distress: fur erect, baring of teeth, ears back, retreating from the common fence line and backing into her nursery den box. Mom Tara chuffed to Lily immediately, with absolutely no signs of aggression. The dad, Charlie seemed ambivalent however marked territory, (sprayed urine) on the fence and/or Lily. During the next two months the tigers familiarized themselves and now chuffs are heard from all, cub no longer baring teeth, putting ears back or retreating. Charlie was still marking territory.

And those were my notes on Phase 1. I visited Lily through out the winter. Vicky, Karen Talasco, Sierra, Jackie, Lindsey and Dominic would all brave the winter cold and snow drifts to come see Lily. Hunter and Doug saw her daily during feedings and cleanings. Lily developed a warm thick coat, so fuzzy she looked like a stuffed toy tiger! Her orange colors became more vibrant, her white, snow white and her black stripes gave her wonderful definition. I purposely would pet Tara and Charlie and Lily at the fence separation at the same time to show Lily that Tara and Charlie were my friends. I don't know if Lily understood my English, but she could surely see my actions were safe.

I gave Lily road killed dead squirrels to play with all winter. What fun to watch. Ya know, true happiness *is* a dead squirrel. Hunter and Doug would change Lily's den hay the same way I did in the nursery. First with a bottle, then just feeding her in the den. Lily was happy and getting to know her neighbors. And the neighbors, Lily's parents, were getting to know her. The other phases would take place in the spring of 2014. I had faith in my research, and in the phases I outlined, but there was still a huge element of worry. Siren's memory plagued me. Stay tuned…

Doug and newborn Tiger Lily
Photo by Lori Space Day

Zoo Momma

Chapter 65 My New Friend Paul

Doug and I look forward to our vacation every year in Canada. It is so relaxing to get away from the daily hustle and bustle of the zoo. I worry about my babies while I am gone, but there is always Dad as a back up if anything goes wrong. After all, he taught me what I know. This year I had my intern Vicky 'Cinderella' to cover the zoo nursery. In previous years Jennie Beckman would stop by a couple of times a week to help with the parrots, but she has her job at the Animal Hospital of Sussex County with Dr. Ted. Dad and I (!) are getting older, so the whole intern concept worked for me. So all was set for us to go on vacation.

Jackie and Mark were in the process of moving to Boston to earn the Masters in their fields. They were actually moving the very day we left Beemerville headed for Canada. The day was bright and beautiful, sun plentiful with a slight breeze in the sky. The kind of day that was going to be busy at the zoo. Oops forgot, I was on vacation, no zoo thinking.

I was reading a book, while Doug drove our blue Hyundai. My vacation starts the moment we get in the car. Doug has to wait until we drive to Canada. Happily reading a trashy romance novel, I had just started to rinse out my busy brain when I heard a loud POP! I looked up and saw a man on a nice Harley, (I think), motorcycle entering Route I- 81 from the ramp on the right, near Lafayette, N.Y.. A plastic grocery bag had flown out of his brown saddlebag on the back of his bike, grabbed by the wind. That had been the sound of the loud POP. I saw the man on the motorcycle look over his shoulder towards the back of his cycle. He was traveling fast, to speed up to the oncoming traffic, which was Doug and I in our Hyundai. The tall Biker misjudged the distance to the road. Complicated by his speed, he crossed over the two lanes of highway in front of us. The Biker headed straight towards the massive silver guard rail separating the north and south bound traffic.

"Oh, honey, he's not gonna make it, he's gonna go over the rail!" I exclaimed. "Oh whew! He is ok. He's upright," I continued. In the time it took me to speak the brief sentences, the biker had gone across the two lanes into the shoulder of the road, and avoided crashing into (or over) the protective galvanized guard rail. Just bumped the guard rail a little bit. The Biker wobbled on the bike and then was upright and traveling up the highway right in front of us.

"He's not Ok," Doug replied. "Gasoline ain't red! He's dripping blood." Doug barely had time to say before the Biker pulled over.

"We better stop, see if we can help," I spoke as Doug already had our car's blinker on. I saw the Biker stop on the right hand shoulder of the highway. Poised with his white sneakered right foot on the ground for balance of the bike, he took off his helmet. It fell to the ground. The blood dripping man then took his left leg and tried to put down the motorcycle's kick stand. But he had no foot!

At this point the man fell to the ground, I don't remember how far he was from his precious Harley, the bike was no longer in my visual field. Doug pulled our car to a stop and put the hazard lights on. Cars pulled up behind us on the shoulder of the road and a few in front of the Biker. As Doug and I exited our car and I saw how bad off the guy was, I started barking instructions. *Sorry but that is what I do in an emergency, I bark.*

"Doug, give me your belt, he needs a tourniquet," I barked to Doug. Doug started to take his belt off of his khakis shorts as we ran towards the injured man. The profusely bleeding man was flat on his back, and attempting to take off his own belt, which was a good sign. At least he was conscious.

I took his belt from him and quickly wrapped it around his upper thigh, and cinched it tight. The folks from the other cars started to gather around us. I know I was barky, like I said that's what happens to me. *Sorry Folks!*

"Doug, call 911, here's my phone," I fumbled in my pocket while holding the belt as tight as I could.

"I can call 911," stated a female voice.

"Ok" I nodded. " You," I barked to someone else, "Get a paper and pencil, we need to get info before he passes out." I tipped my head to one guy in particular, as my hands were busy. That young man headed off towards his parked car. The blood was still spurting out the bottom of the handsome man's leg. I could not cinch the belt any tighter. *Note to reader, none of the first aid instructions for the tourniquet procedure mentions the fact that a belt may not have holes in it where you need a hole to hold the belt tightly in place. You have to keep your hand on it cinching it tight.* I took my other hand and placed more pressure, with the weight of my body behind it, on his femoral artery. Now I had both my hands in the crotch of the strange man's jeans.

''What's your name, hon," I asked.

"Paul," he replied, giving his last name also. *I don't know his address to get his permission to put his last name in this book.*

" Do you know your blood type? Any blood borne diseases? Do you have any allergies? Who should we call? Where do you live? " I rapid fired questions as the young man I had sent for paper and pencil took notes as Paul spoke.

Another man came upon the accident scene and asked "Does anybody here know first aid?"

"I'm not certified, but I think I'm faking it pretty well," I jokingly quipped under pressure. "Any helpful hints? Jump right in!" He agreed with my assessment and procedure so far. He had first aid training. Someone else brought Paul a blanket, and something for under his head. While we waited I chatted with Paul to keep him conscious and had time to survey his lower leg.

Paul saw me looking and tried to sit to look also.

"You don't want to look right now Paul," I warned him. Paul glanced once and laid back down. "I have the bleeding slowed down. Hang in there, the ambulance is coming." Paul's good leg with jeans and a sneaker started to twitch. Shock was setting in.

I could hear the conversations around me but my focus was on Paul. He was becoming ashen in color, probably from the loss of blood. Police had arrived.

There was a large pool of blood on the road, under - where his foot should have been. His jeans were ripped and torn and mixed in with the white sinew, clear connective tissue, deep burgundy muscles and pulsing veins and arteries. I could see his tibia and fibula bones sticking out of his lower leg. Pretty gory if I say so my self. I had seen a lot of road kill deer in my life, so had Doug, so maybe that is why the grossness of it did not bother me, and this was an emergency situation. I started to loose the circulation in my hand that tightly held the brown leather belt in place.

The other man with first aid experience offered to take over for me. I moved slowly away as he took over the cinching process. I stood and walked a few paces away. My muscles cramped from sitting in our car for three hours before I kneeled on the uneven graveled shoulder of the road.. The fire department and ambulance were on the scene within maybe ten minutes. The helpful crowd were hovering around, one lady offered me a bottle of water.

I looked up to see where Doug was in all the hellabaloo. My Doug, the mechanic, was directing traffic until the fire trucks and ambulance showed up. I walked into his conversation with a fireman. They were discussing where the foot might be. The other firemen were looking across the highway from where Paul lay.

"No, his foot is gonna be way back there, across from the entrance ramp," Doug was pointing as we all started to walk. A few of the firemen were almost to the designated spot. It felt good to stretch my legs out, so I followed along. We had walked halfway to the entrance ramp when a fireman passed us in a blur. He held a bloody white sneaker with an anklebone perched on top. I assumed the rest of Paul's foot was inside the red streaked white leather sneaker. He had found the foot right where Doug had said it would be.

Doug and I walked back to where the police were interviewing the witnesses. We were first on the scene and had witnessed the entire thing. The police wanted us to stay until another ambulance came to help wash the blood off of us. I looked down at my hands. And I did not have a speck of blood, neither did Doug. My hands, after all, were in Paul's jeans covered crotch. The police man gave us some hand sanitizer. We gave the police our information. After an hour and a half stop with my new friend Paul we were back on our way to vacation in Canada. We had a lot to talk about as we decompressed.

That is how I met my new friend Paul. Paul is a fireman with the Cambridge Massachusetts's Fire Department. Doug looked up the info on line, there was a small article in the Syracuse newspaper. Paul was on his way home to see his family. I wrote the Cambridge Fire Department and the Chief told me Paul planned to complete rehabilitation and go back to work at the fire department. Ironically Jackie moved to Boston that very same day. She can see Cambridge from her apartment window, and walks past the Cambridge Fire Department on her daily walks. Somehow I feel she is safe there.

My new friend Paul is a now member of a very exclusive club.

Chapter 66 Rattling Rattle Snakes!

Very serious and dangerous procedures take place here at the zoo. Most of the time everything turns out ok, and hopefully we can laugh about it after the adrenaline wears off. The previous spring the kitchen was re-vamped from a hamburger, hot dog fast food place to a pizza restaurant. This brought in all new staff for the kitchen.

I needed to clean the six foot boa constrictor while my Dad was not there to be my second, watching the snake for my safety. So I enlisted Shawn Demarest out of the kitchen. Shawn is slight of frame, with an artist's dark goatee and glasses. Shawn is my height, but one third my body size. He was not to do any dirty work, just tell me what the snake was doing. I needed to know prior to my opening the case door-when I could not see the snake. Shawn was positioned in front of the snake case and gave me the update on the position of the snake.

After the snake had grabbed on the rabbit, Shawn joined me on the backside of the cases. I heard the beep, beep, beep of the zoo gate's automatic opening. I saw the green John Deere with Doug in the drivers seat patiently waiting to enter the zoo. Someone is in or out that gate fifty times a day so I paid little attention to what Doug was doing. I had my eye on the snake as we changed the water.

The tractor rumbled by.

Shawn was on my right when I heard the first rattlesnake rattle.

"Get out of here!" I ordered. I slammed the door on the red tailed boa's case. I moved to run out from behind the row of cases. "Faster, Move!" I demanded as I shoved Shawn none to gently towards the three feet gap between the brown cases and the stone wall of the building. *When had that rattlesnake escaped? Where was he?* My hand on the middle of his back, Shawn propelled forward, arms akimbo, legs trying to catch up with his rocketing upper body. Shawn nearly took a face plant on the concrete back porch floor. I did not know where that escaped rattle snake was, I had only heard him. But I knew the one thing to do was to get out of the confined area with a pissed off, scared, therefore rattling dangerous snake. And Shawn was not moving fast enough for me to escape too! We heard the rattling sound again as we quickly cleared the cases.

And then Shawn and I both broke into hysterical laughter. At the end of the driveway in front of the large Snake Den Doug had stopped the tractor. He had climbed off the tall tractor. My husband was re-arranging the rattling dried corn stalks on the back of the manure wagon being toed behind the tractor. I looked towards the gate that the tractor, the manure wagon full of dried brown corn stalks and Doug had just come through. He had lost a dozen or so crispy corn stalks right in front of the boa's case also. I hadn't seen them pass, my eyes were on the snake. The long brittle corn stalks dragging on the ground was obviously the rattle snake sound I had heard. Shawn and I could hardly contain our laughter as we spit out the funny story to Doug. Doug nonchalantly shrugged his shoulders, rolled his eyes at our goofy laughter and climbed back onto the massive tractor.

Adrenaline is always funny, after the fact.

The Space Farms Snake Den

Photo by Lori Space Day

Zoo Momma

Chapter 67 The Barnyard Nursery Barn

When Parker and Jill decided to bring in the Extreme Pizza franchise in to replace Gramma's hamburger and French fries restaurant many things changed. The one thing that effected the Nursery was that the Extreme Pizza franchise did not need fresh eggs. The chickens in the Zoo Nursery had been supplying Gramma's kitchen with eggs for breakfast sandwiches for, well forever. Now, suddenly I had a lot of fresh eggs on my hands. *For once on my hands and not on my face! Oh Funny me!* Dad and I had a discussion and we decided that we could sell the eggs, all the local farmers' wives did, and we had a bigger audience/customer base. So I became a chicken pimp. Daily I would collect the eggs and wash them. We would sell out at the admissions desk daily. Dad and I put the money in a special fund, as I wanted a new barn to replace the Nursery shed that had been built forty years before. Fine in it's hayday *(pun intended)* the shed had become shabby with the effects of time.

Again, we had to wait until fall to start that project. Doug and Hunter would need to remove the guard fencing on the blacktop side of the Nursery. Tiger Lily was in the center section, so we could not do that while the zoo was open to visitors. Lily was scheduled to move to the adult enclosure, so we just had to wait for safety of our visitors.

In September of that year I went to Broadhecker's a local farmer that also sells small barns, horse sheds, chicken coops, rabbit hutches, and the regular assortment of animal feeds. I know Tom and Jane Broadhecker well, having sat on the Sussex County Board of Agriculture with them. Their son Phil is taking over the business of farming.

The warm weather animals were put away to winter quarters as soon as Hunter and Doug could after the zoo closed for the season. Then they got to work. Mutt and Jeff, -tall thin Hunter and his buddy, stocky shorter Uncle Doug-, came to disassemble the Zoo Nursery four foot high chain link fence by the blacktop. A lot of cursing, and joking, listening to Hunter and Doug is just plain funny and endearing. I have corrected Hunter and Doug on cursing when the visiting public are at the zoo, but when we are closed or the guys are alone, boy the language changes quick! The fence came down in one afternoon, with a colorful conversation.

The next day we moved Tiger Lily.

The day after Tiger Lily's graduation to the adult zoo I started to dismantle the old run down shed. Sledge hammer, regular hammer, screw gun, and screw driver. I did that job very intently. My aging body hurt for exercise I did not normally perform. I had a passion for the work I was doing. I had wanted a new barn for the Barnyard Nursery for years, but other projects always took priority. This was the year. My hens had earned their new digs.

I took apart the sides first, salvaging what T- 111 I could. My dad lived through the Great Depression. He taught me to save what you can to recycle long before recycling became politically correct and ecologically necessary. If I had a

288

problem the five pound sledge fixed it. I toppled the roof section to the ground but could not dismantle it. I had to admit that I needed help. That was hard for me, but I called Doug and Hunter. They came by shortly after. Now reader, read this part very carefully. Hunter and Doug chain sawed the roof into smaller sections -SO *I* COULD LOAD IT ONTO THE PICK-UP TRUCK!   Such help mates gentlemen! But that is the code I taught them. I asked for help cutting the roof. I did not ask them to help put it on the truck. Sometimes I am my own worst enemy.

When the old shed was on the pick up truck, I looked at the stained white wall behind it, and said "Hummmmmm…..". I had a week or so until the new barn was due to arrive. My dream barn, a red with white trim barn complete with a cupola and a rooster weather vane on top. Yeah the cupola and weather vane were extra $ but I had waited a long time to get this new addition to 'my' nursery. Singular of purpose, I started to paint a mural on the blank white wall. *A mural would be better than just another white wall, dontjathink?* The project went fast, the weather held and within a few days the mural was complete. Doug was a saint when his supper was repeatedly delayed because I stayed until dark to paint at the zoo. I was in 'my zone'. Good thing he understood.

When Phil Brodhecker called to say the barn was in I was elated. Hunter had brought me a couple of skid loaders of beautiful white sparkley crushed stone to put down under the barn as per Phil's instructions. I was ready.

Phil brought the barn on the back of a roll off truck. Now I can back up a pick-up truck like I was raised on one, because I was. Phil's truck was huge, and with my brand spanking new red barn on it, backing up was a mirror only job. I was impressed with Phil's driving skills and Phil in general. Blonde, handsome and more importantly: smiling and enthusiastic, Phil's attire was up-scale farmer. Then again clean jeans and a clean shirt is up-scale for zoo folks in the off season. Phil expertly backed up my hen's twenty foot by ten foot red barn castle right into the spot I requested. Wow! Aside from his obvious intelligence, Phil could park a barn! I had not worked with Phil before, he was Parker's age, about fifteen years my junior. I had known his parents for years, but not Phil.

After the barn was completely on the ground in spot, Phil decided to measure the distance from the wall of the building to the barn. And Hot Darn! He was only ½ inch off from left side to right side of the barn, which was like nothing. Wow! That was impressive. It was almost dark when Phil left the zoo. Doug's supper was going to be late again. Oh well.

The night would be cool and clear, so my lady hens did not need a barn over night. The next morning Doug cut a two foot by two foot hole in my new red barn's door for the chickens, roosters, ducks and surprisingly kid goats, (the next spring), to climb in and out of. I painted and sealed the floor a matching barn red color. I built a shelf inside adding milk crates with fresh hay for chicken nests. Chickens were in the nests before I exited the new fancy barn. The white cupola with black rooster weathervane was just the right touch and stood out against the countryside mural. I was happy. My new nursery was complete. I was bone weary but also proud to the bone that this undertaking had succeeded beautifully.

Zoo Momma

Chapter 68 Post Holiday Scene

2013 Post Holiday Scene
Relax, sit down, grab some coffee my friend,
Its time for our yearly chat once again.
There's been blizzards and boy it's been cold,
Lets warm it up, like friendships of old.
So howyaben? I've really missed you, I have been so busy here at the zoo.
Hope all is well with you and yours,
Done with your day, completed your chores?
Good lets get started, I'll tell you mine,
And please write back when you have the time.
Doug had a heart attack last January, Boy oh boy that sure was scary!
I thought he was joking, "Walk it off" I said,
I'll not live that down until I am dead.
3 stents in his heart, quit smoking -new diet
Almost a new man, but still very quiet.
His heart stopped a total of three times, It's hard to put my fear in rhyme.
Was a tough one for a while, He still makes me laugh and my heart smile.
We celebrated thirty years last spring,
Looking forward to what the future brings.
Spring rolled around and boy was I busy,
A day in my life would make anyone dizzy.
Parker and Jill bought a pizza franchise,
No more buffalo burgers and French fries.
California hit men stripped Gramma's kitchen,
My opinion not asked, so no use bitchin'.
Threw it all in boxes, no reverence or care,
I had to be tough, not to show my despair.
I sorted, then kept, some of Grams kitchen treasures,
Our Gram's kitchen memories - they have no measure.
Tara our Tiger had lost mate Khyber, So we got another boyfriend for her.
Sometime last March Charlie Tiger made magic:
Turned Tara into a cougar, Now that was some trick!
We didn't know, no one had seen ,
Surprised were we when cubs made the scene.
One cub had trouble, birth trauma ya know,
But boy oh boy did Tiger Lily grow.
She started at two pounds, now is Shepard size,
She seems to grow right before your eyes.
So say a prayer that all goes fine, When it's parent and cub reunion time.
Something new I learned this year: Don't house emu with white tail deer.
Emu chased and killed all of the fawns,
Did not think they'd have such brawn.

Zoo Momma

But the deer did have their revenge,
this fall rut the buck gored an emu in the 'end'.
Learn something new every day! Some lessons are learned the hard way.
Jackie and Mark moved to Boston, yeah, cool.
Both going to BU in master's school.
She's working hard, job and school, Call home now and then the only rule.
I miss her terribly, every mother's lament,
my empty nest syndrome still not spent.
They're happy, in love, it's so nice to see,
I remember young love between Doug and me.
Hunter chain sawed his knee, then came to find (who else but) me?
He passed out, came to and passed out some more,
The first sight of blood and he hit's the floor!
Seventeen stitches but he is now fine,
He works well with Doug and that's a good sign.
Lindsey's has a boyfriend - Dominic. A cuter couple I could not pick.
I took on an intern , her name was Vicky,
Great gal, enthusiastic, reminds me of me.
Figured I knew enough to teach someone else,
In real world, not a book that stays on the shelf.
She learned a lot, she lightened my load,
And lifted spirits on my life's road.
Seems life's a trade, a duty to pass knowledge on
And then all too quick the summer was gone.
Vicky went back to school, but I seen her now and then
I know she'll do well, she's now a friend.
The day Jackie moved, we were on our way,
To Canada for our annual vacaaaaaa..
When suddenly a biker crossed our lane, Traveling fast, was he insane?
He crossed, looked back then hit the rail,
Stayed upright, His balance never failed.
I thought he was fine, 'til Doug said:
"He's in trouble, 'cause gasoline, it ain't red".
Biker pulled over to put down his kick stand,
But had no foot to put on the sand.
Doug and I were first on the scene,
I used a belt tourniquet, you know what I mean.
My new friend Paul, from Cambridge Mass.,
(Across from where Jackie goes to class),
Doug looked it up on line, My friend Paul is doing fine
Recouping in Syracuse after traumatic amputation,
Paul hopes to return to his fire station.
Still working on my next book, when I'm done I'll let you all look.
The pizza place does not use real eggs, So I was really scratching my head.

291

Zoo Momma

What in the world should I do, With all the hens that lay eggs at the zoo?
In past the hens furnished the restaurant,
But now, the pizza place didn't want.
By the dozen we decided to sell, Farm Fresh, free range, organic as well!
If we made enough, I'd buy a new barn for my hens,
My girls did their job laying again and again,
They sold like hotcakes here at the zoo,
So put on my resume, I'm a chicken pimp too!
I took down the old barn, wall behind looked yucky,
Decided to mural it, if I was lucky
The weather would hold, but just not quite,
Even though I worked to the end of day light.
So next spring I'll finish the mural behind the hen's barn,
And this is the end of my yearly yarn.
Finished that coffee? Ok what's next:
Send me a letter, email or a text.
Let me know what's up with you,
And when you'll come visit us here at the zoo!

Love, Lori and Doug.

Our Chicken's new barn in the zoo nursery.
Photo by Lori Space Day

Chapter 69 Lily's Reunion

The winter closed season passed slowly with lots of snow over 2013-14. Lily was safely in her auxiliary enclosure parked at the far end of the tiger's former grassy compound. When the heaviest of snows came, I took out sheets of plywood and boxed in the sides of the enclosure, so only the front was open to Lily's parents. On sunny afternoons we would take down the plywood on the western side so Lily could enjoy the sun on the high platform in her enclosure. Lily grew like a weed, and her winter ruff around her face was phenomenal. Petting - feeling her fuzzy fur on my finger was a delight. She loved her 'scratches'. The dampness of the snow enhanced Lily's tiger smell. *Yes every animal specie has it's own distinct smell.* The grassy compound was now covered with snow, but Lily's parents Tara and Charlie would constantly visit Lily through the double fence. Due to the depth of the snow, we did not start phase two of the cub reunion until the first of March 2014. Lily had been cooped up in the smaller auxiliary cage for the previous four months. Lily no longer showed any sign of fear when her parents approached. Charlie was still marking territory on Lily which was a good sign, he was marking her as his. Charlie the tiger would never have turned his backside to Lily if he thought she was any kind of a threat.

The first phase of the reunion was complete. Lily had lived next to her parents for months, everyone seemed to get along.

In preparation for the second phase, the guys had installed a water dish on the concrete section. The second phase was easy, Hunter called the parents up onto the concrete patio and den section to feed them. He then pulled the slide on the chute (tunnel between the grassy section and the patio) to lock the parents into the concrete patio section of the enclosure. The patio included the spacious hay filled den so the large cats still had lots of room, and their familiar den.

When that was completed. Doug and Hunter opened the sliding door between the auxiliary enclosure and the grassy section they had installed on the far side of the tiger enclosure back in November. All of this took a lot of behavior research and planning. I stood on the outside of the fence about ten feet away from the open door. Lily did not hesitate and bounded out to see me. After a minute of scratches and reassurance, she was happy to have the area to run. Lily ran a lap around, then stopped dead in front of the lions that had gathered at the communal dividing fence. The male lion, Attila, hissed and bared teeth at Lily while pawing at the ground by the fence. Lily bee-lined back to me waiting on the opposite side of the enclosure. Her ears were laid low, fur raised on the back of her neck and her tail between her legs. She was scared. All the while the parents were chomping on their food on the patio, watching, but not responding to Lily's presence in the grassy area. That was a good sign. I knew that Attila, the huge maned male lion could not hurt Lily through the fence. All the neighbors would have to get used to each other. I left Lily to learn her new territory and the way back to her den. Lily stayed on the far side of the tiger's grassy enclosure, far away from the common fence with the African Lions. As I left Lily was stretching her legs, running in her new freedom, an orange, white and black striped streak on the white snow covered ground. All was well, I slept better that night.

As planned, Phase 2 lasted two weeks. Lily learned the enclosure and would freely walk back into her den in the auxiliary enclosure on command. That was important just in case things went wrong in Phase 3. We would be able to call Lily back into the auxiliary den and shut her in if Mom Tara or eventually Dad Charlie seemed intent on harming Lily. Exactly what we would do after that we had no plan, but I would have to find/send my baby to another zoo. So it was very important that Lily go to her den on command.

Phase three made me worry days in advance. Keep in mind we were opening the zoo to the public in less than a month. We had to have the auxiliary enclosure out of the way so we could re-install the guard fencing. No visitors could get close enough to touch the tigers by New Jersey state law. And our lawyers!

The appointed Monday dawned bright and clear. Not that I had slept much. I had been fine all winter with Lily being next to her parents. Now that it was time to let Mom Tara meet Lily face to face, well, I hadn't slept well for the previous days. Because, you see, reader, once a big cat fight starts there is not much you can do. If you had a strong water supply you can hose the cats down to break up a fight, but we did not have that type of city water supply. Parker, Hunter, Dad and I all discussed having the fire trucks from the Beemerville Fire Department (that our Grandfather Ralph had founded), come and stand by just in case. We all agreed that would put the tigers more on edge because they had never seen a fire truck. And we wanted those tigers calm. Sedatives were offered when I previously discussed the reunion with Dr. Ted. The four of us decided against that because a doped up animal is often afraid, because they don't know what is happening to their bodies. Eventually the sedative wears off and then what? If Lily was doped up would she respond to my voice commands if we needed her to go back to her den? You can tranquilize during a fight, but the reader must realize it takes up to forty minutes for a dart to take effect. A lot of damage can be done with teeth and claws in forty minutes. Unsalvageable damage.

My trauma with Siren haunted my dreams. I needed the sedative, not the tigers. So here I was once again, perched by the side of the enclosure. I watched Tara slowly approach Lily after Hunter let only Mom Tara come down the chute through the narrow, one animal at a time, one way tunnel. Dad was in his car, with the shotgun, once again, right behind me. Hunter passed behind me, and stood guard with Doug by the sliding door to Lily's auxiliary enclosure, just in case we had to order Lily in for her own safety. Tara slowly approached Lily, who was standing right beside me separated by the chain link fence. Tara by tiger standards was an old lady, but she could cause damage if she wanted to. Tara being older was a slight bit slower on the chase also, which gave Lily the escape advantage.

Dad could not hear me, I was not facing him. I was chuffing to Lily and Tara. Chuffing sounds like a horse blowing raspberries. In the tiger language chuffing means, "Hello, all is well. All is good, all is at peace." An all purpose word like "Aloha".

"Chuff, Good girl Tara, Chuff, Good girl Lily, Oh what good girls I have, Chuff, Chuff, Chuff," was my mantra.

"Talk to them Lori, they will respond to your calmness," Dad encouraged and urged.

"I know," I responded between chuffs. "I am," I turned my head towards Dad so he could hear my response. I realized he had not heard my chuffing.

Phase three moment of truth had arrived. Again I had a front row seat. My heart was in my throat, but I knew like Dad had said, I needed to stay calm. As I am their mother, both young Lily and Mom Tara would read my attitude. I chuffed more, and spoke more. And chuffed again.

Lily stayed by my side. Tara did not run but sashayed towards Lily, a good sign. A run would designate an attack. When the moment arrived and Tara was right next to us, Tara chuffed back to me, chuffed to Lily and then to Tara. Tara smelled then rubbed her forehead head on Lily's nose. Lily's ears went back, took a step backwards and just as quickly resumed her peaceful stance. Lily and Tara chuffed while smelling each other. Everything seemed fine. Which was good, because my lips were becoming numb with all the chuffing I was doing. I continued to pet and chuff to both of my big orange babies. I stayed a couple of minutes and then heard Dad behind me.

"Lori, you have to leave now," Dad, ever the teacher said. "They are focusing on you and they need to focus on each other. Since no fighting ensued, Doug announced he was not needed, left Hunter at the sliding gate and went on to whatever work he was involved in. Parker left at that time also.

"I know, Dad," I simply replied. "They should be fine now, right?" I wanted verification from the only expert there, my Dad. Dad nodded. It was hard to turn my back on the tiger reunion and walk away on the crunchy snow. I walked to the gate, both Tara and Lily following me along their side of the fence.

"Where you going now, Leaving me with HER?" Lily chirped as if to say. I walked out the guard fence and up the icy hill and hid behind a large oak tree. *Yeah, Hunter it was a huge tree.* I stayed behind the tree for about a ½ hour. Dad still in his car beside the tigers and Hunter standing guard by the sliding door to Lily's auxiliary home.

Tara was following Lily around the snow covered grassy section. Not chasing, just sorta following. Every now and then Lily would turn around and follow Tara. A gentle dance. So we all left them alone and went about our business.

I walked to the top of the hill twice that afternoon. Lily and Tara doing the same getting to know you dance. Just before I left for home, at dusk, I walked out and could not see either of the big orange striped cats. So I walked down the hill. I was so relieved to see Lily laying in the doorway to her hay filled auxiliary home. Hearing the crunch of my Bean boots on the icy snow, Lily sat up at attention, not leaving her spot. Tara was farther inside the auxiliary den, stretched out, happily lounging on the fresh hay. The look on Lily's face said it all:

"MOM! She's in MY room, and you aren't doing anything about it?"

Lily's eyes were all adamant questions. "Whatdayamean, she's gonna stay here too? This is my room!"

I chuckled to myself and left my two girls to work it out. I slept just fine that night. Chufffff.

Phase four rolled around a week later. Charlie had been anxious to join the girls out in the snow. Lily and Tara slept every night in the auxiliary enclosure, together. Not cuddling, but in the same space. Hunter, Parker, Dad and I were all there for the last big moment. I stood halfway down the fence, Lily by my side inside the fence and Tara up closer to the tunnel gate. When everyone was in position, Hunter opened the tunnel gate. Charlie came bounding out. He walked straight to Lily, gave her a sniff, a chuff and immediately waltzed over to Tara and started to breed her. How anti- climatic! If any thing bad was going to happen, it would of at that time. Lily seemed non-pulsed, Tara receptive, (I noted to start counting the days again) and Charlie? He looked like the smiling Cheshire cat.

We all congratulated ourselves on a job well done. I was quietly elated and so relieved. I believed my plan would work, I really did, but there is always that nagging chance that things could go drastically wrong. Dad and I stayed about a ½ hour again, while the guys went back to work. I checked on the tiger trio a couple of times that afternoon, all was well. At dusk, I was back at the tigers, all three were in Lily's auxiliary enclosure, Charlie up on the sun shelf, Tara and Lily laying together down on the hay. The auxiliary den was left at the tiger enclosure for another week, then it was time to move it back across the street and re-install the guard fence. Doug and Hunter did such a good job of re-installing the guard fence. The only trace was the disruption of the grass where the den had been. Good job, guys.

All through the multiple phases I had not mentioned the other surrounding animals at the zoo. Anything that happens at the zoo, the other animals know. For those who have not been to our zoo (please come), the lion and tiger enclosure is within eye sight distance of the Japanese Hokkaido bears, the fallow deer, the Mountain Lions, the black leopards, the jaguar, and the tigers' communal fence neighbors - the African Lions. Every day at feeding time, all the animals are alert. Just a truck driving by, they will look up. But start doing a procedure on an enclosure, they pay attention. Bring in a new animal and the entire zoo is on high alert, watching, peering, sniffing the new smell.

During the cub's reunion, the closest other animals are the African Lions that share the common fence in the middle of the two enclosures. Attila the big male lion sure wanted at Lily. From the first day he saw her in the snow covered grass until months after Lily walked into the big tiger den, Attila would make aggressive overtures. That surprised me as Attila had previously made kissy face - rubbing on the fence with Tara on the other side. Lily stays clear of Attila. Lily still hesitates to go onto the concrete section, up by the den until the lions go to sleep in the den for the night. She often stays outside in the bitter winter weather. It is now three years later and Lily still does not like to go up on the patio, if she can see Attila. Dad and I are discussing making an auxiliary den for her on the far side of the tigers' grassy section.

I love my tiger girls, and am so happy that Lily was successfully reunited with her parents. I would of fallen apart if things went wrong.

Charlie and young Lily exchange greetings.

Photo by Jessie Goble

Chapter 70 Gotta Love Spring

Someday I won't look forward to raising the spring babies on a bottle. And then I will quit. It is a lot of work, and though I hate to admit it - I am getting older. I enjoyed Intern Vickie the previous year, with her perky personality, having someone to help with the zoo nursery work, and being able to teach someone who really wanted to learn. Yes, everyone wants to play with the infant animals, but so few are willing to work with both ends of that critter. So I decided to accept another intern. I get multiple email requests a year. The internship is non-paying. Doug and I helped our daughter with college finances so we know how expensive that is. I really only wanted help for the mornings, teaching about the babies and the zoo. In the afternoon I work visitor relations when we are busy. Keeping all of that in mind, I want my intern to have time to get/keep to a paying job if they have one. Distance is also a factor. So I picked an email from a local girl, Stephanie, who was at Penn State and going to become a Vet. I emailed her back to stop in for an interview (I wanted to make sure she looked strong enough and presentable for the job). She emailed me back saying she would be available after Memorial Day.

A couple of weeks or so later, the beautiful young lady stopped in and came to me saying she was interested in the intern position. She was tall, thin, long dark hair, gorgeous and seemed perky. She certainly looked like she could haul a bucket of water. We chatted as we worked and she told me all about Penn State and the Veterinary program.

"Great, when can you start?" I asked.

"What about next week?" The PreVet replied.

"Ok, I thought your would not be available until after Memorial Day?" I asked

"I'm done with school, no use sitting around getting bored," she replied.

My kind of girl I thought to my self.

Pre Vet showed up the next week and we started my teaching process of what to do in the nursery. Imagine my surprise when two weeks later, Stephanie stopped by for an interview! Stephanie also was tall, long dark hair, gorgeous, thin and vivacious. Pre Vet was actually E-VET, Yvette Gramingnano! I had gotten the emails and the girls goofed up. Now I had two interns! Both in college at Penn State both Pre-Vet programs. Now how do you choose, and send one home? I couldn't do it. It was my mistake, so I explained my mistake to the girls and that is how I ended up with two interns. I felt like I was constantly repeating my self. They would alternate days, and some days one would stay later than the other. So often in my teaching aspect, I was repeating my self. Then I worried that my age was making me repeat myself. Gotta laugh at yourself sometimes.

Both interns were sharp, very intelligent, absolutely gorgeous gals. All of a sudden I had lots of help from the guys already employed at the zoo. Such is life.

One afternoon that July, Yvette was still at the zoo and Hunter needed my help with an animal situation. Seems a sika deer buck, still in velvet had gotten baler twine twisted around his antlers and stuck on a giant log in the mucky steam of the enclosure. Well, the stream was not mucky until the buck was thrashing in it.

I grabbed a razor knife, a scissors, Yvette and met Hunter out at the sika enclosure. My green Zoomomma jitney sped though the zoo. The sika paddock is about an acre large, rimmed in tall green trees, with a stream running though it to a larger pond area. The black silt of eons of swamp debris layers the bottom of little pond. When I was young this whole area was all swamp, and undeveloped. Swamp is mucky and easy to sink in up to your knees. The buck had been thrashing trying to unhitch himself from the six foot long log. The three of us approached cautiously. The dark brown buck alternated standing still and then bursting into another bout of fighting with the baler twine. When the buck saw us coming he swung to the pond side to try to get away from us.

"Hey Hunt, let's approach from the pond side, so he doesn't drag that log and us into the pond," I suggested. I looked at Yvette's feet to see what kind of shoes she had on. She saw my glance.

"Don't worry, these are barn boots," Yvette's enthusiasm shone in her eyes.

"Yep," Hunter replied, not concerned with attire. *Typical male!* "Ready?" And Hunter took off at a run. He is the fastest one on the farm, but Yvette with her long legs was right behind him. Muck flew from their boots like the backwash from an four wheeler. Bravely and with no hesitation Hunter grabbed the buck by the velvet antlers and twisted. Yvette grabbed one side of the antlers. Between the two of them they twisted the neck of the hundred and fifty pound buck placing the buck, not so gently, on his side. Right on the bank of the free flowing stream. The buck gave up quickly. I doubt that the buck knew we were trying to help him. The previously thrashing adult buck was just done out, exhausted. Hunter and Yvette held the buck's head, while Hunter also had his body over the buck's panting body. Hunter's legs were dangling in the cool muddy stream. *So much for our clean presentable clothes.*

I started with the scissors and quickly switched to the razor knife. The balled up baler twine was originally orange but now was mucky mud gray. Trying not to cut into the external circulatory system of velvet I cut the wound up baler twine as quickly as possible. Soon the buck would have rested enough to catch his breath and might start to thrash again. The process maybe took two minutes.

"Done Lee?" Hunter asked, as the wrestled buck began to stir. I nodded. "Ok we are off on Three!" Hunter counted, and we all jumped out of the way on three. The muddy buck lay still for a few seconds then realized he was unrestrained. The buck jumped up, and calmly trotted back to the rest of the herd that had watched the whole incident from the tree line in the paddock.

We congratulated ourselves on a job well done and then laughed at our muddy, dirty, wet clothes. I checked us for leeches. *God ! I hate leeches.* We all went home to clean up, change clothes and come back to the zoo. I rarely go home clean. All in a days work.

Chapter 71 The Human Corral

The previous year I had started a fun event for the children that visit the zoo. This spring I would do the same. Every year we have a number of Mouflon lambs that need human intervention, or kid goats, or fawns etc. The infant hoof stock farm animals are able to be petted by the visitors according to N.J. State Law. I have fed so many babies on bottles. I can actually feed seven bottles at a time, but it is not easy. So I frequently recruit human children to help. Everybody wants to volunteer. The problem is I often have more children volunteer than I have babies on a bottle. So I came up with process that keeps everybody happy.

Yvette, Stephanie, Sierra, and I were raising three little Mouflons, and four baby goats that spring. The Mouflon lambs are born in March, so they grow up fast. The baby goats did not come along until May so they were a little smaller during the summer. After the animal infants were good on a bottle we would ask the visitors to help.

One of my interns would stay by the Nursery fence gate until my signal. The rest of us would organize the visiting kids into a circle. I would hand out bottles at 12, 3, 6 and 9 on the circle and give these instructions after introducing ourselves.

"OK everyone, we are going to play a game like hot potato. In a moment we are going to let the babies out and they will come running to the bottles in your hands. When the baby goat/lamb comes to you, just point the bottle down at their nose. They know what to do. Now Parents if you want to take a picture of your child you need to be on the opposite side of the circle from your child. So move now." And the crowd would shift.

" You don't have to worry, my babies are small and don't have enough teeth to bite you," I would calmly state. You can hear the laughter mixed with sighs of relief from a few petrified children. My interns would spot the kids that might need help by the scared look on their faces and stand by that child.

"When we let them out, the babies will run into the circle through the gate people I assigned. Then the gate people need to close up the circle. My interns will help me get the babies on the bottles, so just stand still in your human corral. Don't break the corral, and let them run you are all fence posts. Then on the count of three give your bottle with the lamb still sucking to the child on your right. We will keep doing that until everyone has a turn." And all the human kids that were not holding a bottle suddenly break into huge smiles.

"There is only one steadfast rule," I would state loudly. "No pictures of my butt on Facebook!" and everyone would laugh.

"Ready?" And I would thumbs-up signal whomever was on the gate. Often it was Sierra, Stephanie, Yvette, and sometimes even Dad. Everyone was well trained. The stampede of brown, white, black and sometimes silver infants would begin. The livestock babies would run into the circle, tails wagging, ears flopping, looking for bottles. Nudging with noses. The human kids would squeal with delight, as the livestock babies would seek out a bottle. It is pandemonium for a few moments until every baby gets situated. Then we pass the bottles, child to child with the baby animals still nursing. And every Facebook picture got us more publicity.

After the bottles are empty and every human child has had a turn we walk as a herd back to the Nursery gate. I'm not sure who enjoys it more, the animal babies, the human kids or me. I have bottle fed so many animals, it is actually more fun for me to watch the joy on the faces of the kids that will only get to do this once in a lifetime.

Young Kelsey Space and Buttercup the kid goat.
Photo by Lori Space Day

Zoo Momma

Chapter 72 You Still Want a Bottle?

Every spring I have white tail deer fawns on a bottle. They are usually born between May 15th and June 15th. Each fawn has it's own characteristics, special markings that only the experienced eye can detect. Chocolate brown eyelashes, white stripes on the hooves, no spots on the neck, longer curly hair, pink freckles on the normally black nose, all are the special differences that help me distinguish the fawns from each other. If one doesn't eat, you have to know which one it is to watch out for it at the next bottle. We bring in some of the fawns out of our adult paddock of white tail deer, every year. The interns and I learn the markings after seeing the fawns every two hours dawn to dusk. I do the dawn and dusk rotation of bottles.

But this chapter is not about fawns, other than to say we let visitors help after the fawns are good on a bottle and not afraid of humans.

I had just fed the fawns in the tall overgrown green grass of their paddock on the hill by the Tool Museum Barn. Coco the fawn did not drink on that hot afternoon. This was not uncommon for her, I would make sure she ate at the next feeding.

I was carrying my small black Zoomomma bucket of empty plus one full bottle of milk down the hill accompanied by the folks that helped me feed. Everyone had enjoyed their experience. Another visitor passed us, asking:

"What you gonna do now? Feed the tiger cub?" he questioned. Lily was famous from her birth the previous year. Everyone was happy to see Lily with her parents. Especially me. We were at the Y in the path by the round Snake Den.

" Sure, why not?" I answered. "I have time." And the troop of folks followed me up the hill past the sunning Syrian grizzlies.

As we crested the hill, Lily spotted me immediately and ran as close as she could to me in her enclosure. I chatted with her as I unlocked the chain link guard rail gate. The bottle was only lukewarm. I approached the chain link fencing. Now reader please to realize that I had not given lily a bottle since the November before, when she was still in the auxiliary den, nearly 10 months previously. I didn't expect her to remember the bottle or be interested. Silly me.

"Here, baby girl," I said as I offered Lily the bottle through the chain link. "See if you remember this." Lily put her nose right up to the chain link. Her pink nose smelled the bottle and I saw her eyes light up. I slipped the bottle nipple end through the three inch wide chain link, letting Lily have the nipple. Imagine my surprise when she not only put her huge whiskered white muzzle on the nipple, but she actually rolled her huge tongue around it and sucked! *Wow cool!* I tried to remain professionally nonchalant. *But I was giggling inside.* I watched to make sure she did not bite off the rubber nipple. She could probably pass it through her system easy enough, but I would have to worry about that.

Tara, ever inquisitive, had heard my voice and the nosy old lady interrupted her nap to saunter outside to see what was going on. Tara joined us at the fence line. I was doubly surprised when Tara growled and pushed Lily out of the way to suck on the bottle herself. Lily paced behind Tara wanting the bottle back, but knowing not to interfere with Tara, the alpha female.

It had been ten months for Lily, but the last baby bottle full of milk Tara had received was FIFTEEN YEARS before! *Holy Mackerel!* I divided the bottle up between the two snarling cats. Snarling tigers less than ten inches, - the length of a baby bottle- away from my hand! Tara the alpha female got the last drops. *Wow!* I could not contain my amazement that Tara remembered.

The assorted visitors and I chatted all the way back to the main building. They learned a lot about tigers that day. And I had a fantastic great day!

The next afternoon I went back to my giant girl kitties and took two bottles. It was a hot sunny day so I made the girls trod all the way to the shade tree on the back of the enclosure. This time I had Lily stand on her back feet and raise up for her bottle. Tara, due to her age was not asked for the Patty -Cake stance. I was chatting with the visitors as I spoke to my girls, both my interns and the tigers. Lily was familiar with the Patty-Cake stance, she was trained to do that so I could visually inspect her belly side. It is impressive to see how tall Lily has become. I am five foot seven inches, and I have to hold my hand above my head to hold the bottle for her.

Charlie the male tiger approached us. I had not bottle raised Charlie, he was raised by someone else, but was raised by hand on a bottle. I totally did not expect Charlie to come to me for a bottle. He never came to me for scratches or petting. And much to my astonishment, Charlie came and pushed Tara off the bottle. Amazing.

So now I take out three bottles of goat milk for my big orange striped kitties. Got to love 'em.

Lily, my big baby, loves her bottles!
Photo by Sierra Walsh

Chapter 73 Australia!

Every zookeeper's dream is to go to Australia. Every animal person I know dreams of going to Australia. Some of the species found there are found no where else on earth. We had kangaroo at the zoo, which we paid dearly for. Emus, a large rattite bird, from Australia came to the Americas as an agricultural product. They were going to replace the beef industry with low cholesterol red meat. Well that did not happen. We still have emu at the zoo. Emu are so plentiful in the US they have been taken off the exotic list and placed on the agricultural classification of animals on our licenses. But I had never seen a Kola, wombat, Tasmanian Devil, seals, or penguins in the wild. Never seen emu or roos in the wild either. Australia had always been a dream of mine. Dad and Mira went to Australia, and so did Parker and Jill on their honeymoon. I was totally surprised when Dad announced at the previous traditional Christmas breakfast at my house that his gift to Doug and I would be a trip to Australia! WOW!

Australia's seasons are the reverse of ours, Dad suggested we go in our spring, Australia's fall. The animals would be in full glory with their cooler season coats, the landscape in the fall more colorful. Well, in the planning stages of January, I just could not leave the zoo when we did not know how Tiger Lily would adjust to being with her parents and vice versa. Tiger Lily weighed heavy in my equation. Now that I think of it maybe Dad was trying to get rid of me just in case things went wrong with Lily's re-introduction? Springtime is also loaded with whatever babies God sends my way. My spring days are very busy and full. I just didn't want to go then. So I set up the trip for the fall of 2014, which was spring in Australia.

The flight there was, well it was a long flight. Thirty hours from bed to bed. Long time sitting in the plane, especially for we whom are used to walking and working all day long. We landed in Sydney, seeing the iconic Opera House on our way down. I did not want to go to a lot of city buildings type stuff. I was there for the animals. We had picked a bus tour by AAT Kings That would start in Sydney, hug the southeast coast and end up at Kangaroo Island.

When we first arrived in Sydney we checked into our hotel and took a nap. Nearby was a zoo and an aquarium. Now you didn't think I was going to pass those up did you? I love aquariums since my days in the pet shop. And the indigenous zoo gave us the first glimpse of the animals we came to see in the wild.

After a good night's sleep we were up and out to join our bus tour group. We would spend the next ten days with these folks, and we met some very nice people. I think Doug and I were the youngest people on the trip, and we were 59 at the time. I didn't want to fly around Australia and miss seeing the countryside. The tour was great. We stopped in little towns all along the way, getting the flavor of the friendly Australian people. I learned a lot about the history of Australia. It was interesting to me as my mom's side of the family had English convicts that were sent there years ago. So somewhere, I had family there. Maybe next trip.

Our guide and bus driver were great. They knew every spot that the animals would be. We went to a province park and to my amazement saw mobs (the name for a group) of gray kangaroos. Taller than me, they looked like giant rabbits with long thick tails. The roos did not seem to be afraid of us, they moseyed on into the field. Very alert, I could see ears communicating to one another. After a few moments the mob would calmly hop away. The entire bus of tourists, and yes that was me too, quietly walked and snapped photo after photo. I can not express my joy of that moment.

As we rode in the bus along the highway, I got a kick out of the kangaroo road crossing signs. They were just like our deer crossing signs, in bright yellow diamond shape warnings. We also saw the dead kangaroo on the road that had not learned to read those signs. There were also wombat crossing signs, kola, and emu signs. They were all a chuckle to see. A gentle reminder that Australians have their problems with cars hitting wildlife just like the deer that get hit by a car here in N.J..

The amount of wildlife was astounding. Our bus would be going down the road, and I would see boulders in the massive fields up ahead. I learned that many of the massive 50 acre greening fields were forests when Australia was first settled. English convict labor cleared the fields by hand with axe, saws and horses. When our bus got closer, those huge gray boulders would stand up and move on long legs with backward knees. The sunning flocks of emu would stand, stretch and start to walk away. We saw a huge mob of kangaroos, maybe fifty in total, hop in unison in one direction then, just like a school of fish, they quickly, deftly, synchronized and moved in another direction. Fascinating. We saw lots of troops of kangaroo, some red, and some smaller gray kangaroo, all with different numbers of individuals. Wallaby, the smaller version of kangaroo were plentiful also.

The guide Paul pointed out the Kolas in the trees. Since Kolas are nocturnal, they just looked like fuzzy bowling balls sleeping in the crock of a tree. We did stop at a few animal sanctuaries. In Australia there are lots of native animal sanctuaries, here in the states you would call them a rehabilitator. The native Australians know that if they hit a kangaroo with their car, they are to check the kangaroo's pouch for a baby roo. There are sanctuaries every hundred miles or so. A lot of the rehabbers have opened to the public, to make some cash to support their passion. Just like my grandparents did years ago. We stopped at one sanctuary. I got to hold a kola bear and get my picture taken. I reviewed my pictures in order to write this chapter. Boy I look old and wrinkled, but very happy holding that kola bear. A once in a lifetime, treasured moment for me.

The tour stopped at a sheep station, station being the word for a farm or ranch in Australia. I enjoyed the demonstration of the extremely well trained sheep dogs collecting the sheep. We also got to watch a sheep sheering demonstration. I've seen it here at the zoo, but with the numbers that a sheep station has, I can see it is back breaking hard work. Enjoy those sweaters, folks.

The tour included a number of stops at National Parks, one in particular was in the rim of an extinct volcano. An Aboriginal man was a ranger there. He taught us how to throw a boomerang, I think it is a law that all tourist must try! I spoke to him at length about our emus chasing down the fawns. He had never heard of emus taking prey larger than snakes or lizards. So maybe our emus were just playing? Oh Whell.

We stopped at Port Campbell National Park and saw the mammoth rock islands of "The Twelve Apostles". Eons of erosion had created them. Cool. Again, the scenery was breath taking. One picture I took had a kangaroo with the ocean as a background.

Again the red or gray kangaroos all over the place fascinated me. Here at Space Farms Zoo we paid a lot of money for kangaroos. In Australia the farmer's shoot them like vermin. The dumbest roos were splattered across the roads.

While skirting the ocean we stopped at a spot where the New Zeeland seals came to shore. Wow! Their park rangers were very strict as to where you could walk along the shoreline. There must have been at least a hundred seals of all sizes. This particular herd of seals were the only seals not hunted out of existence when Australia was young. That was because of their location with a reef slightly offshore to prevent the ships of sailors from landing on shore to kill them for their fur. I was in the end of the tour and could not quite hear the ranger's speech. I'll admit I was bad and I walked closer to one seal to snap a few shots. And the Ranger yelled at me. OOOPPS! Sorry. *NOT Really. Yeah and at work I hate people that don't follow the rules!*

In one costal town there was an older gentleman who fed the pelicans every day. Dressed in waterproof bibs, a windbreaker jacket and a goofy hat he was very entertaining. Every day just like Doug and I work, every day, Christmas, Easter, New Years Eve, etc. Every day he feeds the pelicans at 5 pm. Every day hundreds of white and gray pelicans come flying in right at 5 pm. What a hoot! Pelicans landed on his head and shoulders. Noisy, messy, and smelling like dead fish, of course!, the pelicans were a much bigger bird than I thought they would be. Some were as tall as the man's waist. I loved the way their lower beak pink skin expanded with the food. Some had holes in their beak skin. All were noisy begging for food. I've not had any experience with pelicans, so that was neat.

One of the things Dad had advised us to see was the penguins come ashore on Prince Phillip Island. I am glad we did not miss it. The little penguins roll in on the surf at night. I would see the bubbly white crest of a wave hit the shore and disperse. Then some of those white surf bubbles would stand up and walk towards shore. The little blue (really dark black) penguins would scramble to get on their feet and head towards the elevated boardwalk especially built for us visitors. Built for the visitors - but also to let the penguins pass underneath us though penguin made paths through the scrub brush. *Sooo cool.* When the momma penguin got close enough for her baby to hear her, the momma would chirp. Then and only then would a fuzzy gray little baby penguin waddle out of what looked like a woodchuck burrow in the side of the hill. The momma would waddle up to the youngster. The youngster would peck at momma's mouth and open wide. Then momma would regurgitate her stomach content into the mouth of the baby.

Yummmy, recycled fish! Hungry kids? After an obviously huge gulp on the baby's part momma and youngster would waddle into the home borrow. One baby per hole, one family per hole. We spent hours watching. We were not allowed to take pictures, as all of this happened at night. The flashes would cause the penguins to become disoriented. So Ok I saw it for real, it was fantastic. As we were leaving, Doug pointed out a sign to me. It was a drawing of a penguin hiding under a car and two words. 'Please Check'. *Jeeese oh Man, if I knew it was that easy I could of scooped a couple up and brought them home. Well not really, but let me think on it....*

We had penguins here at Space Farms when I was a kid. I remember they got out of their area in the pond and we had to go out with a row boat to try to catch them. We would row right up to them. Those penguins were smart. They would let us row up right next to them and then dive under water, then surfacing on the other end of the two acre pond. And we would row again. It was the look in their eyes that let me know they knew, they could outsmart us. I think the penguins got quite a kick out of us trying to catch them. They died after being in zoo residence for a couple of years. Someone threw the old fashioned rip off pop tops off of soda cans in the water of their exhibit. That tells you how long ago it was. The pop tops looked like fish descending therefore the penguins ate them. It killed both of the penguins. I knew we have no place to keep them now, but the penguins were cool.

I had my sixtieth birthday in Australia. We were on Kangaroo Island at a very nice restaurant. I had searched menus since we arrived in Australia for kangaroo meat dishes. *Gottta try it, ya know?* On my birthday, ten days into the trip, there was kangaroo steak on the menu. I ordered it medium rare. The folks at the next table suggested I order it rare, as it is tough meat. I did. The meat tasted just like venison I've had at home. Australia was a great place to turn sixty. The best thing about my birthday in Australia? I was far away from those pesky brothers and sister that would have thrown me a horrible you are getting old party. I turned sixty watching kangaroo and seals play in the daytime, and dining on 'roo steak at night. Sixty's not so bad now, 'ay Mate?

After the AAT Kings tour was over at Kangaroo Island, we flew back across the Australian continent to the Great Barrier Reef. The fight was interesting as we got to see from the sky the vast stretches of many hues of brown desert landscape we all hear about, the 'outback'. We had been hugging the coast where the rain and ocean gave life to the land. The interior was dry and desolate. I would not want to be an Aboriginal having to live off that impossible landscape.

The Great Barrier Reef is by the Equator so we were immersed in jungle heat and humidity as we exited the plane. The parts of Australia we were in were much more temperate climate, and plant/tree structure, just like home here in N.J.. So the jungle was a pleasant change. We stayed overnight and the next morning got on a large fast speed boat that took us out to the Barrier Reef. Set up on an oil platform was it's own little island for us tourists. From that spot we took an glass submarine voyage around the reef. As Doug and I both had a tropical fish background, we marveled at all the fish we were familiar with, and those we were not. The thickness and pale gray/blue tint of the plexi glass dimmed the colors of the fish as we knew them. *But we don't snorkel. Sooo.* We had really wanted to see the Great Barrier Reef, and knew that we might not ever get back to Australia.

Lunch was on deck and I sat down next to a man who was a friend of the secretary of Agriculture for Australia. He was in the wine business. As our spouses ate we looked out at the vastness of the turquoise blue ocean. He and I discussed the potential of importing kangaroos to the U.S.. He gave me his card, said he would help point me in the right paperwork direction. So maybe someday in this lifetime, maybe after I finish this book, I will get back to Australia and adopt a batch of rehabilitated kangaroos, to start a kangaroo farm. Who knows? Like my Gramma Lizzie always said, "If you're gonna dream girl, dream big!"

Petting a koala was a life long dream.
Photo by Doug Day

Zoo Momma

Chapter 74 Fire!

My cell phone rang after ten p.m., the caller ID announced "Call from Parker." Any phone call after ten p.m. is an emergency in my world. How about yours? Doug had gone to bed an hour before. I was in my sewing room watching TV. I picked up the phone.

"Ask Doug to come down here right away," I could hear the tension in Parker's voice. "The feed house is on fire and I need him to go turn off the electric." I was at full attention fast. I ran to wake up Doug and explain the situation. Doug groggily put on his clothes, as I donned mine. We grabbed the first clothes we could put our hands on, so the clothes were a colorful miss match, but we knew to dress warm. It was December, freezing cold and snowing like blazes. Doug was out of the house before me. He was down the road in the gray dead deer pick up truck before I got in our car to follow. *Yeah right! Like Doug thought I would stay home! Hump!*

The feed house is an U shaped building across the street from the zoo itself. The original building was an old school house that Ralph and Elizabeth Space bought back in the 1938. The same school that my great grandfather, grandfather, Ralph and Dad, Fred, attended until 8th grade. My Dad went on to graduate High School in Sussex. The building is part concrete and part timber framed. Over the years the school house was expanded to include a section to eviscerate animals for food for the zoo, and multiple large walk in freezers, to hold that meat until we needed it. Hence we call it the feed house. The upstairs had a small apartment, and the multiple rooms where we spent our youths every fall skinning the twenty thousand mink we produced at the Space Farms Mink Ranch. I knew first hand the grease/oil that the mink produced. I had skinned my fair share. The oil from the mink carcass is used in many cosmetics. The floor and other wooden construction was permeated with the smelly oily residue. In short, the wood structure was like a candle, wood soaked in oil.

I pulled in the driveway across from the zoo by my Dad's house. I parked far away from the feed house. When I arrived I saw one bright red Beemerville Fire Truck parked in front of the feed house. Parker was in the back section of the truck by the nozzles. I saw my 18 year old nephew Hunter in full fireman gear talking to Doug and Parker. Then much to my worry, Hunter pulled down his fire facemask and went into the feed house. Next Doug disappeared from sight. Other trucks were starting to pull in the driveway, along with all the local volunteer firemen. I watched helplessly as the brave firemen of the Beemerville Fire Department pulled in and got organized.

The elderly mom and son that lived in the apartment were out, safe, sitting in their car and gabbed with me. The Auxiliary came and Jill opened up the main building for them to work out of, making sandwiches and lots of warm coffee for the firemen. Doug came back out to join me. We sat in the gray truck, front row seats to the activity in front of us. Parker called Dad's house to tell him about the fire. Located on the other side of the driveway, I was surprised that Dad had not heard (then again he is hard of hearing) or seen all the fire department's colorful lights. The snowy ground was slippery, and more snow was falling. The water being pumped on the fire was freezing on the ground. Dad started to walk around the huge feed house complex to see what was happening. My grandfather had started the fire department in the 1930's, and Dad had taken a turn as chief, as my brother, Parker, had also. I walked with Dad, to keep him upright on the slippery surfaces. Parker was busy with the fire, and I had not seen Hunter again. I was starting to worry.

A few minutes later Hunter came out of the building, dirty, covered in soot. He asked me to call Samantha, his girlfriend, and Jill to tell them he was alright. So that became my next job after Dad decided to sit in his warm white Explorer. I alternated carrying instructions from whomever, to calling Sam to let them know the guys were ok, every time I saw them. Jill, Sam and the Beemerville Ladies Auxiliary kept the coffee flowing and goodies available for the firemen.

"Are there any dangerous animals loose in the zoo?" Post Ex-Chief Charlie, from the Beemerville department asked me. "Or is there any thing roaming around that might hurt the firemen?

"No of course not!" I did not understand the necessity of the question. The fire was across the street, far away from the zoo. Then a red fire truck went into the zoo, through the zoo gate. Firemen cut a hole in the pond fence and started pumping water from the zoo pond. The fat yellow fire hoses were laid around the main building, out the zoo gate and across the street to another pumper truck that forced water to other fire trucks which flushed gushes of water on the now flaming building. Wow! What a system.

As the night continued, I saw ladder trucks stretched up to the second floor to the pelt room section. Intrepid firemen scaled the ladder, with long, heavy chain saws to cut holes in the one year old bright red tin roof. Sparks flew, and as soon as the roof was open the fire was liberated, blazing, reaching far into the night sky. I remember being amazed at the dichotomy, fire and snowflakes at the same time.

Doug and I sat in the dead deer smelly gray truck to warm up, watching the firemen from ten different neighboring town departments. I knew most of the firemen from Beemerville, and some of the guys from the other departments. Everyone was cautious, but knowledgeable on exactly what to do. The fire blazed long into the night. Firemen from Beemerville, Colesville, Andover Township, Branchville, Frankford, Hampton, Hardyston, Lafayette, Montague, Sandyston and Sussex had all responded to the call. There must have been at least a dozen fire trucks, pumpers and fire related vehicles. Beemerville was lit up like a gaudy Christmas tree by the flashing red white and blue lights on the vehicles. The lights and sounds echoed off the surrounding white buildings and chrome festooned yellow and red fire trucks, magnifying the colorful display. State Police cars added to the vivid array. Doug and I were both amazed at the synchronized efforts of the fire departments. They worked together so well. Every volunteer fireman had a job and did it coordinating with his fellow firemen.

Zoo Momma

It takes a special kind of courage to walk into a burning building when the average man's natural instinct is to run in the other direction. All our volunteer firemen had gone through years of training, and it showed. I was impressed. I had been a member of the Ladies' Auxiliary when I was younger, but had not rejoined after returning from Pittsburgh. I had served coffee and goodies way back then also. But times had changed and the training and equipment had changed drastically. When Hunter took the lead on the exploration of the building he knew so well, I worried along with Sam, his girlfriend, and of course, Jill, his mom. In my eyes Hunter went into that building a boy and walked out a man. I had never seen him in that capacity before. And I was proud. I'm just his aunt, but I am proud.

Doug and I went home at four in the morning. Some of the fire trucks had gone back to their home bases. Sleep came quickly. Later that morning I surveyed the damage, the center part of the u shaped building was lost. Frozen turkeys that we had stored for the local charities to hand out at Christmas were charred and tossed on the ground. Pieces of the building were strewn on the ground. The upcoming year's worth of frozen venison for the animals' diets was smoked. Animals don't eat smoked meat. All ruined. The fire caused massive destruction. But thank God no lives were lost.

My frozen rabbits were lost in the melee. Now Hunter will laugh at my mentioning rabbits, but I had lost a years worth of frozen rabbits in Hurricane Irene, and again the next year in Super Storm Sandy. Now I had just lost another year's supply for the big snakes, one more time, to a fire. *Maybe God is telling me something?*

I was just an observer during the fire, filling in where I could help. I take no credit for more than that. The firemen were amazing. My brother Parker, handled the insurance claims, and the rebuilding of the feed house complex which took a year. When bad things like this happen, you just be thankful no one got hurt, wake up in the morning and start cleaning up. *Come on now girl, let's get going ! We've got animals to feed.*

Zoo Momma

Chapter 75 Great Balls of Fire!

Great Balls of Fire!
Grab some coffee, OJ or maybe some tea,
It's time for a visit, just you and me.
Let's see what's happened for the past year,
As I send you this note of holiday cheer.
A five month process to put Tiger Lily in, with her kin
It worked, with worry , and chuffing of chins.
They are all happy now, get along fine,
Thank goodness, I worried such a long a time.
Had Molly the Mouflon who refused to die,
Every morning she would bellow and cry.
Gave her a bottle, she could not walk, but boy oh boy did she talk!
So I put her in a box and made her a sling,
waited to see if she'd walk last spring.
I tortured Unsinkable Molly Brown with lots of PT,
now she can run, as good as can be.
Raised goats, for the kid's circle, oh what fun,
Every kid feeds a bottle when all's done.
Each mom snapping pictures for face book,
Then their 300 friends get a good look!
Advertising you just got to love it,
Good word of mouth, can't get enough of it.
Raised rabbits and fawns and my sweet Tiger Lily,
300 lbs, takes a bottle, how silly.
The visitors they love it, they oooh and ahh,
Then mom Tara come by with her chutzpa
Stole Lily's bottle so now when I go,
I take out three bottles, -yes that three,
One for Lily, one for Tara , and one for Charlie.
Three adult tigers on bottles, when the bottles are drunk
Visitors clap and smile, it amazes ME, whodathunk?
Summers are busy, visitors, babies, and projects,
you never know what will happen next.
I wrote for the press, chatted on radio,
and did some time on the Pet Stop show.
I took on two(!) interns this year, cramming all my info in their young ears.
Delightful entertaining, they brightened my day,
Lightened my workload, While I taught them my 'way',
Some call it voodoo medicine, just old farmer I say!
Stephanie is off to Vet School, Yvette back at Penn,
I hope to see them soon again.
Sierra, a local young gal, has been helping too,

Zoo Momma

there's always so much to do at the zoo.
Monkey's with mites and the coatimundi,
interesting challenge for my gals and me.
Training baboons to go into a box,
Oranges, bananas and fruit, it took quite a lot.
Jack's still in Boston, working on her masters,
she'll finish this spring, I'd hope faster.
Mark and she are quite the pair,
she's gorgeous, they're smart, and he's so debonair!
Two young urbanites on the education quest,
out on their own with their own little nest.
I miss her much, I wish they lived near,
who knows its only for another year.
Doug's doing fine, we grow older by the day,
our bones ache and creak what can I say?
He's handsome as ever, when he cleans up,
though his language is colorful redneck - yep!
Hunter works full time on the farm,
we love his sense of humor and his strong arm.
He's helpful with a lot of good ideas,
Doug and he have grown close over the years.
Our vacation this year was truly a wonder,
we went to the marvelous land down under!
Wow, what a trip the things we have seen ,
Amazing fantastic, really cool and keen!
Kangaroos by the hundreds, cockatoos by the flock,
Seals, wallabies, sheep, koalas, wombats and sea lions on a dock.

The sights were glorious, each glance photo worthy
Quite the trip for a country gal like me.
And emu, did I mention them, We saw them again and again.
Was nifty to see them freely roam,
and the other species that call Australia home.
I turned 60 in Australia and the best thing about it,
I was in Australia, my brothers could not shout it!
Was a fabulous trip, I recommend it highly,
Was the trip of a lifetime, for a zookeeper like me.
Thanks Dad. Speaking of Dad,
Dad had back surgery recovered just fine,
So he can go hunting all the time.
He's 86 , up and out every day, working is what he considers play.
I hope I'm that able when I am his age, Arthritis is the family plague.
Mom's fine, her back often hurts, we lunch once a week
We keep in touch, every other day we speak..

313

Zoo Momma

When dealing with parents I try to keep in mind
(Poor Jackie!) Someday it'll be my time.
Just before Christmas Oh boy did we have a night,
A five alarm fire the men came to fight.
Five fire departments were here,
to put out a fire in the freezer of dead deer.
No humans were hurt, nor animals either,
but we lost our supply of meat in the freezer.
And 150 Christmas turkeys destined for the poor,
toasted, smoked, thrown out the door.
A long tough night, some things just hard to see,
Like watching Doug walk in to turn off electricity.
And young Hunter decked out in full gear,
leading men in a burning building, no fear.
He knew the lay out, we've all worked up there,
now you can see straight up in the air.
The fire it burned all through the night, our hamlet bathed in colorful lights
From the many fire departments to whom we all give a cheer,
Their bravery and training, remarkably clear.
We lost the freezer and wood shop, the animal food and the tools within.
No one was hurt, so now clean up can begin.
Alas my friend that's been our year, thus ends my note of holiday cheer.
Though often at night my ass is draggin',
while my wrinkles are perpetually saggin',
Remember I am more than just what you see,
With a wink from the pixie that still lives in me.
Write me a note, if you have the time,
I'd love to hear from friends of mine.
Love Lori and Doug

Chapter 76 Three Little Bears

The snow fall over the winter of 2014 -2015 was heavy. The guys needed to use tractors and backhoes in the zoo to manage the snow. Remember carnivores and omnivorous animals eat six days a week, the day we skip is not always the snow day. Snow drifts settle in certain spots in the zoo, especially in the valley sections and behind dens where the incessant wind swirls the snow.

The Kodiak bear den is on top of a hill. The specially designed enclosure is actually two 'condos' with separate entrances for male, boar, and female, sow, bears. My Dad designed the enclosure and dens with the specific requirements of bear reproduction in mind. Everyone has their favorite specie, and for my Dad, it is bears. Each condo den has two doors. One door enters into the grassy enclosure and the other door can be opened from the outside. The doors entering inside the enclosure are left open and the bears can go in and out at their discretion. The doors from the outside are kept locked. Those doors are only used in case of new bears being put into the enclosure or if there are babies to check on.

The last set of Japanese Hokkaido bear cubs born here at Space Farms were in the large turf enclosure. We could not inspect them due to the construction of the that enclosure. But they were fun to watch grow up. Those bears did just fine without human intervention. Same as the bears in the wild. Animals need less intervention than the average person would think.

We had acquired a new set of Kodiak bears from the Rix Bear Ranch in Middletown, N.Y. My Dad and Al Rix went way back, and the next generation of bear experts, Al's daughter Jeannette had an extra pair of Kodiak bears for us. We moved them into the large redesigned Kodiak bear pen in the fall of 2013. The bears came in a rolling steal bar transport cage, which the guys rolled, (*with some trouble from the soft grass turf)*, right up to the outside door of the den to insert the bears into their new home. Each bear came individually caged so it was a process to put the bears in one at a time. The bears were retired show bears so they had worked with humans before. Once the bears decided to leave the den, they frolicked in the new addition of natural turf that Doug, Hunter and Parker had designed. Gone was the old concrete floor section by the pool, though the pool was saved and utilized in the new section. Hunter has an eye for enclosure design. The new section featured a huge rock pile to climb, the pool, and a natural log shade area in the grassy ½ acre enclosure. The new Kodiak bears loved their spiffy spacious home. They frolicked in the pool and ran between the two sections, that were divided by the 'condo' dens. The bears did all that bears do...

Kodiak bears or Ursus arctos middendorffi, also called the Kodiak Brown bear are grizzly bears. The islands of the southwestern Alaskan Kodiak Achipelago formed a geological barrier and fostered the Kodiak breed of grizzly bears. There is very little genetic diversity within the population. The Kodiak bears vary in colors from dark brown, orangey to blonde tipped on dark roots. The adorable cubs often have what is called a white natal ring or collar in their coloration for the first few years.

Sows reach 500 to 700 pounds, while boars reach 800 to 1,500 pounds in weight. Goliath was a Kodiak bear my Dad raised and he reached a Guinness Book world record of over 2,000 pounds. Most mature male Kodiaks weigh around a thousand pounds.

Denning is the time the bears sleep in the winter. Most females den up with cubs late October and stay in the den until warmer June with their cubs. Those cubs drain the mother's resources. During the denning they live off their accumulated body fat and loose 20 to 30 % of their total body weight. I was surprised to find out that ¼ of Kodiak bears do not den up. Dad said the weather is not quite as severe in that part of Alaska. *Well, whadayaknow!* After denning the bears eat anything they can find, ravenous from the winter's lack of food. Carrion, seaweed, berries and growing vegetation, satiates the bear family until the pacific salmon come upstream - May through September. It does not surprise me that the Kodiak bear does not hunt deer or mountain goat, as the deer and the mountain goat have mobility and speed over the bear. Not that a bear can not move fast, however bear are not stealthy enough to stalk or have the stamina to chase fast for a long enough time to catch a deer or goat. However, carrion deer or goat is fair game or game fare!

There is an intense hierarchy often exhibited at the salmon river fishing spots. Verbalization and body posturing declare who gets the best spots on the fishing stream.

Mating occurs in May and June, the embryo not implanting until fall. The average litter is three cubs. Cubs are born in late January or February. Each cub weighs about 10 oz. and grow very quickly on mother's rich milk. Grizzly milk is 40.6% solids, of which 55% is fat, 28% is protein and only 1% carbohydrates. My grandmother's home made bear cub formula and the professionally processed formulas I have worked with are like pudding at room temperature. You have to warm the formulas up to liquefy them for the cub to suck them out of a bottle. Cubs are born hairless, eyes sealed shut and look like baby piggies. Their hair starts to grow immediately, with soft brown (or black according to the breed) fuzz. They hum when they nurse. NummmmmNummmmmNummmmm. That hum sounds like a person saying no at the same time they are humming, with a u sound instead of an o. The noise is distinct. Eyes open at four weeks old. On the rich milk babies grow fast and by the time they are six weeks old they are the size of a bread box. Do not let their cuteness fool you into thinking those cubs are lovable. I have watched my grandmother try to start bear cubs on a bottle at six weeks old. They fight back with gums and claws, refusing the rubber nipple until they get hungry enough.. My grandmother wore opera gloves with her jeans to wrestle the cubs into position. At six weeks old those cubs were tough, and stubborn. Once they were taught to suck on the bottle the game was not over. Noooo way. The cubs often fought for the bottle, just like they would push their siblings away from their natural mother's nipples. You could not feed one bear cub with other cubs around. We always had to separate them and feed them one at a time. And with the gloves, because the natural instinct of the cub is to push on momma bears breast to make the milk come out. If the milk was in a bottle the cubs would push on your arm, and on the end of those adorable little paws, were sharp as razorblade claws.

Not all bear cubs live in the wild. Half of all bear cubs born in the wild die before their third birthday. Cubs will stay with mom until they are three years old. Young bears have a high death rate. After three years old, only 56% of the males born and 89% of the females survive. Matter of fact the biggest killer of young bears is the father or other male bears. They will kill off any cubs they find to bring the female back into estrus. Therefore the momma bears keep their cubs away from poppa bear. Boar bears will kill any male they can as to limit the competition for breeding. There is no Daddy bear in a happy bear family. Sorry kids, the whole Goldilocks story is a fake. But bears do like porridge.

Luckily President Franklin D. Roosevelt created Kodiak National Wildlife Refuge in 1941, protecting the home range of the Kodiak bear. Approximately two million acres are part of the southwestern Alaska Refuge. This includes 2/3 of the Kodiak island from which the bears get their name and other islands in the Archipelago chain. The refuge is overseen by the Kodiak Archipelago Bear Conservation Management Plan with human representatives from twelve different very diverse groups. This area is currently used for hunting and tourist viewing of the famous Kodiak bears.

This brings us back to our two retired traveling bears at the zoo and the snow drifty winter. Yes they had done what bears do, and birds do and bees do. We had watched the sow den up separately in her own 'condo' room. That was our clue that she was pregnant. So we locked the boar bear back into the bachelors quarters of the enclosure. Now don't go feeling sorry for the bruin, He had his own quarter acre to romp and play in also, and a giant tub for splashing fun.

Dad and I had discussed many possibilities and watched and waited. Come the first of March, Yvette, my intern, was visiting on her college spring break. Dad and I had coffee with her in the am. Dad was lamenting the depth of the snow, as he at 86 years old could not get close enough to the bear den to determine if there were cubs. Yvette and I volunteered to go see if we could hear any thing. I knew the sound to listen for from my youth spent helping my grandmother.

We were dressed head to toe in snow gear as we waddled through the zoo with restricted movement like two overdressed kids . Or at least I was. Yvette had the advantage of long legs. As we approached the Kodiak den we weighed our options. We could go in through the guard fence gate and trudge twenty five feet to the outside den door through waist high snow. Or we could jump (who me?) the chest high guard fence opposite the den door and trudge through the massive waist high snow drifts. We decided to jump the fence. *Yeah great for Yvette with those long legs. She jumped the fence, I sorta rolled over it, totally graceless! Not my finest ballerina moment.* After swimming through the cold white snow drift we stood silently at the den door.

"I'll knock, you help listen, in case your hearing is more acute than my old lady ears," I joked before knocking. I knocked, Yvette and I listened intently.

Zoo Momma

And we heard the "nummmmmmmmmm". Yvette's eyes twinkled and I'm sure mine were filled with glee also. After a moment I knocked again. "Nummmmmmmmmmm!" I had made no bones about it, raising a baby bear by myself, not with the aid of my grandmother, was on my 'bucket list'. Every body knew it at the zoo. MY plan was to let the Momma Kodiak raise them until they were 4 weeks old or so and then inspect the litter. At this point we did not know how many or what sex the offspring were.

Yvette and I reported back to Dad. Dad and Parker had a conversation about the bear cubs. The next day Parker duct taped, *Dontja just love that stuff?*, his cell phone to a long pole climbed on top of the green cinderblock den, lowered the pole to the den door and snapped a few shots. But Momma Kodiak's back was to the camera, cubs were nursing on her belly side hidden from view. But you could hear that nursing noise. If there was more than one cub, we would take some and raise them by hand, and leave one female with Momma Kodiak. We would be able to trade the hand raised cubs to other zoos. It is a lot easier to transport a golden retriever sized handleable bear than a wild mother raised full grown bear. Not to mention the fact that Momma was not going to give her babies up easy. At six weeks old the cubs are still den bound, but Momma comes out to eat, so we could locked her out and inspected the cubs through the outside door. Like I said those were my plans that I discussed with Dad previously.

Dad thought the little bear cub(s) would be a great show with the Momma Kodiak, who's name by the way was Susy Q. Daddy bear is Buddy. Another week rolled by quickly. I called all the newspapers and TV folks I knew, we were proud of our new offspring. Each of the three major papers got a scoop of their own. The Herald got a great photo of Momma Suzy and the cubs waiting in the doorway of the den. The Advertiser News got a wonderful photo of mom grooming one of the cubs. And the Star Ledger got to see all three cubs! Yes, I said three, I was surprised at that also, we knew there were two. I have to hand it to the photographers, they braved cold weather and an eight foot ladder way above an electric fence wire.

A true Space, I hate to admit when I am wrong, but Dad was right. It was wonderful to watch the cubs play and frolic all summer long. At six weeks old the cubs just started to come out of the den. Each had a distinctive cream colored natal ring on milk chocolate brown fur. We did not know what sex they were. I asked Jessie Goble and Mike Tracy, (two season pass holders that are members of a local photography club), to keep an eye out to see where the cubs peed from. A squat would be a female, a squirt from the middle of the belly would be a male. Two girls one boy.

Under momma Suzy's protection the cubs would come out to play. If the slightest thing was 'off', Suzy sent the cubs a single grunt and the three cubs would run back into the den. As the cubs got older they became bolder and bigger, eventually chasing the black vultures that tried to steal their food. The three little bears romped and played all day. One thing I learned, momma bears do not take any grief from a cub. A number of times the young male would pester to nurse

318

when momma Suzy was not so inclined. She would take her paw and swat that cub. And I mean swat hard, enough to lift the cub off the ground and toss it ten feet or so. But Suzy was also very protective. When the photographers were there, Suzy charged the fence a couple of times. Channel 9 WPXI 's photo-journalist and I got the bejesus scared out of us. I joked that we should of brought a change of pants! The cubs <u>were</u> fun to watch.

I had put the word out through the zoo community that we had the cubs. Anyone interested? One zoo from Washington State called, and it turned out my Dad had known the founder years ago. His grandson contacted us after Labor Day, and the cubs had just grown too big to fly. At this writing the cubs are now a year old, just about half as big as momma Suzy. They grew really fast, and did not den up much this last winter, we only had one big bad snow storm. Momma Suzy will feel the instinct to run her children off by this fall. The guys separated Suzy and moved her into the bachelor's pad with her Buddy. The cubs are adjusting to living with out mom. They have nothing to worry about, compared to wild bear cubs. Anyhow, right now, the grass is greening up, and the three not-so-little bears are romping, rolling, play fighting, frolicking, swimming, and having one heck of a good time. Really now, isn't that what life is all about?

This little bear is quite the acrobat!

Photo by Michael Tracy

Chapter 77 My Spring Lesson

Spring came with the usual assortment of infant animals that needed my help. Mouflon lambs, and a couple of kid goats started the year for the nursery. Our red foxes had aged out, so Doug and I took a run out to Pennsylvania and met my now-after-all -the-years friend, Gary Sunderland, the fox farmer, to pick up two ten day old red fox kits. It was April 14th, my sister's birthday, so it seemed appropriate to name one of the foxes after her. My sister's name is Renee Rabell, her middle name came from a lovely lady mink rancher my parents knew back in the day. My parents liked the name. Naming a fox Renee would be too confusing in the family so I called the male kit Rebel. My grandfather Ralph, (a known philanderer), always called a good looking woman a "Tootsie". And so the little girl fox had a name too.

Tootsie and Rebel were sweet little foxes, Doug and I stopped at Dr. Ted's Animal Hospital for a quick inspection according to state law. The little foxes were raised in my house like all the foxes before them and most of the infant animals under my care. Good thing my house was on Space Farms Zoo property.

Dr. Ted and I made the trip to Channel 12 in Edison N.J. to take the foxes, Mouflons, and kid goats on The Pet Stop" with Dr. Brian Voynick. D.V.M.. It is great publicity for the zoo and lots of fun for the day. Still work, but a different kind of work.

On the way home, Dr. Ted mentioned that his son Matt was looking for an internship. Matt came for an interview. I had five applications on my desk but agreed to take Matt on. Matt started a few days later, his life became a blend of zoo nursery work, college, and working on horses with his dad, Dr. Ted.

I was unsure about taking on a male intern, but figured, what the heck, I would treat him just like working with my nephew, Hunter. Hunter had become an integral part of the workforce and we worked together well. Matt was tall, thin and strong like Hunter. Matt had his father's recognizable loping gait and the same cadence to his familiar voice. Matt had short dark hair and piercing blue eyes with an easy grin, and was somewhat shy. The young single girls in the pizza shop immediately took notice and so did every single girl visitor. Matt was great with educating the public on the animals in the nursery, especially if the visitor was female! I expected that. Education is part of the intern experience, so Matt was at my side learning how to raise foxes, the Mouflons, rabbits, goats, and peacocks. Matt would help, like all the other female interns would help give bottles to the adult tigers during a demonstration. Matt also helped prepare fruits and veggies for the parrots, Rhesus monkeys and baboons. I had prided myself on teaching my previous female interns how to do every thing, including carrying buckets of water, bales of hay, and the proper way to hold an alligator. Well, Matt was a farm boy so all those things were no problem AND he knew how to drive a truck and tractor. We got along just fine, though every now and then I would loose Matt, later to find him checking out the antique guns in the museum or playing with the foxes. I barked at Matt once too often and then my Dad would bark at me.

Zoo Momma

"Give the kid a break," Dad instructed. "He is a volunteer."

So I tried. Often Hunter would stop by and borrow Matt to help load a couple of wagons of hay into the hay mow. And Matt would go with Hunter to feed the carnivores. With his easy going funny personality, and adventurous spirit, Matt's company made everyday chores a lot more fun. I was leery of loosing my male intern to the more macho parts of the adult zoo, but I have to admit, Matt hung in there with me. And I was glad to have him.

Matt taught me a lot, Hunter nicknamed him Mr. Wickapedia. In the daytime we would chat about a certain specie, then at night Matt would look it up via Google, giving me a more in-depth report in the morning. It always surprised me how much I knew! Does that make sense? But there is a lot that Google reveled. After five days a week all summer, Matt and I covered just 'bout every animal at the zoo. Matt left after lunch every day to go to college, he only had one semester left until he graduated in animal science.

One Sunday zoo visitors called the admission's desk to let us know that a litter of assorted colored piglets had been born and one black one was wounded. Matt and I zoomed in my Zoo Momma Mobile to the pig paddock by the elk. Matt being the unpaid intern was not allowed to participate in any thing dangerous, so he was to be the receiver. I unlocked the gate, and walked to the momma black sow who, fortunately, was nested by the fence. Matt stayed outside the fence to receive the wounded offspring. I knew the momma sow, I had helped raise her in the nursery a year or so before. Sammy had ten piglets in her litter. And one did have a nasty gash. A V shaped flap of skin hung down off it's hip. I grabbed the scared -read that suddenly squealing at the top of it's lungs- piglet with my Phylstrom tongs (snake grabbers). I did not want to risk my hand that close to a momma of any specie even though I had helped to raise her. I quickly moved away towards the fence with piggy in my hand, and handed it to Matt through the larger fencing on top. I could see Sammy Sow getting agitated by her panicked, squealing piglet. I moved quickly out of the way and out of the rock strewn acre large paddock.

Matt and I performed first aid on the screaming piglet on the picnic table by the famous Space Farms Snake Den. I was trying to Q-tip out debris from the wound when Matt chimed in.

"I've seen my father use a syringe with water to flush out a wound," Matt quietly suggested between piggy squeals.

"Great idea," I left Matt with the wiggly piggy who quieted after I stopped poking his raw meat with a scratchy Q-tip. I returned with a syringe that did the job with more finesse' and less pain, therefore less squealing. After a good dose of betadine, I used a piece of duct tape (again- donchyajust love that stuff?) for a bandage, to cover the wound from dirt, flies and possible maggots, and to tightly bind the three inch flap of skin to the piggy's body so it could re-attach. I saw Matt raise a single eyebrow. I explained that duct tape is the only thing that will hold a bandage on a tiger. The sticky part would also stay on the piggy when he was back with Sammy sow. Matt and I successfully re-placed the little black piglet with a five inch strip of gray shiny duct tape back with mom. As we left the pig paddock the duct taped piglet was nursing right next to his siblings. I thought the silver duct tape gave the piggy a punk rock look. Now I keep a supply of neat colored duct tape on hand- never can tell when you might need a little peacock or leopard colored duct tape.

All our work was for naught by the next morning. We checked on the new litter and the entire litter was missing. Carried off by black vultures in the night. I hate those birds. We have a depredation permit, but they are sneaky sons'o guns.

The Unsinkable Molly Brown, a little Mouflon Yvette, Stephanie and I had raised the year before had a baby of her own. But Molly was not doing well, she kept bloating up. Matt and I went out to rouse her and get her on her feet so she could fart out the gas. Matt came in one day and had Googled the answer, mineral oil. So we gave Molly a baby bottle full of mineral oil. She would still take a baby bottle from me. That worked for a couple of weeks. Great job Matt. I do not think 'Google it' in those scenarios, that is a millennial generation kind of thinking. Then a couple of weeks out, Molly bloated up again, when we were off and I did not catch it. She was dead the next morning in behind the shed.

This is where I started to learn a lot about myself. I had lost animals in front of my female interns, and shed tears in front of them and with them. I lost Molly who had struggled with life from day one, I nursed her through her first few rough weeks of infancy to adult hood and saw her through her first lambing. She died despite what Matt and I had done for her. I sent Matt to the far side of the zoo with a fabricated chore, and I went into the ladies rest room at the zoo and had a cry. I did not want Matt, my male intern to think of me as a softie. I wanted him to think of me as a professional. But my gal interns would have understood. Probably so would Matt, but I did not give him the chance. A zoo visitor came into the zoo rest room, saw me crying, and asked if I was ok. I said yes, but then explained about loosing Molly. She wrapped her arms around me and we both had a good cry. Then I felt better, splashed cold water on my face and went about my workday.

I started to notice after that, there were subtle ways I was treating Matt, my only male intern differently than my gal interns. We raked the barnyard every morning, washed bottles and collected eggs. I would have Matt do the 'manly' raking, while I washed bottles. He could go get bales of hay, while I retrieved the bales for my female interns. Little things like that. I understood why Matt wanted to go work with the guys in the zoo, and allowed it, but would have been angry if my gal interns left as frequently to do so.

Jackie was home visiting one time and saw me dusting dirt off of Matt's back. Who knows where the dirt came from?

"Mom!" Jackie reprimanded. "You just can't touch him like that."

"Why not? He has dirt, dust and maybe ticks or spiders on his back," I replied, still looking at Matt's dusty T-shirted back.

"You have to ask permission first!" Jackie my consummate professional stated.

"Ted told me to treat him like I would treat Hunter," I sheepishly replied.

"It's ok, Lori," Matt forgave me. "My mom does that too." He grinned.

So after that I would simply state "Jackie's rule" and then go ahead and dust Matt off, or do such other motherly things. I would often take photos of Matt holding animals and grab his phone out of his pocket, but I did always ask first. If he was holding an animal with two hands, it was tough for him to get his own phone out of his pocket to take a selfie without dropping the animal. So "Jackie's rule" came into existence with Matt, whereas with all my gal interns I just pick pocketed the phones. Zoo keeping, and especially zoo keeping in the nursery is a very hands on job. I have become very close with all my interns in a mentor, motherly, fun and kooky aunt kind of way.

Matt's mom, Jennifer came and had lunch with us a few times and my animals had more check ups from Dr. Ted in that summer than ever before. Matt and Ted made a great team trimming miniature horses' hooves.

Dr. Ted had warned me ahead of time that Matt hated snakes and would not work with them.

"Don't worry about that," I said. "I'll have him over that in a short time, it is part of the job." Matt was hesitant at first but by day three on the job, he was handling Charlie the king snake. Taking pictures and sending them to his petrified mom. *Told you so Ted!* After that Matt assisted me with all the snake jobs, including helping my Dad with the big snake clean out jobs.

One day Dad and I had just started to clean the albino 8 ft python. I asked/ordered Matt to get a bucket of water. Before Matt took five steps towards the bucket, Dad chipped in.

"Don't be so bossy," Dad instructed. "I want to show Matt something, you get the water." I 'harrumphed' and went to get the water at the side of Grammas house, twenty feet away from the snake cage. I'm older, but my hearing is just fine and was fine tuned by my seething anger of being stepped over, again.

"This snake hook, here, look Matt," Dad started to explain. "This snake hook was made by my father Ralph from the brake rod of an old Model T Ford back in the 1930's. This is a piece of history here at Space Farms."

Matt intently listened. And I must say innocently unaware of my flash of anger. I was a card carrying member of the National Organization of Women , N.O.W. in the seventies and am a dyed in the wool feminist. I am capable of doing any job at the zoo. Where the men folk use their muscles, I have learned to use other methods, animal behavior and tools. But I can do it. My Grandfather Ralph told me that when I was five.

Now does anybody else see the problem here? Matt was MY assistant, twenty two *(read that stronger than me)* years old. Dad wanted ME to fetch the bucket of water, while he told Matt , a young MAN, about MY family history. A tidbit of info that I had not heard before. Yeah, I might not be into mechanical stuff, but I am into snakes and I know the family history with snakes, and the Model T tie in was interesting for me also. But nooo. Lori go do the work, we have guy things to talk about. Not Matt's fault at all. Just another example of my father's un-self-recognized misogynistic behaviors and beliefs. And as I said before, I had some of those beliefs also. Matt unknowingly taught me that.

I enjoyed having all my interns, Jennie, Sierra, Vickie, Yvette, Stephanie, Matt, Alison, niece Lindsey and nephew Hunter. I feel it is important to pass on the knowledge, especially the special hands on nuances of nursery zoo keeping that so many folks overlook or just don't know. And part of that comfort is in the touch of a mother's (or father's) gentle paw or human hand.

Chapter 78 Titus and Osman

My cell phone rang as I was putting on my running sneakers at 7:15 a.m. on July 13th. *No I don't jog, I just run all day long!* I had packed the car with the luggage and fishing supplies that Doug and I would need for our week's vacation fishing at the Mountain River Lodge in Deep River, Ontario Canada. We look forward to the week at our favorite vacation spot all year. I had to get to the zoo to do my zoo chores before we took off at noon. "Sharply at noon!" I believe were Doug's exact words. Doug was already at work at the zoo.

My pesky cell phone announced the caller: "Call from: Hunter the Great". *Hunter had originally programmed his name and number into my phone. He was younger and it was cute - then.* I immediately, instinctually worried about Doug and his heart. Doug had watched his diet, taken all the medications, quit smoking and done all the right stuff. But once you've witnessed a loved one's heart attack, that nagging thought is always in the back of your mind. And everyone knows not to call me in the morning before 8 a.m. if it is not an emergency.

"This is either tiger cubs or a heart attack," I cryptically spouted as I grabbed my keys. "And it damn well better not be a heart attack!" I quickly added thinking to un-jinx my husband.

"It's tiger cubs, and we're having problems with Lily," Hunter said quickly, "Can you come down right now?"

"My sneaks are on , I'm out the door." I stated as I grabbed my keys. As I started my car, I called Dr. Ted. Got him first ring.

"Your kid is about to have the experience of a lifetime. Tiger cubs coming in tell Matt to get here, ASAP," myonegiantrunonsentence to Dr. Ted.

"OK," was all the time I could allot to Dr. Ted to reply as I clicked my cell off. *I have a short driveway.*

I drove the two blocks to the zoo, used my gate zapper inside my car and made sure the gate was closing before I left the kitchen door area. *Never can tell what might happen and we did not want tigers running out of the zoo. Just kidding. Well, think about it, not really kidding.* It was a quick drive past the Syrian Grizzlies and over the hill to the lions/tigers. At the top of the hill, I saw Hunter at the bottom of the hill, waving me to the lions' side of the condo-den section. I noticed the lions were locked out into their grassy section. I was still in the car as Hunter began to speak.

"Lily had them outside, and we can't get her up on the concrete," Hunter's voice was full of the excitement we all felt. "And the black vultures …We need to lock her up on the concrete, see if you can call her in. "

"Ok." I said as I put the car in park in the middle of the green lawn. I got out of my navy blue SUV and approached the lion's side of the concrete section. Doug was standing at the chute gate on the other side All three tigers knew him well and were not afraid of him. They usually obeyed him, but not today. I saw Lily out in the grassy section, at the beginning of the chute. I could hear the cubs screaming in the far section of the ¼ acre grassy paddock. But the big boy, Charlie tiger was just standing inside the chute facing toward the grassy section, blocking Lily's entry.

"Charlie!, Back it up Charlie, come on big boy back it up!" I loudly commanded. Once again the big tiger surprised me. I had not raised this tiger, and did not interact with him on a daily basis. Charlie, tossed a look over his shoulder at me, and backed up out of the chute onto the concrete section.

Lily peered at me from the far side of the chute. As soon as Charlie cleared the chute, when she and I had eye contact, I called her in.

"Lily, hey big girl, come on over here," I cooed to her affectionately. And she happily plodded up the chute onto the concrete towards me. Doug pulled the horizontal slide door and locked it into place. Everyone breathed a sigh of relief. I walked to the tiger side to give Lily loves, her positive reward. The men entered the grassy section in search of the noisy cubs. Lily seemed her normal self, not agitated or even slightly off kilter after just having delivered cubs. The underside of her tail was a little bloody, in a normal delivery kind of way.

Doug, Hunter and Ed entered the grassy section to retrieve the two sandy brown and black striped cubs that Ed had first heard, then seen. After they brought me the two cubs, the rest of the large grass tufts and the fallen logs were searched for more cubs. No other cubs were found. Tigers have one to six cubs, one or two being the norm for first time moms.

Dad, Hunter, Ed, Doug and I inspected the cubs. Two tiny tot tiger males in very good shape.

"Your call, Lori," Dad quietly said. "Lily did not have them in the den, and the vultures are flying." Everyone knew Doug and I were leaving for Canada at noon. If we put them in the den, the cubs would have Tara and Charlie (both with no milk) but there was no guarantee that Lily would go into the den. Lily had been hesitant to go into the den since the male lion Attila had scared her upon her first entrance a year ago. Even with the visual barrier the guys had erected, Lily would still sit outside in the grass in the rain and snow. *So do tigers in the wild by the way.* In my heart, mind and professional opinion there was no choice. The vultures were circling, the cubs were crying, Lily was an inexperienced mother, and not exhibiting any normal maternal behavioral markers. Eventually the two male cubs would have to come out anyway or Charlie the alpha male would eliminate his competition upon the two cubs' maturity.

"Call Lindsey, Hunter," I asked. "Matt is on his way. I have prepped the two kids for the job. A job that they are now going to learn real fast." And the tiny tiger cubs were placed in my arms. *How can I get out of a fishing trip?* My mind was a jumble of thoughts as I drove to the office nursery. *Doug will be so angry if I don't go.*

"Hey Hunter, want to go on a free fishing trip to Canada?", I half joked to Hunter. You've got four hours to pack your bags."

" I would Lee, but with Doug gone…" Hunter's eyes were glittering with laughter, he knew my vacation was no longer a priority for me. *Ok, Darn!* "Besides you've got to teach someone someday." *Truer words were never spoken.*

Zoo Momma

Yeah, he was right.

I drove to the office nursery which had been prepped the week before. The cubs were no surprise for me. Doug had reported to me that he had seen Charlie breed Lily on April 1st. I thought he was pulling an April Fool's Day joke, until I saw the activity myself the next day. Three and a half months gestation would bring us up to mid July. But I had counted days so many times before with Tara and nothing had ever happened. Lily was very young to breed, maturity in female tigers is usually at three years and Lily was only two. Oh Hell!

I had ordered in the special Zoologic Milk Matrix, 25/42 made for big cats. I had written a three page *(yeah I know, I didn't know that I knew three pages worth)* what to do list for newborn cubs and gone over the info with Matt, Lindsey and Hunter. I could not think of one person that would or could drop everything and go on a sudden fishing trip with Doug. My Dad would be around and he taught me everything about raising animals. If something went wrong, Dr. Ted is on everyone's speed dial. I told everyone not to hesitate to ask questions of Dad or Dr. Ted if even the slightest doubt arose. I would be a cell phone call away. I constantly reminded myself that kids Lindsey and Matt's age have human babies and raise them just fine. So everyone was prepped, except for me. I was not prepared for the sense of abandonment I was feeling. And I was the horrible abandon-er!

Anyhow… Matt got to the zoo first, followed momentarily by Lindsey. I had put the two cubs in the incubator to warm up the screaming and cold cubs. We went step by step just like I had written for the kids, who were by the way 19 and 22 years old. First we checked each cub for birth wounds. Lindsey worked with one cub, Matt with the other. Each taking a turn at the incubator. No puncture wounds or other issues.

The umbilical cords were long so Lindsey held down her cub while I tied it off. Then we switched, I held the cub still while she cut the cord within two inches of the tiny cub's body. Repeat with Matt and his cub. I stressed to the kids that the cubs need to eat, pee, poop and sleep. So be careful not to over handle. I fetched warm water and wash cloths. I let the kids stroke down the cubs in a stimulating, mother tongue manor, read that not too gently, but a good stiff rub down. It was killing me not to do the work myself. It was so hard to standby and watch them do the job that I love. I mixed up formula and gave Matt and Lindsey each a bottle. I pointed out the nipple cuts and the black magic marker line on the nipple for the full bore open position. The cubs drank voraciously, a few drops less than the two ounces I put in the bottles.

"How did you know they would drink only two ounces?" Matt questioned.

"Magic," I chuckled. "Ok just experience, I guess," I answered Matt. "These are tigers number 14 and 15 for me, but it never gets old!" Then a question dawned on me. Matt liked to fish! He fished a couple of times a week on the Delaware river only ten miles from the zoo.

"Hey, Matt, want an all expense paid fishing vacation in Canada? You

327

like to fish. How fast can you pack?" I asked hopefully.

"No, thanks," Matt laughed, he, Lindsey and I knew this was going to be a great, possibly once in a lifetime experience for them. I was having no luck finding someone to go fishing in Canada with Doug. I don't think the detriment was Doug, I know the anchor was the cubs.

We weighed the cubs, 2 # and 2# 1 oz. Good sized cubs. We chatted gleefully about the cubs, Lindsey and Matt working out a babysitting schedule. The cubs were not supposed to leave the Space Farms property according to state law. Lindsey would take the cubs home to her dad Parker's house at night. Parker lived on Space Farms property just like Dad and I. Feedings were every two hours around the clock until about midnight. Then start again at 6 a.m. Matt would be at the zoo every morning at 8a.m to cover my work and take care of the cubs until he left to go to his summer college courses at noonish. Matt and Lindsey would cover the cubs for the next seven days straight, Parenthood does not take a day off. That would give Lindsey time to work the admissions desk from 9 a.m. to 4p.m every day, and the second person at admissions desk would come in at 11a.m.. Lindsey would feed the cubs whenever Matt was not there. What a schedule, and what a responsibility placed upon the two 'kids'. *Then I would think: But wait a minute here, Lor, you raised your first lion cub at age 19, they can do this. They have the same advantage that you had, my dad Fred, plus they have Dr. Ted, Matt's dad. You better go to Canada.* I told the kids what I had thought. The banter in the nursery was upbeat, positive, Rosie the Riveter "You can do it!" kind of attitude. I'm not sure whom I was convincing, Lindsey, Matt or myself.

I stayed with Lindsey and Matt and the cubs until their second feeding. Sierra stopped her outside volunteering and came to see the cubs also. All was going well. I reiterated the need for sleep for the cubs. In the wild mom nurses and licks them clean, stimulates for pee and poop, then the cubs sleep until they are hungry again. All the food energy is needed to grow. If you handle them too much the energy is used up in fighting the stress of being jostled around. These cubs were also immunologically challenged, not having received colostrums of the natural mother's first milk. The less hands and exposure to germs the better for the cubs. Sometimes love is letting them be.

Matt and Lindsey were confident in their work, Lindsey had helped me with Lily two years before and Matt had helped with the fox kits that spring. I told them both they could call my cell any time day or night, and I would be in touch via my tablet, email or Facebook.

I left for my house, about fifteen minutes after I saw Doug speed up the road. Yeah, I was late, and I still had to pack the car with frozen food items before we left. Doug's healthy heart diet required low salt, so I cooked and froze vacation food ahead of time. Doug was in and out of the shower. We drove out of Beemerville at 12:30. I was only a half hour late. I could not find anyone to go on vacation with Doug.

The trip to River Mountain Lodge was uneventful, which was good, I had an exciting morning. I slept a little. We stopped at Watertown, N.Y. for the night. I called Lindsey and was relieved at the sound of her calm voice and that the cubs were doing well. Matt and Lindsey had named 'their' respective tigers: Titus and Osman.

Every other year the fishing vacation at the River Mountain Lodge was a relaxing wonderful week. This time it was the worst week ever. I had to keep myself perpetually busy to keep my mind off the cubs. I only had cell reception at the lodge, not out on the wilderness lakes where we fished. *Daaahhh why didn't I think of that ahead of time?* My tablet got goofed up and lost all my email addresses. But I could message via Facebook and kept in touch with Lindsey every morning before Doug and I left for fishing. I checked in again after we got back from the lakes. The weather was gorgeous all week, the fish were biting like crazy. Doug had a great time, even though I was very distracted. I fished, painted rocks, read trashy novels, and sunbathed a little bit. As soon as my mind had a still moment, I wanted to be back in Beemerville. It was a tough emotional week. All seemed fine with the cubs. I just did not want to be on vacation.

I kept up with the publicity that was running though the papers and TV with the cubs, Lindsey and Matt were on the cover of the New Jersey Herald with the cubs! Lindsey and Matt did a wonderful job with the cubs. I could not have done better myself. Dr. Ted checked on the cubs daily with or through Matt. Even Sierra pitched in. Jennie Beckman had helped with numerous cubs before, she stopped by frequently. Victoria Ciccolelle, my intern the year Lily was born, also stopped by to help. Every one was 'on call', the cubs thankfully had no medical issues.

When the weather forecast in Canada called for the last two days of our vacation to be rainy, I hemmed and hawed and tried to find a way to tell Doug that I wanted to go home. Needed to go home. I wanted this torture-cation to end. We were discussing the weather at dinner and what to do for our last two days. Usually if it rains we relax, stay in, he reads and I shop, read or paint for the day. Suddenly Doug just blurted out.

"Want to go home in the morning?" He gently suggested. There was not a speck of anger in his voice, for me wanting to cut his precious fishing trip short to go back to the zoo for the cubs. He knew me well. *What a great guy! To give up the last of his favorite fishing vacation days so I can go to my passion, the cubs at the zoo! Not a lot of men like him that's for sure!*

"OH Babe, you know me well!" I chimed in. "I can be packed in two hours, you go square up at the desk." Terri and Diane, the owners, knew our family, our family business, knew of the tiger cubs being born and they would understand.

We left at four a.m. the next morning. I called Lindsey from the road when we got to Watertown, ½ way home. I told her we would be home by 5 p.m. ish. I had worried that Lindsey would not want to give up the cubs. I had to come to terms with the possibility of the next generation taking over my job that I loved so much. *Well, more sleep for me I figured.* I could tell from Lindsey's voice that was not the case.

"Awesome, Lee, can I take the cubs up to your house?" she asked. " I can have them there at four."

"Sure, make yourself at home, kid," I told Lindsey. " We'll be there ASAP.

"Fabulous!" was Lindsey's reply.

We arrived home as predicted and beautiful raven haired Lindsey and her handsome boyfriend Dominic, (think Leonardo Di Caprio) were sitting on our couch watching TV when we walked in. Titus and Osman were sleeping off their last bottles in their warm cozy brooder box, electric heating pad plugged in. The cubs looked chubby and clean. *Great Job Kids*! Lindsey, Dominic and I chatted while Doug unpacked the car.

"I never realized the stress level," Lindsey suddenly blurted out. "It is not the cubs, they were doing fine, it was the people. Every one wanted to touch them and I had to be the one to say no. That was tough!"

We commiserated over the myriad of problems dealing with family, friends, reporters and the general public when raising immunologically challenged cubs. And then there is N.J. state law that says no one but keepers get to touch exotic animals in N.J. Once the word was out via news media and social media the visitors to the zoo increased. Everyone wanted to see the cute cuddly cubs. I was the only one who could understand what Lindsey and Matt had gone through. The worry about the health of the newborn cubs and the stress of dealing with humans is overwhelming. Worrying that something would go wrong, and then YOU have to explain to hundreds of people what went wrong, on top of feeling bad about the death. *Yeah I know that worry! I live with that stress with every baby I raise*. Lindsey was glad I was home too, I think. Lindsey and Matt had become very attached to their charges, and that would continue as long as the cubs were with us at the zoo. Lindsey and Matt had earned their stripes.

I was glad to be home, I was where I was supposed to be doing what I was called to do. The cubs progressed according to all the normal developmental markers for tiger cubs I had experienced before.

Due to the timing of the cubs birth on July 13th, my weeks torture-cation, and the deadline of the newspaper that goes between the zoos, I was at my desk the very next morning putting an ad in for the cubs to find a new home. After that ad is placed all we can do is wait and see what zoo wants the cubs. As I finished my phone call to the inter-zoo paper, Dr. Ted stopped by to see the cubs and Matt.

"Right back at it? Huh Lor?" Dr. Ted joked with me, he knew the zoo/animal business does not stop for vacations, neither does his vet business. "How was the fishing?"

"Fine," I curtly stated, momentarily saddened by the call I had just made. "Let's check on the cubs." We walked to the office nursery a couple of steps away. We chatted about the cubs and the minor staffing issues that happened while I was gone.

"Matt has really enjoyed this," Dr. Ted suddenly turned into Daddy Ted, beaming and proud of his son.

"The kids did a great job," I said. " I was just putting the word out that the cubs were available." He and I knew we could not keep the tiny tigers, we had three adult tigers. Charlie the male would not accept the young males back into his territory. The cost of making a new enclosure for two more tigers was prohibitive. The cubs would be placed at another zoo.

"Let me know when you need a health certificate," Dr. Ted said, "These cubs are in great shape, your cubs always are." *Awwwhh Gee, thanks Ted.*

"It will be a while, they can't leave on a plane until they are eight weeks old," I mentioned. "Unless the new parent zookeepers want to drive here…"

We chatted about other things, our families the kids, and the cubs, while Dr. Ted did his physical exam of the cubs. All was great. Next we would check on the skin condition of the Rhesus monkeys, which had been steadily improving all summer, and the rescued miniature horses with over grown hooves.

Dr. Ted stayed for a soda then started back to his office at the Animal Hospital of Sussex County. Matt was leaving to float horse teeth for a client.

Visitors to the zoo were increasing, so I started to do a tiny tiger talk during the feedings. The cubs were still too small to be outside, they could barely crawl at one week old, so they were in the office nursery incubator. I have used the incubator since Newton Memorial Hospital donated it to us when they re-vamped their maternity wing. The addition of clear Plexiglas sides allows the visitors to see the infants inside. I would stay inside, nurse and clean the tigers. Matt or Sierra would go outside and tell the visitors what we were doing. Or Matt would feed and I would talk. Until one day I had to bright idea to use a baby monitor system. I put the speaker outside the nursery window. True credit for this idea should go to Randy Cosh, Ed's wife, who was our next door neighbor and came to watch a tiger feeding while, her son slept. In her hand was a baby monitor. *Now why didn't I think of that years before? And I have been shouting through windows!*

At two weeks old the tiny tiger tots started to walk, their eyes opened, full of wonder. Titus started to shed out his hair. Now the walking, and eyes opening are right on developmental schedule for tigers. The hair shedding doesn't usually start until ten weeks old. The subtle browns of the 'puppy fur' act as camouflage in the wild, the hot orange color would stand out in the green jungle or beige savannah. Shedding is usually so gradual you don't notice except for the hair on your clothes. The brighter orange color slowly replaces the softer rusty brown hair. But Titus was almost bald! In just a couple of days! So I started Titus on a vitamin A D &E regimen, those being the vitamins most helpful to skin and hair.

Lindsey, Matt, Dr. Ted, the tiger cubs and I were scheduled to go down to "The Pet Stop" on Channel 12 News 12 New Jersey based in Edison N.J.. The cubs behaved well, and I picked the brains of our Dr. Ted V.M.D. and Dr. Brian Voynick D.V.M. on Titus's hair loss during lunch. Hormonal or dietary. I could not see how it was dietary as I was using the same diet that I used on the other fourteen tigers I had raised, with nary a problem. Hormonal, well, there was nothing I could do about that, just wait it out and help him get through it. *Nothing like an embarrassed tiger with low self esteem due to patterned baldness!* I continued the vitamins, I did not know if it helped but it could not hurt. Titus's new orange fur grew in within two weeks, but he sure looked funny during that time.

Meanwhile Osman and Titus continued to grow. At three weeks old they were adorable fluff balls. The cubs graduated to the outside nursery as soon as I thought their mobility was up to par. They could move out of the hot sun and into the shade of their grassy enclosure easily. Matt, Lindsey and all my other previous interns all played with the tigers to make them handle-able by any future keeper. According to schedule the cubs were started on ground venison at four weeks old, when their carnasial teeth came through the gums. They also enjoyed chewing on leg bones with some raw meat still on the bone. *Yummmm!* The cubs were still coming home with me at night, even though the nights were plenty warm in July and August. The night bottles and play time with me is MY special time. Time for me to just kick back and play with my babies. Time eludes me in the daytime, but the cubs had the interns to play. So the nights belonged to me, and I treasured every moment.

During one of the daytime playtimes with Yvette, my intern from the year before, she noticed a little bump on Titus's right side just behind his shoulder blade when the cubs were six weeks old. We inspected it. It looked like an ingrown hair bump. I kept an eye on it and showed it to Dr. Ted on our next visit. He suggested we bring the cub in for a visit and take a sample of the area. Dr. Ted was going on vacation, so Dr. Pam Schott would take care of the minor procedure. I knew Dr. Schott, I had compete faith in her, she is a great Vet, with a wonderful reputation. I had worked with her many times before.

I took both cubs with me to Dr. Pam, if they were separated they just cry, since they had been together since birth. After being weighed and cuddled by the veterinary technicians, Dr. Pam took a scraping sample of what now looked like a dime sized raspberry birthmark, you know the kind you see on human kids. It would be sent away for pathology.

A couple of days later, the report came back. The bump had become a fatty mast cell tumor. These mast cell tumors were common. Even though Dr. Schott was confident that if left alone, it would go away, I was devastated. No one was going to want a cub with a tumor. Even if it was a temporary birthmark kind of tumor. What if the tumor did not recede? What would we do with one lonely cub? I had hoped to place both cubs at the same facility, so they would not be lonely. Now what was I gonna do?

Dr. Spinks returned from his vacation and stopped by to see the growing tigers and do a 'walk through' of the zoo. A 'walk through' of the zoo is the term used for a general inspection, where Dr. Ted's trained eye may pick up something with the animal collection that we zookeepers did not. No new problems were found, the animals were hail and hearty, the monkeys were in fine fur, the baboons les antsy with the new toys provided. Rescued mini horses hooves needed to be trimmed again, and we set up a time for that procedure.

I had told Dr. Ted about the problems of placing a tiger cub with a potential tumor and expressed my concern for Titus's future.

"Why don't I perform cryosurgery on the mass?" Dr. Ted asked. "I have the equipment, it's quick, easy, pain free and we can do it right here at the zoo."

"Let's do it, no one is going to want a cub with a tumor," I worried.

The next Sunday at 8 a.m. Dr. Ted performed the cryo surgery in the zoo on top of a folding table right outside the admissions door near the colorful rental strollers. Matt, Parker and I were there. Cryosurgery is done with only a local anesthetic for the normal adult cat or dog patient. Anesthesia in cubs is different, and always dangerous. So the decision was made to go without anesthesia, the freezing part would not be painful and very quick. No that would not be painful. But restraining a twenty pound tiger cub that had never been restrained was not easy. It took Parker, Matt, and myself to hold the small cub down and absolutely still while Dr. Ted froze the now nickel sized spot. Wow, never thought Titus would be that strong, but take my word, he was. He did not like being restrained and he let us know it by whimpering, whimpering very loud.

The whole procedure took only three minutes. When Dr. Spinks was done, the cryosurgery had frozen a circle the size of a fifty cent piece.

"The tumor will die along with a few adjacent cells and grandulation, (grow new tissue and fill in), will follow with complete healing in two to three weeks," Dr. Ted explained.

I cuddled Titus, consoling him, and he immediately licked my face. He seemed unaffected by his so recent surgery. I carried him to the office nursery so he could relax out of the sun and prying eyes. I put Titus in the black wire doggie corral I had set up for him with all his favorite blankets and toys. He made one circle around the corral, inspecting the contents of the toy box. Then Titus flopped down on the entire pile of stuffed animals and fell asleep. He had just had a rough wrestle with three humans, and was most likely exhausted for expending the energy physically and the mental energy of not knowing what was going on. He needed a nap.

Dr. Ted and I checked on him an hour later. As we opened the door to the office nursery, Titus came bounding towards us! Happy to see us, chuffing, and ready to play. The frozen deep red tumor had fallen off when Titus climbed out of the four foot high corral. What had been fifty cent sized was much smaller when it thawed. Dr. Ted was happy with the surgery, and told me to keep the area clean. Which was not going to be a problem as Titus was licking the area as we spoke. All was well when we placed Titus back with Osman for the rest of the day. I had bought green low pile carpeting for the cage in the nursery, so Titus would not get dirt in his surgery site. The two tiger tots played the day away as if nothing had happened.

Intern Matt's special job that day was to keep an eye on the tiger cubs, and break up any rough housing or anything that may hurt Titus' wound. Tough job, but somebody had to do it!!

All I had to do now was wait for the phone calls to determine where Titus and Osman would go. I had received one phone call, for one cub. I was holding out. I expected more calls on the cubs, I wanted them to go someplace together. Male tigers in the wild live solitary lives, except for the brief mating time. If a zoo wanted two male tigers they had to get them as sibling cubs and keep them together. Strange male tigers would fight to the death if put in the same territory. And I did not want my babies to face a lifetime alone. All I could do was wait and pray for the right phone call….

Lindsey Space and Matt Spinks hold Titus and Osman a pair of tiger cubs.
Photos by Lori Space Day

Chapter 79 Road Trip!

In 2003 Tara had three litters of cubs, totaling ten cubs. I found homes for all of them within two weeks of their births. The cubs did not always leave right then, some cubs I kept for up to twelve weeks old due to transportation or other issues. With each cub birth, no matter what kind of cub, lion, tiger or bear, *OH MY!*, as soon as I knew the cubs were healthy and eating well, I would place an ad in the zoo newspaper that went between the zoos. I would also call the five zoos we dealt with on a regular basis to see if they wanted cubs or knew another zoo that wanted them. So after I placed Tara's ten cubs I had a list of about fifteen places to call that wanted cubs in the future. That was as of 2003.

In 2003 the number of wild tigers was exceeded by the number of tigers in captivity. There were less than 7,500 tigers left in the wild. Fast forward, to 2014 and the wild numbers had dropped to 3,200, according to the National Geographic website. There are more tigers than that just in the state of Texas. Texas also has the most liberal wildlife ownership laws by the way. *Someday I want to live there, just me and my animals, oh, pipe dreams!* The decimation of the wild population is due to the human overpopulation encroaching on the tigers territory, bringing humans and tigers n closer proximity. The other main cause of the lower population of tigers is the poaching of the tigers for folk lore medicine. You would think the invention of certain little blue pills for men would have saved the tiger!

Anyhooo… according to U.S.D.A. law, which issues our licenses to operate a zoo, Titus and Osman could not go on an airplane until they were eight weeks old. That was just fine with me, as the cubs would stay with me*, oops I mean the zoo*, until after Labor Day. That would be great for the zoo visitors and ok, lets face it, great for me too. I love my babies. I do realize how special it is to raise the big cats and the myriad of other animals at the zoo. It is a special privilege granted to me by God in granting me the advantage of my birth within our unusual family.

When I placed the ad in the zoo newspaper after returning from Canada, I expected an avalanche of phone calls. Surprise, I got one call from Georgia, a man with a delightful southern accent. He wanted one cub. We chatted, exchanged information and photos via emails. He wanted one cub. I really wanted both cubs to go together, so the one left over would not be lonely. I told the southern voice that I would not ship a cub until it was eight weeks old. I took his phone number.

"Yes Mam' Miss Lori," he softly crooned and we ended our conversation. I waited for more phone calls on the tiger cubs. I was getting very attached, how could one not? Adorable, affectionate and cuddly, the tiger tykes were playful and just plain fun. I wanted the best for my babies. And not one more phone call came in for the cubs! Wow. I expected an avalanche. After five weeks had passed, I pulled out my waiting list that I had kept since 2003 and started to make the phone calls. All of the private zoos had gone out of business, and the big city zoos were stocked with adults and did not want more cubs.

Zoo Momma

Especially two male cubs.

In the meanwhile the cubs were growing, Osman much more aggressive than Titus, each cub developing it's individual personality. Titus was a lover, but had that dime size strawberry birth mark. Now who was going to want a tiger with a potential tumor? The cubs had been together since birth, but who would take Titus? Many a night I worried my self to sleep over that one. Dr. Ted and Dr. Schott reassured me that Titus would be fine. All these thoughts crossed my mind. I had called the Southern Gentleman back and left multiple messages, but had not heard back from him for a couple of weeks. Great! Now I had no home for the twosome tiger cubs.

Amazingly, the Southern Gentleman, (SG), called me back just after Labor Day. I thought he didn't want either cub so he didn't call. I was wrong, SG's father had been sick, so he hadn't had the time to call me back. Did he still want the cub? Yes! Hallelujah. And I wound up my pitch, giving the personality traits of both cubs. I did lay it on thick on how loving Titus was, (which he is), and that Osman was a little more independent, (assertive?). Osman seemed smarter, while Titus was a follower. I also told SG in full disclosure about Titus' birth mark, and volunteered to fax him the report from our vets, saying exactly what the birthmark was. I told the SG that Dr. Spinks was going to cryosurgery the birthmark off, but I had no home scheduled for the tiger tyke.

"Would you consider taking them both?" I pleaded. "One would be so lonely with out the other, and until you get a female for breeding, you could keep them together."

"I could build a bigger cage," SG pondered. We chatted about what he would need if he adopted two cubs.

"You should see them play together!" I purred, "it's so much fun to watch, and they burn off play energy on each other instead of you."

"Alright, I'll take them both," SG was grinning - I could hear that southern smile through the phone! It was not really hard to convince him, he wanted both right from the start, he just didn't know it.

We discussed air plane flight possibilities and we hung up so I could make the arrangements.

Talk about things changing since 2003! Prior to 2003 I had shipped out many cubs, and knew all the rules. Yes, we had to have a wooden crate, with air holes, water refill accessibility, and a pad locked door. We would need to take the crate empty and fill it with bedding, water dish and animal in front of security officers. That was instituted after 9/11. Do not ship any powdered milk. Well, the rules had changed. I would not be able to ship the two cubs together, because they weighed over ten pounds each. This was a major problem for me. The cubs had never been separated. If we separated them at the airport, they would just cry for hours. In today's world of cell phone cameras in every airport employee's pocket, this was a public relations nightmare waiting to happen. I could imagine the headlines complete with screaming cubs photographs in my mind: "Pitiful Crying Tiger Cubs from Space Farms…" And the cost of shipping was prohibitive also.

The SG had the easy answer the next time we spoke.

"Can I talk you into meeting me halfway?" SG asked. " I can drive up half way and you drive down to meet us. Easier on the cubs that way, easier on the pocketbook, easier on us for the worry of an airplane trip."

"Oh Yeah," I stammered, why didn't I think of that? "Let me talk to Dad and figure out a half way point. You can't exactly trade tiger cubs at a rest stop on the highway. I'll call you right back." The solution was so simple, but would be hard on me. You see reader, I hate to drive. Almost to a phobia point when driving in the city or on the Jersey Highways. But I have no problem driving west. But this was south. But I had been on both the major highways I would need to travel. I kept talking my self into bravery. "I can do this!" said my inner Rosie the Riveter.

Dad suggested we meet at the Natural Bridge Zoo in Virginia, it was about halfway. Sounds like a plan. That was a Friday morning, I called SG back and we set up for a Sunday ride to the Natural Bridge Zoo. I called the Natural Bridge Zoo, and left a message for the owner, Karl Morgenson, a long time friend and associate of my Dad's that we would be stopping by with the cubs on Sunday.

Ok, so for me to leave the zoo I have to have all my other work covered. Sierra could do my other nursery work in the morning, Sierra's dad would bring her to the zoo. My Dad would help Sierra if she needed him in the nursery. I wanted someone to ride along, and Karen Walsh, Sierra's mom was willing to make the day long trip. Karen was a bus driver and would have to be home on Sunday night to drive school bus in the morning of Monday. Karen and I had become friends over the years that Sierra became a Junior Zookeeper. Ok let's do it.

Doug, my mechanical hero husband, checked our car out for oil, tire pressure and all the manly stuff men do with cars. He made sure every thing was in good order. I had no car issues to worry about.

I was sorry that Lindsey and Matt would not get to say goodbye, but both kids had gone back to college. The way it goes sometimes.

I had my paperwork in order to bring the cubs, both Veterinary Health Certificates, USDA transport papers, copies of our permits, both Federal and State, info on SG's and transfer of possession papers. I had the car packed with the two crates, extra formula, spare towels for poop clean ups, and toys. I slept fitfully that night, I had my GPS set, a paper map and had map quested the simple directions. Karen met me at my house at 5 am on Sunday the 13th. I let the tigers out in the back yard to pee and poop after Karen and I fed them. We packed up two tigers, two women and left.

Afterward when I discussed my surprising lack of apprehension *during* the drive with Dr. Ted, he told me that I was on a mission, and my zoo mommaness superceded my fear. Ok so maybe. Back to our story...

I was so right on with the behavior patterns of Titus and Osman. I had packed them in separate crates with full bellies hoping they would sleep. I didn't want any stray poop getting in to Titus' open wound from the cryosurgery. Or Osman to rough house in close quarters and rip it open. The wound was healing nicely. Sleep? No go. I swear and Karen will attest to this; those cubs cried for two hours. Karen and I have known each other for about eight years and we both have the gift of gab. We started talking, but very quickly discovered that when the cubs heard my voice, they would cry. So we rode the seven hour trip to Virginia in silence, playing the radio or cds. If you know me personally, you know how hard it is for me to stay quiet for that long. If we needed to communicate we whispered, or faked sign language. Karen is about ten years younger than me, with streaked blonde long hair, she is tall and a genuine sweet person. We did break into laughter when we crossed in to Virginia and John Denver's "Country Roads" started to play.

We took one or two potty breaks for us, and a breakfast break at McDonalds. Karen went into Mc D's to order while I opened the hatch of my SUV and fed the cubs though the front grate of the large pet taxis. Feeding both cubs at the same time, my back was to the restaurant. I did not think a thing about it until the flash of a phone camera went off. I turned around, and saw about twenty people watching me feed the cubs. The cubs were still in their pet taxis, I did not take them out, but I guess it was kind of novel to see two tiger cubs getting a bottle in the parking lot of Mc Donald's. Karen came back with our food we would eat in the car, my turn for a potty break and we were back on the road. Fifteen minutes tops.

We arrived at the Natural Bridge Zoo right at estimated time of noon. Karl met us at the front gate and we waited about twenty minutes for SG and his gorgeous wife to arrive. When SG got out of his truck, he looked like the cover of one of the trashy romance novels I read on vacation. Tall, blondish, worn faded baseball cap, small blue plaid collared shirt tucked into his faded snug jeans, snazzy belt buckle and cowboy boots. Swoon and Sway! His wife looked like she had stepped off the fashion runway also, tall, dark wavy long hair, nice crochet sweater and blue jeans. I knew they had three children from our conversations on the phone. You would never have guessed that she had even one with her fabulous figure. She could have been Miss Georgia! But his voice, cut through me like a hot knife through butter. I love a southern accent.

"Well, nice to meet you Miss Lori," SG said. "Yes Mam that was a long trip!"

I introduced SG and his wife to Karl. We put the tigers' crates into the back of the SUV. We all drove into the zoo proper to Karl's private home area within the center of the zoo. On the way to his home we toured the zoo via his SUV. Karl is well known in the zoological world, he is an expert on many species. He has a reputation for good healthy strong animals. His zoo is open to the public and he does a lot of breeding to help endangered species numbers. I am always fascinated by the amount of tropical birds he has. *Ok maybe a little jealous,* Virginia has much milder weather than we do in N.J. therefore Karl can keep those tropicals with less trouble. Karl has giraffes, which I have always wanted but again the weather is an issue for us.

We let the cubs out to play in Karl's private green grassy island home inside the zoo itself. Other zookeepers gathered around to observe and help wrangle the cubs. The cubs had been cooped up in their large pet taxis for the seven hour trip and wanted to roam around. All of we human travelers were in need of a good stretch too. After Titus and Osman had a good pee and poo, they started to play with whomever was nearby. Karen was in her glory to play with the cubs. I was glad to see SG and his beautiful wife, sit down and interact with both cubs. I knew SG had big cat experience, and could tell by his gentle but stern manor with the cubs he was going to be a great new parent for my cubs. I explained the basic commands I had taught the cubs, "No Bite, No Claws, Open, Sit, Come, Nice and Gentle". I don't know how to explain it, but both cubs gravitated to SG and his wife in a giant hug fest. The feeling of relief that came over me is hard to explain. I knew in that moment my cubs would be just fine. And they would be together.

"These cubs are in great shape," Karl gave me a fantastic compliment, it meant a lot to me, coming from him. I knew they were in great shape, and their training was spot on, but it was nice to hear from a fellow professional. We all chatted about the cubs, their training, eating, sleeping and personalities. I showed the new parents the shrinking cryosurgery wound and explained that Titus was doing great licking it clean, so Dr. Ted (and I), did not feel it needed additional medication. Dr. Ted had assured me that there would not be a recurrence. We all played for about two hours. Then it was time to go to our respective homes. SG and I transferred the cubs' pet taxis into the back of his SUV, where his wife would sit and talk to the cubs. I heard later that they were out of the crates and on her lap half way home. I hope they didn't cry too much. We finished up the traveling paper work on the hood of his huge black SUV.

I said good by to Karl, who sent his regards to my Dad. I hugged SG and his gorgeous wife emphasizing they could call me at any time with any problems or questions. Their new mom climbed in to sit by the cubs. I said my good byes to my boys in the back of a SUV, whispering.

"You be good boys, and make me proud," I was holding back tears all of a sudden, don't know where they came from, I was feeling great about the placement of my guys with these new parents. I was giving a generous amount of kissy noises. "Be nice to each other, no squabbling. You make me proud. " With that said, I rapidly turned on my heel and quickly strode to my blue Hyundai. Karen followed.

We started traveling down the road, to get something to eat, it had been a long time since the breakfast at McDonalds.

"You OK?" Karen was so sweet to ask.

"I'm fine, the cubs will be fine, I really liked the new parents didn't you?" I asked Karen rapid fire. My welled up eyes had receded. We grabbed sandwiches from a local deli and hit the highway once again, eating on the road. This is where it was very good to have a gabby friend like Karen on a trip like this. In as much as Karen and I had to stay quiet on the seven hour trip with the cubs, we gabbed the whole way home. Karen kept the conversation moving along, chatting about everything under the sun. We were both getting tired of the road, and the emotional let down of the departing cubs made us a little silly. But it was all good. Without Karen, if I was alone on that long trip, I would have dissolved into a mud puddle on the side of the highway. But we had a purpose to get the cubs there, and now the purpose was to get home so Karen could drive bus in the morning.

We had left my house at 5a.m. and we got home at 11:30 p.m. 18 ½ hours total on the trip. We were exhausted physically and mentally. Doug was asleep in his chair when we got home, he woke up to say good nite, give me a hug and go to bed. *Well, He sort of waited up.*

Dr. Ted was right, we were on a mission. Mission accomplished. I hit the sack hard that night, and got to the zoo a half hour late the next morning to do my chores. But there was a smile on my heart, my boys would be fine.

Special thanks to Karen for seeing me through this trip.

Chapter 80 Sorry Charlie!

Everyone's ears perked up when the two cell phones went off simultaneously. One is an interruption, now two phones? That means trouble. I watched as Parker and Hunter both reached through their fall jackets for their cell phones. Dr. Ted looked at them, then me with a question in his eyes.

"Must be a fire call," I calmly stated, though calm was not what I was feeling. The six of us stood still, waiting to hear. We were getting set up to neuter Charlie the tiger. There were no homes available for tiger cubs, we found that out with Lily's first litter of Titus and Osman the previous summer. We had three tigers, Tara was an old lady at 18 years old. Charlie and Lily were young. With our average tiger longevity, we would have them for another twenty years. Yes, they might actually outlive me, for a change. IF the world of tigers came to that point, Lily could be bred up until she was fifteen.

This was the time of year to do this operation. It was a warm winter day in early December. There were no flies to lay maggots and complicate healing. Tara and Lily would be able to sleep outside the den, the weather called for no rain. The forecast was for warm weather for the next week to ten days. Charlie could stay in the den, the ladies outside. The planning to put this day together was extensive, from weather to Dr. Ted's schedule, everything was carefully orchestrated.

"Gotta go!" was the simple statement. Parker and Hunter jumped in the Kabota (jitney) and took off for the firehouse. I watched our muscle men ride off over the hill past the rhesus monkeys. We had gathered all the equipment we would need. The list was long: Stretcher, jab pole, tough strong table, blankets, a squeaky toy, lights, generators, buckets, towels, and Dr. Ted had his truck into position. His Vet truck is a rolling magic machine, if Dr. Ted needs anything, poof! Jennie can find it in the truck. Ok so it is not magic, it is the intelligence of planning, of knowing what he will need. And of all the possibilities that could go wrong, and what you would need to fix that problem. No magic, just good planning that comes with experience. Just seems like magic. My Dad's car had the ultimate medicine, if things went drastically wrong or dangerous, the shotgun on the seat. *Well, if you want honesty in my stories, you have to be able to handle the potential possibilities.*

All the supplies were in place, with the exception of the big spot lights and generator. Vickie Cinderella (Ciccolelle), my former intern, came to help and observe for the day. *I mean like really, how often you get to watch a tiger neutering?* Vickie had driven Matt DeBlock in my jitney back to the office to get the beat up old gray Ford pick up with the last two items. Dr. Ted had his generator reved up. Parker and Hunter had been gone a few moments when Hunter called me on my cell.

"We're gonna be a while, there is a chemical spill," Hunter continued but my brain had fuzzed out. *Damn! We've got every thing set up and NOW there is a fire call?* "You can handle it without us." *Damn! There goes our muscle! Double*

Damn! That is one heavy tiger!

"Ok," I hung up as I turned to Dr. Ted, Jennie Beckman, Aisling Howe, (both vet techs), and Dad . "We are on our own, we just lost major muscle, but I can lift, Matt will be back, Jennie? Do we need more muscle than that ?" I looked towards Dr. Ted with my question.

Later both Jennie and Vickie would tell me the look on my face said it all. I was not worried about the procedure, I had total faith in Dr. Ted. It was the lifting of the 500# plus tiger onto the table. Oh and by the way, the life and limb danger if something went wrong. I was glad Parker and Hunter had faith in us to carry through.

"We can neuter him on the floor, then we would not have to lift him," Dr. Ted stated. "We should be fine. Jennie hurt her back so no lifting for her."

"Sounds like a plan!" I was relived that Dr. Ted did not want to reschedule.

Suddenly Matt careened over the hill, pulling onto the sloping grass by the tiger den a little too fast. The beat up gray truck bounced to a stop. The emergency light on it's three foot high orange tripod crashed and fell down in the back of the truck. Our giant heavy generator slid from one side of the dead deer road kill blood stained truck bed to the other. I could see my 87 year old Dad getting hot under the collar before he even spoke.

"It will be ok, Dad, let's just see if the light still works," I calmly stated.

"I've got a light," Dr. Ted chipped in.

"Ooops," Matt DeBlock sheepishly shrugged his shoulders as he approached our group. I was glad Matt was working at the zoo. Bruce and JoAnn DeBlock, Matt's parents had worked for Space Farms also. They were friends of mine and the family. I had worked with them for years. Bruce and JoAnn had passed away within five years of each other, leaving four teen age kids to grow up fast. The four lived in one of the Space Farms rental apartments. Matt was a middle child, tall, strong, and had blonde curly hair women would pay a fortune to have. Matt is soft spoken and soft in his step. I threatened many times to put a tack on his heel so he could not sneak up on me. *I spook easy.* Matt was also a relatively new driver, so his inexperience gave him a break from the steamed cursing I had cut off from Dad. Matt up righted the light and joined the group discussion of how to proceed.

Dr. Ted took charge. Charlie had been locked into the den early in the morning by Hunter. The den is twenty feet long by six feet wide. There was a huge cage inside the concrete den. with a three foot walkway on the door side. The wide 8X4 inch fencing would allow Dr. Ted to use the jab pole, (a long pole with a syringe on one end). All the equipment was checked, in working order. Dr. Ted, without hesitation started the process.

Filling the hot orange punch pole with anesthesia. *Now why make it hot orange, any animal sees that and is gonna know trouble is coming.* Dr. Ted and I entered the den.

My job was distraction. I held the squeaky toy and talked to Charlie, showing him the toy. Dr. Ted got in position to jab the syringe pole in Charlie's rump. It would take two shots for the initial knock down, as the punch pole syringe only held so much fluid anesthesia. Both times the squeaky toy served it's purpose. I felt like a traitor, but it had to be done. I'm sure Charlie sensed the anxiety cloud around us. Dr. Ted and I exited the den, giving Charlie the peace and quiet he needed to sleep.

The anesthesia equipment had already been unloaded. The long wooden table that we were going to lift Charlie on became a catch all for equipment. Jennie and Aisling organized what Dr. Ted would need. I surveyed the scene, it looked like a medical yard sale with items strewn across the green grass waiting to be used. I had to chuckle, when I saw Dr. Ted pull out two lawn chairs from his truck for himself and Dad. We all knew it would take at least forty minutes for Charlie to be totally asleep. Well, Dr. Ted was prepared alright, a real Boy Scout! He and Dad sat down comfy cozy chatting about our families, hunting and fishing. And me, I was busy worrying, occasionally peeking in the den door.

The entire procedure of the neutering is dangerous when you are talking a tiger. However the initial knock down is very important. The dosage of the anesthesia is never exact because we do not have an exact weight of the tiger. Dad and Dr. Ted are very good at estimating. Once the big cat is asleep, someone has to be the first into the locked cage to make sure the cat is asleep. In the past that was Parker, followed closely by Dr. Ted. This time it was Dr. Ted, and myself. Charlie had fallen asleep with his head towards the den door. We wanted his tail end towards the den door. Dr. Ted was going to perform surgery with the tigers tail by the door, just in case any of us needed to make a quick escape. So Dr. Ted first checked Charlie's eyes, and confirmed that Charlie was out.

"The blink response is the last to go to sleep," Dr. Ted instructed as we worked. "He's out. Let's move him around." So Dr. Ted and I grabbed giant fuzzy paws the size of dinner plates and twirled the sleeping giant around on his back. His tail was now to the door and his head by the inside fencing next to the walkway. The external anesthesia machine was hooked up to Charlie's face though the fencing. Matt DeBlock was assigned to kneel on the floor outside the internal den cage (in the walkway) to hold the anesthesia's face mask on Charlie.

Dr. Ted and Aisling were kneeling on cold concrete, *(Oh so sorry Ted, who is about my age, I know those knees are going to hurt),* just inside the den cage door at the giant tiger's exposed tail and testes. I think the tiger grew in those moments. When you kneel next to a tiger, you realize how big they are and this was a full grown, very healthy, 600 lb tiger. Charlie's white belly seemed pristine at that moment.

Dr. Ted was giving instructions to his staff, and again my job was just to worry and maybe fetch. Dr. Ted adjusted his head lamp, did the final check of equipment and looked around.

"Every thing go?" He stated more than questioned. "Let's do it."

The initial cut was made and the operation proceeded. I walked over to Matt.

"If Charlie so much as moves a whisker, I want to know," I firmly stated. "And Matt- talk loud, don't mumble!" Which Matt was prone to do. *Or maybe my ears are getting older...* Matt nodded, vigorously.

Vickie, Dad and I stood by the den door trying not to be in the way but we wanted to see everything also. Vickie was a saint and retrieved my camera for me, multiple times so I could take pictures. There was no spot to leave my camera in the den. If Dr. Ted asked for something we all 'jumped to it'.

Jennie was retrieving items for Dr. Ted out of his magic medical truck. Aisling was assisting Ted with the operation, yes there was blood to begin with, then Doc tied off the vessels and the bleeding was reduced. I was surprised at the size of the testes themselves, I expected them to be larger. Each testes was about the size of half a Hostess Twinkie. Kind of puny compared to those of a boar pig. Oh well, nature is a wonderment.

The operation was a success, and all happened so quickly. After the tiger was asleep, maybe the surgery took a half hour. Maybe less. Long time on his knees on cold concrete for Dr. Ted, but I never heard him complain. After the last suture was in place every one stood and collected the medical debris. We rolled Charlie over onto a clean bed of fluffy second cut hay and covered him with a blanket for warmth. Hypothermia is a major concern, we needed to keep Charlie warm.

Jennie brought in a warming machine, which would blow hot air into a plastic blanket like balloon. Neat-O invention. We fished it through the fencing where the anesthesia machine had been removed. Again all of this was done very quickly, Charlie would wake up fast once the anesthesia machine was removed. The humans were out of the den, and the den door padlocked before the first whisker twitch. When Charlie started to move around we fished out the plastic hot air blanket. Charlie woke up, Dr. Ted observed him for a few moments and decreed that Charlie would be fine.

We were a well coordinated team. Dr. Ted and I commended every one on a job well done.

We packed up the strewn equipment, lifting the heavy anesthesia machine and the compressors. The debris in the grass was picked up. We packed the heavy table in the back of the pick up truck, the heavy table we never used to hold a huge tiger.

This was Aisling's first time to assist at a zoo procedure. After all was said and done, I asked her if she realized just how unique the opportunity was.

"Once we got into it, the procedure went so fast, there was no time to think about it, " She said. "Now, it seems pretty darn cool!" *I know the adrenaline rush, the danger, and the excitement of zoo work. It does make the time fly by.*

Parker and Hunter returned from the chlorine chemical spill by the school, that the HASMAT trained firemen, (Parker and Hunter included) had helped clean up.

Hand shakes all around, and pats on the back. Charlie was going to be fine, and no school children were harmed.

We kept Charlie in quarantine in the den for a week while his sutures healed. We did not want Lily roughhousing with Charlie and ripping his surgery site open . Hunter gave Charlie antibiotics in his food every day.

All's well I guess. But there will be no more baby tigers for me to raise. The thought saddens me. Not for just me, but the world of the tiger is shrinking so rapidly. Zoos are a gene repository, a living museum of certain species. Without the extended gene pool that zoos keep alive, the tiger specie's days are undoubtedly numbered.

So Sorry Charlie.

Chapter 81 Christmas Mouse

The Christmas Mouse
"Tis two nights after Christmas, and all through the house,
Not a creature is stirring, not even a mouse…"
I've trapped them all out , taken 'em down to the zoo
Those rattlers and moccasins like Christmas dinner too!
Jackie just left back to Boston, so I'm feeling quite blue.
Thought I'd write my note to good friends like you.
So flash me a smile, and we'll chat a while.
Let's see - raised four lambs and two red fox kits
Five fawns, some duckies and peacock chicks.
Oh! And lest I forget-momma Kodiak raised three little bears
Who frolicked while folks came from everywhere.
And then in July, surprise, surprise,
joy came to my heart from adorable eyes!
On our first day of vacation, Doug and I were to leave the nation.
Hunter called me, was I dressed yet? Fear for Doug at the zoo?, you bet!
"Nope, not that, but we think there's two,
You better get down here to the zoo."
Two little cubs waited for me, offspring of my dear Tiger Lily.
Lily's very young at only two and didn't know just what to do.
So niece Lindsey and Matt my intern, Stepped up, pediatrics to learn.
We examined, trimmed umbilical's, and we fed them twice.
I left for Canada, my heart in a vice.
(I did not want to go, yeah go figure that!)
The cubs did great, I was in constant touch,
Must admit I did not relax much.
Matt and Lindz did wonders, the tiny tiger tots did fine,
With long distance tutorage of mine.
Doug and I were back in a week -well a couple days less-
Doug did not complain, with him I am blessed.
Was hands on learning for Matt and Lindsey,
The stress outstanding -cub care was easy.

It amazes me how rude people can be;
"Why aren't they with mom tiger?" accusingly.
Oh whell! they don't know, and that is also part of my job,
To teach and explain to preconceived snobs.
We poured love into the cubs have no doubt,
And found them a good home, that is what it's about.
I drove Ozzy and Titus to Virginia , nineteen hours on a mission,
Met the new parents, Mercer and Alex, watched cubs enjoy the kissin'.

Zoo Momma

New parents met us halfway, cubs were in Georgia by the end of the day.
My good friend Karen Walsh rode with me, not an easy ride,
I needed her gab so I didn't cry.
Karen's daughter Sierra helped me at the zoo again this year,
Love that kid, she's always full of good cheer.
Dr. Ted has been here quite a bit,
His patience and intelligence just does not quit.
He examined monkeys, woodchucks, fox pups, tigers, and whatever else,
He is a great comfort to my babies and myself.
We did TV twice which always fun, days "off " from our days on the run.
Dr. Ted neutered Charlie the tiger dad, needed done but none the less sad.
A fire call for Parker and Hunter, they came back to the zoo much later.
Meanwhile it was Dr. Ted, and me, Ashlin, Jenny and sleeping Charlie.
So Titus and Ozzy just might be - the last little tigers raised by me.
Now instruction of how has all been written,
For the next person so zoo smitten.
(not that I'm going anywhere soon, but…)
Lily is three, tigers live 18 to 22, - do the math, with my age, can you?
Then came Paul Truman Peacock late in the year,
But has given us all a whole bunch of cheer.
He's become a pet, and flies on command,
To your arm when you hold egg in your hand.
What a hoot! (or a peck) but his story is not complete yet.
Doug picks up dead deer and doing heart great,
Finds lots of neat places for our Tuesday dates.
My computer guru, he is quite the guy,
He constantly keeps me wondering why,
Or how - he thinks is a mystery, the man constantly baffles me!
Graying and grizzly but a true gentle man,
We go out to dinner whenever we can.
I've developed an aversion to cooking, and he understands…
I worry about him constantly, but then he just makes fun of me.
Hunter watches over him, his buddy and workday kin.

With her Masters Jackie graduated, in Public Health she matriculated.
So Doug and I took a ride, and watched Jack graduate BU with pride.
She and Mark are still together, Not I'm not allowed to ask -so whenever.
Jack still working at Planned Parenthood,
Helping women for the greater good.
They are looking forward to their next step,
In relationship or career, either not determined yet.
And so Doug and I , we wait to hear…maybe next year.
Dad's doing fine slowly aging, for 87 years old, he's quite amazing.
Up and out at the zoo every day,

Zoo Momma

Opinionated, feisty-always something to say.
We took Angie Cockatoo to the TV station,
To hear Angie and Dad a singing sensation!
Still hunting and trapping, and out on the tractor,
Age is not his limiting factor.
Arthritis is the family curse, I'm sure in a few years mine will be worse.
Mom is doing much better, still knitting grandbaby sweaters.
Her health is good, we walk when we should.
And the rest of the whole fam-damn-ily,
Is just the same, oh joy to me!
So thanks to Lindsey, Matt, Shelly, and Sierra too,
And all of the characters here at the zoo,
Jenny, Melissa, Vickie, Steph, Yvette, and others I've not mentioned yet.
I've made it through another year, to write my letter of Christmas cheer.
So take a moment now my letter is done,
And write me back that you've had fun,
A note, an email or a phone call will do, I really want to hear from you.
'Tis two nights after Christmas and all through <u>my</u> house,
Not a creature is stirring, For sure no darn mouse!
Love Lori

Photo by Michele Mulder

348

Zoo Momma

Chapter 82 I Just Can't Wait!

Part of my work at the zoo is to help with medications and routine wormings. I also prepare fruits for the primates to augment their dry prepared primate chow. The baboons, Rhesus monkeys and Ring tailed lemurs all get extra fruits and veggies. All the nutrition they need is in the prepared primate chow, but who wants to eat a dried pellet food for all of your life? Now that would be boring. I was preparing the fruits, veggies and the monthly worming medicine for the baboons and Rhesus. I mixed the appropriate amount of wormer for each animal in some peanut butter and put the spiked peanut butter between two Ritz crackers. *(Now there is an advertising possibility!)* I plunked the Ritz cracker sandwiches on top of the three kiddie sand pails of fruits and veggies clearly marked for each set of animals. Walking through the main building towards the kitchen, I saw my Dad had come back from picking up a dead deer. His signature faded bibs were stained with. deer blood, His woodland camouflage jacket appropriately smelled like dead deer.

"Hey Pop! We need to feed the cotton mouth moccasins today, can you help in a minute?" I asked loudly as Dad's hearing loss has become more pronounced. We need two people, one to call out where the snakes are in the display case before you open the door from the back. You see, the door on the back has no windows. You can't see before you open the door if a venomous snake has moved closer to the door. So if you don't have someone to look from the front window you could open that door and have a venomous snake literally in your face.

"Yep, but can we do it right now?" he asked as he eyed my blue sand buckets full of fruit. "I'm going out to lunch in a little bit."

"Sure," I replied as I placed the buckets on the nearby table. " Let me step into the other room and get the mice."

"Ok, I'll just sit here and rest a bit," Dad stated as he sat down in the chair. He was after all, 87 years old.

I headed into the next room four steps away and got a bucket, opened a mouse tank and quickly counted out eight mice. I was maybe two minutes away from Dad in the next room. Carrying the bucket 'o mice, I walked back through the door to where Dad was and stood still in absolute shock!

"NOOOOO DAD!! Don't eat the crackers!!" my loudest voice boomed. My eyes could not believe what they saw. My Dad was eating the medicated crackers! Now there was enough medication for 100 lbs of animal in those crackers and Dad weighs well, twice over that, and then some. But Dad is on all sorts of medications. I worried about drug interactions. Dad just sat there laughing, licking his fingers. Obviously tormenting me. He had only eaten half of a cracker, and I thought to call his doctor. Then I figured his doctor might not even know what ivermectin wormer is. So just not to worry, I called Dr. Ted. I gave him the nutshell version, in between my consternation and laughter. Dr. Ted reassured me that Dad would be ok. And yeah, Dr. Ted was laughing too.

Dad was fine. He reported to me the next morning that he was a little gassy the previous night, but he felt fine. The twinkle in his eye let me know he was ok.

"Well, Dad," I could not resist, "You always have been full of hot air!!"

You know what reader? I get out of bed every morning and just can't wait to get down the zoo and see what's gonna happen that day. There is rarely a dull moment.

See you at the zoo!
Love, Lori

My Dad, Fred Space in his volunteer fireman dress uniform.
(Sans worms!)
Photo by Lori Space Day

Bibliography

Burton, Maurice & Burton, Robert. Encyclopedia of the Animal Kingdom. London: Phoebus Publishing Co., 1976.

Cobon, John. The Atlas of Snakes of the World. Neptune City, N.J.: T.F.H. Publications, 1991.

Hediger, H.. Wild Animals in Captivity: An Outline of the Biology of Zoological Gardens. New York: Dover Publications Inc. 1964.

Hickman Sr., Cleveland P., Hickman Jr., Cleveland P. & Hickman, Frances M.. Integrated Principles of Zoology. St Louis: CV Mosby Co., 1974.

Keeton, William T.. Biological Science. New York: WW Norton & Company, 1972.

Miller, Stephen A. & Harley, John P.. Zoology: The Animal Kingdom. Dubuque, IA,   Bogata, Boston, Buenos Ares, Caracas, Chicago, Gilford, CT, London, Madrid, Mexico City, Sidney, Toronto, Wm C Brown Publishers, 1996.

National Geographic Society. Wild Animals of North America. Washington, DC: National Geographic Society, 1987.

Romich, Janet A., An Illustrated Guide to Veterinary Medical Terminology, Second Edition, Thomson Delmar Learning, Clifton Park, N.Y. 2006

Rue III, Leonard Lee. Pictorial Guide to the Mammals of North America. New York: Tomas Y Crowell Company, 1967

Rue III, Leonard Lee. Sportsman's Guide to Game Animals: A Field Book of North American Species New York, London: Outdoor Life Books, 1968.

Rue III, Leonard Lee. Furbearing Animals of North America. New York: Crown Publishers, 1981.

Space, Fred T.. Facts About Snakes of the North East U.S. A.. Sussex, NJ: Fred T. Space, 1969.

Teitler, Risa. Taming and Training Macaws. Neptune City, NJ: T.F.H. Publications Inc.,   1979.

Wikipedia and other sites on the internet

Zoo Momma

Dear Reader,
Again I must reiterate: Learn from the elder experts that surround you. They may be the generation before me/us that did not have computers and/or the inspiration to write it all down. You can learn a lot from them. Ask then listen. And observe, be aware of your surroundings and what happens within them.
Sincerely,
Lori